The
GOSPEL
COMMISSION

The

GOSPEL

COMMISSION

Recovering God's Strategy
for Making Disciples

Michael Horton

BakerBooks

a division of Baker Publishing Group
Grand Rapids, Michigan

© 2011 by Michael Horton

Published by Baker Books
a division of Baker Publishing Group
P.O. Box 6287, Grand Rapids, MI 49516-6287
www.bakerbooks.com

Paperback editon published 2012
ISBN 978-0-8010-1390-4

Printed in the United States of America

The Library of Congress has cataloged the original editon as follows:
Horton, Michael.
    The gospel commission : recovering God's strategy for making disciples / Michael Horton.
      p. cm.
    Includes bibliographical references.
    ISBN 978-0-8010-1389-8 (cloth)
    1. Discipling (Christianity) 2. Evangelistic work. 3. Missions—Theory. 4. Mission of the church. I. Title.
    BV4520.H66 2011
    266.001—dc22   2010043420

green press INITIATIVE

Contents

Acknowledgments

It is impossible to thank all those pastors, missionaries, teachers, and fellow saints who have formed my interest in this topic. I am especially grateful to Lesslie Newbigin, late missionary bishop in India, for his friendship and instruction. Thanks also to my colleagues at the White Horse Inn and Westminster Seminary California, as well as Pastor Michael Brown and the faithful saints at Santee. I am also grateful to the fine team at Baker, especially Robert Hosack and Wendy Wetzel.

Introduction

A gracious disturbance is at work in the world today. With the resurrection of Jesus Christ, the age to come has broken into this present evil age. It's not business as usual. God isn't coming alongside us to empower us for our projects of personal and social transformation. God did not become flesh and suffer an ignominious death at our hands so that we could have sprawling church campuses, programs, and budgets. There's something more profound—more radical—going on. But what is it?

In Christ, God has broken into our world of sin and death and is even now bringing the powers of the age to come into the present age by his Word and Spirit. It is a profound disturbance of our lives and our world: disorienting, dividing, and delivering us from the supposed givens of what we thought were "reality."

But for that reason, it's a *gracious* disturbance. God is interrupting the regular news to bring us a special report and through us is bringing this report to the ends of the earth. Around this news from heaven the Spirit is gathering a colony or embassy of grace in a world of fear, guilt, rebellion, and distraction. Jesus's mandate in the Great Commission is a lodestar for refocusing our mission as Christians and as churches on the central calling for this time between Christ's two comings.

Why another book on the Great Commission? Like others, I am concerned that we are being distracted in our churches today by "mission creep." According to Wikipedia, mission creep is "the expansion of a project or mission beyond its original goals, often after initial successes." The term was originally coined in a 1993 *Washington Post* article on the UN Peacekeeping mission in Somalia, in which the writer argued that a humanitarian mission turned into a military operation which did not have clearly spelled-out goals and for which the soldiers on the ground were not prepared.[1]

In *Christless Christianity*, I paint an unflattering but documented portrait of the message that seems to pervade contemporary churches. Following closely on its heels, *The Gospel-Driven Life* focuses on the core Christian message and its radical implications for our lives in the world. My goal in *The Gospel Commission* is to call us away from mission creep, centering our discipleship and our churches on the very specific sources, goals, strategies, and methods that Christ mandated for this time between his two comings.

The Empire to Which We Are Sent

When I was growing up, nearly everyone in my immediate and extended family on both sides was raised a Southern Baptist or at least an evangelical of some sort. Today, some are hostile toward Christian institutions and official doctrine. Others affirm a childhood experience of "getting saved" with fond recollection, even if this experience is apparently irrelevant to their current beliefs and commitments. But when the conversation moves to the deep end—namely, to doctrine and discipleship (especially in relation to the church)—everybody crawls out of the pool as if someone had cried, "Shark!" Kept to the level of slogans and experiences, "spirituality" is fine. The problem is "organized religion," which usually means anything associated with actual beliefs and practices that are shared by a specific, concrete, and visible community of Christians. Some of these relatives have not been to church in years but would be deeply offended at any insinuation that they might not be Christians. So we mostly avoid the topic. They're family, but when it comes to the faith, it's easier to talk to a stranger on a plane. I could relate similar stories of friends with whom I graduated from a conservative evangelical college.

These experiences are far from unique in our culture today. This story will resonate with people who grew up in Roman Catholic, Orthodox, mainline Protestant, evangelical, and Pentecostal families.

In fact, it's interesting how many of America's pop culture icons have a conservative Protestant background. Ted Turner, the CNN founder who famously said "Christianity is for losers," attended a Christian school in his youth. Actress and New Age advocate Shirley MacLaine was raised in a staunch Southern Baptist home. *Playboy*'s Hugh Hefner relates, "I was a very idealistic, very romantic kid in a very typically Midwestern Methodist repressed home. There was no show of affection of any kind, and I escaped to dreams and fantasies produced, by and large, by the music and the movies of the '30s."[2]

Raised in a Progressive Missionary Baptist church, Oprah Winfrey loved to quote Bible verses and relate Bible stories—sometimes even in church, where she says she began her public career before an audience. In fact, her friends at school dubbed her "Preacher Woman." As LaTonya Taylor relates, "To her audience of more than 22 million mostly female viewers, she has become a postmodern priestess—an icon of church-free spirituality."[3]

In a denomination in which liberal is the new traditionalism, retired Episcopal bishop John Shelby Spong boasts appearances on *Larry King Live*, attacking the Christian creed with a blend of sarcasm and poor scholarship. The author of *Rescuing the Bible from Fundamentalism* (which, as it turns out, means Christianity), he was raised in a fundamentalist home and church.

Similar hostility toward "organized religion" (especially Christian orthodoxy) was evident among the pioneers of the Enlightenment and Romanticism. Thinkers like Kant, Lessing, Hume, Hegel, Schleiermacher, Feuerbach, Marx, and Nietzsche were reared in evangelical pietism. Many were children of pastors, and most of them even pursued theological studies in preparation for the ministry. Successive waves washed away layers of Christian consciousness: from the Christ of the creed to the inner experience and piety of Jesus as moral example, to the rejection finally of both—in favor of nature-mysticism or atheism.

As Unitarian rationalism spawned a homegrown Romantic movement known as American transcendentalism, writers like Henry David Thoreau and Ralph Waldo Emerson called readers to turn away from everything external in religion—Scripture, church, creeds, and sacraments—and fix their attention on "the infinitude of the private man," as Emerson put it. Not even God stands outside of us and over us, but God is simply the divine energy that pulses through all living things. In his famous "Harvard Divinity School Address" (1858), Emerson announced,

The Puritans in England and America, found in the Christ of the
Catholic Church, and in the dogmas inherited from Rome, scope for
their austere piety, and their longings for civil freedom. But their creed
is passing away, and none arises in its room. I think no man can go
with his thoughts about him, into one of our churches, without feeling, that what hold the public worship had on men is gone, or going.
It has lost its grasp on the affection of the good, and the fear of the
bad. In the country, neighborhoods, half parishes are signing off, to
use the local term.[4]

Meanwhile, on the American frontier, revivalism was also turning
attention from God and his grace to the inner experience, free will,
and moral action of the human being.

In many ways, this long march of secularism (or at least "spiritual but not religious" approaches) should be seen less in terms of
the invasion of a foreign army than as a teenage rebellion in the
evangelical house.

Of course, part of the hostility is directed at the particular claims
of the faith, but I would venture to say that most of those who have
turned to eclectic spiritualities, agnosticism, or atheism today are not
reacting against a clearly understood Christian creed. Often they refer
to their upbringing as involving strictness combined with hypocrisy.
For a host of reasons—real and imagined—growing up in a Christian environment is perceived by many of our contemporaries as a
negative experience.

Surrounded by people who are pretty much like ourselves, we can
easily see the mission field as a distant place to which we send heralds.
However, all of that has changed. Our lives are bound up socially with
non-Christians. Some have experienced the church as a negligible or
even harmful influence in their past. Many of us have experienced
enough of that ourselves to sympathize with them. Like any family,
churches can be embassies of grace or prisons—and much in between.
However, in my own experience at least, today we are more likely to
encounter people (at least those of post–baby boom generations) who
only know "Christianity" from TV preachers and political debates.

The challenges that have drawn me back to a close examination of
the Great Commission are not primarily external attacks of "secular
humanists" but a gradual decline in the health of evangelical witness
in American churches. Secularization—that is, the gradual conformity
of our thinking, beliefs, commitments, and practices to the pattern of
this fading age—is not just something that happens *to* the church; it

is something that happens *in* the church. In fact, it's difficult to think of secularism as anything other than a Christian heresy.

In its lust for cultural relevance, mainline Protestantism squandered its inheritance. Conservative Protestants today are also in danger, not so much of being attacked by New Atheists as of surrendering a robust confidence in God and his Word to a culture of marketing and entertainment, self-help, and right-wing and left-wing political agendas. If mainline bodies sold their birthright to the high culture, are evangelicals in danger of selling theirs to popular culture?

The growth of evangelical churches throughout the baby boomer era has tapered off and shows signs of precipitous decline. According to one study, 60 percent of American young adults raised in the church are no longer active participants (much less members) in their twenties.[5] While many Christians abandoned mainline Protestant denominations for evangelical churches, a growing trend is reported of evangelicals quitting church altogether.[6] While cautioning against overly dramatic conclusions, researcher Ed Stetzer observes, "Southern Baptists, composing the largest Protestant denomination in the United States, have apparently peaked and are trending toward decline. The same is true of most evangelical denominations." He adds, "The bigger concern is that people who identify themselves as Christians (and even evangelicals) do not evidence the beliefs historically held by Christians."[7]

Instead of reaching the lost, are we losing the reached? Or are those reared in our own churches being truly reached in the first place? Do they know what they believe and why they believe it? Are we making disciples even of our own members—our own children—much less the nations?

Add to this massive group of burned-out Protestant, Catholic, and Jewish Americans the rediscovery of Eastern religions in the 1970s and the burgeoning religious diversity of our neighborhoods, and we have a pretty good idea of the challenges and opportunities before us as we hear and explore our Lord's Great Commission.

But the promise is not only "for you and for your children"; it is also "for all who are far off, everyone whom the Lord our God calls to himself" (Acts 2:39). The "other" is no longer an abstraction, an anonymous category of "the lost," in which religious identity often gets caught up with ethnic, cultural, and even political differences. Similar to the early days of the church, it is more apparent today that "those who are far away" may be living next door or even under our own roof. In this context, we can no longer just *assume* that these wonderful people who enrich our lives are "strangers to the covenants of promise, having no hope and without God in the world" (Eph. 2:12). We have to be *convinced* of this all over again, persuaded by the clear testimony of Scripture. The fact of religious pluralism has always been with us, but now we are staring it in the face in our daily lives.

The Embassy of Peace

It's not surprising that the church shares with secular politics terms like "mission," "ministry," and "ministers." In state diplomacy, a mission can be a specific course of action or a permanent office, such as an embassy or consulate. The same is true of the church. It is both a *people* deployed with a task and a *place* where God is at work through official structures and offices. Diplomats, ambassadors, official heralds appointed by the head of state to announce something of great significance for individuals and for the whole world—this is the analogy that the New Testament employs for the work of fulfilling the Great Commission. Even the term "gospel" was a secular term in Greek that referred to the good news that an official was sent to announce back in the capitol: namely, that there had been victory on the battlefield.

Ambassadors do not create their own policies, usurping the role of their head of state. They do not negotiate the terms of the peace treaty, but communicate them. They are under orders. Ambassadors aren't merely private individuals who share their personal beliefs and experiences with others. They do not send themselves, but are officially commissioned and sent. The apostles were sent directly from Christ, as "eyewitnesses of his majesty" (2 Peter 1:16; see also Luke 1:2), while the ordinary ministers like Timothy were trained and then called and commissioned by Christ "when the council of elders [*presbyterion*] laid their hands on you" (1 Tim. 4:14). Christ still sends his ambassadors out on his mission, proclaiming the Good News, baptizing, and teaching everything that Christ commanded. And he still calls his whole body to witness to God's saving love in Jesus Christ through word and deed.

The Great Commission is given within the wider context of the covenant of grace that was initiated with God's promise of a redeemer in Genesis 3:15, reaffirmed in the covenant with Abraham, and fulfilled in the new covenant. In the political treaties of the ancient Near East, a great king (emperor) would graciously deliver a smaller kingdom from invaders and then incorporate that kingdom into his empire. In these treaties, there was a clause that gave the lesser king the right to invoke the great king in the case of future threats. It was referred to as "calling on the name of (the great king)."

This political relationship became the template for the covenant of grace. Quoting Joel 2:32, Paul declares, "For 'everyone who calls on the name of the Lord will be saved'" (Rom. 10:13). We do not have to attempt to ascend to the heavens or descend into the depths to attain salvation; rather, God comes down to us, not only rescuing us but delivering the Good News that reconciles us to him. Paul adds the following links in the chain of his argument:

> How are they to call on him in whom they have not believed? And how are they to believe in him of whom they have never heard? And how are they to hear without someone preaching? And how are they to preach unless they are sent? As it is written, "How beautiful are the feet of those who preach the good news!" . . . So faith comes from hearing, and hearing through the word of Christ. (Rom. 10:14–15, 17)

The church is Christ's embassy in the world. Elsewhere Paul relates,

> All this is from God, who through Christ reconciled us to himself and gave us the ministry of reconciliation; that is, in Christ God was reconciling the world to himself, not counting their trespasses against them, and entrusting to us the message of reconciliation. Therefore, we are ambassadors for Christ, God making his appeal through us. We implore you on behalf of Christ, be reconciled to God. For our sake he made him to be sin who knew no sin, so that in him we might become the righteousness of God. Working together with him, then, we appeal to you not to receive the grace of God in vain. For he says, "In a favorable time I listened to you, and in a day of salvation I have helped you." Behold, now is the favorable time; behold, now is the day of salvation. (2 Cor. 5:18–6:2)

Like their Lord, the directly appointed ambassadors of Christ were beaten, flogged, imprisoned, and even martyred. Instead of calling on the name of the Lord through his delegated representatives, the kingdoms of this age responded to God's embassy with hostility. And yet the Great Commission bore and continues to bear fruit among Jews and Gentiles to this day. "For I am not ashamed of the gospel, for it is the power of God for salvation to everyone who believes, to the Jew first and also to the Greek" (Rom. 1:16).

After his resurrection, our Lord commissioned his apostles to go throughout the earth making disciples by preaching the gospel, baptizing, and teaching everything he has delivered for faith and practice. There is a lot of rich substance packed into that mandate. Motivated by a sense of urgency, Christians for two millennia have made enormous sacrifices—including their own lives—in order to bring the saving message of Christ to every person on earth.

Our Embassy to the Empires of This Age

With new challenges come new opportunities. In many ways, this is a better time to take the Great Commission more seriously. Once we begin to see ourselves as belonging to a minority within a predominantly pagan society with vestiges of cultural Christianity, we are freed up to reorganize our beliefs and practices in a more distinctly biblical pattern. Discipleship cannot mean going with the flow; it requires swimming against the current not only of contemporary culture but often of contemporary church life and experience.

The central point of this book is that there is no mission without the church and no church without the mission. As evangelicals we have tended to see the church and its public ministry of Word, sacrament, and oversight of spiritual and material needs of the body as "maintenance" for those who were evangelized once upon a time. They're already in. But evangelism and mission have to do with going outside the church and its ministry to say and do something else. The cleavage between church and mission is often stated explicitly in evangelistic appeals: "I'm calling you to believe in Jesus, not to join a church." But what does it mean to make disciples—what does that really look like on the ground? Furthermore, how do we deal with the challenges of religious pluralism and the rising sentiment in evangelical circles that salvation does not require explicit faith in Christ? In the following chapters we explore the strategies Christ instituted that make the church his mission in the world—for lifelong believers as well as strangers to the gospel—as well as the relationship of evangelism and social justice. Along the way I interact with evangelicals today who are offering a different interpretation of the Great Commission.

The central mandate of the Great Commission—to proclaim the gospel to everyone in the world—used to be taken for granted by Christians, especially by evangelicals. Convinced that salvation comes through hearing and believing the gospel, generations of ordinary Christians left the comfort of kith and kin to hazard unfamiliar and often unwelcoming engagement with those who had not yet heard the Good News. Many of my generation grew up singing "We've a Story to Tell to the Nations," and we felt a connection to the missionaries who returned on furlough with their slides and reports. They were like heroes to us kids.

We also had a sense, however naïve, that we lived in a Christian country and sent missionaries to other nations where Christ is not known. Of course, we knew that the light was dimming in secular Europe, but a vaguely conservative religiosity and morality numbed us to the reality that our own American culture is entering that twilight. Alternating between fundamentalisms and liberalisms of various sorts, American Christians nevertheless seem increasingly aware of the reality that the West, including the United States, hosts a religiously diverse culture. Sociologists like Peter Berger have pointed out that modernity led to radically different trajectories in Europe and America. Europe has become secularized: modernity and unbelief went hand in hand. Yet American religion has thrived under the conditions of modernity. Liberal democracy, free enterprise, pragmatism, consumerism, and the triumph of a therapeutic worldview have been seen as allies rather than enemies of evangelical faith and mission. Somehow we adapted instead of becoming extinct. Or so it seemed until recently.

So amid the whirl of spiritual movements in America today, the question is properly raised: how much of this is recognizably *Christian*? "But it's *working!*" no longer resonates as it did only a couple of decades ago. As self-described evangelicals fall away from regular church attendance and many churches themselves seem distracted from their primary calling, the light is dimming and the salt is losing its savor. Increasingly, Christians in North America who want to recover vital faith and practice recognize that they too are "strangers and exiles" (Heb. 11:13) in this present age. And actually, this recognition may be a healthy prelude to a fresh era of mission.

Throughout this book, I will be interacting with primarily Western voices and trends, especially those in North America. I do not pretend to understand sufficiently, much less to write from the perspective of Christians in other contexts. Nevertheless, having spent some time living in Europe and ministering in Africa, South America, and Asia,

I can say that whenever the United States has a fever, the rest of the world begins to cough. Along with the gospel, homegrown American aberrations (like the prosperity gospel) are spreading like wildfire in the two-thirds world.

I write out of a concern to see us recover clarity in our message, focus in our mission, and commitment to the specific strategies laid out by our Lord. While *Christless Christianity* and *The Gospel-Driven Life* focused on the central *message*, this book explores the central *mission* in an age of "mission creep"—that is, a tendency to expand the church's calling beyond its original mandate.

I believe that in our passion for relevance, we are subordinating the strategies that Christ promised to bless to our own action plans. Just as it's easy to take the gospel for granted and to turn it into a story about us and our efforts rather than Christ and his saving work, a similar temptation is always present with respect to the Great Commission. Today this mission creep takes many forms, but as in earlier periods the tendency is usually to expand the Great Commission to include a host of enterprises that Christ did not mandate. Many of these operations throughout our history have been well motivated, and some have even been successful in their positive cultural impact. Others have led to bloody wounds and indelible scars, not only on the face of civilization but on the visible church. Yet the deeper question is whether we are losing our focus on the mission that Christ gave us for this "intermission," the time between his two comings.

The empire to which we are sent is no longer the Roman Empire or Christendom but the powers and principalities of modernity, which are often hailed as "postmodern." Whether we call it modern, postmodern, or most-modern, this culture is forged largely as a culture of rebellion against orthodox Christian faith and practice in the name of progress and emancipation. Sometimes this rebellion has taken an explicitly anti-Christian form, but more often it has been motivated by a concern to adapt Christian faith and practice to the norms of modern Western culture. In fact, from the Enlightenment to the "emerging church" (or "emergent") movement, the West has experienced successive calls to "a new kind of Christianity" even in the name of mission. The appeals are often urgent: Christianity must either wither or adapt to the new conditions.

In spite of the apparent success of evangelical movements and megachurches, the United States seems increasingly unevangelized. While the West stews in the juices of growing secularization, the center of gravity for growing Christianity has shifted from the northern hemisphere to the global south: Africa, Asia, and Latin America. Citizens of Pakistan may be more likely to encounter Korean than American missionaries today. Churches in China are now becoming sending centers for missionaries throughout the world.

The students in my seminary classes who come from Nigeria are often more serious about their faith and practice in the face of their native paganism than I am in the face of mine. They are evangelistic and they don't just make *converts*; they make *disciples*. Like the ancient Christians, they baptize adult converts and their children only after a lengthy period of instruction (catechesis), prayer, and wrestling with the spiritual forces that refuse to surrender to Christ without a fight. They know firsthand what it means to forsake father and mother and even be persecuted by members of their own household. Upon his conversion to Christ, one friend, a former Sharia lawyer who had witnessed and approved the execution of Christians, was given one day to leave his Islamic country or face beheading. His family disowned him and stayed behind.

In many ways our era is more similar to the first-century context than it is to any period since the Constantinian fusion of Christ and culture in "Christendom." On one hand, the gospel is spreading in many places around the world, despite the imminent threat of persecution and martyrdom. On the other hand, like a lot of Christians in the first-century Roman Empire, most believers in Europe and North America face disapproval, distraction, and disbelief more than martyrdom. We are threatened more by a broad cultural sentiment against strong truth claims that might upset the vague spirituality that holds the empire together than by secret police.

When the Visigoths sacked Rome in 410, the church realized how many nominal Christians were in the empire. In fact, many Romans turned back to paganism, blaming the catastrophe on the abandonment of the gods in favor of Christ. Much like the conditions that provoked Augustine to write *The City of God*, our context affords a marvelous opportunity to recover the sharp distinction between the kingdom of God and the kingdoms of this present age. While Jerome lamented, "What will become of the church now that Rome has fallen?" the bishop of Hippo realized that God had brought the mission field to the missionaries.

Like George W. Bush, Barack Obama invokes the time-honored rhetoric of America as a redeemer-nation, "the last best hope for the

world," along with the post-9/11 language of religious pluralism: that
we all—at least the "Abrahamic faith traditions"—pray to the same
God and share the same hope for a better world, so let's make that
the tie that binds and reject any stronger cords that would threaten
the greatness of America's mission in history. We hear this from all
quarters of culture, both high and low, and we even hear it increasingly from some Christian leaders.

In this context, we feel a lot of pressure to sand down the rough
edges of our message, toning down both the seriousness of God's
judgment and the wonder of God's grace in Jesus Christ. To some
extent, this is understandable. Over the last several generations, many
churches have given the impression that *God's judgment*—which leaves
nobody standing—is actually *our own judgmentalism* and the gospel
is "Pull yourself together!" rather than the Good News concerning
Christ's redeeming work. Our neighbors are often turned off by the
most visible representatives of Christianity. Many who inveigh against
the departure from "Judeo-Christian values" are exposed for their own
immoral lifestyles, and statistics tell us that evangelical Christians do
not live much differently from non-Christians.

So why not just bloom where you're planted? Especially when our
neighbors have seen so much hypocrisy, why not tone down the rhetoric
and just live as Christ's disciples among them? Let's not talk about
God's wrath and judgment, repentance, and faith in Christ, but instead
let's show them that following Jesus makes a real difference in our
lives here and now. You don't have to actually profess faith in Christ
publicly. Baptism and church membership are optional extras. This is
no longer merely what our non-Christian neighbors tell us; it's what
a growing number of professing Christians believe—and many more
seem to assume in practice.

However, the more we really understand that God's judgment strips
us of our self-righteousness and his gospel clothes us with Christ,
the better prepared we are to be *more* radical in our witness and in
our discipleship.

While my previous two books urge us not to take the gospel for
granted, my concern in this book is for us to not take the Great Commission for granted. We have an occasional missions conference, we
offer short-term missions trips for the youth, and we support missionaries to discharge the duties of the Great Commission. All of this
is important. However, especially in our contemporary context, we
need to become more broadly aware of the fact that we are living in

a culture and increasingly in churches that for various reasons seem distracted from the message and realities of Christ's kingdom.

There is a big difference between saying that pastors discharge an essential ministry by *making us disciples* and quite another to say that they are *vicarious disciples*, studying, praying, meditating, and witnessing in our place. We can easily assume that we have discharged our duty by paying "church workers" to be disciples for us.

Meanwhile, the various ministries of our churches here at home often focus on attracting and satisfying members with something other than the gospel and the means of grace that we expect the missionaries to take to other nations. The Great Commission and its mandated methods of proclaiming the gospel, baptizing, and teaching becomes a mandate for foreign missions, while in our own congregations we assume that everybody already gets the gospel and is well-taught in the Scriptures. A cleavage between the Great Commission and the regular life of our own churches grows into a gaping chasm. As I will argue in this book, the Great Commission is a call not only to bring the gospel to other parts of the world but also to plant and to faithfully maintain churches where disciples are made and witness expands both at home and abroad.

A lot of proselytizing and catechizing is going on today. Other religions and an increasingly secularist ideology are often aggressive in their campaigns. Not only our neighbors but we ourselves are immersed in daily news, commentaries, marketing, and conversations that presuppose a world without God, without the gospel, without Christ, and without the hope of resurrection in a new creation. There is never a good time to take the Great Commission for granted, but particularly in an age like ours.

The Outline of the Book

This book is divided into three sections. Part One focuses on "The Great Announcement." The Great Commission itself begins with the triumphant announcement that all authority in heaven and on earth belongs to Jesus Christ. The gospel that brings salvation also drives the church in its mission. Tracing the thread of Christ's person and work from John the Baptist to our Lord's ascension and the sending of the Spirit, this section provides a sketch of New Testament teaching concerning the kingdom and the church that the following chapters build upon.

Part Two examines "The Mission Statement" that lies at the heart of the Great Commission, while Part Three investigates "The Strategic Plan" that Jesus includes in his mandate. What does it mean to "go into all the world and make disciples of all nations," preaching, baptizing, and teaching everything Christ commanded (see Matt. 28:19–20)? What does it mean especially when many Christians today believe that being a disciple doesn't necessarily mean belonging to a church—or even, in the view of a growing number, that personal faith in Christ is not necessary for salvation? How does the gospel itself encourage plurality without falling into the relativism of religious pluralism? What is the relationship between "the gospel" and particular cultures in "all the world"? And what does gospel-centered and mission-driven church life look like in practical terms on the ground? Along the way, I interact with contemporary trends in discipleship.

As this exploration opens with the Good News that grounds the church's mission, it ends with Jesus's promise to be with his church until the end of the age. The imperative to go into all the world and make disciples is supported by the two bookends of Christ's gracious promise. But what does it mean for Christ to be present among us, drawing sinners to himself, when he is absent from us in the flesh since his ascension? The final chapter examines the difference that it makes for our mission here and now when we realize that Christ is building his church and the gates of hell will not prevail against it.

I write this book as a pastor: that is, as a missionary who wants to assist fellow believers in that amazing work of preparing the whole body for its mission in the world. As I have been working on this book, my own understanding of and amazement at the Great Commission has grown. The issues that face us are critical. The paths we choose to take at this point are of enormous long-term importance. My prayer is that readers will come away, as I have, with a fresh appreciation for the message, mandate, and methods that Christ has ordained for his continuing mission in the world.

The Great Announcement

All authority in heaven and on earth has
been given to me.

Matthew 28:18

The Great Commission actually begins with a great announcement. Before there can be a mission, there has to be a message.
Behind the sending of the church lies the Father's sending of his Son
and Spirit. Before we go, we must stop and hear—really hear—what
has happened that we are to take to the world. The evangel comes
before evangelism. We must hear this gospel not just at first, for our
own conversion, but every moment of our lives if the Great Commission is to be a joyful delight rather than an intolerable burden with an
impossible goal. Hear it again, with all of the supporting evidence of
Christ's incarnation, life, death, and resurrection: "*All authority in
heaven and on earth has been given to me*" (Matt. 28:18).

1

Before You Go

I am a pretty impulsive person. If there is a check I need to take to the bank, I rush out the door, jump in the car, and am halfway to my destination when I realize that I've forgotten the check. The most humiliating part of it is that I will have to return home and face my wife greeting me at the door, grinning, holding the check and saying, "Did you forget something?"

Just go. Just do it. "Get 'er done," as they say. Reflection slows you down.

The same thing can happen with the Great Commission. We think it doesn't really matter if we don't get all the details right, as long as we are zealous. It is easy to subordinate the message to the mission, the evangel to evangelism, as if being busy with outreach could trump the content of what we have been given to communicate.

Of course, it can work the other way too. We can be preoccupied with getting the message *right* without actually getting it *out*. The evangelist D. L. Moody once quipped to a critic of his methods, "I like my way of doing it better than your way of *not* doing it." If "zeal without knowledge" is deadly (see Rom. 10:2–3), then knowledge without zeal is dead. The Great Commission doesn't give any quarter to either of these extremes.

"Go therefore into all the world and make disciples." This is the version of the Great Commission that many of us memorized. However, it leaves out a great deal. To begin with, it leaves out the whole rationale for the Commission in the first place. Although it sounds a little corny, a good rule of thumb in reading the Scriptures is that whenever you find a "Therefore," you need to stop and ask "what it's there for."

When we see an imperative like "Go therefore," we need to go back and look at what has already been said leading up to it. There is no reason for *us* to go into all the world as Christ's ambassadors apart from the work that *he* has *already* accomplished.

The Great Commission actually begins with the declaration: "All authority in heaven and on earth has been given to me" (Matt. 28:18). This is the rationale for everything that the church is called to do and to be. The church's commission is indeed *directed* by a *purpose* ("making disciples of all nations"), but it is *driven* by a *promise*.

Grounding Purposes in Promises

Like our own lives, the church is gospel-driven. Every new-covenant command is grounded in the gospel. We love God because he first loved us (1 John 4:10, 19). We choose Christ because he chose us (John 15:16; Eph. 1:4–5, 11; 2 Thess. 2:13). We are called to holiness because we are already declared to be holy in Christ, clothed in his righteousness (Col. 1:22; 3:12; 1 Cor. 1:30). Because we have been crucified, buried, and raised with Christ, we are no longer under the tyranny of sin and are therefore to offer up ourselves in body and soul to righteousness (Rom. 6:1–14). In view of "the mercies of God," we are called to "present [our] bodies as a living sacrifice" (Rom. 12:1).

Similarly, in our corporate calling as the church, we are always responding to a state of affairs that God has spoken into being rather than creating that reality ourselves. The church's mission is grounded in God's mission, which he fulfilled objectively in his Son and whose subjective effects he is bringing about in the world through his Spirit. Because the Father sent the Son and then the Spirit, we are sent into all the world with his gospel. So being *mission*-driven is really the same as being *gospel*-driven. As believers and as churches, we are motivated by the mission of the Triune God, as the Father, the Son, and the Spirit save us and send us with that saving message to our neighbors.

All of our spiritual blessings are found in Christ, not in our individual or collective decisions, experiences, efforts, or ambitions. We confess our faith in "one holy, catholic and apostolic church" not because we can see it nor because of any vain confidence that we can build it. Our unity is based on the fact that there is "one Lord, one faith, one baptism" (Eph. 4:5). Despite all appearances to the contrary, we believe that this church is catholic, because it is not a communion of friends I chose for myself but a family that God has chosen from all of eternity in his Son. We believe that this church is also holy, not because of its empirical piety but because God has made Jesus Christ our wisdom, righteousness, holiness, and redemption (1 Cor. 1:30). And finally, the church is apostolic not because we can identify living apostles in the world today but because it proclaims the apostolic doctrine in the power of the Spirit.

Far from eliminating our own responsibility, this Good News concerning God's work in Christ is what liberates and propels the church out into the world. Only because it is in Christ is there an assembly of sinners drawn from every people and language that has been transferred from the kingdom of death to the kingdom of everlasting life.

The Original Missionary

Many of us grew up with missions conferences where a handful of Great Commission verses were repeated in order to justify the missionary imperative. Sometimes we got the impression that God has done his part (providing the opportunity for salvation) and now the rest is up to us. We become the main subjects of the Great Commission.

However, as Christopher J. H. Wright has pointed out in his remarkable book *The Mission of God*, the whole Bible is about *God's* mission, with Christ as the central character.[1] In his postresurrection appearances to the disciples, Jesus not only preached himself as the center of Scripture (Luke 24:27, 44), but he made their proclamation of him part of that mission as well: "This is what is written: The Christ will suffer and rise from the dead on the third day, and repentance and forgiveness of sins will be preached in his name to all nations, beginning at Jerusalem" (Luke 24:46–47 NIV).

So it's not only that there are a few major verses justifying missions. Rather, the whole Bible is about God's mission: sending his Son, then sending his Spirit, and sending his people out as his disciples. In fact, as Wright points out, the Bible itself is a missional document, arising out of and keeping up with the history of God's missional activity in the world. The messianic center of Scripture is inseparable from its missional context and thrust.[2]

And this missionary God is not one person but three. Every person of the Trinity is involved in every work—creation, providence, redemption, consummation—yet each in his own way. The Father begets, the Son is eternally begotten, and the Spirit is breathed out by the Father in the Son. Every work of the Godhead is done from the Father, in the Son, through the Spirit. The Father is the origin, the Son is the mediator, and the Spirit is the perfecting agent who ensures that the Word will not return empty-handed from its mission. From eternity, then, God's missions have always been based on an essential unity with a plurality of persons-in-relationship. The character of that relationship is covenantal, with mutual giving and receiving: no debts, just an everlasting exchange of gifts.

We are God's analogy, created in his image to reflect in our own creaturely manner that covenantal relationship of male and female in a mission. Just as God completed all of his work and then entered his Sabbath enthronement, Adam—with Eve at his side—was to lead creation in triumphant procession into the consummation: everlasting confirmation in immortal glory. Long after the original treason of this royal couple in Paradise, the Last Adam appeared. Jesus Christ is both the missionary God and the human representative who fulfilled the mission for which we were created. The whole story of the Bible turns on the merciful determination of this Triune God to redeem and to restore sinful creatures and the creation that lies in bondage because of the curse. In spite of every failure, disloyalty, and unfaithfulness of the human partner in the covenant, God will complete his mission. And in the person of Christ, he has also fulfilled the mission that he assigned to humankind in Adam: to lead creation into the everlasting blessing of immortality, forgiveness, righteousness, and peace.

Calling Abram out of a moon-worshiping family, God kept the promise alive even after the fall. Like Jesus's disciples, Abram went to a place about which he knew almost nothing, simply on the basis of God's word. God promised Abram that he would be not only an earthly father of Isaac and his descendants in an earthly land but also a spiritual father of heirs from every nation who would be blessed through his seed. In spite of his people's covenant-breaking, the missionary God kept calling and sending prophets not only to indict Israel on the basis of its violation of the covenant made at Sinai but to renew God's pledge to the Abrahamic promise through a new covenant. God himself would descend in judgment and redemption. The God of Israel would complete the mission that Israel, like Adam, failed to fulfill.

The Gospel-Driven Church

The church in the new covenant is no less "prone to wander" than the church in the old covenant. And it is therefore no less dependent entirely on the faithfulness of the Father, in the Son, by his Spirit. The promise of the Savior has always created, sustained, and expanded the kingdom of God. When Israel violated the covenant of law that they swore at Sinai, the prophets nevertheless proclaimed God's faithfulness to the Abrahamic covenant. This divine oath would be realized in the new covenant, when God would forgive their sins and give them a new heart (Jer. 31).

We must never take Christ's work for granted. The gospel is not merely something we take to unbelievers; it is the Word that created and continues to sustain the whole church in its earthly pilgrimage. In addition, we must never confuse Christ's work with our own. There is a lot of loose talk these days about our "living the gospel" or even "being the gospel," as if our lives were the Good News. We even hear it said that the church is an extension of Christ's incarnation and redeeming work, as if Jesus came to provide the moral example or template and we are called to complete his work. But there is one Savior and one head of the church. To him alone all authority is given in heaven and on earth. There is only one incarnation of God in history, and he finished the work of fulfilling all righteousness, bearing the curse, and triumphing over sin and death.

We use the verb "redeem" too casually today, as if we (individually or collectively) could be the agent of this sort of action. God has already redeemed the world in his Son, having "ransomed people for God from every tribe and language and people and nation" (Rev. 5:9). On this basis, the Spirit is at work applying this redemption, drawing sinners to Christ, justifying and renewing them, in the hope that their bodies will be raised together with an entirely renovated creation (Rom. 8:16–23). The church comes into being not as an extension or further completion of Christ's redeeming work but as a result of his completed work. Heralds *announce* victory; they don't *achieve* it.

Jesus Christ has been given all authority in heaven and on earth to judge and to save. This great announcement that launches the Great Commission is anticipated throughout the Gospel of John.

Although the Word was made flesh, his own did not receive him. "But to all who did receive him, who believed in his name, he gave the right to become children of God, who were born, not of blood nor of the will of the flesh nor of the will of man, but of God" (John

1:12–13). We do not have the ability or authority to make ourselves children of God, but Jesus exercises his authority to give life in the power of the Spirit. Jesus told Nicodemus that apart from this new birth from above, no one can enter his kingdom (John 3:5).

In John 5, Jesus said, "For as the Father raises the dead and gives them life, so also the Son gives life to whom he will" (v. 21). The Father has given all judgment into the hands of the Son (vv. 22–23). Then in chapter 6 Jesus says,

> All that the Father gives me will come to me, and whoever comes to me I will never cast out. For I have come down from heaven, not to do my own will but the will of him who sent me. And this is the will of him who sent me, that I should lose nothing of all that he has given me, but raise it up on the last day. . . . No one can come to me unless the Father who sent me draws him. And I will raise him up on the last day. (vv. 37–39, 44)

In chapter 10, Jesus says,

> I am the good shepherd. I know my own and my own know me, just as the Father knows me and I know the Father; and I lay down my life for the sheep. . . . My sheep hear my voice, and I know them, and they follow me. I give them eternal life, and they will never perish, and no one will snatch them out of my hand. (vv. 14–15, 27–28)

Again in chapter 15 he reminded his disciples, "You did not choose me, but I chose you and appointed you that you should go and bear fruit and that your fruit should abide" (v. 16). Then, on the verge of Good Friday, Jesus prayed,

> Father, the hour has come; glorify your Son that the Son may glorify you, since you have given him authority over all flesh, to give eternal life to all whom you have given him. And this is eternal life, that they know you, the only true God and Jesus Christ whom you have sent. . . . I am not praying for the world but for those whom you have given me, for they are yours. (John 17:1–3, 9)

So there is a thread running throughout John's Gospel that testifies to the eternal covenant of redemption between the Father, the Son, and the Holy Spirit. The Father chose a people in Christ from the mass of fallen humanity, giving them to Christ as their mediator, with the Spirit as the one who will give them faith and keep them in that faith to the end. Not one of those whom the Father gave to the Son will be lost.

Given the unity of the Bible's witness to Christ, this thread of passages in John's Gospel helps us to understand what Jesus meant in the Great Commission. Although this commission is not repeated in the same form in Luke or in John, the basic substance is found in their concluding chapters as well (Luke 24:44–53; John 21:15–19). "All authority in heaven and on earth has been given to me" (Matt. 28:18). What an announcement! It presupposes everything from our Lord's conception in the womb of the Virgin Mary to his ascension to the Father's right hand. And it anticipates his return in glory to judge the living and the dead. He alone has all authority to judge and to save.

In his opening vision in the Apocalypse, John hears these words from the glorified Son: "Fear not, I am the first and the last, and the living one. I died, and behold I am alive forevermore, and I have the keys of Death and Hades" (Rev. 1:17–18). It is this triumphant indicative that grounds Jesus's command to John: "*write therefore* the things you have seen" in this remarkable book (v. 19, emphasis added). In the same way, his announcement that all authority is in his hands is the rationale for the Great Commission's "*Go therefore . . .* "!

Given the fact that we—and those to whom we are sent—are "dead in the trespasses and sins" (Eph. 2:1), we do not have the authority or power to save ourselves or even to respond in faith apart from God's gracious liberation (Eph. 2:5, 8–9). The Great Commission would be a futile task if the ultimate power and authority lay in our hands or in the hands of those to whom we bring the gospel. Jesus Christ did not make it possible for us to be saved. He did not begin a work of redemption. He did not do "his part" so that we could do ours. Rather, Jesus Christ has accomplished everything. He has assumed our flesh. He has fulfilled all righteousness in our place and has borne the judgment for every one of our sins as our substitute. And he has been raised as the firstfruits of a whole harvest, the beginning of the resurrection from the dead. There is no more redeeming work to be done!

I'll never forget when this marvelous truth of Christ's objective, completed work really gripped me. My well-meaning pastor once asked me, "When were you saved?" Without intending to be clever, I heard myself answer, "Two thousand years ago." At first, I was as surprised at the remark as my pastor. A lot of our talk about "getting saved" in evangelical circles focuses on the day that we did something:

we invited Jesus into our heart, said a prayer, went forward, or otherwise evidenced a decisive conversion experience. However, this shifts the concentration from the gospel itself (Christ's saving work) to our experience of the gospel. We are commanded to believe the gospel, but the gospel itself is an announcement concerning Christ's all-sufficient achievement for us.

Not even the new birth is the result of human decision or effort. We are not given steps for "How to Be Born Again." Jesus's statement in John 3, that one must be born from above in order to enter the kingdom of heaven, is not an *imperative* (i.e., command) but an *indicative* (i.e., statement of fact). That is, it simply declares the state of affairs. We are not born again by our decision, as John had already indicated in chapter 1 (v. 13). Rather, says Peter, "you have been born again . . . through the living and abiding word of God. . . . And this word is the good news that was preached to you" (1 Peter 1:23, 25). The gospel is *for* us, not *about* us. It isn't about anything that we do, feel, or choose. It is the Good News about Jesus Christ and what he has accomplished for us.

Of course, the new birth evidences itself in conversion: a lifelong response of repentance and faith. God does not believe for us, but we do so because we have been redeemed already by Christ and are given the gift of faith. All of our salvation is found in union with Christ. It takes a miracle to believe in Christ—and he is still a wonder-working Savior whose miracle of the new birth is greater than all of the signs he performed in his earthly ministry.

Because all authority in heaven and on earth is given to Jesus Christ, we are sent into the world with confidence that God's mission will be accomplished. Paul preached the gospel to Lydia and "the Lord opened her heart to pay attention to what was said by Paul" (Acts 16:14). After explaining that God "saved us, . . . not because of our works but because of his own purpose and grace, which he gave us in Christ Jesus before the ages began" (2 Tim. 1:9), Paul—on the verge of his execution in Rome—assured Timothy, "Therefore I endure everything for the sake of the elect, that they also may obtain the salvation that is in Christ Jesus with eternal glory" (2 Tim. 2:10).

The greatest missionary in the history of the church was driven by the gospel indicatives. Because God had chosen sinners from a mass of spiritual death, Christ had saved them, and the Spirit gives them faith through the preaching of the gospel, Paul could go on, enduring persecution, knowing that God's purposes would be realized. Neither

Caesar, nor the Jewish leaders, nor the sinners to whom he preached possessed this authority. With the other apostles, Paul was entrusted with the keys of the kingdom—that is, the gospel itself. However, not even he could open the sealed tomb of the fallen heart. The preaching of the gospel seems weak and foolish in the eyes of the world. "But I am not ashamed," he tells Timothy, "for I know whom I have believed, and I am convinced that he is able to guard until that Day what has been entrusted to me" (2 Tim. 1:12).

A missionary friend once said that when his plane approached the Mumbai airport and he saw the masses of people below, he was overwhelmed with the impossibility of his task. Then he remembered that he was not commissioned to save these people, or even to open their hearts to believe the gospel, but simply to proclaim it, and God would gather his people. That made all the difference, he said, and he was liberated to fulfill his calling. There can be no recovery of delight in the Great Commission without a renewal of the church's conviction that it not only came into being but is sustained in every moment by the will and work of the Father, in the Son, by the Spirit. It is this confidence that motivates a missionary in Saudi Arabia to labor for years before witnessing a single conversion. So why do so many of us, as American Christians, measure success in our own churches by other standards, based on what we can accomplish and see on an impressive scale?

Christ's ascension to the right hand of the Father creates the confidence that our going will not be in vain, whether we are sent to China or to our next-door neighbor. The same Word that creates and sustains the church's own existence and growth is proclaimed to the world so that Christ's kingdom expands to the ends of the earth. The Father's decision is irrevocable. Christ's mission is accomplished already, and the Spirit will be just as successful in his labors. Therefore, the Great Commission cannot fail.

Jesus had already prepared the disciples for his departure and the sending of the Spirit (John 14–16). He had told them, "I will build my church, and the gates of hell shall not prevail against it. I will give you the keys of the kingdom of heaven, and whatever you bind on earth shall be bound in heaven, and whatever you loose on earth shall be loosed in heaven" (Matt. 16:18–19). Christ himself has redeemed his church and is now building his church in the power of his Word and Spirit. It is not a kingdom that we are *building* but a kingdom that we are *receiving* (Heb. 12:28).

In Heaven and on Earth

The titles "Lord" and "Savior of the world" are familiar in our Christian vocabulary. Apart from the unfolding drama of redemption, they are mere slogans. In fact, these phrases have taken on a less radical meaning in our ordinary usage today. We often speak of "making Jesus our personal Lord and Savior," but this obscures two important points.

First, we do not *make* Jesus *anything*, especially Lord and Savior. It is because he already is Lord and Savior that we are freed from the fear of death and hell. *All authority* belongs to him already.

Second, the gospel announces Jesus Christ not only as your personal Lord and Savior or mine, but as *the* Lord and Savior of the world. All authority *in heaven and on earth* belongs to him. As the risen Lord, he is given by the Father the power to judge and to justify. Salvation is not just "fire insurance" or "sin management." The gospel promises far more than going to heaven when you die. It is an all-encompassing pledge from God for the total renewal of creation. It involves the resurrection of our bodies and the liberation of the whole creation from its bondage to sin and death. What insurance plan, global market, or government agency can claim this kind of authority over life and death? When he returns, Jesus will judge every person and nation and consummate his kingdom in everlasting righteousness and peace. We cannot limit salvation to our private world of the soul; the whole cosmos was created by the Father, in the Son, through the Spirit, and it is upheld and finally redeemed in the same way.

The privatized view of Jesus merely as "personal Lord and Savior" does not really provoke controversy today. After all, our non-Christian neighbors shrug, "Whatever works for you." However, these ascriptions of praise to Jesus Christ were subversive on the lips of early Christians in the Roman Empire. After all, they were titles that Caesar had ascribed to himself. People could believe whatever they wanted to in private. Whatever they found morally useful, therapeutically valuable, or spiritually and intellectually enlightening was fine. In fact, when it came to gods, the more the merrier! The Roman Empire was a melting pot of cultures and religions. However, whatever varied religions and spiritualities it tolerated, Rome insisted that they contribute to the civil religion that included the cult of the emperor. God could have his heaven, or the inner soul, but Caesar was "lord of the earth."

The early Christians were not fed to wild beasts or dipped in wax and set ablaze as lamps in Nero's garden because they thought Jesus

was a helpful life coach or role model but because they witnessed to
him as the only Lord and Savior of the world. Jesus Christ doesn't
just live in the private hearts of individuals as the source of an inner
peace. He is the Creator, Ruler, Redeemer, and Judge of all the earth.
And now he commands everyone everywhere to repent. All idols are
shams. All power and authority not only in heaven but on earth is
Christ's. He has cast Satan out of the heavenly sanctuary, where he
prosecuted the saints day and night (Rev. 12). And now, having bound
the strong man, he is looting his house on earth, taking back what
rightfully belongs to him (Matt. 12:29).

We can only imagine the offense that such testimony as the following might have aroused in Caesar or his emissaries:

> For by him all things were created, in heaven and on earth, visible and
> invisible, whether thrones or dominions or rulers or authorities—all
> things were created through him and for him. And he is before all
> things, and in him all things hold together. And he is the head of the
> body, the church. He is the beginning, the firstborn from the dead,
> that in everything he might be preeminent. For in him all the fullness
> of God was pleased to dwell, and through him to reconcile to himself
> all things, whether on earth or in heaven, making peace by the blood
> of the cross. (Col. 1:16–20)

Later in Colossians Paul writes,

> And you, who were dead in your trespasses and the uncircumcision
> of your flesh, God made alive together with him, having forgiven us
> all our trespasses, by canceling the record of debt that stood against
> us with its legal demands. This he set aside, nailing it to the cross. He
> disarmed the rulers and authorities and put them to open shame, by
> triumphing over them in him. (Col. 2:13–15)

The "rulers and authorities"—whether sin, death, and Satan themselves or their earthly lackeys who spread destruction to the ends
of the earth—are already divested of their ultimate power. Like the
deceiver himself, they fall over themselves in a stupor of pride, oppression, and persecution of the church, but they will all be brought
down; their time is short (Rev. 18). Even in his "weakness," God has
made a mockery of the powerful of this age (1 Cor. 1:25–29).

Caesars may still rule and demand the proper temporal allegiance
of their subjects (Rom. 13:1–7), but they rule at the pleasure of the

Sovereign of the universe. Disease may stalk and death may claim our bodies, but it no longer has the last word: "O death, where is your victory? O death, where is your sting?" (1 Cor. 15:55). Our fate does not lie in the impersonal forces of nature. We are not at the mercy of insurance companies and health care providers. Not the invisible hand of the market but Jesus Christ is Lord of all powers and principalities.

Of course, devout Jews agreed that there was only one universal sovereign, Yahweh, and stoutly refused any collusion with Gentile idolatry. However, they just as sharply rejected the apostles' transfer of the name of Yahweh in the prophets (Joel 2:32) to Jesus (Acts 2:21; Rom. 10:13). They regarded as blasphemy such statements as we find in Acts 4:12: "And there is salvation in no one else, for there is no other name under heaven given among men by which we must be saved."

The boundaries of Israel are now redrawn around Jesus Christ. There is a new kingdom, from heaven, spreading its dominion in this world. It is not a kingdom of power and glory, with an earthly capital. It is a kingdom of grace and forgiveness, overcoming the death and condemnation under which the world lies helpless.

Are you rattled by the magnitude of opposition to the gospel, increasingly even in the nations once nominally committed to a vaguely Christian culture? Does the Great Commission seem threatened by the gathering forces of secularism, militant Islam, consumerism, violence, and moral relativism? These are among the "principalities and powers" that Christ has vanquished objectively, although their effects have not yet been finally and forever eliminated.

New Testament scholar Oscar Cullmann compared Christ's resurrection and return in glory to "D-day" and "V-day" during World War II. The landing assault broke the back of the Nazi forces, but insurgent battles raged until victory in Europe was fully realized. Even now, Christ has crushed the head of the serpent and is setting prisoners free. All authority in heaven and on earth is given to him. Are you distressed by your lack of understanding, zeal, or faithfulness in your own discipleship, much less in your appreciation for the Great Commission? Christ is Lord! He has forgiven you all of your sins and has given you a new heart. In spite of every setback, you are assured that your Shepherd-King has already won the war!

2

Exodus and Conquest

The Gospel and the Kingdom

Jesus possesses all authority in heaven and on earth, but what does that mean for us here and now? This chapter offers a map of redemptive history, locating our position ("You are here") and the coordinates for our mission in the world today. What is Christ's kingdom and is it here now—and if so, in what sense? Today, on the left and the right, there are interpretations of the kingdom that seem closer to the misunderstanding of Jesus's contemporaries. Retracing the unfolding plot is vital for understanding the context of the Great Commission.

The Big Map: Exodus and Conquest

"Of course Jesus Christ has all authority in heaven and earth—he's *God*." This is true enough, but it is only part of the story. The New Testament attributes this status as much to his *humanity*:

> And being found in human form, he humbled himself by becoming obedient to the point of death, even death on a cross. *Therefore* God has highly exalted him and bestowed on him the name that is above

every name, so that at the name of Jesus every knee should bow, in
heaven and on earth and under the earth, and every tongue confess
that Jesus Christ is Lord, to the glory of God the Father. (Phil. 2:8–11,
emphasis added)

Similarly, we read in Hebrews that although "we do not yet see everything in subjection to him," we do "see him who for a little while was
made lower than the angels, namely Jesus, crowned with glory and
honor because of the suffering of death, so that by the grace of God
he might taste death for everyone" (2:8–9).

Our Lord has accomplished something in history—in his life, death,
resurrection, and ascension—that qualifies him to be the judge and
justifier of the ungodly. Jesus is both the Lord of the Covenant who
commands and the Servant of the Covenant who fulfills all righteousness and wins for us forgiveness, the new birth, resurrection,
and the renewal of the whole creation. As God, he *is* Lord; as human,
he "was declared to be the Son of God in power according to the Spirit
of holiness by his resurrection from the dead" (Rom. 1:4).

Exodus and Conquest in the Old Testament

Starting with Matthew's Gospel is like walking into a movie in
the middle. We have to go back to the Old Testament in order to see
the thickening plot of which Jesus Christ is the central character.
The exodus-conquest motif unfolds from Genesis to Revelation,
but if we do not see how it plays out differently in our era between
Christ's two comings, our interpretation of the church's mission will
be skewed.

In one sense, we can trace the exodus-conquest story all the way
back to creation, when God separated the waters to create dry land:
a holy place for fellowship with his covenant partner. Taken from
"darkness" and "void" (Gen. 1:2) to a lavish garden, the world was
fashioned into the glorious theater of God's kingdom. God himself
passed through the waters, fulfilling his mission of creating the cosmos, and then entered into his royal enthronement with the earth as
his footstool. As God's viceroy—and our representative head—Adam
too was to fulfill his commission and win the right for himself and
his posterity to eat from the Tree of Life. Adam and Eve were given
the mandate to be fruitful and multiply, to rule and subdue, driving
out God's enemy who would corrupt the garden and tempt God's
covenant partner into rebellion.

Yet the central event in the Old Testament, which reverberates throughout the history of Israel, is the exodus from Egypt. The Song of Moses recounts, "The LORD is a warrior; the LORD is his name. Pharaoh's chariots and his army he has hurled into the sea" (Exod. 15:3–4 NIV). God remembered his covenant oath to Abraham in Genesis 15. The covenant with Abraham was an unconditional pledge. Beyond an earthly seed and land, God promised Abraham and Sarah a seed who would bring everlasting blessing to the families of the earth. Moses too was a beneficiary of this promise, but the covenant that he mediated at Mount Sinai was temporary and conditional. It pertained to the nation of Israel and depended on the nation's strict observance of the law mediated by Moses.

Between the exodus and conquest lay a vast desert, where God met his people through Moses at Mount Sinai and then on the way to Canaan, where God pitched his tent "outside the camp" (Exod. 33:7). Yet even though they had been eyewitnesses of God's miraculous deliverance from Egypt, the people continually questioned God's purposes and Moses's leadership. Like Adam, they demanded the food they craved instead of relying on God's Word and Spirit. Consequently, that entire generation—including Moses—was barred from entering the land of Canaan.

Under Joshua, a new generation of Israelites entered the Promised Land, driving out the idolatrous and violent nations against whom God had been storing up his wrath. Again we hear echoes of the original commission given to humanity. Like Adam, Israel is to subdue the enemies of God, driving out the serpent from God's holy garden, and to participate in God's just judgment of the nations. Repeatedly, the kingdom of God in the land of Canaan is likened to a feast: eating and drinking with God and each other in a land flowing with milk and honey. Psalm 68 recounts the march of God's kingdom, from the exodus to the conquest of Canaan.

Eventually, when the temple was also constructed as a more permanent residence, God commanded it to be built with three major areas: the outer court of the Gentiles, the inner court of the Jews, and the Most Holy Place where the high priest entered once a year to offer the atoning sacrifice on the horns of the altar, above the ark of the covenant containing the tablets of the law.

Yet even in the Promised Land, Israel lost the point of the story. Psalm 78 recites this history, moving back and forth between the repeated failures of God's people and the unfailing faithfulness of the

Covenant Lord. Instead of allowing the types and shadows of the law to point them to the coming "Lamb of God, who takes away the sin of the world" (John 1:29), they turned to the idols of the pagans whom they had failed to drive out of the land. "For I desire steadfast love and not sacrifice, the knowledge of God rather than burnt offerings. But like Adam they transgressed the covenant; there they dealt faithlessly with me" (Hosea 6:6–7). Like our own first parents, Israel demanded the food they craved instead of sharing in Yahweh's feast. On the basis of the oath that Israel swore at Mount Sinai, there is no hope. The prophets are sent as God's covenant attorneys, prosecuting the case and invoking the sentence: exile from the land. The northern kingdom was taken captive to Assyria, and eventually Judah too was carried off into Babylon. For the end of exile nothing less is required than a faithful Adam, a true Israel, an obedient son.

Exodus and Conquest in the New Testament

Moses prefigured Christ in many ways, but the typology (foreshadowing) is never complete. God gave his law and promises through Moses. When Israel sinned, the mediator could prevail in his plea that God would restrain his wrath for the moment. The elaborate ceremonies and sacrifices that God delivered through Moses provided a temporary "covering over" of transgressions. These rites directed Israel's faith to the true Lamb of God. Yet Moses's mediatorial ministry was partial and temporary. Neither Moses nor the priests could forgive sins or heal the straying hearts of God's people. Moses's ministry was great. However,

> Jesus has been counted worthy of more glory than Moses—as much more glory as the builder of a house has more honor than the house itself. . . . Now Moses was faithful *in* all God's house as a servant, to testify to the things that were to be spoken later, but Christ is faithful *over* God's house as a son. And we are his house if indeed we hold fast our confidence and our boasting in our hope. (Heb. 3:3, 5–6, emphasis added)

An Old Testament "type" is like a trailer for a movie. While the Red Sea was a preview, Christ's cross was the ultimate judgment itself. And unlike Moses and the Israelites, Jesus passed through this sea only by first being drowned in it. Paul even identifies the cross as his Red Sea crossing (1 Cor. 10:1–6). But also unlike Moses, Jesus was not barred from entering the Promised Land, but opened the gates of Paradise for his people and entered as their conquering pioneer.

Like Moses and the Israelites, Jesus was tested in the wilderness—his forty days recapitulating Israel's forty years. Instead of demanding the forbidden fruit (like Adam) or the food he craved (like the unbelieving generation in the wilderness), Jesus answered Satan's temptation with God's Word. All of Jesus's replies to Satan in the temptation (Matt. 4:1–11) are taken from Moses's speech in Deuteronomy 6:13, 16; and 8:3.

After his faithful completion of the trial, enduring temptation and fulfilling all righteousness, Jesus bore our judgment in his own body. And then he was raised by the Father and the Spirit into the Sabbath rest of everlasting glory. This is the *real* exodus, through which the Son "ransomed for God people from every tribe and language and people and nation" (Rev. 5:9). And now, in the last scene of his earthly ministry, Jesus is about to ascend, commencing the *conquest*: this time not merely of a sliver of real estate in Palestine, through the military sword, but of the whole earth, through the sword of his Word and Spirit.

Ascended in Conquest

It is not surprising that if Jesus had to correct the disciples' misunderstanding of the nature of the real exodus, some serious instruction was necessary on the meaning of the real conquest, to which the conquest under Joshua merely pointed as a type and shadow. The last question the disciples ask Jesus before he ascends is, "Lord, will you at this time restore the kingdom to Israel?" (Acts 1:6). Before we turn to Jesus's answer, it is important to remind ourselves what was behind their important question.

The Kingdom (Conquest) They Were Expecting

The messianic kingdom of peace is anticipated in many places, especially in Isaiah 9:11; 11:9–10; 32; and Micah 5:1. The redeemer-king will come from David's house, enthroned in majesty (Pss. 47; 93; 96; 97; 99). Jesus himself appealed to Daniel 7 for his title as Son of Man. God *is* king in status, governing all of history for the ultimate purpose of establishing his universal reign. However, on the last day he will finally be *acknowledged* as king in all the earth. He will reign not only as Creator, Provider, and Lawgiver but as Redeemer, Judge, and Consummator. Ranking next to the Shema found in Deuteronomy 6 ("Hear, O Israel, the LORD our God is one . . ."), the Qaddish is a Jewish prayer that arose in the Babylonian captivity. It reads,

> Glorified and sanctified be his great name in the world he has created according to his own pleasure. May he establish his royal dominion and start his deliverance of his people, and may he bring his Messiah and redeem his people in the time of your life, and in your days, and in the time of the life of the whole House of Israel, with haste and in a short time; and thou shalt say Amen.[1]

Jesus knew this prayer well, and the Lord's Prayer echoes its petitions.

Before and immediately after Jesus, various claimants to the messianic title arose, launching campaigns to drive out the Romans. In fact, even the more moderate Pharisees were trying to get everybody to rededicate themselves to the Mosaic law in all of its details so that the Messiah could come. However, the problem is that on the basis of the covenant of law that Israel swore at Sinai ("All this we will do"), Israel has no hope. On that basis, *Israel* stands condemned, "in Adam," like the rest of the human race.

Nevertheless, the prophets proclaim a "new covenant" (Jer. 31:31–34). This is an oath sworn by God rather than by Israel, with his promise to forgive his people and to give them new hearts. God himself will raise "a righteous Branch" from David who will be called, "The LORD is our righteousness" (Jer. 23:5–6). This new covenant looks back to the promise that God swore to Abraham and forward to the coming of the messianic Son of David, who will judge and save (Isa. 40–55; Obad. 21; Micah 4:3; Zeph. 3:15; Zech. 14:16–17). He will regather his scattered sheep, fulfill all righteousness, clothe them in his holiness, forgive all their sins, and make the whole earth the theater of his grace and glory forever. This final act of salvation and judgment will not be a dress rehearsal or type, like the holy wars that God commanded against the idolatrous nations inhabiting Canaan. It won't be a preview of coming attractions. It will be the real deal. It will result not merely in temporal life and death but in a final and everlasting verdict.

In spite of diverse interpretations of the prophets about the end times, this era of first-century Jewish expectation was dominated by a distinction between "this age" (under the reign of sin, death, and oppression) and "the age to come" (under the reign of righteousness, resurrection, and peace).[2] Yet these were usually seen as clearly marked eras with an obvious and clean dividing line in history. This age is all exile for the people of God, but in the age to come there is nothing but blessing, righteousness, and peace.

There are two very "Gentile" misunderstandings of the kingdom to be avoided here. *At one extreme is the idea of the kingdom as a purely spiritual reality, equivalent to the Greek idea of the immortality of the soul.* In Greco-Roman mythology, virtuous and heroic souls were thought to ascend to the Elysian Fields, and "salvation" was the release from the body, which Plato among others called "the prison house of the soul." There are many similarities between Eastern and Western versions of this story. This vision of the "afterlife" has been a tough habit to break in the West. For many of our neighbors—perhaps even Christians—the kingdom of heaven is a place of disembodied bliss, with images of angels playing harps and bouncing from cloud to cloud. Salvation becomes equivalent to "going to heaven." The phrase "passing away" has become part of our vocabulary even as Christians, although it was introduced by Christian Science founder Mary Baker Eddy. Death is not real—or at least it is not an ominous threat but the portal to liberation from this world.

The biblical story line is radically different. It speaks of the kingdom of heaven not as an escape from this world but as a completely new form of existence for the world and its inhabitants. Except for the Sadducees, most Jews in Jesus's day expected the coming kingdom as a total renewal of creation: the resurrection of the body, global peace and justice, fertile vineyards and lavish banquets. The contrast is not between this "lower world" of matter, time, and space and the "upper world" of timeless spirit but between "this age" (dominated by sin and death) and "the age to come" (dominated by righteousness and life).

These categories—*this age* and *the age to come*—were widely employed in Jesus's day, and he and his apostles drew on them explicitly (Matt. 12:32; 24:3; 1 Cor. 2:6; Gal. 1:4). It is a new creation, a new covenant, and a new heavens and earth that is promised in the new age. In fact, in the book of Revelation (especially chapter 21), not only do the kingdom's horizontal boundaries between nations disappear; so too does the vertical boundary between heaven and earth. Finally, God will dwell in the midst of his people as their source, center, and circumference. There will be justice and peace. The lion will lie down with the lamb, and warriors will beat their swords into plowshares.

In the New Testament, death is a tragedy—the result of sin. Yet all who trust in Christ will be raised in the likeness of his glorified body to eat and drink forever in the presence of God. God guards the souls of his saints upon their death, but, in the words of the Apostles' Creed, the ultimate hope of salvation is "the resurrection of the body and the life everlasting" in a renewed creation (see Rom. 8:23–24). Death is neither unreal nor a natural stage of life. It is a curse for breaking God's law—the ultimate exile. Only in Jesus's exodus from the waters of judgment can we be brought safely into the age to come.

At the other extreme is the idea of the kingdom as merely the moral development of the human race toward a world of love, peace, and justice. This view, often associated with the Enlightenment and Protestant liberalism, assimilates the radically God-centered vision of the prophets to the human-centered march of enlightened progress. However secularized, this vision is in many ways a legacy of "Christendom." If the first "Gentile" mistake is to imagine an escape from this world through the soul's ascent, this second error identifies the kingdom with the gradual ascent of humanity toward a kingdom of love, justice, and righteousness.

For the prophets, it was *God's* kingdom—descending from heaven, not evolving on earth. It would bring a final heavenly judgment to the earth, resulting in everlasting life and death. God's claim on the whole earth was even more comprehensive than that of Alexander the Great and Rome's emperors, but only God could actually bring it about. The happiness and flourishing of humanity and the rest of creation is the result, but God's glory is the motive and the goal. Forgiven and renewed, the heirs participate in the advance of this kingdom. Nevertheless, its saving realities are brought to earth directly by God, not attained by human striving.

The prophets proclaimed the forgiveness of sins, the granting of new birth, and the gathering of a remnant from all nations to Zion together with the resurrection of the dead, the final judgment, and entrance into the heavenly Sabbath as *one event*. Yet "double fulfillment" is a characteristic of biblical prophecies. Kim Riddlebarger has compared it to driving to the mountains. From the valley floor, it looks like there is one range, but as you get closer you recognize multiple peaks, each behind the other.[3] Salvation and judgment indeed form one event, but in two distinct stages. As we see below, Jesus himself distinguished between aspects of his kingdom that are already present and its consummation yet in the future.

Jesus's disciples, apparently like John and his disciples, interpreted Christ's ministry within the exodus-conquest plot. Though less radical than the revolutionary zealots, the Pharisees were calling all Israelites to radical recommitment to the Mosaic law in all of its details so that Messiah could come. This included ratcheting up the purity laws, barring everything unclean from the temple: anyone sick, handicapped, or diseased, and certainly all moral outcasts.

Into this environment came the last of the old-covenant prophets, John the Baptist, preparing the way for the Messiah out in the desert. However, John was not preaching revolution—the overthrow of the Romans. Instead, he was warning of the imminent judgment of Israel, preaching, "Repent, for the kingdom of heaven is at hand" (Matt. 3:2). Clearly, he was not simply warning them that they needed to ask Jesus into their heart before they died, nor was he inviting them to participate in making the world a kinder, gentler place. Like the prophets, John announced an imminent judgment *on earth*, but *from heaven*. While welcoming repentant outcasts—even prostitutes— John rebuked the religious leaders for their smug reliance on their pedigree as the descendants of Abraham and announced imminent judgment—even within the household of Israel (Matt. 3:9–10). "I baptize you with water for repentance," John declares, "but he who is coming after me is mightier than I, whose sandals I am not worthy to carry. He will baptize you with the Holy Spirit and with fire. His winnowing fork is in his hand, and he will clear his threshing floor and gather his wheat into the barn, but the chaff he will burn with unquenchable fire" (Matt. 3:11–12).

This kingdom has not yet arrived but is *near*, John announces. It is time for all of Israel to mourn over its unfaithfulness to the covenant and to be prepared for the Messiah's arrival. This kingdom that is "at hand" is nothing less than the advent of "the wrath to come" (Matt. 3:2, 7). Judgment begins in the house of the Lord, with the arrival of the one who will baptize with the Spirit (salvation) and with fire (condemnation).

Then one day, the Messiah came to the Jordan River to be baptized by John, and the Spirit descended as a dove and the Father declared from heaven, "This is my beloved Son, with whom I am well pleased" (Matt. 3:17).

So it is hardly any wonder that John the Baptist would have expected *all of this* to happen in his lifetime, or at least in the earthly ministry of Jesus. Yet as time wore on, Jesus's ministry seemed to fall short of John's expectations. If Jesus is the Messiah, why has the resurrection of the dead and the last judgment not yet taken place? Why is Herod still on his throne, along with his equally wicked queen who has demanded John's beheading? In prison awaiting his execution, John sent his disciples with a provocative question: "Are you the one who is to come, or shall we look for another?" (Matt. 11:3). In other words, "Just let us know now if we've been putting our hopes on the wrong messiah."

Jesus answered, "Go and tell John what you hear and see: the blind receive their sight and the lame walk, lepers are cleansed and the deaf hear, and the dead are raised up, and the poor have good news preached to them. And blessed is the one who is not offended by me" (Matt. 11:4–6). Jesus turned to the crowd and spoke concerning John the Baptist. No prophet has arisen greater than John, he said. "Yet the one who is least in the kingdom of heaven is greater than he" (Matt. 11:11). Jesus added, "From the days of John the Baptist until now the kingdom of heaven has suffered violence, and the violent take it by force" (Matt. 11:12).

The coming "wrath of God" of which John spoke is not a replay of the holy wars that God commanded in Israel's conquest. Just when it seemed that the crowds were ready to renew the Sinai covenant, Jesus gave them a different sheet of music. Jesus's reply—namely, that the gospel is preached to the poor, with various healings as its validating signs—hardly seemed to qualify as the cosmic renewal that was promised by the prophets. Yet this seems to be exactly the character of the kingdom in its present phase.

In his first coming, Jesus is the Suffering Servant who fulfills all righteousness and bears the curse. His resurrection is the dawn of the age to come, as he is made the "firstfruit" of the raised and glorified saints. However, only in his second coming will there be a consummation of the kingdom's blessings. All of the dead will be raised, the Messiah will take his throne for the last judgment, and he will welcome his sheep into the kingdom prepared for them from the foundation of the world. When he comes again in judgment, the campaigns of Joshua will pale in comparison with "the wrath of the Lamb" (Rev. 6:16). Yet *for now* it is a kingdom of grace, as Christ gathers a people through the Spirit for the everlasting feast.

This is precisely what stumped everyone, including his own disciples. Jesus comes, proclaiming the forgiveness of sins as the message of his kingdom, and nobody seems to be happy. Explaining the differences between John's "forerunner" ministry and his own, Jesus says (it seems with some frustration),

> But to what shall I compare this generation? It is like children sitting in the marketplaces and calling to their playmates, "We played the flute for you, and you did not dance; we sang a dirge, and you did not mourn." For John came neither eating nor drinking, and they say, "He has a demon." The Son of Man came eating and drinking, and they say, "Look at him! A glutton and a drunkard, a friend of tax collectors and sinners!" Yet wisdom is justified by her deeds. (Matt. 11:16–19)

John came with the message of imminent judgment, with the deportment of a lamenting prophet, while "the Son of Man came eating and drinking." Jesus comes with the gospel of forgiveness. The groom arrives for his wedding feast, dressing his bride in festive garments (Matt. 22:1–14). However, the one is too gloomy and the other is too joyful. The bad news can't be *that* bad and the good news can't be *that* good. Nobody seems to be up for either a funeral or a party!

Through his preaching and deeds, Jesus had inspired his followers to anticipate the imminent consummation of the kingdom. The disciples had missed the point of Jesus's journey throughout his ministry. The mother of James and John asked Jesus if her sons could sit on Jesus's right and left when he comes in his kingdom, but Jesus replied that she didn't know what she was asking: namely, that they be crucified on his left and right (Matt. 20:21–22). Every time Jesus brings up his death and resurrection, Peter tries to change the subject and Jesus rebukes him (Matt. 16:21–28; 20:17–28; 26:30–35). Although Jesus said, "For this purpose [his death] I have come to this hour" (John 12:27), the disciples were still thinking of a kingdom of power and glory. The symbol of failure rather than triumph, the cross was the last thing on their minds. They fled his crucifixion in fear and despair: "We had hoped that he was the one to redeem Israel" (Luke 24:21).

Yet on this same Emmaus road (in Luke 24), Jesus proclaims himself from all the Scriptures, and the disciples recognize him as their resurrected Lord in the breaking of the bread. Now they understand the real meaning of the *exodus*, but surely the *conquest* would finally mean the overthrow of the Romans and the restoration of Israel. Yet at this very moment, their "Joshua" announces his departure. Right up to the moment of Jesus's ascension, the last question that his own disciples ask him is, "Lord, will you at this time restore the kingdom to Israel?" (Acts 1:6).

The Kingdom (Conquest) That Came

So now Jesus stands before the apostles and, right at the commencement of the conquest, leaves! In Acts 1, Luke reminds the recipient of his report, Theophilus, that his Gospel narrated "all that Jesus began to do and teach, until the day when he was taken up, after he had given commands through the Holy Spirit to the apostles whom he had chosen. To them he presented himself alive to them after his suffering by many proofs, appearing to them during forty days and speaking about the kingdom of God" (vv. 1–3).

Jesus was raised "after his suffering." There is no exodus without the Passover. The original event was the trial by which the Spirit of God passed over the houses in Egypt whose doors were sprinkled with blood and brought death to the rest of Egypt's households. The old-covenant Passover was the annual participation of Israelites in that event of judgment and deliverance. Especially poignant is Isaiah 53, prophesying the advent of the Suffering Servant who will bear "the sin of many," will "make many to be accounted righteous," and "makes intercession for the transgressors" (vv. 11–12).

Instituting the Supper on the eve of his crucifixion, with the ambient noise of bleating Passover sheep, Jesus said, "This is my body, broken for you; my blood of the new covenant, shed for many for a remission of sins" (see Matt. 26:26–28). This last will and testament was put into effect at the cross (Heb. 9:15–22). While the sacrifices of the old covenant covered over sins until the day of final redemption, Jesus Christ offered himself, once and for all. "Therefore he is the mediator of a new covenant, so that those who are called may receive the promised *eternal* inheritance," not just the inheritance of the land of Israel, which was only a type (Heb. 9:15, emphasis added). Our High Priest entered not the earthly replica but the heavenly sanctuary itself, with his own blood, "now to appear in the presence of God on our behalf" (Heb. 9:24).

Even after his exodus through the waters of death, Jesus led his disciples through a new wilderness in forty days of preparation prior to his ascension. There were ten appearances of Jesus Christ after his resurrection, including his appearance to five hundred people in

Galilee (1 Cor. 15:6). Now there is an intense period of instructing the disciples "and speaking about the kingdom of God" (Acts 1:3). It was like a Berlitz seminary education in just over a month.

Joshua and Jesus are really the same name in Hebrew (*Yeshua*, meaning "God saves"). And now, just as the first Yeshua led the Israelites into Canaan at the end of forty years, the second Yeshua ends his forty days by entering into the heavenly Canaan by conquest.

I mentioned above the significance of the theme of "eating and drinking with God" in the Old Testament. This "eating and drinking" formula is not merely a sign of fellowship but a covenant-making meal. Adam and Eve ate without God, as they chose the fruit he had forbidden, and the lush Garden became a wasteland. Moses, Aaron, and the elders "ate and drank with God" at the top of Mount Sinai. The theme continues with the vision of eating and drinking with God in the land of Canaan.

However, Jesus brought the new wine of God's kingdom. The mourning ministry of John the Baptist is overcome by the merry ministry of Jesus. In fact, disciples of John asked why Jesus's disciples do not fast, even though they and the Pharisees do. "Can the wedding guests mourn as long as the bridegroom is with them?" Jesus answers. "The days will come when the bridegroom is taken away from them, and then they will fast" (Matt. 9:15).

During these forty days between the resurrection and ascension, meals—eating and drinking in the presence of God—are central. In Acts 1:4–5 Luke reports, "And while staying [or *eating*] with them he ordered them not to depart from Jerusalem, but to wait for the promise of the Father, which, he said, 'you heard from me; for John baptized with water, but you will be baptized with the Holy Spirit not many days from now.'"

In Luke 24:36–43, the eating and drinking is especially stressed, first, as an occasion for Jesus to prove that he is not a ghost. "Does a ghost eat and drink? Does a ghost have flesh and bones as you see that I have?" Peter reports later in Acts that Jesus appeared "not to all the people but to us who had been chosen by God as witnesses, who ate and drank with him after he rose from the dead" (Acts 10:41). But this eating and drinking is also emphasized as a new-covenant meal through which Christ assures his disciples of their forgiveness of sins. The words and actions of Jesus in these postresurrection meals follow the formula that Jesus used in the upper room when he instituted the Holy Supper.

Table fellowship is a central motif for the joy of the kingdom (international banquet), and it is rightly included as a central part of new-covenant worship ("the breaking of bread" in Acts 2:42). Just as the two disciples whom the resurrected Jesus meets on the Emmaus road in Luke 24 hear him *expound himself from all the Scriptures* and then recognize him in *the breaking of the bread,* so too in the upper room again we see Jesus's ministry of the Word and the Supper as the double assurance of—and sharing in—his victory. Paul would tell the Corinthians that the cup of blessing and the bread that is broken are a "participation in" the body and blood of Christ (1 Cor. 10:16). In a covenantal context, the meal ratifies the treaty toward all who embrace its promise. So even in the ambiance of a feast, we are still in the world of foreign diplomacy: the covenantal environment of a peace treaty.

Luke continues his postresurrection narrative by reporting that Jesus "ordered them not to depart from Jerusalem" but to wait for the promised Spirit (Acts 1:4). Joshua had been told by God to give instructions to each of the twelve tribes before entering Canaan in conquest, and Jesus gives instructions to his twelve apostles (minus Judas, of course). They too are to wait for heavenly empowerment to take possession, this time of the whole earth, not by sword but by the word of their testimony to Jesus Christ. Now it is not only Jerusalem and Judea but "the ends of the earth" that are the field of conquest.

But first they must learn. Apostles (ambassadors) are *sent*; they do not send themselves. Before they go, they need to be prepared by Jesus's instruction and the Spirit's empowerment. While John the Baptist spoke of the Messiah as the one who baptizes with the Holy Spirit *and with fire,* Jesus assures his disciples that they will be baptized with the former rather than the latter. The Spirit will descend in blessing upon those whom Jesus has clothed with his own righteousness. *Then* he will return at the end of the age to judge the world.

In the upper room (John 14–15), Jesus had already prepared the disciples for his departure and the arrival of the Spirit. "It is better that I go," Jesus said. "When I go to the Father, I will send you the Holy Spirit" (see John 14:16, 26, 28; 15:26).

What could be better than Jesus's continued ministry among them? How could there be a new conquest without Joshua leading the troops? Jesus had already answered this in his upper room discourse (John 14–16). He would ascend to the Father, and he and the Father would send the Spirit on his mission of earthly conquest. Jesus calls the

Holy Spirit "another *parakletos*" (attorney), who would bring inward conviction of sin and faith in the gospel while Jesus himself interceded in the heavenly courtroom. The same Spirit who clothed the Servant in our flesh and then clothed him with heavenly power for his earthly ministry will "clothe" the disciples. At the conclusion of his Gospel, Luke reports Jesus's words, "I am sending the promise of my Father upon you. But stay in the city until you are clothed with power from on high" (Luke 24:49).

Imagine what would have happened if the one event of final judgment and salvation had occurred in Jesus's first advent. There would have been no break in the clouds of judgment, with a space opened up for repentance and faith in Christ. The gospel would not have been preached to Israel and the nations, with now two millennia of a Spirit-led ingathering of the harvest. Then and there, the world would have been confirmed in everlasting guilt and judgment, with no hope of forgiveness and entrance into the new creation.

Yet the last question that the disciples ask Jesus before his ascension is, "Lord, will you at this time restore the kingdom to Israel?" (Acts 1:6). It's a great question. No doubt it was even provoked by Jesus's emphases in his forty days of instruction, "speaking about the kingdom of God" (Acts 1:3). It reminds us what the story is all about, its central plot that unfolds from the promise to Abraham all the way to the resurrection of the dead and life everlasting. It is not about merely "going to heaven when you die." It is not just an individualistic thing. It's a lot larger than that. It's about a cosmic, sweeping, historical re-creation.

Of course, a lot had already happened to turn the disciples' expectations on their head. Christ inaugurates his kingdom by dying on a Roman cross, becoming a curse for us. He is raised, but why aren't the *rest* of the dead raised? Why are we still living in exile, with the Romans occupying the holy land? All of these questions percolate and are expressed in this single query.

Jesus answered the disciples' last question of his earthly ministry: "It is not for you to know times or seasons that the Father has fixed by his own authority. But you will receive power when the Holy Spirit has come upon you, and you will be my witnesses in Jerusalem and in all Judea and Samaria, and to the end of the earth" (Acts 1:7–8).

This indicates the form that his kingdom-conquest takes in this present age. Like the Great Commission, it centers on the Spirit-empowered witness to Christ, taking the gospel to the world. Only in Jesus Christ, the true Temple, can the dividing wall that separates the court of the Jews from the court of the Gentiles—and both from the Holy of Holies—be broken down. Only in Christ can the borders of Israel be expanded to encompass the whole earth. He is the seed of Abraham and Sarah in whom all the nations of the earth are blessed. His kingdom is not a revival of the old-covenant theocracy that *Israel* swore at Mount Sinai but the realization of the Abrahamic covenant that *God* swore and to which the Sinai covenant pointed. Having fulfilled its role, the old covenant is now "obsolete" (Heb. 8:13). The kingdom has no borders. It is no longer a geopolitical entity but a global embassy of grace. The Father sends the Son, the Father and Son send the Spirit, and the Triune God sends the disciples out on this mission of salvation. "As you sent me into the world," Jesus prays to the Father, "so I have sent them into the world. And for their sake I consecrate myself, that they also may be sanctified in truth" (John 17:18–19).

The nature of this new-covenant conquest is clear. The disciples must wait in Jerusalem until the Spirit comes to make them *witnesses* to Christ. He doesn't dismiss their question. Rather, he answers by saying, "The Holy Spirit will come in power and make you my witnesses to the world." It may not be the answer they were expecting, but it is indeed an answer—*the* answer that continues to propel the kingdom vision of Christ's disciples.

"And when he had said these things, as they were looking on, he was lifted up, and a cloud took him out of their sight" (Acts 1:9). The ascension is not just something that the disciples experience subjectively or interpreted in their hearts. It is an event that they witness together "as they were looking on." The cloud in which Jesus is wrapped is nothing less than the Glory-Cloud: the Spirit who had hovered over the waters in creation, who led Israel through the Red Sea and wilderness, who filled the temple and then evacuated it when Israel violated the covenant. And the same Spirit of Glory who envelops Christ will be sent to envelop his co-heirs at Pentecost.

The resurrection is the watershed in history, with the dominion of sin and death falling into oblivion, losing its grip on its terrified subjects, and righteousness and life coming to reign. The descent of the Spirit is the event that renders all subsequent time "these last days." The clock is running down on this present evil age. The firstfruits of the harvest, Jesus Christ, has been raised, entering the everlasting Sabbath rest in conquest. The war in heaven is over, though insurgent battles must still be waged on earth. The lame were excluded from the temple courts as a sign of corruption, but already in Acts 3 a lame man is healed within the temple courts (3:1–4:31). It's already happening—"on earth, as it is in heaven."

Jesus is really gone now: "a cloud took him out of their sight" (Acts 1:9). He is truly absent from us now in the flesh. In church history there have been various attempts to downplay this fact of Jesus's bodily departure until his return at the end of the age. The two Gentile misunderstandings of the kingdom I mentioned above are at play here. Defaulting to our Greek philosophical heritage, we can speak as if Jesus is still present with us spiritually on earth, the way that a deceased loved one is "still with us" as we gather together at Thanksgiving. We can do something like this by saying that since Jesus is omnipresent in his divinity, it does not matter that he is bodily absent. Perhaps even the church takes his place as the visible embodiment of its ascended Lord. It's easy, then, to see the *church* as the replacement for Jesus in the flesh. The glorified Son may reign in heaven, but the church (or perhaps an earthly head) reigns as his vicar (meaning substitute) on earth. It has even been argued recently that Christ's second coming is fulfilled in the world-transforming activity of those who continue his redeeming and reconciling work.[4] Jesus simply vanishes and "returns" as the community of his followers.

However, neither then nor apparently afterward did the disciples look for, much less find, any adequate substitute for Jesus and his return in the flesh. Jesus was raised bodily and he ascended bodily. He is indeed forming a covenantal body for himself in this age, by his Spirit, but his natural body is now glorified at the Father's right hand. He does not walk with us and talk with us in a garden, as he did with his disciples, but he is exactly where we need him most. In our human flesh, glorified in immortality, our living head guarantees our own resurrection, interceding and reigning.

This point is emphasized by the two angels who appear—perhaps the same ones who appeared to the women at the tomb in Luke 24. In that earlier scene, the women go to the tomb with the customary burial spices, and Jesus's body is gone. "While they were perplexed about this, behold, two men stood by them in dazzling apparel. And as they were frightened and bowed their faces to the ground, the men said to them, 'Why do you seek the living among the dead? He is not here, but has risen'" (Luke 24:4–6). Now, at the ascension, the two angels said, "Men of Galilee, why do you stand looking into heaven?

This Jesus, who was taken up from you into heaven, will come in the same way as you saw him go into heaven" (Acts 1:11). He has been "taken up from you" bodily, and he will return in exactly the same flesh. They are not to pitch tents at the ascension site and build a shrine, reminiscing about the good old days when Jesus was among them. There is no time for that—the plot is still unfolding. Rather, they are to go to the upper room—Christ's earthly embassy—and await the Spirit's empowerment for their mission. The story is not allowed to come to a halt at the ascension; it has only begun.

Luke reported the same event in the closing verses of his Gospel: "Then he led them out as far as Bethany, and lifting up his hands he blessed them. While he blessed them, he parted from them and was carried up into heaven. And they . . . returned to Jerusalem with great joy, and were continually in the temple blessing God" (24:50–53). They would eventually be cast out of the temple and the synagogue, just as Jesus told them in his Olivet discourse, along with the prophecy that the temple itself would soon be destroyed. It was completely leveled under the emperor Titus in AD 70. Yet the true sanctuary—Christ with his people—would continue to be erected "without hands," by the Spirit.

Arraigned before the Jewish council (Acts 7), Stephen recalled Israel's history, with Christ as its fulfillment, including the prophecy of the end-time temple not "made by hands" (v. 48). And he beheld "the Son of Man standing at the right hand of God'" (v. 56). Participating in Stephen's execution that day was Saul, who would be converted (and renamed Paul) through a similar vision as Stephen's (vv. 54–60).

In Acts 2:42 we read that the believers gathered daily and were devoted "to the apostles' teaching and the fellowship, to the breaking of bread and the prayers." In this assembly, Jesus would be in their midst. Though he would not descend bodily until his return, Jesus pledges his uninterrupted presence by his Word and Spirit. For now, he makes himself the meal; when he returns bodily, he will eat and drink with us at the everlasting feast.

In the Meantime Jesus Opens Up a Fissure in History

Jesus does not abandon the disciples on the verge of the conquest. Rather, he enters the true sanctuary—heaven itself—in royal triumph. There is now a gap between Jesus's earthly ministry in the past and his return in the future. And our history is now taken up, with Jesus's glorified body, into the age to come. This is why Paul can even speak of our being "seated . . . with him in the heavenly places" as a present reality (Eph. 2:6). "If then you have been raised with Christ, seek the things that are above, where Christ is, seated at the right hand of God. . . . For you have died, and your life is hidden with Christ in God. When Christ who is your life appears, then you also will appear with him in glory" (Col. 3:1, 3–4).

This delay between Christ's two advents—the kingdom of grace and the kingdom of glory—is a stay of execution, affording an opportunity for repentance. As we see below, Jesus taught (especially in the Olivet discourse) that during this era the kingdom grows through proclamation of the gospel even as it suffers persecution. Christ's universal reign will be far from obvious to the world. There are wars, famines, earthquakes, hatred—all the way until Christ's sudden and surprising return. There is no indication that we will reach a golden age on the earth and that the nations will welcome Christ at his return. Quite the contrary, Peter reminds us, scoffers mock, "Where is the promise of his coming? For ever since the fathers fell asleep, all things are continuing as they were from the beginning of creation" (2 Peter 3:4). Yet they overlook the fact that the delay of Christ's return in judgment creates a space in history for repentance and faith in Christ.

Jesus was not leaving the battlefield but taking the seat of heavenly command, securing our place, while the Spirit led the ground campaign. Satan has been defeated, cast out of the heavenly courtroom where he accuses the saints day and night. At the Father's right hand is the seat of all power where our defense attorney sits enthroned, interceding for us. "Who shall bring any charge against God's elect? It is God who justifies. Who is to condemn? Christ Jesus is the one who died—more than that, who was raised—who is at the right hand of God, who indeed is interceding for us" (Rom. 8:33–34).

As the conquering King, Jesus Christ distributes the spoils of victory to his companions below who are still engaged in the earthly conquest. This is how the New Testament interprets the "Psalms of Ascent" (especially Psalms 24 and 68). Jesus enters the heavenly sanctuary announcing, "Behold, I and the children God has given me" (Heb. 2:13). Interpreting Psalm 68:18, Paul explains, "'When he ascended on high he led a host of captives, and he gave gifts to men.' (In saying, 'He ascended,' what does it mean but that he had also descended into the lower parts of the earth? He who descended is the one who also ascended far above all the heavens, that he might fill all things.)" (Eph. 4:8–10).

What compensates for the bodily absence of Jesus from the earth right now? *Nothing!* One medieval theologian said, "He who looks at the church looks directly at Christ." That is simply not true—and it's a good thing, given the church's checkered past. It is the Spirit who causes the church to look up to its ascended head in faith, confident in his Word and eagerly expecting his triumphant return. The Spirit testifies to Christ and empowers the Spirit-filled church to do the same.

Israel's downfall began when it demanded a king like the rulers of the nations instead of being satisfied with its true, heavenly King. Similarly, whenever the church tries to make Christ's kingdom visible through its own decisions, programs, and methods, it becomes assimilated to this passing evil age, swallowed in the sea along with Pharaoh's mighty men. Yet whenever the church proclaims the gospel, baptizes, teaches, and administers the Lord's Table, the powers of the age to come break into this present age, and the light of the new creation dawns.

Pentecost: The Sending of the Spirit

Only when we face with all seriousness the ascension—the absence of Jesus Christ in the flesh—do we realize our dependence on the Holy Spirit as the one who now mediates his active presence in the world. "It is to your advantage that I go away," Jesus instructed, "for if I do not go away, the Helper will not come to you. But if I go, I will send him to you" (John 16:7). Jesus does not leave us orphans but goes to prepare a place for us and reign on our behalf at the Father's right hand, and so that the Spirit can draw the nations to Christ.

The Holy Spirit's Long and Fruitful Career

The Holy Spirit's earthly ministry doesn't begin at Pentecost: "In the beginning, God created the heavens and the earth. The earth was without form and void, and darkness was over the face of the deep. *And the Spirit of God was hovering over the face of the waters*" (Gen. 1:1–2, emphasis added). The Spirit's work is always associated with *completion*: bringing about the effects of the word spoken by the Father in the Son. This is why the sending of the Spirit is treated by the prophets as the sign of the consummation, the sign that the "last days" have dawned (see Joel 2:29). This is true already in creation: the Spirit was at work in the creation to bring it to the place where it could become the stage for God's unfolding plan and covenant relationship with his creatures.

The exodus account (Exod. 19) also invokes this creation imagery with the Spirit descending, hovering over the waters, and separating them in order for dry land to appear, then leading the redeemed host by pillar and cloud to the Sabbath rest. The Spirit also descends over, upon, and within the tabernacle and then the temple, as well as resting upon the prophets for their unique mission.

This same Spirit separated the waters in a virgin's womb, as it were, to make the "dry land" appear not only for divine-human communion but for the Son's assumption of our humanity. When Mary asked, "How will this be, since I am a virgin?" the angel answered, "The Holy Spirit will come upon you, and the power of the Most High will overshadow you; therefore the child to be born will be called holy—the Son of God" (Luke 1:34–35). In Matthew's Gospel, before the engagement or any conjugal union with Joseph, Mary "was found to be with child from the Holy Spirit" (Matt. 1:18).

The Spirit "overshadows," bringing to completion the creative word of the Father in the Son, sharing in the Triune benediction: "And God saw everything that he had made, and behold, it was very good" (Gen. 1:31). Echoes of Genesis 1 and 8 (including the benediction formula) are evident in the report of Jesus's baptism: "And when Jesus was baptized, immediately he went up from the water, and behold, the heavens were opened to him, and he saw the Spirit of God descending like a dove and coming to rest on him; and behold, a voice from heaven said, 'This is my beloved Son, with whom I am well pleased'" (Matt. 3:16–17).

After his baptism by John, Jesus, "full of the Holy Spirit, . . . was led by the Spirit in the wilderness for forty days, being tempted by the devil" (Luke 4:1–2; cf. Matt. 4:1). In these forty days he recapitulates Adam's trial and Israel's forty-year trial in the wilderness. Jesus's self-consciousness as the Servant of the Lord prophesied by Isaiah is inseparable from the endowment of the Spirit. In his first public speech, Jesus takes up the scroll in the synagogue and reads Isaiah 61:1–2: "The Spirit of the Lord is upon me, because he has anointed me to proclaim good news to the poor" (Luke 4:18). Then he announces, "Today this Scripture has been fulfilled in your hearing" (Luke 4:21).

Jesus performs his miracles by the Spirit—in fact, attributing them to Satan is "blasphemy against *the Holy Spirit*" (see Mark 3:28–30; Luke 12:10). Jesus also bestows the Spirit on his disciples (John 20:22). In Exodus 19, the momentous event of the Spirit's descent is represented by the sound of winged creatures in a moving cloud, a scene that is repeated throughout Ezekiel and will return at Pentecost with the erection of the end-time sanctuary "made without hands" that Ezekiel prophesied.

To the Spirit particularly is attributed the dignity of transforming created space into covenantal place: a home for communion between Creator and creatures, extending to the ends of the earth in waves of kingdom labor. In the prophets, the Spirit is associated with a glory-cloud (Isa. 63:11–14; Hag. 2:5) and divine wind or breath—*ruach*, the same Hebrew word for spirit/the Spirit (Ps. 104:1–3). It is, in fact, by this Spirit that all things are created and renewed (Ps. 104:30). The presence of the Spirit always signals the arrival of God's kingdom in judgment and salvation.

The Spirit who clothed Christ in our flesh and in consummated glory now clothes us with Christ. Adam became "a living creature" when God "breathed into his nostrils the breath of life" (Gen. 2:7). Here "breath" (*ruach*) is the same word used to refer to the Spirit of God, and with many of the church fathers I interpret "the breath of life" here as "the Spirit of life." We hear echoes of this in the Spirit's filling of the temple in Ezekiel 37 and in John 20:22 as Jesus Christ breathes on the disciples and they receive the Holy Spirit.

In all of these events in the history of creation and redemption, the Spirit is sent as the divine witness or covenant attorney who sends the human witnesses (prophets and apostles). Throughout the prophets, "the day of the Lord" is the final judgment. Already in Genesis 3:8, God arrives to arraign Adam after his disobedience "in the Spirit [*ruach*] of the day." Although this is commonly translated "in the cool of the day," *ruach*—the same term for the Holy Spirit elsewhere—is used here. This is why Jesus calls the Spirit "another *parakletos*," meaning "attorney." The Spirit's arrival announces judgment and justification.

The Creator Spirit is, even in the very beginning, a divine witness to the goal of creation: namely, the consummation. Forfeited by Adam in the first creation, this goal is finally achieved by the Last Adam in the new creation, but he accomplishes this as our representative by constant dependence on the Spirit. *The age to come is Christ's to win;*

it is the Father's to give; and it is the Spirit's to bring into the present, even in the midst of this present evil age.

It is no wonder, then, that the outpouring of the Spirit is identified with the "last days"—specifically, the last days *of this present evil age,* prior to the entrance into the everlasting Sabbath (the age to come). The Spirit comes from the consummated future of Sabbath glory, like the dove that brought Noah a leafy twig in its beak as a harbinger of new life beyond the waters of judgment. Already in creation, therefore, we meet the Spirit of promise: the one who propels creation toward its goal, which is nothing less than the consummation at the end of the trial. This interpretation of the relationship between the Spirit of Glory and judgment is especially supported by 2 Corinthians 3 and 4. In Christ, the veil that prevents us from seeing the glory of God in the face of Christ is now removed by the Spirit of God (2 Cor. 3–6).

Like a ripple effect, this Spirit-filling expands to all of those gathered in the upper room at Pentecost. And now we are called to "put on" Christ, wearing his righteousness as a royal robe, and the Spirit begins gradually to conform us to his image (Rom. 13:14; Gal. 3:27; Eph. 4:24; Col. 3:10). The indwelling of the Spirit even now is a down payment on our full re-creation in Christ's likeness, as we "put off" death and "put on" immortality and glory (1 Cor. 15:53; 2 Cor. 5:2–5). This is what it means for us to become "partakers of the divine nature" (2 Peter 1:4). In Christ, and by his Spirit, believers are even now "the image and glory of God" (1 Cor. 11:7).

The Spirit evacuated the earthly temple, exiling Judah to Babylon, and now the Spirit returns to fill his true and everlasting temple. However, this time it is the real thing, the end-time sanctuary: Christ and his "living stones." Echoing the original creation, the Father and the Spirit issue their heavenly benediction on Jesus in his baptism (Mark 1:11), repeated by the Father testifying from heaven at the transfiguration (Mark 9:7). Nevertheless, since the hearers are "dead in trespasses and sins" (Eph. 2:1), there must be an inner work of the Spirit, convicting them of sin and giving them faith to trust in Christ. Even after spending three years at Jesus's side, the disciples' understanding of, much less testimony to, Christ's person and work depended on the descent of another witness from heaven: the Holy Spirit.

The church fathers (especially Irenaeus) spoke of the Son and the Spirit as the "two hands" of the Father. With these two hands, the Father draws us to his breast, so that we may share in that exchange of gift-giving love that the persons of the Trinity have enjoyed from all of eternity. After the Spirit clothes them, the disciples—themselves drawn into this communion of love—will be the emissaries sent out as God's witnesses for the final ingathering.

Therefore, it is not surprising that Jesus referred to the Spirit as "another attorney/witness [*parakletos*]," "even the Spirit of truth" who illumines the hearts of his people to understand Christ's teaching (John 14:16–17, 26). And John writes,

> The Spirit of truth, who proceeds from the Father, he will bear witness about me. And you also will bear witness, because you have been with me from the beginning. . . . And when [the Spirit] comes, he will convict the world concerning sin and righteousness and judgment: concerning sin, because they do not believe in me; concerning righteousness, because I go to the Father, and you will see me no longer; concerning judgment, because the ruler of this world is judged. I still have many things to say to you, but you cannot bear them now. When the Spirit of truth comes, he will guide you into all the truth, for he will not speak on his own authority, but whatever he hears he will speak, and he will declare to you the things that are to come. He will glorify me, for he will take what is mine and declare it to you. (John 15:26–27; 16:8–14)

And now in the last recorded words before the ascension, Jesus tells them, "You are witnesses of these things. And see, I am sending upon you what my Father promised; so stay here in the city until you have been clothed with power from on high" (Luke 24:48–49 NRSV). The Spirit brings about within us the "Amen!" of faith to all that Christ has accomplished. In the cosmic courtroom, the Spirit is the divine Cloud of Witness whose animating agency creates an ever-growing cloud of witnesses in heaven and on earth.

As John the Baptist announced, Jesus baptizes with the Spirit and with fire, and as Jesus confirmed in John 14–16, the Spirit comes with both salvation and with judgment. But this single event is unfolding in various stages. It requires patience.

We recognize the close connection between the Spirit and judgment in Peter's Pentecost sermon (Acts 2:14–41), where he announces the fulfillment of Joel's prophecy, which itself is unmistakably judicial in character (Joel 3:4, 12). In fact, Peter's explanation of the Spirit's outpouring harkens all the way back to Numbers 11:1–12:8, in which a weary Moses longs for the day when all the people are filled with the Spirit. The new creation has dawned and the Spirit descends in judgment, but this time not to scatter the proud nations and divide their languages (as at Babel) but to unite them in all of their diversity by the gospel. Because they are clothed with Christ, the Spirit's judgment turns out to be a benediction even greater than the one pronounced at creation. As Raymond Dillard comments, Joel prophesied that multitudes will come in that day "not to *make* a decision, but to *hear* the decision of God"[5] (see Joel 3:14). Pentecost inaugurates the day of reckoning—not the final day of judgment, but its prolepsis, as Israel and the nations are gathered to be judged and justified in these last days before the last day in which only judgment will prevail.

Through the Spirit's work of convicting sinners and uniting them to Christ for justification, the verdict of the last judgment is already rendered in the present: "There is therefore *now* no condemnation for those who are in Christ Jesus" (Rom. 8:1, emphasis added). Through this union also the Spirit makes us share in Christ's new-creation life, raising us from spiritual death and indwelling us as the down payment on our bodily resurrection in glory (Rom. 8:11, 23).

The Spirit at Pentecost

Israel's harvest festival of ingathering was always directed by the prophets to the coming day when a remnant from all nations would worship in Jerusalem. Just as Pentecost came fifty days after Passover in the Jewish calendar, the new Pentecost—the real Pentecost—comes fifty days after the Passover Lamb's sacrifice.

Jesus ordered the disciples to remain in Jerusalem "for the promise of the Father": the baptism with the Holy Spirit "not many days from now" (Acts 1:4–5). About 120 people were gathered in the upper room, near the temple, where pilgrims had gathered for the feast from far-flung regions.

> When the day of Pentecost had come, they were all together in one place. And suddenly from heaven there came a sound like the rush of a violent wind, and it filled the entire house where they were sitting. Divided tongues, as of fire, appeared among them, and a tongue rested on each of them. All of them were filled with the Holy Spirit and began to speak in other languages, as the Spirit gave them ability. (Acts 2:1–4 NRSV)

Astonished that uneducated Galileans were proclaiming the gospel in their own languages, the visitors' reactions ranged from "amazed and perplexed" to outright incredulity: "They are filled with new wine" (Acts 2:12–13).

Just as the Spirit's presence in Christ's ministry was identified with his proclamation of the gospel (Isa. 61:1–2; Luke 4:18–21), the consequence of the Spirit's descent at Pentecost was not unrestrained pandemonium but the public proclamation of the gospel by Peter, with the other apostles standing at his side (Acts 2:14–36). The one who had cowardly denied Christ three times was now risking his life for the message that the one who had been crucified only a short distance from where he was speaking had been raised and was at God's right hand. Stringing together a series of citations from the prophets and the Psalter, Peter proclaimed Christ and this remarkable descent of the Spirit as the fulfillment of everything the Scriptures had foretold. "Cut to the heart," three thousand people embraced Peter's message and were baptized (Acts 2:37–41). Thus began the fulfillment of the Great Commission.

Nothing like that had ever happened in Jesus's ministry. In John 6, Jesus drew his largest crowd by feeding the five thousand, but then he drove all but the Twelve away when he preached the difficult doctrines. Jesus had promised his disciples, "Truly, truly, I say to you, whoever believes in me will also do the works that I do; *and greater works than these will he do, because I am going to the Father.* Whatever you ask in my name, this I will do, that the Father may be glorified in the Son" (John 14:12–13, emphasis added). The Spirit was upon Jesus but did not yet indwell his hearers. Not until Jesus went through his exodus ordeal and his conquest of the heavenly sanctuary could the Spirit be sent to fill, indwell, and empower the disciples for the conquest on earth. Only the Spirit could unlock human hearts to understand and to receive the gospel.

Jesus Christ is the Word of the Father, but the Spirit makes that Word bear fruit in the hearts of those who are spiritually dead. With the Father, the Spirit gave the Son to sinners in the incarnation ("conceived by the Holy Spirit"), and in the upper room discourse (John 14–16) Jesus promised that when he ascends he will give the Spirit. We are the beneficiaries of this exchange of gifts between the persons of the Trinity.

Because of the Spirit's work, Christ himself is present in his Word, in baptism, and in the Supper, and he is present in the brothers and sisters who enrich us by their fellowship. He is our *prophet* through the lips of ministers, our *priest* through the service of deacons, and our *king* in the discipline of elders. In this way, the church does not replace

Jesus, but its ministry is the means of grace through which *he himself* creates, sustains, and expands his body. In this way, the Spirit makes of all Christians in their general office prophets, priests, and kings.

We have seen that God created humankind as an analogy of his own trinitarian life. We were meant to lead creation, with all of its varied parts, in a chorus of praise and thanksgiving. It is human beings, in their rebellion against God, who have "talked back," as it were, instead of answering back in obedient love. Instead of answering God's call with the proper response of a covenant servant—"Here I am; let it be done unto me according to your word"—we have built towers of Babel, aspiring toward a homogeneous unity in a Promethean attempt to conquer heaven as well as earth (Gen. 11). This parody of God's kingdom swings between individualistic anarchy and totalitarian unity. Although God still preserves and authorizes the secular state, it cannot create peaceful communion, a real fellowship of diversity in unity and unity in diversity. However, the same Spirit who descended on Babel's tower, confusing the languages and scattering the people, descended at Pentecost to form a genuine unity that preserved the rich diversity of language, culture, and custom (Acts 2:1–13).

The Spirit does not *replace* Jesus; he *gives* us Jesus, uniting a still weak body to its glorified head. The disciples must wait for the Spirit, but when the Spirit comes, they are on the move.

This is why the ascension narrative is followed by the replacement of Judas by Matthias. Why, in the run-up to Pentecost, does the church busy itself with details of church government? It's because the church is not just an invisible movement but a visible institution founded by Christ with the apostles as the foundation. In Acts 1:2 Luke reports that Jesus was "taken up, after he had given commands through the Holy Spirit to *the apostles whom he had chosen*" (emphasis added). Not surprisingly, then, the post-Pentecost church gathered regularly for "the *apostles' teaching* and the fellowship, to the breaking of bread and the prayers" (Acts 2:42, emphasis added). They are *authorized* to pass on what they have been taught by Jesus himself. This is the Great Commission: to go into all the world preaching the gospel, baptizing, and teaching everything Jesus had commanded. And their written testimony forms the canon or constitution that authorizes and defines all subsequent Christian witness, worship, doctrine, and practice. Nothing in Scripture is to be omitted and nothing is to be added. It is Christ's kingdom and he has given us his constitution, which is to endure without amendment until he returns.

We know that Christ's kingdom is at work in this world because sinners are being reconciled to God. From Peter's Pentecost sermon to the end of the book of Acts, the success of the kingdom is identified by the report, "And the Word of God spread." From Jerusalem to Rome and beyond, there is already a growing multitude who hear the Word, trust in Christ, are baptized, and begin their pilgrimage together—refreshed along the way by that same Word, fellowship in the Spirit, the Lord's Supper, and the prayers. Baptized into the new creation—that is, Christ—through faith, they form a nucleus of the church that will reach the ends of the earth.

This forgiveness of sins and the raising of those who are spiritually dead is a greater miracle than the raising of Lazarus. It is nothing less than the dawn of the new creation. In Ephesians 4, Paul highlights the significance of Christ's ascension in terms analogous to the conquest of a general who then distributes the spoils of victory to the soldiers—namely, pastors and teachers whose ministry of Word and sacrament builds up the whole body into its head through the truth.

As the writer to the Hebrews tells us, the powers of the age to come are breaking in on this present age in the power of the Spirit through the Word and sacraments of Christ in his kingdom of grace. The prophets identified the last days with the outpouring of the Spirit on all flesh. Because the Spirit has come, we are in "these last days." The rest of the book of Acts is the answer to the disciples' question, "Now are you going to restore the kingdom to Israel?" (see Acts 1:6).

The temple undergoes a makeover. It's no longer a local building but a worldwide house. No longer stationary in Jerusalem, the Spirit is once again on the move, "in Jerusalem and in all Judea and Samaria, and to the end of the earth" (Acts 1:8). This is why a central subplot running throughout Acts is Paul's effort to make it from Jerusalem, "the city of the Great King" (Ps. 48:2), to Rome, the city of Gentile power, the real "court of the Gentiles"—indeed, "the uttermost parts of the earth."

Peter declares,

> You yourselves like living stones are being built up as a spiritual house, to be a holy priesthood, to offer spiritual sacrifices acceptable to God through Jesus Christ. . . . But you are a chosen race, a royal priesthood, a holy nation, a people for his own possession, that you may proclaim the excellencies of him who called you out of darkness into his marvelous light. Once you were not a people, but now you are God's

people; once you had not received mercy, but now you have received mercy. (1 Peter 2:5, 9–10)

As word of this kingdom spreads, the temple grows, expanding, with each living stone reflecting the Light of the World through the indwelling Spirit.

Intermission: "You Are Here"

Now we can locate our place on the map of redemptive history. As I noted at the beginning of this chapter, there are two extremes in contemporary Christian interpretations of the kingdom. One extreme is to say that the kingdom is not present at all, but is an entirely future reality. "The kingdom, however, will also be a period of failure."[6] Thus, even in this future millennial kingdom the purpose is not only to dispense Christ's gifts, which he has already won by his own trial, but to provide "the final form of moral testing."[7]

The other extreme is to say that the kingdom is present in its all-encompassing form, transforming the kingdoms of this age into the kingdom of Christ. In this perspective, the main calling of Christians and churches is to redeem the culture and extend Christ's kingdom over politics, the arts, entertainment, sports, economics, law, and every other aspect of public and private life. We've gone from "soul winning and waiting for the rapture" to "kingdom transformation" in the blink of an eye.

The Great Commission is given to the church for this time between his first and second comings. It is an *intermission* between his accomplishment of redemption and his return to consummate its blessings. However, this intermission isn't a time for loitering in the lobby as consumers; it is a time of joyful activity on behalf of our neighbors: loving and serving them through our witness to Christ and also through our daily callings in the world.

This Great Commission is not the "cultural mandate"—the original commission to be fruitful and to multiply, ruling creation as God's viceroys. That is the covenant of creation, in which worship and cultural labors were fused in a vocation whose goal was nothing less than bringing all of creation into the everlasting Sabbath rest. It was this covenant that was renewed as God took Israel to himself as a chosen nation. "But like Adam they transgressed the covenant"

(Hosea 6:7). So once again, God cast his people out of his sanctuary, "east of Eden," into captivity, where they languished in hope for the coming Redeemer promised through the prophets even in the people's dire distress. Nevertheless, God again promised the coming seed who would bring salvation to the ends of the earth. It would be a new covenant, greater than the covenant that Israel swore at Mount Sinai.

The march toward the kingdom continued, even though its typological sign—the land and the temple—lay in ruins. The land of Israel was no longer holy but common. The Spirit had evacuated the temple and Judah joined its northern sister in exile. Yet even in Babylonian captivity, the people received the letter from the prophet Jeremiah:

> Thus says the LORD of hosts, the God of Israel, to all the exiles whom I have sent into exile from Jerusalem to Babylon: Build houses and live in them; plant gardens and eat their produce. Take wives and have sons and daughters; take wives for your sons, and give your daughters in marriage, that they may bear sons and daughters; multiply there, and do not decrease. But seek the welfare of the city where I have sent you into exile, and pray to the LORD on its behalf, for in its welfare you will find your welfare. For thus says the LORD of hosts, the God of Israel: Do not let your prophets and your diviners who are among you deceive you, and do not listen to the dreams that they dream, for it is a lie that they are prophesying to you in my name; I did not send them, declares the LORD. (Jer. 29:4–9)

Living like our exiled parents (Adam and Eve), "east of Eden," the children of Judah are to participate in the common life of the secular city. They find their welfare in the city's welfare and are therefore to pray for the commonwealth. Yet they are also to increase the size of the covenant community during this period, and the greatest threat is not persecution by the ungodly but the internal deceptions of unauthorized prophets. (As we will see, this is precisely the situation of the new-covenant church in its exile, and Jeremiah's exhortations bear striking resemblance to those of the apostles in their letters.)

Although a remnant returns to Jerusalem and seeks to rebuild the walls and rededicate itself to the covenant they made with God at Sinai, they realize that they are still in exile. Ruled by a series of oppressive Gentile regimes, punctuated by false messiahs and attempts to bring in the kingdom by force, the City of Peace is in perpetual turmoil. It is into this scene that John the Baptist steps as the forerunner of the Messiah.

It is this new covenant that forms the basis for the Great Commission: a holy task of bringing the Good News to the world. It is an unshakable kingdom—incapable of being thwarted by our own unfaithfulness—precisely because it is not a kingdom that we are *building* but one that we are *receiving* (Heb. 12:28). It is God's work. Everything that we will be exploring in the rest of this book presupposes the view of the kingdom that is summarized here.

Is the Kingdom Here Now?

How we define the kingdom will have a lot to do with whether we think it is already here and, if so, to what extent. Forgiveness of sins and the new birth are not the only things that God promised through the prophets. As we have seen, it includes a sweeping cosmic renewal, with the kingdoms of this world under the domain of Christ. It is the salvation not just of souls but of bodies, and not just of human beings but of the whole creation. Yet the New Testament teaches that this kingdom arrives in two phases. Like its head, the church suffers now in humiliation, under the cross, in order to reign in future glory with Christ (Rom. 8:17). In this intermission, the kingdom is the gospel and the gospel is the kingdom. Wherever Christ is forgiving and renewing sinners by his Spirit through the ministry of the gospel, the King is present and his kingdom is expanding.

This view focuses most clearly on the character and message of the kingdom that we find in the prophets and the Gospels. In both alternative accounts of the kingdom mentioned above, the emphasis falls on a geopolitical regime, whether it is in terms of a revived theocracy in Israel (including sacrifices) or an ever-expanding, global influence on nations and cultures. Both views identify the kingdom with visible power and glory, overlooking the fact that what we have now is a kingdom of grace that is present wherever the gospel is preached and the sacraments are administered. The preoccupation, in both views, seems to be analogous to the expectation of Jesus's contemporaries (even his disciples) prior to Pentecost.

Jesus and Paul explicitly invoke the distinction between "this age" and "the age to come" (Matt. 12:32; 24:3; 1 Cor. 2:6; Gal. 1:4). However, the contrast isn't as observably cut-and-dried as many had expected. With his triumph over the demonic forces, culminating in his death and resurrection, Jesus has inaugurated the age to come. And yet it is breaking into this present evil age. There is a clash between the realities of the age to come and the bondage of this age. There is an "already" and "not yet" aspect to the kingdom.

John the Baptist announced that "the kingdom of heaven is at hand" (Matt. 3:2), and Jesus announced that it had arrived as he healed the sick, raised the dead, and declared after the return of the seventy disciples from their mission, "I saw Satan fall like lightning from heaven" (Luke 10:18). "But if it is by the finger of God that I cast out demons," Jesus said, "then the kingdom of God has come upon you"; the strong man (Satan) has been bound, so that his house may be looted (Luke 11:20–22). Above all, sinners and outcasts are being forgiven directly by Jesus, without any connection to the temple machinery. With Satan bound, the apostles are called to go into all the world and unlock the prison doors and free the captives. They are given by Christ the keys of the kingdom, to bind and loose on earth what has been bound and loosed in heaven (Matt. 16:19; 18:18; John 20:23). The exodus is past, but now is the era of conquest through the witness of the gospel to the ends of the earth. Only when Jesus returns will the conquest be consummated as the kingdoms of this age are made the kingdom of our God and of his Christ.

In Matthew 24, part of Jesus's Olivet discourse, Jesus taught that he will come on the clouds of glory with all of his elect, but there are stages to be realized before this final event. First, the temple then standing will be completely destroyed (vv. 1–2), as indeed it was in AD 70. Then the disciples asked, "What will be the sign of your coming and of the *close* of the age?" (v. 3, emphasis added). Jesus replied that there will be imposters coming in his name, leading many astray, along with wars, "but the end is not yet. For nation will rise against nation, and kingdom against kingdom, and there will be famines and earthquakes in various places. All these are but the beginning of the birth pains" (vv. 6–8). There will be persecution and martyrdom for his followers, with many deserting Christ's flock. "But the one who endures to the end will be saved. *And this gospel of the kingdom will be proclaimed throughout the whole world as a testimony to all nations, and then the end will come*" (vv. 13–14, emphasis added). On the last day, Jesus will return on the clouds of glory to "gather his elect" from the whole earth and to judge the living and the dead (vv. 29–31). "But concerning that day and hour no one knows, not even the angels of heaven, nor the Son, but the Father only" (v. 36). It will come when people least expect it (vv. 36–44).

Contrary to the expectations of most of Jesus's contemporaries (including John the Baptist and his own disciples), this single event will not happen all at once. It will unfold in a series of fulfillments, and the era that we now occupy is the parenthesis in which the final judgment is postponed so that the gospel of the kingdom can be proclaimed to the whole world.

So we must be careful not to fall into the same misunderstanding of the kingdom that was shared by Jesus's contemporaries. Tasting morsels of that day, with various healings and victories over the demonic forces in the ministry of Jesus and his apostles, we want to see fully realized here and now the consummation to which these signs point. If necessary, we will bring about the consummation of this kingdom ourselves! We must resist this temptation, because it misunderstands that the most crucial vocation of the church in this present age is the proclamation of the gospel. "Being asked by the Pharisees when the kingdom of God would come, [Jesus] answered them, 'The kingdom of God is not coming with signs to be observed, nor will they say, "Look, here it is!" or "There!" for behold, the kingdom of God is in the midst of you'" (Luke 17:20–21).

The kingdom of God in this present phase is primarily *audible*, not visible. We hear the opening and shutting of the kingdom's gates through the proclamation of the gospel, in the sacraments, and in discipline. Taking no notice of the kingdom of God, the nations will be going about their daily business, engaging in violence and immorality as in the days of Lot, "eating and drinking, buying and selling, planting and building" (Luke 17:28), when Jesus will return suddenly. Jesus warned,

> Then if anyone says to you, "Look, here is the Christ!" or "There he is!" do not believe it. For false christs and false prophets will arise and perform great signs and wonders, so as to lead astray, if possible, even the elect. See, I have told you beforehand. So, if they say to you, "Look, he is in the wilderness," do not go out. If they say, "Look, he is in the inner rooms," do not believe it. For as the lightning comes from the east and shines as far as the west, so will be the coming of the Son of Man. (Matt. 24:23–27)

Like the disciples, the church today has to get used to the fact that Jesus is absent in the flesh and there is no substitute. The church cannot fill that gap or seize the glories of Christ's consummated kingdom until his return. In the meantime he carries on his heavenly work for us in his priestly and royal office, with his Spirit leading the ground campaign. Our works cannot fill up this gap between Christ's two advents. Our activity cannot compensate for his return in glory to consummate his kingdom. Rather, we are called to repent and believe in Christ, to make disciples, to be disciples, and to proclaim this gospel to the ends of the earth. The kingdom is *present*, but not yet *fully present*.

Only if we hold in slight esteem the forgiveness of sins, rebirth into the new creation, justification, sanctification, and the communion of saints can we fail to revel in these present realities of Christ's reign. In his resurrection, Christ has inaugurated the final resurrection of the dead. Already the verdict of the last judgment is being rendered in the present. Those who believe in Christ are already declared righteous, and those who do not are already condemned (John 3:16–19, 36). "There is therefore *now* no condemnation for those who are in Christ Jesus" (Rom. 8:1, emphasis added). The decisive verdict of the last day is already known for all who believe the gospel.

Furthermore, the renewal of the whole creation has already begun with the new birth, raising us from spiritual death and seating us with Christ by grace alone (Eph. 2:1–7). The Spirit's indwelling presence in our hearts is the down payment on our final resurrection and the renewal of creation (Rom. 8:20–23), "for in this hope we were saved" (v. 24). Yet we do not yet see these full effects of Christ's kingdom, Paul reminds us. "But if we hope for what we do not see, we wait for it with patience" (v. 25).

Everything that was promised through the prophets (including John the Baptist) is indeed part of the kingdom that Christ brings. In fact, it is true that they belong to *one and the same event*. However, it becomes clearer as the Gospels unfold that the manifestation of this kingdom occurs in *two phases*. At present, the Spirit is raising those who are spiritually dead and giving them faith, uniting them to Christ for present justification and sanctification as well as future glorification. Yet believers, like unbelievers, still suffer common ills as well as blessings. They eventually die, but believers die with the hope of the resurrection in a renewed heavens and earth. By his Word and Spirit, Christ is now gathering a people for himself. Only when he returns, however, will the angel proclaim with a loud voice, "The kingdom of the world has become the kingdom of our Lord and of his Christ, and he shall reign forever and ever" (Rev. 11:15).

Similar to Jesus's Olivet discourse, Paul describes this new creation as occurring in two phases:

> For as by a man came death, by a man has come also the resurrection of the dead. . . . But each in his own order: Christ the firstfruits, then at his coming those who belong to Christ. Then comes the end, when he delivers the kingdom to God the Father after destroying every rule and every authority and power. For he must reign until he has put all his enemies under his feet. The last enemy to be destroyed is death. (1 Cor. 15:21, 23–26)

In a sense, the resurrection of the dead has already begun—with Jesus as the firstfruits. Nevertheless, there is a delay between his resurrection and ours. And in this delay, the harvest multiplies, grows, and ripens.

Until Christ returns, the kingdoms of the world—and our daily callings in them—are common, not holy: working alongside non-Christians "east of Eden." Whether performed by Christians or non-Christians, these works are not a means of cultivating, guarding, and keeping God's holy sanctuary. These activities do not create, build, and expand Christ's kingdom of saving grace. Nevertheless, they are essential means through which our Lord preserves society through common grace. Thus, the Great Commission is qualitatively different from the mandate that God gave to Adam and Eve in the Garden and to Israel in Canaan. In fact, the Great Commission is given to the church only because *the Last Adam* has fulfilled that creation mandate, fulfilling all righteousness, bearing the curse, driving out the serpent, and being raised as the firstfruits of the new creation. Now the command to "be fruitful and multiply" is fulfilled by the Spirit through the raising of a worldwide spiritual family, the true offspring of Abraham. This is God's holy commonwealth in this age (1 Peter 2:9–10), the "Israel of God" (Gal. 6:16).

When we return to Jesus's teaching and actions in the Gospels, we can see this already/not yet tension. No longer "at hand," the kingdom is "here," Jesus announces (Matt.11:5–6; 12:28; 13:1–46; Mark 1:15; Luke 11:20; 15:4–32; 17:20–23). The King is present, inaugurating his kingdom. At the same time, he speaks of its full realization in the future (Matt. 6:10; 16:28; Mark 9:1; Luke 6:20–26; 9:27; 11:2; 13:28–29). The kingdom is coming but also has come (Matt. 12:28–29; Luke 11:20).

The manner in which the demons respond to Jesus shows his authority over them, but not just a raw power: it is his coming in his kingdom of grace and forgiveness that they fear most. Satan and his emissaries are busiest not with plotting wars and oppression; these are symptoms of the sinful condition that human beings are capable of generating on their own. However, Satan knows that if the Messiah fulfills his mission, the curse is lifted, his head is crushed, and his kingdom is toppled.

Through his earthly emissaries, the devil tried repeatedly to intercept the seed of the woman. Cain murdered Abel, but God gave Seth. Pharaoh slaughtered the Jewish male infants, but Moses was secretly rescued. The wicked Queen Athaliah had the whole house of David killed, but young Joash was secretly hidden away. Upon hearing the wise men announce the birth of the king of the Jews, Herod massacred the male infants, but Jesus was carried away with his parents to Egypt.

Now there is nothing Satan can do to keep the Messiah from being born, so he throws all of his energies into seducing him away from his mission. All of his forces are deployed in this last battle for "all authority in heaven and on earth" (Matt. 28:18). All of Jesus's miracles are pointers to this saving announcement; they are not ends in themselves. The kingdom comes with words and deeds. In the miracle stories it is said that Satan has bound these people (see for example Luke 13:11, 16). Christ is breaking into Satan's territory, setting history toward a different goal, bound to his own rather than to demonic powers. This is why Paul's call to spiritual battle in Ephesians 6 identifies the gospel, faith, the Word, and Christ's righteousness as the armor and weapons. Satan's energies are now directed against the church and its witness to Christ. The devil knows his house is being looted and his prisons are being emptied as the gospel is taken to the ends of the earth.

Whatever the salutary effects of this kingdom on the wider society due to Christians living as salt and light, this age cannot be saved. It is dying. Through his apostles, Christ declares to the churches, "Grace to you and peace from God our Father and the Lord Jesus Christ, who gave himself for our sins to deliver us from the present evil age, according to the will of our God and Father, to whom be the glory forever and ever" (Gal. 1:3–5). To be sure, the Spirit is also at work in *common grace*, restraining the spiritual entropy of this present evil age. However, the Spirit's *saving* mission is not to improve our lives in Adam, under the reign of sin and death, but to crucify us and raise us with Christ. Paul reminds us that "the appointed time has grown very short" (1 Cor. 7:29). We marry, live, and work in the world, but without anxious attachment to this present age, "for the present form of this world is passing away" (1 Cor. 7:31). Like God's counsel to the captives in Babylon, Peter exhorts believers to "conduct yourselves with fear *throughout the time of your exile*, knowing that you were ransomed from the futile ways inherited from your forefathers, not with perishable things such as silver or gold, but with the precious blood of Christ" (1 Peter 1:17–19, emphasis added). Fully involved with the common life of our neighbors, we are nevertheless pilgrims who, with Abraham, are "looking forward to the city that has foundations, whose designer and builder is God" (Heb. 11:10).

The Sermon on the Mount is not a generic set of timeless principles for individuals and nations, much less a basis for a "Jesus love ethic" over against the supposedly violent God of Israel. Jesus spoke of his coming judgment as something far more sweeping and everlasting than any of the holy wars that God commanded under Joshua. Rather, the Sermon on the Mount begins with the blessing from the Covenant Lord on his people and inaugurates a new regime of peace that is to be modeled by the citizens of his kingdom as they endure persecution and live together in the love that only Christ can give through his Spirit.

In Exodus 20, God gave his law at Sinai on the basis of his saving work: "I am the Lord your God, who brought you out of the land of Egypt, out of the house of bondage"; *therefore*, "you shall have no gods before Me" (vv. 2–3 NKJV). Summarizing what it means to love God and neighbor, the Ten Commandments are written on the human conscience in creation and remain perpetually binding on all people. However, the civil and ceremonial laws attached to the Decalogue were given uniquely and exclusively to Israel as God's holy nation. Similarly, in Matthew 5 the gospel in the Beatitudes is the basis for the law in the Sermon on the Mount, and the love of God and neighbor is stipulated in a new constitution given uniquely and exclusively to the Israel of God.

Instead of calling down God's judgment and driving out the Gentile nations, Jesus commands us to pray for our enemies. "You have heard that it was said, 'An eye for an eye and a tooth for a tooth' [Exod. 21:24; Lev. 24:20; Deut. 19:21]. But I say to you, Do not resist the one who is evil. But if anyone slaps you on the right cheek, turn to him the other also" (Matt. 5:38–39). God no longer sends plagues among the godless but "makes his sun rise on the evil and on the good, and sends rain on the just and on the unjust," and expects us to imitate his kindness (Matt. 5:45). This is not the time to judge our neighbors,

but to take the log out of our own eye (Matt. 7:1–5), to diligently
seek God's good gifts (vv. 7–11), to enter through the narrow gate
(vv. 13–14), and to bear good fruit (vv. 15–27).

In fact, when Jesus went to a Samaritan village to preach the Good
News and was rejected, James and John wanted to call for fire to fall
from heaven in judgment upon them, "but he turned and rebuked
them" (Luke 9:51–56). Nicknamed "sons of thunder," James and John
were clearly looking for a kingdom of glory all the way to the very
end. They even asked Jesus if they could be seated at his right and
left hand at the presidential inauguration, but Jesus told them that
they had no idea what they were asking for: namely, crucifixion with
Jesus (Mark 10:35–40). Unlike rulers of Gentile kingdoms, Jesus said
that he will reign by sacrificial service on behalf of his subjects, and
anyone who wants to be a leader in that kingdom will choose service
over power (Mark 10:41–44). "For even the Son of Man came not
to be served but to serve, and to give his life as a ransom for many"
(Mark 10:45). In this episode Jesus is simply repeating the themes of
the Sermon on the Mount.

There is no holy land over which to fight. There aren't even holy
places, shrines, or sanctuaries, since Christ and his people together
form the end-time sanctuary. Jesus was announcing the arrival of
the new covenant, which he would inaugurate in his own blood
(Matt. 26:28).

All human beings are still obligated to the moral law, and by that
law they will be judged (Rom. 1:18–19; 2:12–16). Even the ungodly
rulers of the Roman Empire enforce the remnants of this civil justice
as "God's ministers" by maintaining a relative order, justice, and peace
in this in-between time (Rom. 13). However, the church is the fruit
of Christ's ever-expanding reign, where the fellowship of the age to
come is already anticipated in this present age.

Confusing Christ's kingdom of grace with the Sinai theocracy was
precisely the error that Paul addressed especially in Galatians. The
kingdom of God in its present phase simply is the announcement
of the forgiveness of sins and, on this basis, entrance into the new
creation. The signs that Jesus performed were evidence that the age
to come had indeed broken in on this present evil age. That is why
he told John's disciples to return with the news of healings, but especially that "the poor have the good news preached to them," adding,
"And blessed is the one who is not offended by me" (Matt. 11:5–6).
In other words, this is his mission in his earthly ministry, and blessed

are those who are not put off by it, expecting something other than this salvation of sinners. God's kingdom is all-encompassing, yet it arrives in two stages with Christ's two advents.

When Christ returns in power and glory, there will be no need for the proclamation of the gospel, no need for faith or hope. There will only be love, since the reality will be evident and fully realized for everyone to see (Rom. 8:19–25; 1 Cor. 13:8–13).

It's not that the horizon of Jesus's contemporaries was too broad but that it was too narrow. While they were settling merely for a messiah who would restore geopolitical theocracy, Jesus Christ was bringing a universal dominion—not just overthrowing Gentile oppressors but casting out the serpent from heaven and earth forever: "for behold, the kingdom of God is in the midst of you" (Luke 17:21). In the present era, his kingdom of grace is a reprieve for repentance and faith in Israel and throughout all nations before Christ's return. It is a new creation at work in the world, a new covenant yielding new relationships with God and with each other based on forgiveness and fellowship rather than on judgment and exclusion.

After Pentecost: The Kingdom in Acts and the Epistles

A great deal happens in Acts 2. From the throne of the ascended Christ the Spirit is sent, creating and indwelling a body that will witness to Christ from Jerusalem to the ends of the earth (vv. 1–13). Its first sign is Peter's sermon proclaiming Christ (vv. 14–36), from which a new covenant community is born. "Repent and be baptized every one of you in the name of Jesus Christ for the forgiveness of your sins, and you will receive the gift of the Holy Spirit. For the promise is for you and for your children and for all who are far off, everyone whom the Lord our God calls to himself" (vv. 38–39). We are told that "about three thousand souls" were "cut to the heart" by this message (vv. 37, 41). As particular persons, they repented, believed, and were baptized, but they were organized by the Spirit into a new human society. "And they devoted themselves to the apostles' teaching and the fellowship, to the breaking of bread and the prayers" (v. 42). From this shared union with Christ, these pilgrims from faraway regions were so united with each other that the worshiping community itself was a witness to the world. "And the Lord added to their number day by day those who were being saved" (v. 47).

We have seen that the forgiveness of sins and the new birth are at the heart of Jesus's proclamation of the kingdom. Proclaimed first to the Jews, this gospel will be preached to all nations. This is the fulfillment of the prophetic vision of a remnant from every nation—even those nations that had persecuted Israel—seeking the Lord where he may be found. "In those days ten men from the nations of every tongue shall take hold of the robe of a Jew, saying, 'Let us go with you, for we have heard that God is with you'" (Zech. 8:23).

The apostles typically interpreted these prophecies as being fulfilled now in Jesus Christ and his gathering of a remnant from Israel and the nations by his Spirit. Amos 9 speaks of the final restoration of Israel in concrete terms. Yet James interprets this prophecy as now being fulfilled in the kingdom of Christ, through the ingathering of a remnant of the Gentiles into the true Israel (Acts 15:14–18). James's interpretation is typical of the Christ-centered reading of the whole of Scripture that Jesus Christ himself taught his disciples (Luke 24:25–27, 31–32, 44–49).

Pitting Jesus (and the kingdom motif) against Paul (and the emphasis on personal salvation) used to be a hobby of liberal Protestants. Alfred Loissy, a liberal Roman Catholic writer, once quipped that Jesus announced a kingdom, but instead it was a church that came. So on one side is Jesus, with his invitation to humanity to participate in his kingdom by bringing peace and justice, and on the other side is Paul who spoke instead of the church and personal salvation by belonging to it.

Today, however, this contrast is sometimes heard in evangelical circles. "While some Protestants seem to let Jesus be Savior, but promote Paul to lord and teacher," writes Brian McLaren, "Anabaptists have always interpreted Paul through Jesus, and not the reverse. For them the Sermon on the Mount and the other words of Jesus represent the greatest treasure in the world. Jesus's teachings have been their standard."[8] In his latest book, McLaren relates that he used to be a "Romans Christian" who understood the gospel as God's justification of sinners through faith in Christ. "A lunchtime meeting in a Chinese restaurant unconvinced and untaught me. My lunch mate was a well-known Evangelical theologian who quite rudely upset years of theological certainty with one provocative statement: 'Most Evangelicals haven't got the foggiest notion of what the gospel really is.'" After McLaren answered by quoting Romans, his friend "followed up with this simple but annoying rhetorical question: 'You're quoting

Paul. Shouldn't you let Jesus define the gospel?'" And as for Jesus, the friend added, the gospel is "The kingdom of God is at hand." *"The kingdom of God is at hand*, or, in the words of my friend Rod Washington, *God's new benevolent society is already among us.*"[9]

However, the "red letter" (words of Jesus) method of interpretation assumes a deficient doctrine of Scripture. Jesus's words, teachings, and actions were remembered, related, and interpreted *by his apostles*. Just as he had promised in the upper room, Jesus sent the Spirit so that they would remember everything that he taught them and would be able to pass that on to others. If "all Scripture is God-breathed" (2 Tim. 3:16 NIV) and if Paul, having been directly commissioned and taught by the ascended Christ, was an apostle whose writings were recognized as "Scripture" (2 Peter 3:15–16), then to hear Paul *is* to hear Jesus. "Whoever receives you receives me," Jesus told the Twelve when he sent them out, "and whoever receives me receives him who sent me" (Matt. 10:40). The whole Bible is canon, and Scripture interprets Scripture.

Besides revealing a seriously deficient view of Scripture, this contrast between Jesus and Paul rests on a misunderstanding of our Lord's teaching concerning the kingdom. Jesus's proclamation of the kingdom is identical to Paul's proclamation of the gospel of justification. Contrasting the kingdom with the church is another way of saying that the main point of Jesus's commission consists in our social action rather than in the public ministry of Word and sacrament. In other words, it's another way of saying that we are building the kingdom rather than receiving it; that the kingdom of God's redeeming grace is actually a kingdom of our redeeming works.

Jesus's message of the kingdom as the forgiveness of sins and the dawning of the new creation was inseparable from his promise to build his church and to give his apostles the keys of the kingdom through the ministry of preaching, sacrament, and discipline. This motif of the kingdom was hardly lost in the apostolic era. It was this gospel of the kingdom that Peter and the other apostles proclaimed immediately after Jesus's ascension (Acts 2:14–36; 3:12–16; 17:2–3). And this is also the heart of Paul's message (1 Cor. 15:3–4).

If the preaching of the gospel, no less than the miracles, is the sign that the kingdom has come, Paul's message and ministry can only serve as confirmation of the kingdom's arrival. All of the realities that the gospels announce as evidence of the messianic kingdom—judgment and justification, forgiveness, a new birth, the gift of the Spirit, and the gathering of a people for the end-time feast—are central in Paul's preaching in Acts and in his letters.

Sometimes it is suggested that Jesus proclaimed a this-worldly reign, while Paul spiritualized this reign as a purely other-worldly reality limited to personal salvation. Whereas Jesus challenged Caesar's temporal authority, Paul encouraged a passive resignation to secular rulers. However, it was Jesus who famously said, "Render to Caesar the things that are Caesar's, and to God the things that are God's" (Mark 12:17). Before Pilate, Jesus affirmed that he was a king but said, "My kingdom is not of this world. If my kingdom were of this world, my servants would have been fighting, that I might not be delivered over to the Jews. But my kingdom is not from the world" (John 18:36). When he comes in glory, his kingdom will be glorious in power and might.

And although Paul called Christians to submit to secular authorities as God's ministers of temporal justice (Rom. 13), he proclaimed Christ as Lord over all principalities and powers (Col. 1:15–17). Although he never invoked his *apostleship* as authority over temporal government, Paul did invoke his Roman *citizenship* by appealing his case to Caesar over the judgment of the Jewish court (Acts 25:11). Christ is Lord over both the kingdom of grace and the kingdoms of this age, but in saving grace (through Word and sacrament) and in common grace (through government and culture). The church is neither to rule over secular kingdoms nor to separate from them, but to live in Babylon in the active expectation of Christ's return.

Paul too teaches that the new creation/kingdom has been inaugurated in Christ's conquest: the righteousness of God has been revealed from heaven (Rom. 1:16–17), including justification of sinners and new birth, the Spirit and his gifts poured out (Rom. 5:5). Christ has all authority in heaven and on earth (Rom. 1:3–4; Eph. 1:18–22; Phil. 2:9–11; Col. 1:15–20).

Like Jesus, Paul teaches that the in-breaking of Christ's kingdom creates a new society. Remarkably similar to the Sermon on the Mount, 1 Corinthians extrapolates the implications of Jesus's new-covenant ethic. Neither Jesus nor Paul interprets these commands as the *gospel*, but as the law of God's household. It is a law that can only be obeyed because the new age or new covenant has dawned. With the forgiveness of sins and new birth comes a new fellowship of love in the body of Christ. The gospel breaks down the walls not only between Jew and Gentile but also between rich and poor. Instead of mirroring their pagan culture, believers are called to settle their disputes between each other in church courts rather than secular ones. They are not to capitulate to a culture of immorality, divorce, socioeconomic and ethnic hierarchies, and the group narcissism that divides Christ's body into competing sects. Rather, united to Christ by his Spirit around the Word and the Lord's Table, Paul tells the Corinthian saints that they are to grow into his body: an embassy of grace in an empire of death.

The tension between the "already" and "not yet" character of the kingdom that we have discovered in Jesus's teaching dominates Paul's horizon as well as that of the other apostles. As the writer to the Hebrews declares, Jesus Christ is already now "heir of all things," even though we don't yet *see* everything in subjection to him (Heb. 1:1–4). Our riches today are the spoils of Christ's triumph that are poured out by his Spirit upon people "from every tribe and language and people and nation," being made into "a kingdom and priests to our God" (Rev. 5:9–10). Since Christ's ascension and the descent of the Spirit at Pentecost, we have been living in "the last days" (Acts 2:17; 2 Tim. 3:1; Heb. 1:2; James 5:3; 1 Peter 1:20; 2 Peter 3:3; 1 John 2:18; Jude 18), before the "last day" (John 6:39–40, 44, 54; 11:24; 12:28). Christ appeared "at the end of the ages" (Heb. 9:26), yet "the age to come" even now is breaking in upon us through preaching and sacrament (Heb. 6:5).

Paul says that "the end of the ages has come" (1 Cor. 10:11), yet "the day of the Lord will come like a thief in the night" (1 Thess. 5:2). This is precisely how Jesus described his second coming in the Olivet discourse. And one could hardly find better confirmation of Jesus's promise that "this gospel of the kingdom will be proclaimed throughout the whole world as a testimony to all nations, and then the end will come" (Matt. 24:14) than in Paul's mission and message. "For he must reign until he has put all his enemies under his feet. The last enemy to be destroyed is death" (1 Cor. 15:25–26). The presence of the Spirit in our hearts as a pledge of the consummation assures that what he has begun in us he will complete. The Spirit brings the blessings of the age to come into the present, which fills us not only with unspeakable joy but also with unutterable longing for the "more" still up ahead (Rom. 8:18–25).

Whatever its wider effects might be, at present the kingdom of Christ itself is not a geopolitical, economic, or cultural force. Just as Jesus said that his kingdom is not of this world, Paul writes, "For we do not wrestle against flesh and blood, but against the rulers, against the authorities, against the cosmic powers over this present darkness, against the spiritual forces of evil in the heavenly places" (Eph. 6:12). Our only weapons are the Spirit and the Word of the gospel. Through faith in Christ we have "the breastplate of righteousness," "the belt of truth," "the shield of faith," and "shoes" ready to run with "the gospel of peace" (Eph. 6:14–16).

Jesus's announcement that he has bound the strong man so that the veil of unbelief may be torn from the eyes of Satan's prisoners is elaborated by Paul (2 Cor. 4:3). Christ has triumphed over Satan at the cross (Col. 2:13–15) and in his resurrection and ascension frees captives (Eph. 4:8–10). The apostles with one voice declare with their Lord that Christ is now reigning (Acts 2:24–25; 3:20–21; 1 Cor. 15:25; Heb. 1:3, 8, 13; 8:1; 10:12–13). For this reason, Jesus can assure his persecuted saints, "Fear not, I am the first and the last, and the living one. I died, and behold I am alive forevermore, and I have the keys of Death and Hades" (Rev. 1:17–18).

In this interim period, the kingdom advances alongside the suffering and even martyrdom of its witnesses. Yet Christ "will appear a second time, not to bear sin, but to bring salvation to those who are waiting for him" (Heb. 9:28 NIV; see also 10:37). The regeneration of fallen creation works in concentric circles, beginning with the inner person and then, at the consummation, including the resurrection of the body and the complete renewal of creation. Wherever the New Testament treats the complex of Christ's return, the resurrection, and the last judgment, no intervening raptures, resurrections, or judgments are mentioned. Only if we are looking for the kingdom in something other than the reconciliation of sinners to God in Christ can we fail to appreciate its miraculous expansion to the ends of the earth.

The book of Revelation gives us glimpses of the heavenly worship and the earthly contest as simultaneous events, like watching a split screen on television. Cast out of heaven by the conquering King, Satan "was thrown down to the earth, and his angels were thrown down with him" (Rev. 12:9). Yet we read,

> And I heard a loud voice in heaven, saying, "Now the salvation and the power and the kingdom of our God . . . have come, for the accuser of our brothers has been thrown down, who accuses them day and night before our God. And they have conquered him by the blood of the Lamb and by the word of their testimony, for they loved not their lives even unto death. Therefore, rejoice, O heavens and you who

dwell in them! But woe to you, O earth and sea, for the devil has come down to you in great wrath, because he knows that his time is short!" (Rev. 12:10–12)

Heaven is conquered, the temple cleansed forever, with the prosecuting attorney disbarred—and yet earth becomes the theater for his futile fury against the church. Especially for our brothers and sisters suffering persecution—and even martyrdom—around the world today, these words are as relevant as when they were first penned.

The Gospel Is the Kingdom and the Kingdom Is the Gospel

The "gospel of the kingdom" (Matt. 24:14) and the "keys of the kingdom" (Matt. 16:19) are really synonymous. They both refer to the proclamation of the forgiveness of sins and the renewal of all things that has begun even now with the in-gathering of outcasts to Zion. Furthermore, both of these phrases are synonymous with the Great Commission.

If John the Baptist could proclaim with seriousness, "Repent, for the kingdom of heaven is at hand" (Matt. 3:2), it is all the more urgent that we repent and believe now that the Messiah has come. The foundation of this repentance is the forgiveness of sins, as John Calvin observed:

> From this doctrine, as its source, is drawn the exhortation to repentance. For John does not say, "Repent ye, and in this way the kingdom of heaven will afterwards be at hand;" but first brings forward the grace of God, and then exhorts men to repent. Hence it is evident that the foundation of repentance is the mercy of God, by which he restores the lost. . . . [Forgiveness is] first in order . . . so it must be observed that pardon of sins is bestowed upon us in Christ, not that God may treat them with indulgence, but that he may heal us from our sins.[10]

In its present phase, the kingdom is the gospel and the gospel is the kingdom:

> Now the means is His Gospel. Also that is why Jesus Christ spoke so often of the Gospel, calling it the Kingdom of God. "The Gospel of the Kingdom" can also be translated "the Gospel, which is the Kingdom." It is not, then, without cause that the Gospel is called "the Kingdom of God." . . . Jesus Christ always has some company wherever the Gospel is preached. For He is not a King without subjects.[11]

In the West, history is divided into periods: ancient, medieval, modern, and postmodern. Today CNN has its own list of headlines. However, the real turning point in history is the resurrection of Jesus Christ. This turning point is not only celebrated but is deepened and widened in its effects every Lord's Day. Wherever this gospel is taken, a piece of heaven—the age to come—begins even now to dawn in the dusty corners of this passing evil age.

The Mission Statement

Go therefore and make disciples
of all nations.

Matthew 28:19

O n the basis of the great announcement concerning Christ's victory, the church is called to bring this Good News to the ends of the earth. Wide in its breadth ("all nations") and deep in its intensiveness ("make disciples"), the mission statement is delivered with a sense simultaneously of joy and urgent seriousness. What does it mean and how is it pursued today, especially in a context of religious pluralism?

3

An Urgent Imperative

"Go Therefore..."

My children play every day with Muslim neighbors in our backyard. During Ramadan, my wife and I have to make sure we don't cave in to the younger children when they beg for a snack. Our lives are interwoven with a wide diversity of relatives, friends, co-workers, and neighbors. They're gay and straight, Mormons and atheists, New Agers and agnostics—and everything in between.

The "other" cannot be as easily objectified, labeled, and depersonalized as the pagan, the infidel, the enemy far away. What happens to these wonderful people to whom we are bound by friendship and family ties? Can we even imagine that, apart from hearing and believing the gospel, they will be condemned to eternal death by the same Jesus we call Lord and Savior? These are tough questions that touch us at the deepest emotional level. Does Scripture offer clear answers? If not, then insisting upon faith in Jesus as "the only way" is indeed just another form of religious bigotry.

The word "missionary" sounds antiquated—and to some people, arrogant or even violent. Even "evangelism" has increasingly negative connotations in the wider culture and among some younger Christians who have had to explain to their friends at college why "Campus

Crusade for Christ" is not a terrorist organization. Although it is an infelicitous term in any age, especially in a post-9/11 world, nobody wants to have "crusades." And in an era in which the line between God and country is often blurred, non-Christians may be forgiven for fearing martial imagery.

Except in the surviving remnants of the culture wars, the military metaphors of Scripture, which once dominated conservative Protestant preaching and songs, have all but surrendered to friendlier images. The Christian life is described today less in terms of a spiritual battle and more as personal and social transformation.

Given the confusion of Christ and culture, as well as the global threat of religious violence, it's understandable that we would flinch at battlefield language. Yet are we overreacting? Not that long ago, you might have been pigeonholed on the street by a zealous believer, waving a Bible with intensity. That seems like a pretty rare occurrence today. "Let's just let our lives do the talking," we conclude. But is there something in between these extremes?

Many Christians today feel awkward taking stands on doctrinal issues that sound increasingly alien in our pluralistic culture. We don't want to come off as the bellicose and judgmental know-it-all. Even in the church, we often shy away from doctrinal discussions for fear of appearing proud or divisive. In addition, recent conversations between evangelicals and Roman Catholics have softened the urgency and even the propriety of evangelical proselytizing in nominally Roman Catholic as well as nominally Protestant countries.

Yet in reaction against perversions of our missionary mandate, are we in danger of surrendering to a culture that privatizes and relativizes ultimate truth claims? In this environment there is a lot of pressure to downplay the communication of the gospel in favor of simply letting our lives do the talking. It's deeds, not creeds, that count. But is this false humility? Doesn't this approach suggest that our confidence has shifted from Christ's person and work to our own?

The mission statement that Jesus delivered to his church is an urgent imperative to proclaim the gospel to *everyone*, to make disciples of all nations. From the beginning, Christianity has been a missionary faith. Though beginning in Jerusalem, the gospel was brought by the apostles and evangelists to diaspora Jews living in cities throughout the Roman Empire and then spread rapidly to Gentiles ("to the Jew first and also to the Greek," Rom. 1:16). On his way to another persecution of Christians, Saul was transformed by a vision in which he was addressed by the ascended Christ. Changing his name to Paul, the apostle to the Gentiles died as a martyr in Rome. The apostles proclaimed that Jesus is God the Creator and Redeemer (John 1:1–5, 14; Col. 1:15–20). Jesus said, "I am the way, and the truth, and the life. No one comes to the Father except through me" (John 14:6). He is the gate to paradise (John 10:7–9), and all who trust in him will be saved; those who do not believe are "condemned already" (John 3:18).

The Great Commission provoked fresh divisions in families and communities. When I read Christ's announcement about dividing families and the record of the early Christians who were actually turned in to the authorities by parents and siblings, I am ashamed of my reticence to offer a clear testimony to Christ at my own family reunions. And when I hear similar stories from persecuted Christians today, I wonder at my hesitancy over the offense of the gospel.

Yet the gospel also forged a strange unity between erstwhile enemies. Though not without initial conflict, the wall separating Jew and Gentile was torn down. The gospel, not ethnic heritage, united the followers of Christ. The fierce imperial persecution of Christians, sporadic but often gruesome, only fanned the flames of testimony to the Lamb. As the second-century church father Tertullian is said to have remarked, "The blood of the martyrs is the seed of the church."

Onward Christian Soldiers—*Really!*

Everything changed with the conversion of the emperor Constantine in the fourth century. The persecuted church became the favored church, and the kingdom of Christ became identified with the Holy Roman Empire. The martyr's cry for Christ's return ("How long, O Lord?") gave voice to the obvious clash between the powers of this age and the powers of the age to come. However, the paradoxical tension between the "already" and "not yet" surrendered to a triumphalistic spirit. The church's sense of its ambiguous and threatened existence, relying only on God's Word and Spirit, faded, along with any serious distinction between the kingdom of grace and the kingdom of glory, the state of humiliation under the cross and the state of exaltation, the empires of this age and the reign of Christ through the gospel.

It is true enough that Islam is not just a religion but an all-encompassing political, socioeconomic, and legal system. It comes not with a gospel but with a law and with a literal sword to back it up. Yet Islam learned much of this from Byzantine/medieval Christianity, with its fusion of Christ and empire. The ancient church historian Eusebius celebrated his patron Constantine as Christ's earthly image: "Our divinely favored emperor, receiving, as it were, a transcript of the divine sovereignty, directs, in imitation of God himself, the administration of this world's affairs." With divine mandate, therefore, the emperor "subdues and chastens the open adversaries of the truth in accordance with the usages of war."[1]

In the fifth century, Augustine offered a radically different interpretation, distinguishing between the everlasting City of God and the temporal City of Man.[2] However, the fusion of the kingdom of Christ with the empire triumphed. Medieval monarchs fancied themselves King David *redivivus*, driving out the Canaanites with their holy knights with the blessing of the high priest. On a cold November day in 1095, Pope Urban II roused a Christendom plagued by internal wars to take up the cause of holy war against Islam. "If you must have blood," he exhorted, "bathe in the blood of infidels."[3]

In both the medieval Christian and Muslim versions, the basic assumption is the same as that which Jesus's disciples shared with their contemporaries: the kingdom of God is a geopolitical as well as spiritual empire, a revival of the old-covenant theocracy. Passages from Joshua could be invoked by Christians for "holy war." As recently as a 2006 *Time* cover story, one American Catholic scholar said of the pope, "His role is to represent Western civilization."[4] But does anyone—even the pope—really believe that today?

At least the zealots of Jesus's day had more of a right to invoke the conquest narratives and the civil laws given at Sinai. However, the medieval versions simply lifted these passages out of their context and applied them to their own regimes, just as many Protestants in the United States invoke promises like 2 Chronicles 7:14 every Fourth of July as if it applied to America. Although Paul says that "our struggle is not against flesh and blood" (Eph. 6:12 NIV), in both the culture wars at home and the "war on terror" abroad, I have often heard evangelicals speak as if it were otherwise. Perhaps there is no better example of mission creep than "Christendom."

The same confusion of Christ's kingdom with cultural transformation can be seen on the left as well as the right. It's just a different agenda. I believe that Christ's teaching concerning the kingdom is far more radical than anything that we are hearing on either side today. The Lord who gave us the Great Commission not only knows every contingency; he rules over it all. Mission creep is bad enough when you have ambiguous military intelligence, but it is especially unconscionable when our Commander is the one to whom "all authority in heaven and on earth" has been entrusted.

Christ's mission statement is just as urgent and just as universal, yet in entirely different ways and for entirely different reasons, and employing entirely different methods than Islam, secularism, or other principalities and powers at work in the world that oppose the kingdom of God and his Messiah. The mission is urgent because although Jesus Christ has come in humility and suffered to seek and to save the lost, he will return in judgment.

On one hand, we have to defend—on theological grounds—the political freedoms of our non-Christian neighbors. On the other hand, we have to acknowledge to the world with gentleness and humility, but also with confidence in God's Word, that outside of Christ there is no "sacrifice for sins, but a fearful expectation of judgment, and a fury of fire that will consume the adversaries" (Heb. 10:26–27). And as this passage makes clear, this is as true of nominal Christians as it is of Muslims, Jews, Buddhists, and atheists.

The era in which we are now living, between these two advents, is "the day of salvation," the intermission in which the Spirit is bringing a remnant from all nations to Jesus Christ. It is therefore a universal mandate, precisely because the kingdom is identified not with any nation on earth but with God's heavenly mission to all peoples. There is not something called Christianity and then missionaries who spread it. Christianity is in its very essence a mission to the world. If it is not reaching, teaching, baptizing, and multiplying disciples, it is not Christianity.

When Jesus appeared to his disciples in the upper room on Easter Sunday evening, declaring, "Peace be with you," he showed his hands and side. "Then the disciples were glad when they saw the Lord. Jesus said to them again, 'Peace be with you.'" And then he prepared them for their commission: "As the Father has sent me, even so I am sending you. . . . Receive the Holy Spirit. If you forgive the sins of any, they are forgiven; if you withhold forgiveness from any, it is withheld" (John 20:19–23).

Our Savior presides over the expanding economy of forgiveness rather than of debt. There is a holy war, but in it "we do not wrestle against flesh and blood," and the only armor that will serve us in this cosmic battle is God's Word and Spirit, focusing on the gospel of peace that withstands Satan's schemes and overthrows his kingdom (Eph. 6:12–17). We cannot give up the missionary imperative. We cannot negotiate the terms of God's peace treaty with the world.

The Mission Statement

Mark's version of the Great Commission reads, "Go into all the world and proclaim the gospel to the whole creation. Whoever believes and is baptized will be saved, but whoever does not believe will be condemned" (Mark 16:15–16).

Clearly, then, the imperative is *urgent*. As the writer to the Hebrews reminds us solemnly, "Just as it is appointed for man to die once, and after that comes judgment, so Christ, having been offered once to bear the sins of many, will appear a second time, not to deal with sin but to save those who are eagerly waiting for him" (Heb. 9:27–28).

Not only is it urgent; it is *specific*. In this time between Christ's two comings, the church's task is to "proclaim the gospel to the whole creation." There is no mandate for the church to develop a political, social, economic, or cultural plan. Although it teaches the whole Word of God, both the law and the gospel, the church's mission is not even to reform the morals of society. Whatever effects the gospel has in the lives of its hearers and in the wider society in which it is heard, *the Great Commission itself* is a very specific mandate to get the Good News to everyone who lies in darkness, to baptize them, and to teach them everything in God's Word.

Like the gospel and the kingdom of God, the Great Commission is becoming so elastic and general that its focus is blurred. All three of these terms have become a cliché for anything that churches (or individual Christians) want to do that they regard as helpful and worthwhile.

Christians are called to do many things and to work diligently in many vocations, not only as church members but as parents, children, neighbors, co-workers, citizens, and volunteers. However, everything that *the church* is called to do as a visible institution—not only its ministry of preaching but its public service of prayers, singing, sacraments, fellowship, government, and discipline—is to be a means of delivering this gospel to the whole creation. Even those raised in the church must be evangelized every Lord's Day, inserted again and again into the dying and rising of our Living Head. The same message that created faith in the beginning sustains it throughout our pilgrimage. It is the gift that keeps on giving, and it is intended to be given away by us to others outside of the covenant community.

The Original Recipients of the Great Commission

Taken from the language of the battlefield, *euangelion* means "good news" of military victory, which was brought back to the capitol by a herald or ambassador. The Great Commission begins not with an imperative, a plan, a strategy for our victory in the world, but with the announcement that Christ has conquered sin and death. "Therefore, having this ministry by the mercy of God," Paul tells the Corinthians, "we do not lose heart. . . . And even if our gospel is veiled, it is veiled only to those who are perishing" (2 Cor. 4:1, 3). "All this is from God, who through Christ reconciled us to himself and gave us the ministry of reconciliation. . . . Therefore, we are ambassadors for Christ, God making his appeal through us" (2 Cor. 5:18, 20). Ambassadors do not create the constitution. They do not forge foreign and domestic policy or negotiate the terms of God's peace treaty. They simply announce liberation and communicate the new constitution of Christ's heavenly colony on earth.

In these Pauline references, as in the Great Commission itself, the primary audience is the circle of the apostles. Their ministry was extraordinary. Called directly by God incarnate, they were eyewitnesses of his majesty (2 Peter 1:16). They laid the foundation upon which the ordinary ministers would build Christ's end-time sanctuary (1 Cor. 3:11). The ambassadors are commanded to go and speak for the King. "Therefore," says Paul, "we are ambassadors for Christ, God making his appeal through us. *We implore you on behalf of Christ, be reconciled to God.* For our sake he made him to be sin who knew no sin, so that in him we might become the righteousness of God" (2 Cor. 5:20–21, emphasis added). In fact, in the very next verse Paul expresses the close relationship between God's work and the work of the apostles: "Working together with him, then, we appeal to you not to receive the grace of God in vain," but to embrace and keep the testimony to Christ that they have heard (6:1).

Unlike the false prophets in Jeremiah 23, the apostles have stood in the Lord's council, as members of the cabinet with the president, and now they bring the terms of the treaty to the world that is under his authority. They received everything from the Lord directly, and now we receive everything from the Lord through them. Their writings are the canon or constitution of Christ's kingdom, and now the people of God are commanded "not to go beyond what is written, that none of you may be puffed up in favor of one against another" (1 Cor. 4:6). After all, Paul adds, "What do you have that you did not receive? If then you received it, why do you boast as if you did not receive it?" (1 Cor. 4:7).

This *extraordinary* ministry came to an end, but the *ordinary* ministry continues through those like Timothy who were called by God indirectly through the laying on of hands by the body of elders (1 Tim. 4:14; see also 1 Tim. 5:17–19; Titus 1:5; James 5:14; 1 Peter 5:1, 5; 3 John 1:1). In Galatians 1, Paul takes pains to defend his apostleship as something he received directly from the ascended Christ. However, he exhorted Timothy, "You then, my child, be strengthened by the grace that is in Christ Jesus, and what you have heard from me in the presence of many witnesses entrust to faithful men who will be able to teach others also" (2 Tim. 2:1–2). Although the special office of ambassador was entrusted to faithful ministers and elders, the Spirit baptizes every believer into the general office of prophet, priest, and king in Christ.

Because all authority has been given to Christ, the apostles were not simply pleading with sinners, much less negotiating the terms. Rather, they were issuing a command in Christ's name: "Be reconciled to God!" Whereas God worked without human agents when he created the world by commanding, "Let there be light," he condescends to work together with us in his miraculous act of creating light out of darkness: "the light of the gospel of the glory of Christ, who is the image of God. For what we proclaim is not ourselves," Paul adds, "but Jesus Christ as Lord, with ourselves as your servants for Jesus's sake. For God, who said, 'Let light shine out of darkness,' has shone in our hearts to give the light of the knowledge of the glory of God in the face of Jesus Christ" (2 Cor. 4:4–6). As in the original creation, God speaks his new creation into being by his Word and Spirit. When his ambassadors speak this Word, the Spirit actually brings about the new world of which they speak. Because the Spirit works through the Word, it will never return to him empty, without having accomplished its intended purpose (Isa. 55:11).

Not only the apostles nor even the ordinary ministers who would succeed them but *all believers* are endowed with this royal authority to "proclaim the excellencies of him who called you out of darkness into his marvelous light" (1 Peter 2:9). In the Gospels, the circle of witnesses extends from the Twelve to the seventy to the "three thousand souls" who were added to the church through Peter's Pentecost sermon (Acts 2:41). From that point on, we hear repeatedly in Acts that "the Word spread" rapidly. The kingdom continues to spread in the same concentric circles: from Christ to his apostles (the New Testament) to the ordinary ministers to the whole Spirit-filled community of witnesses.

Deep and Wide

First, this Commission is *deep in its intensiveness*. The eleven disciples of the Lord are called to make disciples, not just converts. Second, this Commission is *wide in its extensiveness*. Not only are the nations streaming to Zion; Zion itself is a mobile, Spirit-powered chariot winding its course throughout the earth. In Christ, the "unclean" (Gentiles) are made holy. The promise made to Adam and Eve of a new Adam and to Abraham and Sarah concerning the seed in whom all the nations of the earth will be blessed was renewed by the prophets as they foretold the joining of a remnant from the Gentile nations to Israel.

Christ is now the temple, and through faith in him all peoples have free access to the throne of God. The dividing wall between Jews and Gentiles has been demolished. Echoing the tripartite structure of the temple precincts, Jesus, at his ascension, tells his disciples to wait for the Spirit's descent so that they may become his witnesses "in Jerusalem and in all Judea and Samaria, and to the end of the earth" (Acts 1:8).

The Rise of Evangelical Inclusivism and the Mandate to Proclaim the Gospel to "the Whole World"

Seventy percent of American adults endorse the statement, "Many religions can lead to eternal life," according to a 2008 Pew Forum study; more than half (57 percent) of those self-identified as members of evangelical Protestant churches agreed.[5] And this is not only a growing trend among Western Christians. There is a rising movement of Muslim "followers of Jesus" who nevertheless remain Muslim, provoking debate over whether a public profession of faith in Christ and identification with his church is necessary.[6]

Fueled by ever-changing patterns in immigration, communication, and social mobility, the United States is a nation of choosers, shoppers, and switchers. "More than one quarter of American adults (28 percent) have left the faith in which they were raised in favor of another religion—or no religion at all." If you include changes from one form of Protestantism to another, it's musical chairs for 44 percent of the population.[7]

The mere fact that we live in a religiously pluralistic society today creates new pressures to soften the message, to remove its offense, and to present it as helpful for everybody rather than saving for those who believe.

In recent years, different views regarding the destiny of the unevangelized have been grouped under three classifications: *pluralism*, which holds that all paths lead to God[8]; *inclusivism*, which teaches that although Christ is the only Savior, explicit faith in Christ is not ordinarily necessary for salvation; and *exclusivism*, which maintains that ordinarily there is no salvation apart from hearing and believing in Jesus Christ.

I am not a fan of these terms. Although I believe that the third view is consistently and clearly taught in Scripture, calling it "exclusive" stacks the deck against it. God loves the world and sent his Son so that whoever believes in him has eternal life (John 3:16). God includes in Christ a vast number from every nation who would have excluded themselves were it not for God's sovereign, gracious intervention. It hardly seems appropriate to denigrate this announcement with the epithet "exclusive."

In any case, the emergent movement seems largely committed to inclusivism. The chief reason Brian McLaren prefers the term "missional" is that "it gets us beyond the us-them thinking and in-grouping and out-grouping that leads to prejudice, exclusion, and ultimately to religious wars." He says, "It opens up a third alternative beyond exclusive and universalist religion. Exclusive religion says, 'We're in, you're out.' Good news for us, bad news for you. Understandably, universalist religion reacts and says, 'Everybody's in!'" But this can lead to "magnanimous apathy."[9] McLaren writes,

Missional Christian faith asserts that Jesus did *not* come to make some people saved and other people condemned. Jesus did *not* come to help some people be right while leaving everyone else to be wrong. Jesus did *not* come to create another exclusive religion—Judaism having been exclusive based on genetics and Christianity being exclusive based on belief (which can be a tougher requirement than genetics!). Missional faith asserts that Jesus came to preach the good news of the kingdom of God to everyone, especially the poor.[10]

So, according to McLaren, the gospel is primarily an imperative for us to follow, a work of redemption and reconciliation that we are to complete.

Although universalists are certain that everyone is saved and exclusivists are persuaded that salvation comes only through faith in Christ, McLaren encourages agnosticism in the matter:

> *But what about heaven and hell?* you ask. *Is everybody in?* My reply: Why do you consider me qualified to make this pronouncement? Isn't this God's business? Isn't it clear that I do not believe this is the right question for a missional Christian to ask? . . . Can't we talk for a while about overthrowing and undermining every hellish stronghold in our lives and in our world? . . . More important to me than the hell question, then, is the *mission* question.[11]

The question to be raised at this point, however, is whether ignoring the hell question necessarily makes the mission something other than proclaiming Christ for the forgiveness of sins and new life. Full-scale evaluations of inclusivism can be found elsewhere.[12] I will only offer a few concerns in relation to some of the more popular defenses of inclusivism in recent years.

Silence Where God Has Spoken and Speaking Where God Is Silent

The major problem with inclusivism, in my view, is that *it refuses to speak where God has spoken and speculates where God is silent.* How can we be so confident about the political policies and candidates that Jesus would endorse, while professing ignorance of "the hell question"? The most vivid and lengthy descriptions come from the lips of our Lord (for example, Matt. 5:30; 8:10–12; 13:40–42, 49–50; 22:13; 24:51; 25:30, and parallels; see also Luke 16:19–31).

We are now living in an era of common grace, in which neither salvation nor judgment has been fully consummated. The powers of the age to come (judgment and *shalom* or peace) are penetrating this present evil age through the Spirit's conviction of sin and the gift of forgiveness and new life in Christ. For now, wheat and weeds grow together, but the era of God's patience will come to an end. From the beginning of Jesus's ministry, he was announced as the judge who baptizes with the Spirit and also with fire (Matt. 3:11–12). Jesus explained, "When the Son of Man comes in his glory, and all the angels with him, then he will sit on his glorious throne" (Matt. 25:31). Echoing Isaiah 2 (as well as chapter 11), Jesus says that the nations will appear before the Son of Man in judgment and all will be separated, as sheep and goats, "into eternal life" and "into eternal punishment" (Matt. 25:31–46).

The Epistles reveal the same solemn expectation. God is not ignoring human rebellion: "But because of your hard and impenitent heart you are storing up wrath for yourself on the day of wrath when God's righteous judgment will be revealed" (Rom. 2:5). For the wicked and unbelieving, "there will be wrath and fury . . . anguish and distress" (Rom. 2:8–9 NRSV).

First Thessalonians 5 warns that "the day of the Lord will come like a thief in the night" (v. 2), just when everyone is proclaiming peace and security (v. 3). This event of salvation and judgment will be as final as it is sudden, "when the Lord Jesus is revealed from heaven with his mighty angels in flaming fire, inflicting vengeance on those who do not know God and on those who do not obey the gospel of our Lord Jesus. They will suffer the punishment of eternal destruction," Paul says, "away from the presence of the Lord and from the glory of his might, when he comes on that day to be glorified by his saints, and to be marveled at among all who have believed, because our testimony to you was believed" (2 Thess. 1:7–10).

Jude tells us that Sodom and Gomorrah "serve as an example by undergoing a punishment of eternal fire" and false teachers are "wandering stars, for whom the gloom of utter darkness has been reserved forever" (Jude 7, 13). Peter warns of "the day of judgment and destruction of the ungodly" (2 Peter 3:7).

In Revelation, there is the vision of the powerful and wealthy of all the earth, who have feared neither God nor mortals, "calling to the mountains and rocks, 'Fall on us and hide us from the face of him who is seated on the throne and from the wrath of the Lamb; for the great day of their wrath has come, and who can stand?'" (Rev. 6:16–17). This is followed by the vision of the bowls of wrath, the fall of the great Babylon, symbol of the earthly city in all of its infamous pride, injustice, and immorality, not to mention its persecution of the saints (chaps. 16–18). Finally, Babylon is judged and destroyed, with the saints singing, "Hallelujah! The smoke from her goes up forever and ever" (19:1–3). The marriage feast of the Lamb is contrasted gruesomely with "the great supper of God" (19:17), as the angel calls the birds of prey to feast on "the flesh of all men, free and slave, both small and great" (19:18). This is followed by the destruction of the ungodly by the rider on the white horse, with Satan finally being "thrown into the lake of fire and sulfur where the beast and the false prophet were, and they will be tormented day and night forever and ever" (20:10). The dead are then judged. "This is the second death, the lake of fire" (20:14). It is the finality of this holy war that ushers in the finality of the new heavens and earth, where there is no longer any judgment, war, pain, suffering, or oppression. And it is there, finally, where the Tree of Life yields its fruit for the healing of the nations (chaps. 21–22).

As Larry Hurtado explains, there was no analogy for Christian faith and practice anywhere either in Second Temple Judaism or in Roman religion. A Roman citizen could hold any number of new religions in combination, as long as the civil religion was upheld. "However, unlike nearly all the other religious options of the time (but directly reflecting the Roman-era Jewish tradition in which it emerged), earliest Christian faith involved an exclusivist religious claim upon adherents. In all the earliest sources, the Christian message was about the one God of biblical tradition, and all other purported deities were regarded as mere 'idols' and worse."[13]

It is not only out of faithfulness to God's revelation but out of love for our neighbors that we must say what we have been told to say. We are neither the authors nor the editors of this script. Deuteronomy 29:29 reminds us that "the secret things belong to the LORD our God, but the things that are revealed belong to us and to our children forever." The Scriptures clearly teach that out of the mass of condemned humanity God has chosen people from every tongue for salvation in Christ (for instance, John 1:12–13; 6:38–39, 44; 10:15, 17, 27; 15:16; 17:2, 6, 9; Acts 13:48; Rom. 8:28–34; 9:6–24; 11:5–10, 29; 2 Tim. 1:9; Eph. 1:4–15). However, we have been entrusted with the task of proclaiming the gospel to every creature, not of discovering the elect. God has clearly revealed the Good News, promising that everyone who believes in Christ will be saved.

We know that there are exceptions. David, at the death of his seven-day-old son (with Bathsheba), acknowledged that they would be together one day at last (2 Sam. 12:23). In the New Testament as in the Old, the children of believers are included in the covenant of grace (Gen. 17:7; Acts 2:39; 1 Cor. 7:14). On this basis, Reformed churches confess that "godly parents ought not to doubt the election and salvation of their children whom it pleases God to call out of this life in their infancy."[14]

What happens to other children? Or to those who through a physical disability cannot understand the proclamation of the gospel? We have no passages to turn to on these questions, except to affirm with Paul the Lord's words to Moses: "'I will have mercy on whom I have mercy, and I will have compassion on whom I have compassion.' So then it depends not on human will or exertion, but on God, who has mercy" (Rom. 9:15–16). "Salvation is from the Lord" (Jonah 2:9), and God is never at the mercy of human abilities or disabilities. What Scripture does clearly reject is the salvation of *anyone*, including children or people with disabilities, on any other basis than God's mercy in Jesus Christ shown toward sinners. Furthermore, exceptions do not determine the rule. Mark's version of the Great Commission includes Jesus's words, "Whoever believes and is baptized will be saved, but whoever does not believe will be condemned" (Mark 16:16). Whatever God *may* do in his sovereign grace, the Great Commission is concerned with what God has *promised* in his Word to do for everyone who calls on his name.

The Great Commission is bound up with "the hell question" since it mandates the proclamation of the forgiveness of sins through faith in Christ and warns that all who do not embrace Christ will be condemned. However, where God *is* silent, inclusivists often offer their own speculations.

In the early third century, Origen offered a synthesis of Christianity and Platonism. In this view, all souls (including Satan and the fallen angels) would be finally restored after purgation and spiritual education, through a series of reincarnations. However, Origen's views were condemned at the Fifth Council of Constantinople (553).

Some inclusivists who tend toward universalism argue their case on the basis of what I would call "hyper-Calvinist" presuppositions. Karl Barth and Jürgen Moltmann maintain that God has elected and redeemed all of humanity in Christ, overwhelming their "no" with his "yes." In this perspective, God's sovereign grace is not only the source of saving faith; it makes human response inconsequential. However, Barth (unlike Moltmann) backed away from speculating on whether every person will in fact be saved.[15] According to Moltmann, the idea that people are able to freely determine themselves for damnation reflects a Pelagian confidence in free will over God's grace.[16] A more moderate case for inclusivism on the basis of God's sovereign grace has been thoughtfully argued by Terrance L. Tiessen.[17]

Other inclusivists follow a more Arminian line of argument. Clark Pinnock and John Sanders share the presupposition that all of God's attributes are subservient to his love and that his purpose is to save every person. In fact, Pinnock recognizes that these theses function as presuppositions or "axioms" by which exegesis must be tested.[18] At the same time, human response is decisive for salvation. As Pinnock acknowledges, his version is especially indebted to the "anonymous Christian" concept of Roman Catholic theologian Karl Rahner and the Second Vatican Council.[19] Pinnock appeals to the examples of Melchizedek, Job, and Paul's quotation of pagan poets in Acts 17 to defend the idea that God reveals himself in a saving way outside of biblical revelation.[20]

For inclusivists who believe that some human response is decisive, general revelation is often treated as sufficient. The gospel revealed through special revelation is clearer, but God's grace can be known and embraced apart from it. Brian McLaren refers to Jesus's parable of the wheat and the weeds. In Matthew 13:24–30, a field hand informs the farmer that an enemy has sown weeds in his field, but the farmer insists that they do not pull up the weeds, but let them grow together with the wheat until he comes for the harvest.

However, McLaren says, "I also propose (with Jesus's parable from Matthew 13:24–30 in mind) that we don't seek to root up all the bad weeds in the world's religions (including our own), but rather seek to encourage the growth of the good wheat in all religions, including our own, leaving it for God to sort it all out as only God can do."[21] And, of course, he does not comment on Jesus's conclusion: "at harvest time I will tell the reapers, Gather the weeds first and bind them in bundles to be burned, but gather the wheat into my barn" (Matt. 13:30). In the immediately preceding parable of the sower, Jesus classified his followers into different fields: rocky, where the Word is heard but doesn't take root; thorny, where the plant is choked by temporal cares; and the productive soil, "the one who hears the word and understands it" (Matt. 13:23). The context of the following parable of the weeds, then, is the community of those who were following Jesus. It is not an encouragement to let a thousand flowers bloom in the garden of religion.

Delivered from Idols or Anonymous Disciples of Jesus?
Confusing General and Special Revelation

Throughout the book of Acts we are astonished at the power of the gospel to transform lives. In fact, a riot broke out in Ephesus, the center of the cult of Artemis, when the sizable idol industry was threatened because of widespread conversion to Christ (Acts 19:21–41). Idolaters are excluded from the kingdom of Christ (1 Cor. 5:10; 6:9; 10:7; Gal. 5:20; 1 Thess. 1:9; 1 Peter 4:3; 1 John 5:21). Paul warned the Corinthians with the example of Israel and the golden calf. "Therefore, my beloved, flee from idolatry" (1 Cor. 10:14). There can be no participation in the body and blood of Christ in the Lord's Supper while indulging in "the table of demons," for "Shall we provoke the Lord to jealousy? Are we stronger than he?" (1 Cor. 10:21–22).

In McLaren's view, the Great Commission invites everyone to become disciples (followers or imitators) of Jesus. "I must add, though, that I don't believe making disciples must equal making adherents of the Christian religion." He explains, "It may be advisable in many (not all!) circumstances to help people become followers of Jesus and remain within their Buddhist, Hindu, or Jewish contexts. I don't hope all Jews or Hindus will become members of the Christian religion. But I do hope all who feel so called will become Jewish or Hindu followers of Jesus."[22]

So in this view the gospel itself is no longer an announcement of the forgiveness of sins in Christ's name. Jesus clarifies and embodies this way of living, but in principle at least this gospel is actually the law of love that everyone knows in his or her conscience and that is taught by many religions.

However, especially in Romans 1 and 2, Paul points out that *general* revelation (that which God reveals through creation) is sufficient to leave all people "without excuse" before God's judgment (Rom. 1:20). God has abundantly revealed his existence, power, righteousness, and goodness in nature and in history. Yet Gentiles suppress this revelation. "What then? Are we Jews any better off?" asks Paul. "No, not at all. For we have already charged that all, both Jews and Greeks, are under sin, as it is written, 'None is righteous, no, not one; no one understands; no one seeks for God.' . . . For by works of the law no human being will be justified in his sight, since through the law comes knowledge of sin" (Rom. 3:9–11, 20).

The apostle's point is that apart from the gospel, there is no *saving* revelation. Quite the contrary: general revelation reveals the law, that righteous judgment that condemns us all. What we need is the Good News.

We do not get *news*, much less *good* news, from the law. It is something that we already know deep within us. It is an inner compass that no one can entirely ignore. It is what makes it possible for atheists to be instruments of God's common grace to their neighbors: developing cures, driving school buses, raising families, and offering goods and services pro bono to people in need. Christians were able to work alongside deists in crafting the constitution and laws of a new American republic. There is every reason for Christians in our world today to work with Muslims, Jews, Hindus, Buddhists—and anyone else who wants to further progress toward a more peaceful and just community of citizens. Whether we're looking at the Tao, the Noble Eightfold Path, the Ten Commandments, the UN Declaration of Human Rights, or the Golden Rule, the underlying general revelation of God's moral will in creation is evident.

However, Paul's argument in Romans 1–3 is that this general revelation that makes it possible for Gentile idolaters to exhibit some degree of justice on the horizontal plane does not deliver the news of God's free justification of sinners. "But now the righteousness of God has been manifested apart from the law, although the Law and the Prophets bear witness to it—the righteousness of God through faith in Jesus Christ for all who believe" (Rom. 3:21–22).

This special revelation does not reside deep inside of us. It is not in our conscience or in our culture. We are not born with this knowledge, and we do not learn it from various religions and spiritualities. It has to be proclaimed to us. This is why the Great Commission is to "preach the gospel to everyone." No one will be saved by a zeal for God and neighbor, but only by calling on the name of Jesus Christ for salvation (Rom. 10:1–4, 9–14). That is why we need preachers. "How are they to call on him in whom they have not believed? And how are they to believe in him of whom they have never heard? And how are they to hear without someone preaching? And how are they to preach unless they are sent? As it is written, 'How beautiful are the feet of those who preach the good news!'" (Rom. 10:14–15).

According to McLaren, Tony Jones, and other emergent writers, however, Christ is revealed as Savior even in creation and culture. Tony Jones writes, "Really, the ways that God, in Christ, can be revealed to us are limitless."[23] Furthermore, "To try to freeze one particular articulation of the gospel, to make it timeless and universally applicable, actually does an injustice to the gospel," he asserts. "This goes to the very heart of what emergent is and of how emergent Christians are attempting to chart a course for following Jesus in the postmodern, globalized, pluralized world of the twenty-first century."[24] Often, God's freedom and sovereignty are invoked to override the missionary imperative: "God can forgive whomever God wants to forgive, whether or not the forgiven person has adequately confessed his or her sins."[25] This way of putting it fails to recognize that *no one* has *adequately* confessed his or her sins. We are justified not by the intensity, purity, or even doctrinal sophistication of our confession but by the Christ whom we confess: "if you confess with your mouth that Jesus is Lord and believe in your heart that God raised him from the dead, you will be saved" (Rom. 10:9).

These passages teach us that special revelation (Scripture) not only gives us *more* or *clearer* revelation than general revelation but also gives us a *different* revelation. General revelation makes us aware of God's existence, his righteousness, his power, and his law by which he judges. Only in the gospel do we hear the surprising announcement of God's saving mercy in Jesus Christ.

Confusing special and general revelation, many inclusivists appeal to Old Testament examples of the "noble pagan" (such as Melchizedek and Job or the pagan poets quoted by Paul in Athens and Cornelius in Acts 10). They also point out that not even the biblical patriarchs knew what we know about Christ and his saving work. So how can explicit faith in Christ be the only way of salvation?

However, there are problems with this interpretation. First, although biblical revelation progresses from Old Testament shadows to New Testament reality, the object of faith is the same. Abraham did not have as clear a view of the gospel as the apostle John, but it was the *gospel*. "Your father Abraham rejoiced that he would see my day," Jesus told the religious leaders. "He saw it and was glad" (John 8:56). Paul reminds us, "For the promise to Abraham and his offspring that he would be heir of the world did not come through the law but through the righteousness of faith" (Rom. 4:13). "Know then that it is those of faith who are the sons of Abraham. And the Scripture, foreseeing that God would justify the Gentiles by faith, *preached the gospel beforehand to Abraham*, saying, 'In you shall all the nations be blessed'" (Gal. 3:7–8, emphasis added). Abraham and Sarah are among those who, like Abel, Enoch, and Noah, "died in faith, not having received the things promised, but having seen them and greeted them from afar, and having acknowledged that they were strangers and exiles on the earth" (Heb. 11:13).

However, the religions of the nations are regarded as idolatrous throughout this history. Clark Pinnock's examples cited above do not demonstrate a saving knowledge of God apart from his revelation to Israel.

Second, the other examples inclusivists cite fail to support their case. From what little we know about Melchizedek, he could not have been a "noble pagan."[26] He was "king of Salem" (proto-Jerusalem), "priest of God Most High," and "God Most High" (*El Elyon*) was identified as none other than "the LORD [Yahweh], God Most High" (Gen. 14:18–22). Melchizedek brought Abram bread and wine, blessed him, and received a tributary tithe—all of these actions reflecting a covenantal context in which Abram recognized Melchizedek as his high priest. Drawing on Psalm 110, Hebrews 7 clearly interprets Melchizedek as a type pointing forward to Christ.

Nor can Job qualify as an anonymous believer. Job's allusion to Psalm 8:4 (in Job 7:17–18) and direct quotations of Psalm 107:40 and Isaiah 41:20 (in Job 12:21–24) place him squarely in God's covenant community.[27] This is confirmed in Ezekiel 14:13–14.

Cornelius, a Roman centurion, is described in Acts 10 not as a noble pagan but as "a devout man who feared God with all his household, gave alms generously to the people, and prayed continually to God" (v. 2). The epithet "God-fearer" was used by Jews to refer to Gentiles who worshiped the God of Israel, attending synagogue but not yet circumcised. Furthermore, God appeared to Cornelius in a vision, telling him to send for Peter, who would explain the gospel (vv. 3–8). Peter also received a vision alerting him to this meeting with Cornelius and his Gentile cohorts, and the apostle proclaimed Christ's death and resurrection. "'To him all the prophets bear witness that everyone who believes in him receives forgiveness of sins through his name.' While Peter was still saying these things, the Holy Spirit fell on all who heard the word," and they were baptized (vv. 43–48). However unusual the circumstances, it is clear that Cornelius received the forgiveness of sins when he heard and believed the Good News.

Arrogance and Abraham

Paul quotes pagan poets to his audience of Athenian philosophers in Acts 17 for the express purpose of demonstrating that they are not living consistently even with general revelation. Christians can appeal to non-Christians on the basis of general revelation, as Paul did in Athens and explained in Romans 1 and 2. They can even learn from non-Christians, as Paul evidently had when at some point in his life he took the time and interest to read Gentile philosophers and poets.

Yet in his Mars Hill speech, Paul does not use these sources as a way of reaching interreligious agreement. Rather, he exposes the fact that we all suppress even this general revelation in unrighteousness. When we appeal to general revelation, we are speaking "law," not "gospel." We turn to the resurrection of Christ to announce, "The times of ignorance God overlooked, but now he commands all people everywhere to repent, because he has fixed a day on which he will judge the world in righteousness by a man whom he has appointed; and of this he has given assurance to all by raising him from the dead" (Acts 17:30–31). Paul turns from universal principles known in nature to the historical event that can only be proclaimed by heralds. However lenient God may have been in "the times of ignorance," the appearance of Christ in these last days leaves everyone without excuse. It is the universal and public character of Christ's decisive work and coming judgment that gives to the missionary enterprise the kind of urgency that is found throughout the book of Acts.

It all comes down again to distinguishing between law and gospel. When it comes to ordering our lives, neighborhoods, states, and nations, there's a lot of agreement between Christians and non-Christians. It *is* arrogant to assert that Christianity is unique in its wisdom for living, that Christians as a whole live better than non-Christians as a whole, that only Christians are good friends and neighbors, and that only they really care about—or at least have the right answers for—the pressing issues and temporal needs all around them. Some non-Christians I know have better marriages and families than many Christians. When we defend Christianity as "the only way," we have to be careful to first point out that, properly speaking, *Christ* is the only way, and that he is the only way *to reconciliation with God, forgiveness of sins, the new birth, and all the blessings of our inheritance in the new creation.* Non-Christians can follow good advice; they can turn over a new leaf and improve their actions and even their moral character. The Nation of Islam has a fine track record of turning gang members into upstanding citizens. What these groups, programs, religions, and therapies cannot do is transform people from enemies of God into friends, from condemned criminals into redeemed heirs, and from citizens of the kingdom of death into citizens of the kingdom of heaven. Only in Christ can we be forgiven and made new, not just better.

By distinguishing clearly between the common and the holy, the kingdoms of this age and the kingdom of Christ, culture and the gospel, general and special revelation, we are not engaging in Platonic dualism. On the contrary, we are following the New Testament teaching concerning the different ways in which Christ is reigning right now and will reign at his return in glory. Furthermore, those who mark these distinctions well will testify to the exclusive claims of Jesus Christ without appealing to cultural and political power.

It is arrogant to assert, "I found it!" or to give the impression that we are better people or that we have the truth. It is arrogant to suggest that we are saved by belonging to the right group and performing the right rituals. However, the gospel announces that God has found us—sinners—while we were running from him. The door is wide open to all sinners. There is no path from us to God. However, God has found a path to us in his Son. We are not testifying to our moral, intellectual, or spiritual superiority. On the contrary, we are proclaiming the God of grace who saves sinners. Precisely because the gospel is Good News for sinners and not a good plan for good people and groups, it is not something for which we can assume any pride.

In fact, moral superiority is a danger in the inclusivist view. How do adherents of other religions hear the encouragement to become better followers of Jesus even while remaining Buddhists, Muslims, and Jews? Is this not tantamount to saying that the only thing they lack is the superior moral example that Jesus offers? And is it not arrogant to tell a Jewish person that she really is a follower of Jesus—an "anonymous Christian"—whether she wants to be or not? The Scriptures do not teach that there is more common grace shown to Christians than to non-Christians, but that there is a difference between common grace and saving grace. In our own eyes, many non-Christians are good people. In God's eyes, none of us fits that bill: "None is righteous, no, not one; no one understands; no one seeks for God. . . . No one does good, not even one" (Rom. 3:10–12).

Today we are used to hearing references to Judaism, Christianity, and Islam as "the Abrahamic faith traditions." As children of Abraham, why are we at each other's throats? Paul's straightforward declaration may strike us today as arrogant. Maybe it works when we are talking about a remote culture. We do not really recoil at Paul's ruffling of the feathers of Epicureans and Stoics. However, surely he wouldn't lump the "people of the book" (Jews and Muslims) together with ancient polytheists. Actually, Paul would lump even nominal *Christians* together with those who do not embrace Christ with all of his saving benefits. It is not being an adherent of a religion (mere assent) that constitutes saving faith, but placing our trust in Jesus Christ alone.

We saw in chapter 3 that John the Baptist prepared the way for Jesus by announcing a coming separation of Israel. "And do not presume to say to yourselves, 'We have Abraham as our father,' for I tell you, God is able from these stones to raise up children for Abraham. Even now the axe is laid to the root of the trees" (Matt. 3:9–10). Jesus Christ is "the son of Abraham," the seed in whom all the nations would be blessed (Matt. 1:1; see also Gen. 12:3). Jesus told the religious leaders,

> I told you that you would die in your sins, for unless you believe that I am he you will die in your sins. . . . If you abide in my word, you are truly my disciples, and you will know the truth, and the truth will set you free. . . . I know that you are offspring of Abraham; yet you seek to kill me because my word finds no place in you. I speak of what I have seen with my Father, and you do what you have heard from your father. . . . If you were Abraham's children, you would be doing what Abraham did, but now you seek to kill me, a man who has told you the truth that I heard from God. This is not what Abraham did. You are doing what your father did. . . . Why do you not understand what I say? It is because you cannot bear to hear my word. You are of your father the devil, and your will is to do your father's desires. (John 8:24, 31–32, 37–41, 43–44)

Therefore, Paul is only elaborating on Jesus's message when he says that all who trust in Christ are Abraham's true heirs (Romans 4). "Know then that it is those of faith who are the sons of Abraham. . . . And if you are Christ's, then you are Abraham's offspring, heirs according to promise" (Gal. 3:7, 29). Those who are merely ethnic descendants of Abraham, who are circumcised on the eighth day but do not share Abraham's faith in the promised Savior of the world, are not truly circumcised inwardly (Rom. 2:28–29). They remain under the curse of the law that they have not kept (Gal. 3:10–14). In theological rather than ethnic terms, they are children of Hagar rather than Sarah: slaves rather than sons (Gal. 4:21–31).

And let's be respectful of Judaism and Islam, allowing them to register their "No!" to Jesus Christ and the gospel without telling them that their "No!" is really a "Yes!" According to these religions, the Triune God is an idol. Human beings are not helpless to save themselves but have been given laws for attaining eternal life. The Son's deity, incarnation, atoning death, life-giving resurrection, ascension, and return in glory to judge the living and the dead are blasphemous claims. Even if one were to allow that God reveals himself redemptively in general revelation, these monotheistic religions explicitly *deny* the existence of this God and his saving work in Christ. Recognizing each other's differences is not only the first step toward genuine evangelism; it's a gesture of genuine respect.

Inclusivism in any form removes the urgency of the Great Commission. However, an inclusivism that defines redemption as our completing Christ's work through works of love and service is another gospel. It stands to reason that if the gospel is following Jesus's example, completing his reconciling work in the world, then it is something that we are to do rather than something that we are to proclaim as having already been done.

As taught by the Second Vatican Council and supported by some evangelicals, inclusivism affirms that Christ is the only source of salvation, but explicit faith in Christ is not necessary. Religious pluralism takes the further step, treating all religions as paths to God. It is this next step that writers like Brian McLaren seem to take. In the new kind of Christianity he proposes, evangelism will no longer be an attempt to lead people to Christ for salvation from a future judgment. "It would invite people into lifelong spiritual formation as disciples of Jesus, in a community dedicated (as we've seen) to teaching the most excellent way of love, whatever the new disciple's religious affiliation or lack thereof."[28] In an earlier book McLaren refers to an "agnostic Jewish friend who asked me, 'What's the deal with Jesus?' When I offered him an explanation not unlike what I've shared in these chapters, he said, 'I could believe in a Jesus like that. If I believed in God, I think I could believe in that Jesus.' I hope you can and will. I do, and it has made all the difference."[29] There is no indication here that his friend might have to repent of his agnosticism and call on Christ's name for salvation. After all, if Jesus is primarily a role model and source for our redeeming work, then there is no offense with which one might need to wrestle.

Far from being agnostic, Paul had been a zealous Jewish leader, persecuting the church until the ascended Christ appeared to him on the road. Unlike his opponents, he did not believe that the gospel was Judaism plus Jesus. Rather, he believed, as did Jesus, that the religious leaders were leading the Jewish people away from their own Messiah, away from the end-time fulfillment of that grand drama that had been entrusted to them as guardians. He did not say that his righteousness as a "Pharisee of Pharisees" was insufficient and needed to be completed or perfected by Jesus. Rather, he said that it was "rubbish" (Phil. 3:8; actually, "dung" is a closer translation). Justified in Christ, he now moves all of that righteousness he thought he had accumulated by the law into the *debt and liability* column. And, like Jesus, he believed that everyone (Jew and Gentile) united to Christ through faith will be saved, and all who are not united to Christ through faith (Jew and Gentile) will be condemned.

If inclusivists are correct, then Paul's heart was needlessly broken when he wrote,

> Brothers, my heart's desire and prayer to God for them [fellow Jews] is that they may be saved. For I bear them witness that they have a zeal for God, but not according to knowledge. For, *being ignorant of the righteousness of God*, and seeking to establish their own, they did not submit to God's righteousness. For Christ is the end of the law for righteousness to everyone who believes. (Rom. 10:1–4, emphasis added)

Many people (including some Christians) hear these words as narrow-minded and arrogant. Actually, it is we who are arrogant when we presume to present our own righteousness—or encourage others to present theirs—before God rather than be justified through faith in Christ alone. Before his conversion, Paul's zeal for good works was motivated by spiritual pride, and it issued in violence. Now, however, he knows that the law condemns everyone and the gospel brings justification and eternal life to everyone who believes.

In other words, Paul would have found the charge of arrogance incomprehensible. For him, the nearly impossible thing to believe is not that anyone will be condemned on the last day, but that anyone will be welcomed into the everlasting Sabbath! He is driven by the Good News that even a Gentile idolater can be justified, sanctified, and glorified. For him, the gospel is all about God's inclusion of people from Israel and the nations who, like him, had been stubbornly opposed to God and his purposes in Christ. Deeply aware of his own conversion, Paul knew that no one is beyond the reach of God's grace. He was *delivered* from religious violence by the revelation of Christ!

To be sure, these conclusions are regarded as highly offensive—incendiary—in our world today. However, this charge of Christian arrogance is not really new. The Sanhedrin did not charge Jesus with revolutionary ideas about organizing society or, like Socrates, with corrupting the youth. He was charged with blasphemy, "making himself equal with God" (John 5:18). When Jesus healed the paralytic boy, the religious leaders became outraged not at the miracle but at Jesus's explicit bypassing of the temple, offering forgiveness directly in his person: "Son, your sins are forgiven." Grumbling among themselves, the scribes asked, "Why does this man speak like that? He is blaspheming! Who can forgive sins but God alone?" (Mark 2:5–7). The Romans persecuted the Christians because their exclusive claims concerning Christ were a threat to the civil religion of the empire.

Postmodernism or Most-Modernism?

Contrary to what its evangelical friends and foes argue, postmodernism is not responsible for relativism and subjectivism. If we go back to the leaders of the Enlightenment—the epitome of *modern* thought—we quickly learn that there is really nothing "postmodern" about religious relativism. Immanuel Kant distinguished sharply between "pure religion," which consisted of universal morality ("the moral law within") and "ecclesiastical faiths" that were merely the outward clothing of these eternal principles in the peculiarities of mythological events, messiahs, doctrines, and rituals.

Kant's contemporary, G. E. Lessing, made the same distinction by speaking of love as the inner core of universal morality and of creeds and rituals as merely the outer clothing of each particular religion. The founder of modern theology, Friedrich Schleiermacher, considered pure religion to consist in the pious experience of absolute dependence on God, which different religions express in their own doctrines and sacraments. The main thing is this universal religious experience. All of these thinkers were reared in evangelical pietism, and Schleiermacher continued to think of himself as "a Moravian [pietist] of a higher order."

Lessing staged a play in 1778 titled *Nathan the Wise*. Set in Jerusalem during the Third Crusade, with Christian crusaders threatening Muslim-controlled Palestine, Lessing's play has the Muslim leader

Saladin asking Nathan the Wise which is the true religion. Nathan replies with a parable of a father with three sons. The moral to the story is that each son (Judaism, Christianity, and Islam) was beloved of his father, who simply commanded them to love each other. Settling this dispute between the sons in court, the "modest judge" is, of course, Lessing himself.

For all of his impressive criticism of modernity's dichotomies and hierarchies and his concern to rescue "the scandal of the particular" from modernity's obsession with the "universal," Jacques Derrida's later writings repeat Kant's preference for pure religion over against ecclesiastical faiths. He wrote of a "messianic consciousness"—the universal experience of looking toward the future in hope—that must never announce the arrival of any particular messiah. And his contrast is even defended with the same arguments as Lessing and Kant: the one brings universal peace, while the other issues in division and violence.

In *Finding Our Way Again: The Return of the Ancient Practices*, Brian McLaren tries to show that when we see Christianity as practices rather than a system of belief, there are lots of convergences with other religions. Similar to Lessing's "Nathan," McLaren concludes with the following speculation:

> What if there is a treasure hidden in the field of our three great monotheisms, long buried but waiting to be rediscovered? And what if the treasure is a way . . . a way that can train us to stop killing and hating and instead to work together, under God, joining God, to build a better world, a city of God? What if our suffering and fear are not intended to inspire deadly cycles of defense and counterattack in a vain search for peace through domination, but instead, what if they can serve to break and soften us like a plowed field after rain so that the seed of God's kingdom—a few notes of God's eternal harmony—can grow within us and among us? This is my hope. And this is our hope. Amen.[30]

McLaren still includes himself among those who acknowledge Christ as the Savior of the world (though "salvation" is redefined in the process). Nevertheless, by moving what matters most about Christianity—its public, particular, unique, and exclusive claims—indoors to the realm of inner experience and spirituality, he exhibits the characteristically *modern* allergy to the scandal of the particular. Jesus's kingdom is the ideal of universal harmony, he says, "And maybe imagining that happening is a lot like having faith; in fact, maybe that song was John Lennon's way of saying, beautifully even if imperfectly, 'May your kingdom come, may your will be done on earth as it is in heaven.'"[31]

I'll never forget a series of lectures by a formerly evangelical professor at Oxford. His basic thesis was that all religions—in their most mystical versions (often considered heretical by the establishment)—were really saying the same thing. After his concluding lecture, a few of us—including a Muslim, a Jew, and a Roman Catholic—went to the pub and agreed that he had basically dismissed everything that was important about each of our religions. Substituting his own particular beliefs (characteristic of a white, middle-aged, Western, liberal theologian), our professor imagined that they were the absolute core of universal truth. In the name of tolerance and the pure religion of Lessing's "Nathan," he exhibited intolerance toward any particular religion and its own distinct claims. Unlike the resurrection of Christ, he had nothing to appeal to as a demonstration of his claim—only a confidence in his own superior criteria (morality and mysticism) to identify the purest core of true religion.

Many baby boomer evangelicals, raised in pietism and fundamentalism, are eager to don the accessories of postmodern fashion without realizing just how completely modern they are. John Lennon's "Imagine" may be the ballad of postmoderns, but it is simply another verse in the hymn of modernity—basically a retelling of Lessing's parable. There is nothing radical, much less new, in the contemporary denials of the unique claims of Jesus Christ. In fact, H. Richard Niebuhr's description of the social gospel is just as relevant in our context: "A God without wrath brought men without sin into a kingdom without judgment through the ministrations of a Christ without a cross."[32]

While McLaren praises Harvey Cox's defense of religious pluralism as a deliverance of our postmodern era, Princeton Seminary's George Hunsinger offers a different verdict: "There is really nothing 'postmodern' about it. At best, it simply rearranges the furniture in the old modernist room."[33] Trying to harmonize revelation with human experience, whether that of the individual or of culture, is doomed from the start. As Hunsinger observes,

> The Christ of natural theology is always openly or secretly the relativized Christ of culture. The trajectory of natural theology leads from the Christ who is not supreme to the Christ who is not sufficient to the Christ who is not necessary. . . . "God may speak to us," wrote Barth, "through Russian communism or a flute concerto, a blossoming shrub

or a dead dog. We shall do well to listen to him if he really does so."
No such object, however, can ever be allowed to become a source
of authority for the church's preaching, for no such object can have
independent revelatory or epistemological status. Only by criteria
derived from the one authentic scriptural voice of Christ can we know
if God might be speaking to us in those ways or not.[34]

Hunsinger concludes by appealing to Jewish scholar Michael Wyschogrod: "Wanting to assimilate theology into the foreign mold of the
surrounding culture, Wyschogrod suggests, is an essentially Gentile
aspiration."[35]

The real dissenters in our world today are those who confess the
Christ who was anticipated by the prophets and proclaimed as risen
by the apostles and martyrs. The real arrogance lies not in believing
God's Word and passing it on urgently to others, but in the false humility that denies—on purely dogmatic and subjective grounds—that
any particular creed can be true. In 1908, G. K. Chesterton observed,
"Scoffers of old time were too *proud* to be convinced; but these are
too *humble* to be convinced."[36] Chesterton spoke of the dislocation
of humility in modern thought, and it works as well as a description
of what many people are calling postmodern:

> What we suffer from to-day is humility in the wrong place. Modesty
> has moved from the organ of ambition. Modesty has settled on the
> organ of conviction; where it was never meant to be. A man was meant
> to be doubtful about himself, but undoubting about the truth; this has
> been exactly reversed. Nowadays the part of a man that a man does
> assert is exactly the part he ought not to assert—himself.[37]

Turning inward, to that which is true in all religions and moral visions,
reverses the flow of God's gifts to sinners and turns the missionaries
into pagans.

We are all tired of bellicose evangelists, overconfident apologists,
and pontificating preachers who proclaim themselves rather than
Christ. The virtues of honesty, humility, and decency—listening to others, acknowledging the value of their critiques—are enjoined throughout the New Testament as expressions of love. However, the ancient
church flourished in a pagan environment not only because believers
were willing to die for their faith but also because they were willing
to argue for it. Paul reminds us, "For the weapons of our warfare are
not of the flesh but have divine power to destroy strongholds. We

destroy arguments and every lofty opinion raised against the knowledge of God, and take every thought captive to obey Christ" (2 Cor. 10:4–5). We may learn some important things from the wisdom of the world—ancient, medieval, modern, postmodern, or whatever's next—but it doesn't come close to the wisdom of God revealed in the gospel of Christ. Nothing that *we* want to say is nearly as interesting.

Dinesh D'Souza is right on when he observes that some professing Christians—especially pastors and theologians—"have assumed a reverse mission: instead of being the church's missionaries to the world, they have become the world's missionaries to the church."[38] He calls this a "yes-but" Christianity. Although we can no longer believe in miracles or in a God of sovereign authority and holy wrath, there may still be something worth salvaging—usually a few moral maxims. "This yes-but Christianity is full intellectual withdrawal, and it is also becoming less relevant," empirically verifiable by mainline Protestantism's precipitous loss of members. Undaunted by this tragic example, a growing number of evangelicals seem convinced that retreat is the best strategy for winning the battle for hearts and minds.[39]

A resolve to declare the gospel over against *religious* pluralism must always be accompanied by a resolve to defend *political* pluralism. Religious freedom is a gift of God that is easy to keep for oneself and difficult to give away to others. Even today, this freedom is threatened not only in Muslim, Hindu, or secularist societies but by established or semiestablished churches in the East and the West. Congregationalists came to New England for freedom of worship but executed Quakers and exiled Baptists. The presidential campaigns of John F. Kennedy (Roman Catholic) and, more recently, Mitt Romney (Mormon) and Barack Obama (liberal Protestant) have tested again the commitment of evangelical Christians to this political pluralism. More recently, some Christian leaders have questioned the right of Muslims to build mosques in their communities. With such rhetoric, the exclusive claim of Christ merges dangerously with an exclusionary politics. Vigilant in the defense of our neighbors' freedoms, we must nevertheless use our freedom to proclaim Jesus Christ as the only way of salvation.

As careful as we must be to avoid resorting to hostile rhetoric—much less attempts to use secular power to legislate and enforce Christian faith and practice—there *is* a war going on right now, and it's not only the biggest one we have ever had but also the longest. It is not fought with guns or even with marketing campaigns and political power plays. It is fought with loving, patient, well-informed, and well-argued testimony to Jesus Christ. This is no time to surrender our confidence in the one thing that has the power to liberate both the church and the world from its captivity to alien gods. The gospel is not a comfort for the heart if it cannot be embraced by the mind. Lots of people give their lives for all sorts of worthy and unworthy things.

Lessing's false humility is evident in his conclusion. Pretending to be the "modest judge" who must give way ultimately to a wiser judge in the future, he has already played the latter throughout the parable. However, the modest judge is actually judged as a pretender by Christ. "The times of ignorance God overlooked" (Acts 17:30) are now over. Something has happened in history that cannot be undone. The Son of God has appeared in the flesh—in our history. Fulfilling the law that we have broken, bearing the curse that we deserve, and being raised to the right hand of the Father, he alone possesses the authority to condemn and to save. Jesus Christ is not just a name that Christians happen to use for the one divinity worshiped by all peoples. Rather, it is "the only name in heaven and on earth by which we may be saved" (John 1:12; 20:31; Acts 2:21, 38; 4:12; Rom. 10:13) and his redeemed community is visible only where sinners gather in his name (Matt. 18:20).

Lazy minds breed lazy hearts and hands. The greatest threat to Christianity is never vigorous intellectual criticism but a creeping senility that transforms truths into feelings, public claims into private experiences, and facts into mere values. Christianity is either true or false, but it is not irrational. If its claims are not objectively true, then they are not subjectively useful. If our only reason for believing that Jesus is alive is that "he lives within my heart," then, as Paul said, "our preaching is in vain and your faith is in vain. We are even found to be misrepresenting God, because we testified about God that he raised Christ. . . . And if Christ has not been raised, your faith is futile and you are still in your sins. . . . If in Christ we have hope in this life only, we are of all people most to be pitied" (1 Cor. 15:14–15, 17, 19).

Faith is not an arbitrary decision but a gracious gift of God that comes through hearing and understanding Christ's person and work. It's certainly true that faith is trust in a person, but we cannot trust a person without knowing who he is and what he has done that is worthy of our confidence. Faith is more than knowing and assenting to facts, but it is not less. Even repentance means "change of mind." Before we can bear the fruit of repentance in godly living, our minds have to be changed. We must recover our distinctively biblical commitment to rigorous, inquisitive, and persuasive thinking before there can be a genuine renewal of Christian conviction, faith, repentance, and discipleship. It is time once again to love God with our minds. It is surely not enough to know the truth, but it is the unavoidable place to start.

As Paul said in his Mars Hill address, the historical resurrection of Jesus Christ is *the* question that faces us all. It is not a question of whose religion works best in the long run or which produces the greatest benefits for the greatest number of people. Was Jesus raised as the firstfruits of the new creation? That is the question that pulls all others into its wake. The gospel *addresses* our deepest (though suppressed) existential anxieties about ultimate meaning, life, death, guilt, and judgment. However, it does so precisely because it *announces* a historical fact. Arguments and evidence may persuade the intellect, but the gospel is not only true; it is "the power of God for salvation to everyone who believes" (Rom. 1:16).

If, as I have argued, the law is universally known by every person in his or her inner depths, we should not be surprised at the similarities between religions when we are longing and working together for greater love, justice, and peace in the world. However, it is only in the gospel where we see God's merciful love and pure justice embrace at the cross. Precisely where our message and mission seem most odd, counterintuitive, and even offensive are they the most interesting and relevant. The story we have to tell to the world is not told in different ways in other religions. The gospel is the strangest thing we will ever hear—or tell. And if it isn't true for all of us, then it isn't true for any of us.

4

One Gospel and Many Cultures

Contextualization

E ven if we agree that faith comes through hearing the gospel, the
command to bring this gospel to all nations requires sensitivity
to diverse cultural contexts. At one extreme, we can ignore the reality
of our cultural context, as if we "just preached the Bible" without
any prejudices. This assumption can keep us from taking seriously the
diversity of backgrounds that we encounter even in our own neighborhoods today. Even more ominously, it keeps us from recognizing that
we are conditioned already by our cultural-linguistic, political, and
socioeconomic background. Like everyone else, we interpret reality—
including Scripture—with certain biases that need to be recognized
and analyzed in the light of God's Word. At the other extreme, we
can become so preoccupied with making the gospel relevant that we
assimilate it to our cultural ideologies, preferences, and demographics.

There is *one gospel in different cultural contexts*; this fact is evident
in the New Testament itself. The sermons of the apostles in Jerusalem
and in the synagogues could recount Israel's history and proclaim
Christ as its fulfillment. Yet Paul's speech in Athens arrives at the
resurrection of Christ by way of a discourse on the "unknown God."

The apostles and early Christians usually had to meet secretly, although they proclaimed the Word wherever possible in the synagogue and the marketplace. Fellow believers in persecuted churches today can identify with this situation more than the rest of us. In strict Muslim countries, baptism is of much greater significance than it is in the West. It is usually followed not with a nice lunch for the pastor and relatives but with death threats. Far more than a vague ritual, the Lord's Supper is a dangerous communal meal. Fellow saints in many parts of the world today are more concretely aware than we often are of being made strangers and exiles even in their own native land. Context shapes the way we carry out the Great Commission.

Contextualization is a popular term in Christian circles today. Basically, contextualization is the attempt to situate particular beliefs and practices in their cultural environment. Migrating from the rarified confines of secular sociology to missiological theory, and then to practical theology departments and ministry programs, the imperative to contextualize the gospel has become something of a mantra among pastors, youth ministers, and evangelists.

The recognition of diversity is welcome. As we have seen, the Spirit's work at Pentecost created a unity in plurality and plurality in unity: one gospel, forming one body, yet each person heard this gospel in his or her own language. This unity in plurality is evident in creation, especially in the creation of God's image-bearing humanity: male and female. Yet after the fall, difference became opposition, suspicion, and violence. This tragic course is illustrated poignantly in the tower of Babel. Nevertheless, the Spirit descended at Pentecost not to scatter the proud nations and to divide their languages but to bring together a new humanity *in all of its diversity* around the gospel. Not even in the age to come do we shed our gendered bodies or the cultural and linguistic characteristics that are inextricably woven into the fabric of our identity. We do not escape creation in the age to come; rather, creation—including cultural difference—is liberated from sin and death.

The sinful condition is universal; we are all born "in Adam." Nevertheless, sin is socialized differently from culture to culture. One culture tends to worship order and another freedom, for example. Eventually, one or the other has to go, since the other god grows jealous. Yet in Christ's kingdom there is ordered freedom and liberating order. Just as we cannot let each other off the hook with a shrug, saying, "That's just how she is," it is not enough to describe a culture as if it were a neutral fact. Cultural-linguistic patterns have to be evaluated by the Word of God, not wholly embraced or wholly rejected. Every culture is in bondage to sin and death. And every culture offers rich treasures, given by the Spirit in common grace.

However, proper sensitivity to diverse cultural contexts is sometimes turned into an ideology that leads to distortions of or distractions from the gospel. In an age of niche marketing, contextualizing refers not only to appropriate missionary training but to becoming specialists in the demographics of our own consumer societies in the West.

Many evangelical seminaries today offer a panoply of elective courses on contextualized ministry (e.g., urban, youth, sports, suburban, emergent, African-American, Latino, men's and women's ministry). Obviously, something has to give—the seminary curriculum can only handle so many credit hours. Increasingly, at least from my conversations with friends, it seems that it is the core courses in biblical languages, systematic and historical theology, church history, and more traditional pastoral theology that are being pared down to make room. As a result, many American pastors, missionaries, and evangelists today may know more about their target market than they do about the "one Lord, one faith, and one baptism" that they share with the prophets and the apostles, the church fathers and reformers, or their brothers and sisters in China, Malawi, and Russia.

In the 1920s Princeton New Testament professor J. Gresham Machen was already issuing the complaint that the obsession with "applied Christianity" was so pervasive that soon there would be little Christianity left to apply. Are we seeing the effects even in evangelical and Reformed circles of a pragmatic interest in the methods of ministry that downplays interest in the actual message? Do our pastors coming out of three or four years of seminary education really know the Bible as pastor-scholars ready to proclaim, to teach, and to lead the sheep into the rich pastures of redemption? Or are they becoming specialists in pop culture and demographic marketing? Turning aspiring pastors into connoisseurs of their own consumer profile builds churches with a cultural hegemony (sameness) in spite of sometimes wild diversity in Christian doctrine, worship, and life. By contrast, the gospel creates spiritual unity rather than cultural uniformity.

In some ways, the concern with contextualization has been an understandable response to a naïve modern assumption that truth is grasped intuitively, immediately, and comprehensively in the mind or in our experience. Postmodern theory emphasizes that all of our knowledge is mediated through social, linguistic, and cultural practices. This point should come as no surprise to Christians who believe that God mediates his saving grace in Christ through Word and sacrament.

God is eternal, but he has revealed himself progressively in history. In fact, after "God the Father Almighty," everything else in the Apostles' Creed—from "maker of heaven and earth" to "the life everlasting"—is a historical truth, not a timeless truth in the realm of eternal forms. There is no time when the Father was without the Son and the Spirit, but the Son became flesh in "the fullness of time" (Gal. 4:4). Jesus died for us "at the right time" (Rom. 5:6) and "will appear a second time" (Heb. 9:28). It has been a scandal to Greeks, Romans, and modern philosophers that the core convictions of Christianity are historical truths rather than supposedly eternal truths of reason, morality, and experience.

God has revealed himself through the particular cultures, personalities, and languages of prophets and apostles across a diverse stretch of geography and history. We do not ascend away from the supposed realm of shadows to eternity in speculative contemplation of Unchanging Being. Rather, God has descended to us in the incarnate Word and still speaks to us through ordinary human speech, water, bread, and wine. As the consummate missionary, the Triune God is the master of contextualization. As Calvin remarked, God speaks baby talk, stooping far beneath his loftiness in order to communicate his saving mercies.

We don't just have ideas. Our beliefs are shaped to a great extent by the cultural habits, language, customs, and practices of particular groups. The Bible's covenant theology makes a lot more sense in feudal societies than in liberal democracies. Faith in a God who is King of Kings and Lord of Lords, who saves sinners by his gracious action rather than by putting himself on the ballot for a general election, may be less plausible to successful capitalists and politically empowered feminists than to prisoners or oppressed workers.

The church leaders who welcomed the fusion of Christ and culture under Constantine and his successors were certainly in touch with their social context. However, a lack of clarity about and confidence in the New Testament vision of Christ's kingdom weakened their ability to criticize their location and their own alliances with it. While challenging the confusion of kingdoms in principle, the Reformation did not sufficiently break from it in practice. Just as it is impossible to understand the Reformation apart from the rise of modern nation-states, the rise of revivalism can only be understood in the context of the Industrial Revolution, frontier expansion, and individualism. Similarly, contemporary American evangelicalism has been shaped by the massive technological and social revolutions of recent history. It is easier for American Christians to take contextualization seriously when we are preparing for a mission trip to Africa. We are less sensitive to the ways in which our own faith and practice are shaped for good and for ill by our own location.

The history of missions provides examples of a dangerous confusion of Christ and culture, with the missionary accompanying the conquistadors and merchant ships. Nevertheless, indigenous movements against colonial oppression were often inspired and encouraged by missionaries, and sensitivity to non-Western cultures was pioneered in many ways by modern missions. However one interprets the past, the explosion of Christianity in the two-thirds world today cannot be identified with Western imperialism. Christopher J. H. Wright observes that the twentieth century began with about 90 percent of the world's Christians in Europe and North America, but it ended with "at least 75 percent" in Latin America, Africa, Asia, and the Pacific.[1] Global Christianity has moved south: "the next Christendom," as Philip Jenkins calls it.[2]

To be sure, the developed world—especially the United States—exports its religious aberrations (like the peculiarly American prosperity gospel). Nevertheless, orthodox Christianity is also growing rapidly. The Anglican communion is sharply divided over fidelity to Christian faith and practice. The thriving churches in Africa, Asia, and Latin America are pulling away from the liberalizing and dying bodies in Britain and North America. Conservative Presbyterian and Reformed denominations in the U.S. and Canada number around a half million members, but there are 1.5 million conservative Presbyterians in Mexico. There are more Reformed Christians in Nigeria than in all of North America. "It is the churches of the majority world that are now sending the majority of people into all kinds of cross-cultural mission work," Wright observes. The second-largest missionary-sending country in the world today is India.[3] If anything, churches in the majority world today are shaping Western missions rather than the other way around.

The Incarnational Analogy

Another way of talking about contextualization in Christian circles today is to suggest that we are to "incarnate" God's love, or to live "incarnationally." However, we have to take a step back and interrogate ourselves about these formulas that we take for granted.

The wonder of the gospel is that God became flesh, condescending from the riches of heavenly splendor to poverty and humiliation for our sakes. But what does it mean for me to incarnate myself or live incarnationally somewhere? From what heaven have I descended? How can my belonging to a network of family members and neighbors constitute an act of condescension, laying aside my heavenly glory and bearing human guilt? I think most of the time people mean by these terms that Christians should go as far as they can in making the gospel accessible to particular non-Christians in specific socio-linguistic contexts. However, the result has been a lot of obsessing over *how* to communicate while assuming (mistakenly) that we know *what* to communicate well enough. In Philippians 2 we are called to imitate the *humility* of Jesus in his incarnation, not to imitate his incarnation itself.

When the real incarnation happened, God assumed our humanity. It is helpful to remind ourselves what we believe as orthodox Christians about this event. On one end of the christological debate was docetism, which denied the real humanity of Christ, saying he only *appeared* to be human. On the other end of the spectrum was Arianism, which denied his deity. Another heresy, Eutychianism, collapsed his humanity into his deity, while the "kenotic" christology of German liberalism in the nineteenth century collapsed his deity into his humanity.

In the orthodox consensus, the eternal Son is the proper subject of the event. The Son assumed our humanity. Jesus Christ is not a combination of humanity and deity. Nor did the Son assume *a human person*, but the *humanity* that belongs to every person. There was no transformation of deity into humanity or humanity into deity, but the union of *two natures* in *one person*.

If conservatives can be naïve about the role of socio-linguistic, cultural, and economic conditioning (the equivalent of a kind of docetism), I think that most of the "living incarnationally"–centered approaches to mission today tilt toward the equivalent of something like the kenotic heresy. In this view, God not only assumes our human nature, without any change in his divine essence or attributes, but empties himself of his deity in order to share in the human experience. At least as the analogy is often applied in contemporary Christian mission, the call to incarnational ministry ends up sounding to me a lot like saying that the context not only shapes the humanity in which the gospel is mediated but also determines the source and content of the gospel.

If we travel down this "kenotic" path, our first stop is emptying the Great Commission of its divinely authorized methods. It is often said that the gospel never changes, but the methods are always in flux, determined by whatever we calculate to be the most effective means for the specific demographic we're trying to reach. Beyond the appropriate sensitivity to cultural habits, this often extends to the relativizing of preaching, sacraments, and discipline. We are now at the stage at which some evangelicals argue that the message itself is always changing, since God speaks through culture as well as through Scripture and this event constitutes one unified speaking.[4]

Navigating between these extremes requires that we first of all recognize the limitations of the incarnational analogy. Like all analogies, this one breaks down. There is one incarnation in history. God has condescended to our weakness by becoming flesh. Jesus Christ is the incarnate revelation of God. Second, the Word has not only wrapped himself in our humanity; he has clothed his Word in the words of the prophets and apostles. Their authorized speech, now deposited in the scriptural canon, is qualitatively different from our interpretations. Their cultural-linguistic background was not divinized but was taken into God's service of communication (i.e., made holy) while remaining human. We do not privilege their culture any more than we privilege our own as revelatory.

At the same time, the incarnation does teach us that God fully assumed our humanity in Christ. There is a legitimate analogy between the incarnation and our communication of the gospel. Although Jesus assumed our humanity, he was—and is—a particular person: a Jewish male, a rabbi, and the son of Mary who grew in wisdom and understanding as he was shaped by his genetic lineage and cultural-linguistic environment. The Truth himself is not a disembodied, isolated mind, like Descartes' self ("a thing that thinks"). Reality is always interpreted. Truth is mediated socially through our cultures and languages. Therefore, we have to resist modernist and fundamentalist assumptions that we "just read the Bible" without any

interpretive assumptions. There is no neutral "view from nowhere."
Only God sees reality as it really is, since he created, upholds, and
guides it to its appointed end. We only know what God has been
pleased to reveal, and even that revelation comes to us through the
mediation of human interpretation in the Scriptures. The difference
is that God has inspired and authorized these interpretations, and we
conform our own interpretations to that rule. Whether premodern,
modern, or postmodern, our cultural locations belong to "this fading
age." And we are told not to be conformed any longer to the pattern
of this age but to be transformed by the Word of God (Rom. 12:2).

So on one hand we have to resist the docetic temptation. It is just
as dangerous to assume that we know the truth in an unmediated
and direct way as it is to assume that because truth is always interpreted, it is merely a human construction determined by the language
and culture of a particular people. The late medieval church resisted
Copernicus and Galileo because it failed to recognize its attachment
to philosophical orthodoxies that it had confused with the Bible.
Overlooking the reality of interpretation—and the role of our own
sociocultural location in that act—has contributed to a successive
stream of dogmatic assertions that, ironically, serve merely to undermine confidence in the authority of God's Word.

It's easy for people like me to pick out the distinctive ways in which
"others" (nonwhite, non-Western) bring their biases to the Scriptures.
It is much more difficult for me to examine my own spectacles—
especially while I'm wearing them. This is why we need to read, experience, and live the Scriptures together with brothers and sisters from
other backgrounds. Our African-American brothers and sisters offer
persuasive testimony to the ways in which white Christians systematically suppress some parts of Scripture, taking as biblical givens what
are in fact nothing more than cultural biases.

Yet we must resist the opposite (kenotic) tendency to collapse
God's speech into human speech, God's Word into the community's
interpretation. The basic plot, doctrines, and practices of the Bible
have united believers across all times and places. Standing over every
culture, God's Word has the power to cut through the systematic
distortions of reality that we assume as givens. There are not many
gospels, but one. And there are not many catholic churches, but one
catholic church that is present in a vast plurality of local assemblies
across all times and places. What makes the church *catholic* is not
that it is one organization under a single human head, nor that it is

a decentered plurality consisting of microtheologies based on local cultures or socioeconomic status. It is *God's* work—proclaiming, baptizing, and teaching—that makes the many one without surrendering their diversity.

Advocates for God: Our Most Decisive Location

I have referred to the current fashion, especially among Western Christians, to encourage the proliferation of "contextual theologies" (Asian, African, African-American, Latin American, feminist, etc.). However, as Christopher Wright notes, "This term in itself betrayed the arrogant ethnocentricity of the West, for the assumption was that other places are contexts and they do their theology for those contexts; we, of course, have the real thing, the objective, contextless theology."[5] I would add that this is the inherent danger of taking the incarnation as a paradigm for our lives and mission rather than as a unique event, the *humility* of which we are to emulate. For us there is no condescension, no transition from a state of exaltation to a state of humiliation. None of us has a pure, God's-eye view of reality and then "translates" that for others.

It is important to recognize our cultural-linguistic biases, but it is equally important to criticize them rather than allow them to become normative, like Scripture itself. Liberation theologians are just as convinced as any fundamentalist that they have the right interpretive lens for interpreting Scripture. You only read the Bible faithfully, James Cone seems to suggest, if you interpret it from the perspective of the experience of African-Americans. These voices can help people like me to recognize my own unacknowledged assumptions that systematically distort my reading of Scripture, but shouldn't we all be striving together to hear God's voice above all others?

Wright adds, "What many of these newer theologies have in common is their advocacy stance. That is, they arise from the conviction that it is fundamental to biblical faith to take a stand alongside the victims of injustice in any form. Thus the Bible is to be read with a liberationist hermeneutic—that is, with a concern to liberate people from oppression and exploitation." Yet Wright counsels that "there is no point, it seems to me, in swinging the pendulum from Western hermeneutical hegemony and ignorance of majority world biblical scholarship to the fashionable adulation of anything and everything that comes from the rest of the world and the rejection of established methods of grammatico-historical exegesis as somehow intrinsically Western, colonial or imperialistic."[6]

Modernity tended to suppress difference, while postmodernity tends to suppress the possibility of arriving at a truth that transcends all temporal and cultural boundaries. To be sure, we all have "interests" and biases. Paul's epistles are addressed to "the church of Christ in Corinth," "in Rome," and so forth. However, their primary location is "in Christ." Their ultimate identity as they hear and interpret the Scriptures together is not rich or poor, Jew or Greek, slave or free, male or female, but true children of Abraham through faith in Christ (Gal. 2:20). In the modern era, both on the left and the right, the concern has been to fit God and his Word into our stories. We have crafted various gospels to serve the metanarrative of progress and emancipation, manifest destiny, personal peace and affluence, or global harmony. We can turn the ancient myth of the soul's upward flight into the modern myth of humanity's gradual ascent in history. However, the really radical move is to accept God's judgment on our life stories and cultural metanarratives in order to be written into his unfolding drama.

Union with Christ does not eradicate cultural or social diversity, but the primary location of Christians in any part of the world is not "the poor," "the wealthy," or any other social and cultural demographic. In fact, "in Christ" is the decisive location that Paul appeals to in order to call the Corinthian believers to repent of the sinful patterns and attitudes prevalent in their society.

Wright properly encourages Christians to read the Bible

in the interests of those who have committed their own personal life story into the biblical story of God's purposes for the nations. But it does so with the even stronger conviction that such commitment should be the normal stance for the whole church, for, on this reading of Scripture, a church that is governed by the Bible cannot evade the missional thrust of the God and the gospel revealed there.[7]

It is by taking our place in that story, not in the stories of this passing evil age, that we actually find a hermeneutic for true liberation. It is in Christ's cross and resurrection that the cosmic liberation of creation from sin, death, evil, violence, and oppression was secured. "From that perspective, we are advocates for *God* before we are advocates for *others.*"[8] We are God's advocates in the world. Only when we realize this do we really have any hope for the others—and for ourselves—who lie under the bondage of systematic sin in which we ourselves may wittingly or unwittingly participate.

In my own experience, I have been overwhelmed by the zeal of Christians in other parts of the world for the truth of the gospel. Captivated by the gospel more than by their own culture or demographic marketing, they are focused on the message and mission that Christ delivered. They resist—quite explicitly—attempts to create indigenous Christianities. They bristle at the suggestions, usually coming from Americans and Europeans, to develop a uniquely "African theology," "Brazilian theology," and so forth. They want to be African and Brazilian evangelists of "the faith once and for all delivered to the saints." And it is their churches that are growing.

To be honest, I'm a little skeptical about anyone who claims to speak for a particular group, especially for a race, ethnic community, or gender. I don't think that James Cone speaks for African-Americans any more than does T. D. Jakes. Cone's debt to Karl Marx and liberal-existentialist theologian Paul Tillich is as evident as Jakes's debt to Adam Smith and Kenneth Copeland. Many Christians and church leaders I know in Central and South America are more critical than I am of liberation theologians like Gustavo Gutiérrez. Who is qualified to write an "Asian theology"? Christian orthodoxy is shaped by a long conversation among people from the Middle East, northern Africa, and Europe. It is being enriched and advanced by Christians in Asia, Latin America, the rest of Africa, and elsewhere. Why should Christians in these countries be more open to European culture-shapers like Marx, Durkheim, and Freud or theologians like Schleiermacher, Bultmann, Tillich, and Moltmann than to this culturally broader and richer heritage of orthodoxy?

The same is true of feminist theologies. We dare not turn a deaf ear to the cry of our sisters who struggle against injustice, and their experiences help us all to recognize cultural assumptions that distort God's Word. But is "women's experience" monolithic, or does it often turn out to be a variation of an ideology developed primarily by men like Marx, Freud, and Lacan? And as long as it is "women's experience," can I not, as a privileged male, hold it at arm's distance in studious objectivity without having to deal with it as the concern of a sister who has a claim on me? It would be more genuinely *post*modern to question the totalizing claims of such ideologies. For Christians at least, the goal of discovering our particular cultural spectacles is to look *through* them, not just *at* them. As we become more aware of our healthy and unhealthy biases, we are better able to read God's Word together more faithfully.

If conservative theologies in the West reflect a largely white, middle-class cultural location, liberal theologies are often more condescending in their imperialism. Look at worldwide Anglicanism. What happens when African churches want to be faithful to Scripture in a way that actually binds them to most Christians across all times and places more than it does to fellow Anglicans in Britain and North America? Liberal clerics like United States bishop John Spong accuse them of being backward, primitive, and insufficiently emancipated (by people like him) from their colonial past.[9] Attachment to historic Christianity is "primitive" or perhaps "colonial," while apparently the distinctive cultures and dogmas of liberal Western academies are simply the way things ought to be.

As Wright suggests above, Christians are first and foremost advocates for *God*: his mission, his kingdom, his will, and his gospel. Ours is hardly the first era in which Christians have had to give serious thought to the gospel and their cultural context. The tension of proclaiming the gospel in a pluralistic environment is as old as the church itself. Israel struggled with this tension, as its capitulation to the idols of its neighbors led finally to its exile. It was a tension well known to the earliest Christians. Yet it was "one Lord, one faith, one baptism" that drew them together, calling them to give up their cherished ethnic, socioeconomic, and gender locations as ultimate and normative for their identity.

Postmodern hermeneutics has provided a useful therapy against the modernist arrogance of the post-Enlightenment West. However, if I am going to be liberated from my own distorted interpretations, there is no hope in the fatalism that says that there is no text, nothing standing outside of our interpretations, judging and correcting them. Again Wright is helpful on this point:

> Where the missional hermeneutic will part company with radical postmodernity is in its insistence that through all this variety, locality, particularity and diversity, the Bible is nevertheless actually the story. This is the way it is. This is the grand narrative that constitutes truth for all. And within this story, as narrated or anticipated by the Bible, there is at work the God whose mission is evident from creation to

new creation. . . . This is the universal story that gives a place in the
sun to all the little stories.[10]

This grand narrative is the plot that leads from existence "in Adam"
to existence "in Christ."

"In Adam" I am self-enclosed, in my own identity. Even other
individuals in my circle are accessories of my narcissism, nurturing
my narrow longings, aspirations, identities, and choices. However,
"in Christ" I am an opened-up person, called out of my cocoon of
inwardness to embrace others—indeed, strangers—whom God has
made my new family. Whether "in Adam" or "in Christ," everyone
is a character in this unfolding drama. The call to preach the gospel
to the whole world presupposes not only an irreducible plurality but
a fundamental unity of the human race.

Genuine Catholicity

There is one gospel that is "the power of God for salvation to everyone
who believes, to the Jew first and also to the Greek" (Rom. 1:16).
Because there is one gospel, there is one church. *Catholic* means
"universal," but for Christians it refers specifically to the unity of all
believers across all times and places in the body of Christ. Reflecting the Triune God we confess, this catholicity consists of *a unity of
faith in a plurality of voices.* Catholicity does not mean many faiths
or many gospels, but rather many saints from many times and places
who hear and speak God's Word together.

I am obligated, as a white native Californian born in 1964 to a
lower-middle-class family, to interpret the Bible together with my
African-American, Latino, and Asian brothers and sisters at my local
church each Lord's Day. Yet more is required. My local church is a
microcosm of the whole body of Christ across all ages and cultures.
We need to link up our interpretations with the family of God spread
over seven continents and three millennia.

A common faith is more of a threat to our cherished locations than
are contextual theologies. I might find a "Latin American theology"
interesting, but I am an outsider. I can take or leave it. It's a completely
different matter if brothers and sisters are confessing *the* faith from
their diverse social and cultural backgrounds. Now I too am an insider, and I am obliged not only to listen to these voices but to listen

with them to the voice of God. We are obliged to worship together, to pray together, to study together, and to live together under God's Word. We are no longer allowed to accept the prevailing apartheid of suburban churches and black inner-city churches, youthful and aging congregations (even different services under the same roof), flag-wavers and flag-burners. Gospel-driven unity in Christ's body is uncomfortable. Everyone has to give up their "right" to privilege their culture, generation, politics, or consumer profile over the gospel.

If there is no narrative beyond our competing local and personal stories, then what is the point of listening to each other? Why should we even try to reach *agreement* if there are only "contextual theologies" rather than a common faith? If the same gospel cannot be understood and embraced by people in every time and place, then Christ did not assume humanity, but at most a particular person or race; he is not the Savior of the world, and his Word and Spirit do not in fact break into and break up the present age with the transcendent powers of the age to come.

The injunction to mere politeness toward "the other" is different from the call to all Christians everywhere to hear the gospel and to read the Bible together as his body. This point needs to be heard in my own community: Reformed and Presbyterian churches. Sometimes we refer to our confession as "the Reformed faith." However, there is no such thing. There is only the *Christian faith*. Faithful Reformed and Presbyterian churches embrace the ecumenical creeds and our confessions and catechisms as the secondary standard for our faith and practice. They are authoritative only because they summarize the central teaching of the canonical Scriptures that we share with all believers.

Having creeds and confessions is far from legalistic. In point of fact, it is the confessions that keep us from becoming overly narrow. The Reformed confessions, for example, treat the whole sweep of Christian faith and practice, not just a few doctrines. And yet they do not require submission on divisive questions that many Christians today regard as fundamental.

I often hear the question, "How can a document written by northern Europeans in the sixteenth and seventeenth centuries constitute *our* confession today?" But when we actually read these documents, we realize that they reflect the accumulated wisdom of churches spread out over many centuries and in many diverse places. It is certainly true that they are not acultural or atemporal, but they are transcultural, and they sustain the church throughout the generations. They teach us that the chief end of our creation is "to glorify God and to enjoy him forever" and that our "only comfort in life and in death" is that we belong to Christ, who has saved us and preserves us to the end. What seismic shift in our culture makes these truths untrue or unintelligible to people like us today? If anything, Americans need to hear this God-centered and Christ-focused message more than ever. These truths are not irrelevant or unintelligible to us today; they have always been offensive in their contradiction of the wisdom of the world. We learn—and confess—that there is one God in three persons, one Christ in two natures, and that this God has chosen, redeemed, called, and justified; he is sanctifying; and he will one day glorify us. If it is true that Abraham was justified by grace alone through faith alone in Christ alone, as Jesus and the apostles testify, then it is true in 1561 and in the third millennium.

Though we are more properly sensitive to cultural assumptions, we nevertheless need more catholicized rather than contextualized theologies. We need a faith and practice that is determined by the Word of God as it is interpreted and confessed by many faithful believers across many times and places. I am more at home in the racially, generationally, socially, and politically mixed church in which I am a minister than I am at a family reunion. Yet that can only happen because the blood of Christ is thicker than that of kith and kin. We share one Lord, one faith, one baptism.

In American churches today, believers often live in remarkably narrow and homogeneous environments. In the 1970s the so-called homogeneous church growth principle was even defended as a missiological strategy. As we are not only divided by race, ethnicity, and politics but increasingly by generation, music style, and social demographics, the apostolic ideal of rich and poor, young and old, slave and free gathered together at the font and table is being surrendered to the false catholicity of the marketplace.

To be sure, ethnic hegemony is sometimes due to language barriers of first-generation immigrants. But what happens when it is second, third, and fourth generations of members consisting mainly of one ethnic group? Can we really say that the Black Church or the largely white suburban church, a Swedish Lutheran church, a Korean Presbyterian church, or a Dutch Reformed church is as healthy as it could be if it were less focused on ethnicity, culture, and politics than on the gospel? As a microcosm of the catholic church, each local church should reflect the diversity of Christ's body. A church without older people is as immature as a church without younger people is moribund. When a church is made up of primarily wealthy or poor members, something is missing. Every Lord's Day is meant to be like Christmas, with an exchange of gifts that God gives us to share with each other.

Our "contextualized," niche-demographic churches are more homogeneous—indeed, more narrow—than a confessional tradition. For all of its insightful criticisms of megachurch consumerism, the emergent movement is driven by mostly white, upwardly mobile urbanites in North America who prefer jazz and indie music to country or easy listening and shopping at boutiques rather than Walmart. Tony Jones admits, "Emergent churches are overwhelmingly white, at least thus far in the still-young movement. So white, in fact, that the satirical religious newspaper *The Holy Observer* once ran a story, 'Frightened Black Family Flees Emergent Church.'"[11] I've only visited a few emergent groups, but I don't see a lot of parents and children worshiping together, much less grandparents. A middle-aged guy from Oklahoma might feel as out of place here as he would at a bar mitzvah in Upper Manhattan.

If the magnet of our unity is cultural affinity rather than the Word, baptism, and Eucharist, ecclesial apartheid will continue to fracture the visible church. Each church becomes a circle of friends more than a communion of saints. Tony Jones seems to justify this suspicion when he writes,

> Whereas traditional groupings of Christians are either bounded sets (for example, Roman Catholicism or Presbyterianism—you know whether you're in or out based on membership) or centered sets (for example, evangelicalism, which centers on certain core beliefs), emergent Christians do not have membership or doctrine to hold them together. The glue is relationship. That makes it difficult to put one's finger on just what emergent is; to the question "What do you all hold in common?" the answer is most likely "We're friends."[12]

In this approach (as in others), the church becomes defined more by the common playlists on its members' iPods than by a common faith. The church becomes less the house of God than the house of the group leader and his friends. Could that be why everyone seems to be so similar?

By contrast, the gospel creates a multigenerational, multiethnic, multinational community of forgiven and renewed sinners whose union with Christ and fellowship in his Word and sacraments makes them the strangest and most wonderful family in the world.

I have terrific friendships with non-Christians as well as fellow believers. However, *fellowship in the gospel* is completely different. It's hardly worth alerting the media to the announcement of a get-together of friends. However, the church gets really interesting when Jews and Gentiles show up and find themselves being made one people despite themselves, when blacks and whites share a common cup, and when Republicans and Democrats encourage each other to live out their baptism and teach each other's children catechism after the service.

As many divisions as there are between Protestant denominations, confessional traditions are at least connected to the wider body of Christ across generations and cultures. A common confession contrasts sharply with the narrow experiences and influences of culturally driven movements.

Apartheid in South Africa can serve as a cautionary tale in this regard. According to some of the leading theologians who challenged this racially based system of segregation, apartheid evolved out of a missionary strategy. According to John de Gruchy, Reformed churches were not segregated until the mid-nineteenth-century revivals by holiness preacher Andrew Murray and pietist missionaries. "It was under the dominance of such evangelicalism," says de Gruchy, "rather than the strict Calvinism of Dort, that the Dutch Reformed Church agreed at its Synod of 1857 that congregations could be divided along racial lines." He adds,

> Despite the fact that this development went against earlier synodical decisions that segregation in the church was contrary to the Word of God, it was rationalized on grounds of missiology and practical necessity. Missiologically it was argued that people were best evangelized and best worshiped God in their own language and cultural setting, a position reinforced by German Lutheran missiology and somewhat akin to the church-growth philosophy of our own time.[13]

The "church-growth philosophy of our own time" to which de Gruchy refers is the "homogeneous church growth principle" developed especially by Donald McGavran. In this widely influential model, the sociological fact that people gravitate to people who are like them became a justification for the market segmentation of churches.[14]

When we allow something other than the gospel to determine the identity of the church, our mission becomes an extension of the powers of this present age rather than the in-breaking of the age to come. As a result, our churches are deprived of that genuine cultural diversity that reflects the new creation.

I miss important things, exaggerate other things, and distort still other things simply because of my own socialization. Demographically, I fit more with the emergent church profile than with a lot of churches in my own denomination. However, I need to be shaped and disciplined by other saints who interpret Scripture and our confession from different backgrounds, experiences, and generations. The communion of saints encompasses not only all believers around the world who are alive today but also the cloud of witnesses who have gone before us.

Turning the church into a circle of friends and extended families happens in conservative churches too. What are we saying about the tie that binds us when the American flag is up at the front of the church along with the pulpit, font, and table? Or when we *replace* the symbols of God's means of grace with an organ, a choir, or a praise band? Something changes. The catholicity generated by "one Lord, one faith, one baptism" surrenders to the false catholicity that divides nations, generations, and consumers.

Brought to the United States by Dutch immigrants (mostly post–World War II), the denomination in which I minister has a lot of churches that are entrenched in ethnic peculiarities. Nobody says to "outsiders," "You're not welcome here." On the contrary, I've experienced tremendous warmth, and I've heard the same from other non-Dutch visitors. And yet there's something about the windmills, ethnic rituals and insider banter, "Dutch suppers," and other collective celebrations of ethnicity that may be entirely appropriate for a social club but are out of place in the church. When things are justified by "we've always done it that way," the question arises, "Who is the 'we' you're talking about?"

If you didn't grow up in it, you can get a similar alienating feeling in a church that arose during the Jesus Movement. Once upon a time, the gatherings were "authentic," even if dominated by a narrow demographic of surfers. However, today's aging surfers-for-Jesus are often seen as a cliché by their children, who now attend the cooler emergent gathering down the street. Is there any reason to believe it will turn out differently for the emergent gatherings? "Mom, it used to be cool, but it's not anymore." Having climbed to the top of the charts, each new "reinvent the church" movement eventually becomes just as alienating, out of style, and ingrown as the more traditional churches they left years ago. Often church growth experts, catechized in market research, actually encourage this planned obsolescence. When the party's over, you are faced with a choice: reinvent and relaunch your product, or call it quits and retire.

The church that Jesus is building is a means of God's faithfulness "from generation to generation" and "from every tribe and people and tongue and nation." Rather than the exploitation of the "divide and conquer" strategy of marketing, here we find a succession of the covenant blessings from parents to children. Here we all have to give up our group narcissism and allow the gospel to create the kind of strange community that we would never have pulled together ourselves.

If this is so, then we need fewer *contextual* theologies and more *catholic* theologies that are truly catholic: that is, interpretive communities that are rich enough to offer mutual correction and insight into God's Word from the various contexts of different times and places. Our attachment to the fad of contextualization, I fear, is actually having the opposite of its intended effect. Instead of making us more genuinely plural, multicultural, and diverse in richness, it is making our churches more culturally homogeneous and separate from each other.

All of us need to be not only enriched by the particular contributions of each other's contextual interpretations but also *freed* from the captivities of our own local distortions of the gospel that claim they alone possess the valid universal truth for us all. In the heavenly worship described in Revelation 5:9, this ultimate catholicity becomes the vision for our partial realizations here and now. In that scene, the focus of worship is not the poor or the rich, the privileged or the marginalized, Westerners or non-Westerners, but the Lamb. Arrayed around his throne, the elect sing, "Worthy are you, for with your blood you purchased people from every tribe and tongue and people and nation, and you have made them to be a kingdom of priests to our God. And they shall reign forever." In the next chapter we will explore what it means for us to be made "a kingdom of priests to our God."

5

The Goal

"Making Disciples"

According to numerous studies, most Americans consider themselves "spiritual, but not religious." In other words, they dabble in whatever beliefs and practices they find intuitively valid and useful for daily living, but they resist any threat to their individual autonomy. They are willing to be consumers in the spiritual marketplace, but not disciples of Jesus Christ. However, Jesus warns, "Not everyone who says to me, 'Lord, Lord,' will enter the kingdom of heaven, but the one who does the will of my Father who is in heaven" (Matt. 7:21). Many will be surprised on the last day, Jesus adds: "On that day many will say to me, 'Lord, Lord, did we not prophesy in your name, and cast out demons in your name, and do many mighty works in your name?' And then will I declare to them, 'I never knew you; depart from me, you workers of lawlessness'" (Matt. 7:22–23).

Evangelicals have always been known for taking this warning seriously, aware of the danger of nominal ("in name only") Christian profession. In fact, evangelicalism is a history of successive renewal movements within established churches where being a Christian was simply taken for granted as part of citizenship in a supposedly Christian

133

nation. However, increasingly it seems that evangelicals themselves exhibit a nominal attachment to the faith. Is the salt losing its savor?

This is the concern that drives writers like Dallas Willard, Richard Foster, and other pioneers of the contemporary emphasis on discipleship as inner transformation through spiritual disciplines and that also motivates the emerging church movement. However much these movements stand in a somewhat critical relationship to modern evangelicalism, in many ways they reflect a resurgence of traditional evangelical emphases.

Appearing in 1978, Richard Foster's book *Celebration of Discipline: The Path to Spiritual Growth* quickly established itself as a classic. Joining Foster's wake-up call to become serious disciples was Dallas Willard, with his bestselling works *The Spirit of the Disciplines* (1990) and *The Divine Conspiracy* (1998). Both are evangelicals (Foster a Quaker and Willard a Methodist) concerned that American Christians are consumers rather than transformed followers of Christ and convinced that the monastic tradition of spirituality offers resources for contemporary renewal.

Writers like Foster and Willard are responding to a genuine crisis: namely, the reduction of the gospel to "fire insurance" and "sin management," with the inner life of believers left to the distractions of a culture that prizes busyness in the world more highly than being alone with God in prayer and meditating on his Word. Some believers have been taught that Jesus can be one's Savior without being one's Lord. However, this is a serious error. Discipleship is not an optional extra. Disciples often misunderstand and disobey their Lord, but they follow him. If we are not followers of Christ, we are not his disciples. That is to say, we are not merely "carnal Christians"—second-class believers who are saved but will lose their rewards. Rather, we are not *Christians*.

As critical as one might be of many aspects of the monastic approach to spirituality, we are particularly tempted in our distracted culture to ignore the daily routines of prayer and meditation on God's Word. The pace of life in highly developed economies like ours threatens to squeeze out the daily habits that allow us to take a step back and evaluate the things that really matter most. This is even true for pastors, especially to the extent that they are CEOs and managers in their office or on their cell phones more than shepherds in their study and at the bedside.

At the same time, monastic piety has been somewhat ambivalent about the role of the institutional church, and pietism has contributed a wariness of all external forms. In medieval piety, laypeople, active in the world, were ordinary Christians, while monks and nuns were viewed as serious disciples who embraced and lived out the commands of Jesus, which they called the "evangelical counsels."

A similar view emerged in pietism, as the truly committed formed holy clubs, cell groups, or a church within the church. Often, believers are encouraged to separate the sheep from the goats by the intensity of inner transformation, dividing the church into higher and lower ranks of "fully surrendered and victorious" and "defeated and carnal." This can lead even to a kind of vigilante operation, where each believer assumes the responsibility of "excommunicating" another: deciding who's in and who's out—who is "really saved"—even if that person is a member in good standing in the church. Baptism counts for nothing. All of that is merely formal and external. Acceptance of a profession of faith by the elders becomes quite secondary to my examination of a brother's or sister's experience and fruit. Regular church attendance is no more a sign of genuine conversion than a machine's being parked in the garage is evidence that it is a car.

Like many others reared in evangelicalism, I grew up thinking that having a daily quiet time was more important than regular church attendance. After all, it's a "personal relationship with Jesus Christ" that really matters. Sunday school teachers, youth, and college workers came to each of us for routine checkups: "How's your walk with the Lord?"—which was code for "Are you having a consistent daily quiet time?" The atmosphere of emphasis on inner experience and character formation was already pretty thick in evangelical circles.

My mother even had a worn copy of Thomas à Kempis's *Imitation of Christ* on her shelf. I recently reexamined that book written by a remarkable late-medieval monk, and it struck me that there was so little about Christ in his saving office. Rather, this bestselling classic is filled with stern warnings to put Christ's example into practice out of fear of judgment and hope of rewards. In church we sang about coming to the garden alone with Jesus, experiencing a joy that was so unique, personal, and individual that "none other has ever known." And asking the question "What would Jesus do?" has been the staple diet in evangelical circles for a long time.

Many of us have overreacted to this background, embracing the gospel and the church's corporate ministry as if they liberated us from obedience and a personal relationship with Christ. This is a false choice. The gospel liberates us *for* obedience, not from obedience, and the corporate ministry of Word and sacrament fuels our devotional life as individual believers. However, if some have reduced discipleship to "fire insurance," the danger in the spiritual disciplines model is the reduction of discipleship to the imitation of Christ. Instead, we need the richness, depth, and breadth of the whole gospel. This gospel is not an answer to "What would Jesus do?" but to "What has Jesus done?" The answer provokes a further question: "How can I receive it?" And this in turn leads us to ask, "How am I to live in the light of it?" Recent writers like James Wilhoit encourage a more balanced way forward, with a more integrative approach to the church and spiritual disciplines.[1] Dietrich Bonhoeffer's *Life Together* remains unparalleled in this regard, showing the wisdom of Reformation piety.

The Anabaptist and pietist streams have fed and shaped evangelical spiritualities for a long time. Yet there were differences even within monastic communities, particularly over the *active life* versus the *contemplative life*. Various medieval orders were founded in defense of one or the other. Many favored contemplation (prayer, solitude, and other spiritual disciplines) as the way of true spirituality, while others, especially the Franciscans (named after Francis of Assisi), emphasized the active life of service, especially to the poor.

Challenging the foundations of monasticism generally, the Reformation taught that all believers were disciples of Christ and that they do not ascend to God by their contemplation or their works. Rather, God has descended to us in Christ, driving us outside of ourselves by his Word so that we look up to Christ in faith and out to our neighbors in love.

First, the Reformers rejected the whole paradigm of Christian Platonism, with its ladder from the "lower realm" of the body and its senses to the "upper realm" of spirit. Second, because Christ has fulfilled all righteousness in our place and fully satisfied for every sin (both what we have done and what we have failed to do), we do not present our works to the Father as a sacrifice for guilt. As a result, there is nowhere for our good works to go except out to our neighbor who needs us. Third, sin is not to be identified with the world as such, but with our own hearts. The goal is not to leave the world and common society, away from the body and ordinary life (including marriage, family, and secular callings). Rather, true discipleship is to receive Christ where he has promised to save and guide us in communion with Christ and each other, especially in the public service and family worship. And it is also to immerse ourselves in God's Word and in prayer so that we can cling more firmly to Christ and bear the fruit of faith in loving service to our neighbors in the world.

Far from eliminating the goal of forming genuine disciples or downplaying the importance of prayer and meditation, the Reformation opened up the meditative study of Scripture to all believers. The boy working at his plow and the mother taking a break from her labors turned to the Bible in their own common language.

The monastic ideal continued in the Anabaptist and pietist heritage and is clearly evident in contemporary approaches to discipleship in our day. Yet some movements are more oriented to the contemplative life (for example, the spiritual disciplines movement associated especially with Dallas Willard and Richard Foster) and others more toward the active life (evident in the emergent church movement). Willard presses pastors to ask themselves, "Is my first aim to make disciples? Or do I just run an operation?"[2] Discipleship has lost its coinage, Willard judges with insight:

> Discipleship on the theological right has come to mean preparation for soul winning, under the direction of parachurch efforts that had discipleship farmed out to them because the local church really wasn't doing it. On the left, discipleship has come to mean some form of social activity or social service, from serving soup lines to political protests to . . . whatever. The term "discipleship" has currently been ruined so far as any solid psychological and biblical content is concerned.[3]

We will interact with these approaches later, but let's begin with a brief exploration of discipleship in the Scriptures.

Discipleship in the New Testament

Rabbi means "teacher," and in Jesus's day disciples attached themselves to a particular rabbi, coming regularly to the synagogue and sometimes attending the teacher on walks or daily rounds to members of the community. Compared to an ox, the disciple accepted the "yoke" of the master. Hence, in pronouncing his curses upon the religious leaders of his day, Jesus could say, "They tie up heavy burdens, hard to bear, and lay them on people's shoulders, but they themselves are not willing to move them with their finger. They do all their deeds to be seen by others" (Matt. 23:4–5). By contrast, he invites all who are "heavy laden" to come to him for rest: "Take my yoke upon you, and learn from me, for I am gentle and lowly in heart, and you will find rest for your souls" (Matt. 11:29).

Two sisters, Mary and Martha, were among Jesus's closest disciples. We are told that Mary "sat at the Lord's feet and listened to his teaching. But Martha was distracted with much serving" (Luke 10:39–40). When Martha complained that Mary was making her do all the work, Jesus replied, "Martha, Martha, you are anxious and troubled about many things, but one thing is necessary. Mary has chosen the good portion, which will not be taken away from her" (Luke 10:41–42). Disciples are learners first; then they will be servants of their Master.

In Matthew 10:24–42, Jesus teaches us what it means to be a disciple in his kingdom, emphasizing that it is a matter of literally following the Master by learning and living. The Great Commission itself ties discipleship closely to the public ministry: proclaiming the gospel to every person and "baptizing them in the name of the Father and of the Son and of the Holy Spirit, teaching them to observe all that I have commanded you" (Matt. 28:18–20). Being Christ's disciples means bringing people into the sphere of the church's ministry of preaching and sacrament. It involves being instructed not just in the basics of biblical teaching, but in *everything* Jesus commanded for our doctrine and life.

Through these means instituted by Christ, the Master is still with us along the Emmaus road, opening our hearts to receive him and all of his benefits (Luke 24:13–35). Seen in this light, the church is not only the financier and sender of missionaries but a mission station in its own right. The Great Commission is as much the mandate to care for the sheep in a two-hundred-year-old congregation in New York as it is to seek the lost in Nairobi. We never graduate from the school of discipleship until we die.

Our English word *disciple* means "student." To be sure, the context is not that of a lecture hall, note taking, and final exams. Rather, it is of an outdoor, mobile classroom in which the tutorials occur in the context of daily occurrences, interactions, and analogies from familiar experience. Nevertheless, this relationship provokes questions and answers, conversation and even debate. Even our Lord's miraculous signs were always connected to the reality they signified: Jesus as the Bread from Heaven, the Lord of the Sabbath, the Healer who opens blind eyes and preaches the gospel to the poor, the Resurrection and the Life. These signs were not just object lessons but harbingers of the kingdom that he was inaugurating. Yet they were always connected to his *teachings* concerning himself and his mission.

Both his disciples and critics came to him with questions, and much of the sayings related in the Gospels have to do with his answers in the form of "teachings." The disciples learned in the field, watching Jesus inaugurate his kingdom and hearing him explain what was happening. However, even they did not really understand the doctrine he taught until the dramatic events of which he spoke were fulfilled and the Spirit opened their eyes to understand the prophetic Scriptures with Christ at the center (Luke 24). His postresurrection appearances were taken up with teaching, fellowship, and the celebration of the Supper.

Jesus did not imagine that his *example* was enough to win the day. In fact, he knew that he was going to Jerusalem to accomplish what only he could accomplish by himself, upheld only by the command of his Father and the power of the Spirit. The primary sign of discipleship was the acceptance of Jesus's teaching concerning himself. Charges of blasphemy and even the offense expressed by the disciples themselves were due to his *teaching* concerning himself. Jesus prepared his followers for imminent persecution for the sake of his name and in their witness to his saving work. The persecutions recounted in the book of Acts are all said to have been on account of testifying to Christ's person and work. The Jewish authorities did not command Jewish Christians to stop feeding the hungry or improving Jerusalem's culture but charged them to stop preaching Christ as the one on whom they are to call for salvation.

In John 6, Jesus offends the crowd of so-called disciples by telling them that he has come down from heaven to give eternal life to all whom the Father has given him (v. 39). "Truly, truly, I say to you, unless you eat the flesh of the Son of Man and drink his blood, you have no life in you. Whoever feeds on my flesh and drinks my blood has eternal life, and I will raise him up on the last day" (vv. 53–54). "It is the Spirit who gives life," Jesus said to his frustrated disciples in John 6, "the flesh is no avail. *The words that I have spoken to you are spirit and life*. But there are some of you who do not believe. . . . This is why I told you that no one can come to me unless it is granted him by the Father" (vv. 63–65, emphasis added). We are told that many followers turned away at this point "and no longer walked with him. So Jesus said to the Twelve, 'Do you want to go away as well?' Simon Peter answered him, 'Lord, to whom shall we go? You have the words of eternal life, and we have believed, and have come to know, that you are the Holy One of God'" (vv. 66–69). Disciples have to swallow *everything* that Jesus says: hook, line, and sinker. Learning this lesson the hard way, the disciples heard Jesus drive away the crowds of consumers by teaching "hard doctrines."

The book of Acts tells us what this Spirit-filled discipleship actually looked like. Even on the day of Pentecost, as the Spirit was poured out, the result was Peter's public proclamation of Christ on the temple steps, from the Old Testament Scriptures, followed by baptism. "And they devoted themselves to the apostles' teaching and the fellowship, to the breaking of bread and the prayers" (Acts 2:42). If we want to see what the Great Commission looks like on the ground, this is it! And if the extraordinary ministry of the apostles—not to mention the extraordinary event of Pentecost—centered on the ordinary ministry of Word and sacrament, then why should we be looking for more extraordinary missions and methods for the Great Commission?

Both the content of their message and these practices distinguished this community of disciples from the world and were the source and means of their disciple-making in the world. To be sure, the teaching they received radically transformed their practice. As a result, they freely shared their worldly goods with each other, and no one was lacking in temporal things. A surprising gospel created a surprising community, living on the fragrance of the age to come instead of the fading fumes of this passing age.

Throughout Jesus's ministry, we encounter his recurring emphasis on his teaching, his words that bring life. It is through hearing the gospel that sinners are saved and disciples are conformed to Christ's image (Rom. 8:29; 2 Cor. 3:18). When the apostle Paul speaks of "growing up"—becoming "mature in Christ"—his first thought is of our being recipients of "the work of ministry" that Christ gave

> for building up the body of Christ, until we all attain to the unity of the faith and of the knowledge of the Son of God, to mature manhood, to the measure of the stature of the fullness of Christ, so that we may no longer be children, tossed to and fro by the waves and carried about by every wind of doctrine, by human cunning, by craftiness in deceitful schemes. Rather, speaking the truth in love, we are to grow up in every way into him who is the head, into Christ, from whom the whole body, joined and held together by every joint with which it is equipped, when each part is working properly, makes the body grow so that it builds itself up in love. (Eph. 4:12–16)

From this ministry of preaching, teaching, and sacrament—that builds us up into Christ—every member expresses his or her discipleship as new creatures through their daily interaction with believers and their non-Christian neighbors (Eph. 4:17–32). Only then can they follow Christ's example of love and humility: "Therefore be imitators of God, as beloved children. And walk in love, as Christ loved us and gave himself up for us, a fragrant offering and sacrifice to God" (Eph. 5:1–2). Notice from this passage that we are to imitate God's love in Jesus Christ, not to imitate his redeeming work.

We offer up ourselves not as an atoning sacrifice but as *living sacrifices of praise*, as Paul says in Romans 12, "by [or in view of] the mercies of God" (v. 1). Furthermore, this constant transformation occurs not by avoiding doctrinal investigation, but "by the renewal of your mind" through God's Word (v. 2).

Jesus does call us to discipleship, not just to "making a decision." However, before we can serve, we must be served by our Savior (Matt. 26:28). We must sit, listen, and learn from the Master who calls, "Come to me, all who labor and are heavy laden, and I will give you rest. Take my yoke upon you, and learn from me, for I am gentle and lowly in heart, and you will find rest for your souls" (Matt. 11:28–29). This humble receiving is not a one-time thing at the beginning of our Christian life, so that we can get on with the *real* business of discipleship (namely, spiritual disciplines, ministry opportunities, and social service projects). It is the well to which disciples return every week, every day. It is their daily bread.

Being disciples involves a whole formation of life, with new choices, habits, and virtues that exhibit new character. However, *making* disciples—defined by the Great Commission—depends on the gospel, as it is delivered through Word, sacrament, and discipline. The Great Commission is a specific mandate, with manifold effects and consequent responsibilities.

From Drama to Discipleship: What Distinguishes This Commission from Others?

Successful companies and nonprofit service agencies have a mission statement, vision statement, and strategic plan. Surely the church is no different. But what are they? And are they something each church needs to write for itself, or are they already written by its founder and president?

What distinguishes the church from the Rotary Club, a political action committee, or a multinational corporation? Is it *the antiquity of the institution*? Many organized religions (for example, Hinduism, Buddhism, Judaism) go back to the Axial Age (800 BC to 200 BC) in their origins. As a political institution, democracy goes back at least as far as Athens five centuries before Christ. Is the church distinguished by *its global reach*? McDonald's and Coca-Cola are global powerhouses. Is the church's uniqueness secured by *its eternal laws and principles for human flourishing*? Buddhism, Hinduism, Jainism, and Sikhism share with Judaism, Christianity, and Islam a respect for a universal law that is written into the human conscience. In fact, Hindus often refer to their religion as "Sanātana Dharma" (the eternal law).

What distinguishes the Christian faith from the world's religions and philosophies is *the story it tells about God's mission as Alpha and Omega, Creator, Sustainer, Redeemer, and Consummator*. As it unfolds, this particular drama gives rise to clusters of doctrines that fill us with doxology, which gives shape to a concrete form of living (discipleship) in the world. There is a clear pattern, especially in many of the Psalms and the New Testament epistles: drama, doctrine, doxology, and discipleship. It's not always as formulaic as that, of course. The clearest examples are Paul's letters. In Romans, for example, Paul begins by referring to the *drama*:

> The gospel of God, which he promised beforehand through his prophets in the holy Scriptures, concerning his Son, who was descended from David according to the flesh and who was declared to be the Son of God in power according to the Spirit of holiness by his resurrection from the dead, Jesus Christ our Lord, through whom we have received grace and apostleship to bring about the obedience of faith for the sake of his name among all the nations, including you who are called to belong to Jesus Christ. (Rom. 1:1–6)

Then Paul begins to make his first major *doctrinal* argument: that the whole world is under the condemnation of the law. He moves from original sin to redemption and justification to baptism into Christ and sanctification to glorification, and then, after a doxological interlude, he returns again to God's electing purposes especially in relation to ethnic Israel.

These doctrinal vistas provoke wonder and praise: *doxology*. Like scenic turnouts on a mountain highway, Paul pauses simply to take in the view and exclaim, "What then shall we say to these things? If

God is for us, who can be against us?" (Rom. 8:31). Through these exclamations of praise, the external gospel is internalized. We find ourselves not only assenting to it but trusting, reveling, and dancing in it. Nothing "in all creation, will be able to separate us from the love of God in Christ Jesus our Lord" (8:39). "Oh, the depth of the riches and wisdom and knowledge of God! How unsearchable are his judgments and how inscrutable his ways! 'For who has known the mind of the Lord, or who has been his counselor?' 'Or who has given a gift to him that he might be repaid?' For from him and through him and to him are all things. To him be glory forever. Amen" (11:33–36).

Then, in chapter 12, the focus turns to the ways in which this drama, doctrine, and doxology generate a particular kind of "reasonable service"—the *discipleship*—that we offer in view of God's mercies (v. 1). As those who are chosen, redeemed, called, justified, and being sanctified and who will be glorified in Christ, we are to live out our high calling in our relationships with the state, with employers and employees, with family members, and with fellow church members with whom we differ on matters of Christian freedom.

Drama, doctrine, doxology, and discipleship: these are the aspects of our high calling that must be integrated. Conservatives may be tempted to abstract the doctrine from its dramatic narrative, doxological practice, and discipleship. Much of evangelical worship over the past generation has focused on praise without adequate grounding in the drama, doctrine, or discipleship. And now the current emphasis on discipleship is threatened by an inadequate grounding in these other important aspects of Christian maturity. The danger is that discipleship becomes little more than spiritual exercises or moralistic activism: "having the appearance of godliness, but denying its power" (2 Tim. 3:5).

First we need to learn the drama and the doctrine. In becoming a disciple, you can't just "go." You have to submit yourself to the grammar of Christian faith and practice. This was true even for the apostles, whom Jesus instructed for forty days before his ascension. Like learning Mandarin, dance moves, baseball, or (for some of us) how to use an iPhone, becoming a Christian takes a lifetime. You have to indwell the world that these new vocabularies and practices generate. You can't really play the piano without learning the piano.

We spend our lives as believers learning the plotline and central characters of the story. Then we have to become familiar with the authoritative interpretations and implications (doctrine). Yet it is really when we are led to lament and praise that we begin to internalize the story and live into it. When we are not just imitators of the characters but actually united to the central figure in the plot, we find ourselves actually recast from our own stories about nothing into the greatest story ever told. We say (and pray and sing) *our* lines in the story.

This pattern of drama, doctrine, doxology, and discipleship is not actually followed in stages. It's not as if the first few years of our Christian life are spent only on getting the basic plot of Scripture down and the next decade is spent on the doctrine, and only then do we get around to worship and discipleship. Instead of stages, these are facets of every moment in our pilgrimage. Nevertheless, there is a certain logical order here.

Without the story, the doctrine is abstract. Without the doctrine, the story lacks meaning and significance for us. Yet if we are not led by the drama and the doctrine to mourn and dance, have we really been swept into it—experientially, not just as truth but as good news? Failing to grab our hearts, the doctrine fails to animate our hands and feet. Yet if we concentrate everything on the doxology by itself, we end up trying to work ourselves into a state of perpetual praise without knowing exactly who we're praising or why. And an obsession with discipleship, apart from these other aspects, will generate a kind of mindless and eventually heartless moralism that confuses activism with the fruit of the Spirit.

Christianity is not distinguished from the world religions and civilizations merely by the fact that it has a story that yields particular doctrines, rituals, and patterns of living. Google catechizes its employees in a certain "form of life," and the stock exchange opens each day with a ritual of bell-ringing, words and sacraments, dogmas and habits of daily living that are a "reasonable service" in view of the apparent mercies and mercilessness of the market's invisible hand. Rooted in the story of Muhammad, Islam is strictly organized by a set of dogmas, rituals, and behavioral codes that shape the identity of millions of people around the world. Orthodox Jewish children are taught each Passover to regard themselves as those whom Yahweh delivered from Egypt.

What *does* distinguish Christianity is the specific content of its narrative, its truth claims, and the worship and way of life that these generate. The Christian faith is gospel-driven at its core, with an unfolding drama from Genesis to Revelation. Far from a catalogue of eternal principles and timeless truths, the Bible is proclaimed by the

apostles as the history of God's redemptive purposes. There is genuine movement from creation to the fall to the long and often winding
path from the promise of a redeemer to its fulfillment in Jesus Christ.
This is one of the reasons why a truly historical consciousness
arose in Israel. While the ancient pagan worldviews are cyclical (with
this world as a shadowy image of the eternal movement of the heavenly bodies), the promise-fulfillment pattern of biblical revelation is
oriented toward historical events. While the nations celebrated the
annual cycles of birth, death, and rebirth through the natural seasons,
Israel's festivals arose around new acts of Yahweh's judgment and
deliverance. We're drawn out of ourselves, toward the "new thing"
that God has done and will yet do in the future.

Therefore, later generations were instructed at each Passover to
regard themselves as those who had passed through the Red Sea with
Moses. The exodus was first of all history, but it became internalized
as the living history of the covenant people as they were immersed
in the continuing life of God's covenant faithfulness. It was not only
objective history; it was also *their story*.

Reciting that story was the burden of my previous book *The Gospel-
Driven Life*. Even if we hear it expounded from Genesis to Revelation
for a lifetime, we only begin to plumb its depths. However, it is this
basic plotline that we need to step into. In part at least, this is what
it means to be baptized into Christ, to put on Christ, to become
written into his script by the Holy Spirit. Psalm 78 recites the twists
and turns in God's covenantal story: "things that we have heard and
known, that our fathers have told us. We will not hide them from their
children, but tell to the coming generation the glorious deeds of the
LORD, and his might, and the wonders that he has done" (vv. 3–4).
The psalmist then goes on to recount God's mercy, Israel's transgressions, and God's appointment of David over his house in spite of the
sins of his people.

From this story arise a host of important doctrines. We discern
the attributes of its central actor as God acts in creation, judgment,
promise, deliverance, and consummation of his kingdom. We come
to know God in three persons: the Father, the Son, and the Spirit. We
come to understand who we are as well, both our creation in the image
of God and the tragedy of original sin. Yet we also hear God's gospel,
led by the shadows of the law to Jesus Christ as our prophet, priest,
and king. His incarnation, active obedience, curse-bearing death, and
curse-destroying resurrection, as well as his ascension and return in

glory, gather increasing clarity and fullness as the story unfolds. We discover the meaning of Christ's kingdom and church, its ministry, offices, and government. And we look forward to the future fulfillment of God's promises for the new world.

Along the way, each recital of the story and every deeper understanding of a revealed doctrine leads us to pause for meditation, allowing ourselves to be captivated by revelations beyond words and mysteries too intoxicating to be fully comprehended by our reason. We find our investigations yielding to adoration and praise: knowing God experientially and not just knowing about God.

Now our discipleship makes sense. It is not mere activism but an activity that arises out of having been made passive recipients of a kingdom that cannot be shaken. Now our discipleship is no longer focused on our own inner life, morality, and experience but on Christ's triumph over sin and death.

We are not sent out into the world to change it, to transform it, to make it into the kingdom of God. Rather, we are sent into the world as God's chosen, redeemed, called, justified, renewed people who know that the world's condition is far worse than our neighbors think and God's future for it far more glorious than they (or we) can imagine. Our good works may appear on the surface as no different from those of our non-Christian neighbors and co-workers. We may work alongside unbelievers in caring for a terminally ill child, marching for the rights of an oppressed minority or the unborn, paying our taxes, and helping disaster victims. Yet our way of being in the world—the basic motivations of our hearts—are formed by the drama, doctrine, and doxology that come from being united to Christ by the Spirit. Like our sanctification, the transforming effect of our lives on others will be something they notice more than we do.

From Grammar to Rhetoric: Recovering Lost Tools of Discipleship

In many ways, this connection between drama, doctrine, doxology, and discipleship follows the transition from grammar to rhetoric in classical education. Those familiar with Dorothy Sayers's *Lost Tools of Learning* may recall how she explains the classical educational model of grammar, dialectic (logic), and rhetoric. In our youngest years, we're sponges for the *grammar*—not just of language but of everything. It's the time for learning primary colors, common names for things and proper names for people, how to read books and music, and table manners. If you have more than one child in this phase, you see how they love to point out the foibles of their siblings on these matters. They're learning the grammar that they will use simply as a matter of course throughout their lives. Then there's the stage of *dialectic* (logic), when they love to argue, question, and explore the connections between various subjects. (It's called being a teenager!) Finally they reach the stage of *rhetoric* as they begin to communicate their convictions in their own words, with richer insight, clarity, persuasiveness, and beauty. They become proficient practitioners of a particular language. These stages are reflected not only in thinking and communicating but in living.

As children, we learned to ride a bicycle first by focusing on the pedals and the handlebar, steering with jerks to the left and the right. After we fell a few times, we gradually mastered balance. If we learned a musical instrument, we focused on the keys and the scale, staring intently at the notes on the page. In an obvious sense the music is external to us: an object on a page. Only after a lot of practice do we begin to play the music without focusing on our fingers. Eventually we find ourselves living in the music, indwelling it. It's not as alien. It becomes part of our lives.

The same process holds for learning to read, making a good vintage of wine, taking up a new hobby, or becoming a research scientist. In fact, it is the way we become proficient at anything: as parents, friends, lovers, plumbers, and football players. It's that initial stage of learning the grammar that children find so natural and adults find so challenging, but it is essential if we are going to play the game of life in all of its variety and richness.

Those who have never learned the grammar tend to be always on the outside of a culture looking in. Those who have never learned to think clearly and to relate their knowledge in a coherent pattern often find that they simply have to take the so-called experts' word for things. And those who have not learned to express themselves well—both in words and deeds—often find that they are captives to persuasive powers that may not share the beliefs and practices they say are essential to their identity.

Growth in Christian discipleship can be compared to this model of learning. First, we learn the basic grammar. It certainly includes memorizing. That's why it's important to commit key Bible verses to memory, and it's why the Reformation restored the early church's practice of catechism, in which parents as well as pastors were to teach to the young and old alike.

A lot of us have been raised in the era of modern educational principles, where the child is the center of the universe. In this romantic view of childhood, the idea is often that our precious little ones have everything they need already inside of themselves and the goal of education is simply to unlock their potential. This is usually accomplished with generous doses of gratuitous praise designed to puff their self-esteem. And above all, learning has to be *fun*! There's a lot of "edutainment" out there, promising to eliminate the burden of growing up. It's always amusing to come across studies indicating that even when American high school and college students rank last in actual performance on math and science, they rank first in self-esteem (judging that they did better on the exam than they actually did), while it's exactly reversed for Asians and Europeans.

Of course, the danger is obvious: increasingly, these generations demand quick and easy programs for immediate results. But many important things we need to learn are not fun, quick, or easy: marriage and raising a family, for example. And who wants a doctor who received his medical education by mail order or from distance learning? Yet many Christians are willing to submit to engaging rhetoric without learning the grammar and logic of the faith. If convenience, accessibility, and immediate gratification are our criteria, we'll be left with fast food, cheap wine, and shallow lives. When we bring this lazy approach to life to church with us, we can never rise above the level of consumers to disciples. Like the crowd that followed Jesus as long as they had a free lunch, we will abandon Jesus when he breaks out the tough stuff.

Increasingly unfamiliar with the multiplication table and English grammar, our children are also being denied familiarity with the basic plotline, characters, doctrines, and practices of Christianity. Also, the important emphasis on a personal (individual) relationship with Christ can be falsely interpreted as opposed to learning a shared faith.

The grammar of the faith is not only learned through direct instruction, however. It also happens through watching parents and siblings live out their faith, and by participating in public worship with growing personal understanding and involvement. Children learn the grammar of the gospel through singing, public reading of Scripture, the prayers, and what they can pick up from sermons, baptisms, and celebrations of the Supper—and from the conversations they overhear in the fellowship of the saints. They also learn the grammar by watching how adults use it in their daily lives, faithfully and unfaithfully. This means that they have to actually be around older Christians instead of spending all of their time with children their own age.

Second, we begin to ask questions about what we've been taught. (By the way, for this stage—basically, adolescence—select catechists or Sunday school teachers who will encourage questioning rather than simply parrot and accept the grammar uncritically.) We begin to see connections between one episode in the Bible and another, even if they are in different testaments. The unfolding plot of Scripture begins to make sense, and the various doctrines begin to find their logical connections.

Finally, as Christians mature they confess their faith in speech, song, and prayer, with personal affection, and can share this faith in natural and persuasive conversation with others, being ready to explain and defend the faith (1 Peter 3:15). In this way, they build up other saints with their gifts and introduce unbelievers to Christ. Along this whole process, there really is no clear division between knowing, feeling, and doing. Especially as we mature, doctrine and life become virtually seamless. I don't mean more *perfect*, but more like *playing* baseball than studying the rules. Even when we are not studying a particular truth, we are living, moving, and feeling with it. We begin to learn to play the piano by focusing clumsily on the notes, the keys, and our fingers, and after many years of practice, we find ourselves simply playing the music. Only when we make mistakes do we focus again on the note we missed or the placement of our fingers. We always need to go back to the music book, expanding and deepening our repertoire, but with the goal of actually playing.

Like learning a new language or the piano, a disciple cannot just begin to live the Christian life without learning the grammar and the logic of the Christian faith. We don't just want to "play by ear"; we want to play God's music. Or, to go back to the drama analogy, we don't just want to write our own screenplay for our own life movie; we want to be cast as new characters in God's unfolding drama, learning our role in his script. And this isn't improvisational theater or a one-man show. Disciple formation can only occur in community, in the covenant of grace where the Triune God has promised to save us, to conform us to Christ's image, and to keep us to the end.

Our Western culture has distinguished sharply between theory and practice, and this has affected our view of the relationship between doctrine and life. In the Old Testament, "following after" or "walking after" the Lord involved the head, the heart, and the whole body. It meant understanding and embracing the truth, responding in faith and thanksgiving, and offering one's entire self in obedience. Faith comes by hearing, not by contemplating, speculating, or imagining. God's Word has to be understood, but this growth in grace occurs through a coordinated engagement of all of our faculties: ears, eyes, hands, hearts, minds, and feet. Your heart must be moved by something other than emotional exuberance, but how can you say that you know God if you do not trust him or follow his command to love one another (John 15:7–17)?

More Than Imitation

The Scriptures direct us to something far greater, deeper, and more transformative than the *imitation of Christ*. They speak of our actually being *united to Christ*: crucified, buried, and raised with him, living out our lives in the world (not in the cloister) as those who are seated with Christ.

This marvelous truth is the antidote to both laziness and legalism. On one hand, the gospel tells us that everyone who is justified is also renewed and is being conformed gradually to the image of Christ. So there is no place for a believer who is forgiven and yet is not being sanctified. On the other hand, it is not because one is imitating Christ's example that he or she enters into this kind of new creation, but because one is united to Christ through faith alone, bearing the fruit of righteousness. Grace is both God's favor on account of Christ and the gift of Christ with all of his benefits, including the indwelling presence of the ever-renovating Spirit.

While remaining sinful, believers now struggle against indwelling sin. The gospel, not principles for attaining the higher life, is Paul's answer to the question, "Are we to continue in sin that grace may abound?" (Rom. 6:1). The apostle does not separate the body of Christ into carnal and spiritual Christians. Rather, he simply declares that *everyone* who is baptized into Christ is justified *and* renewed inwardly, sharing in his death, burial, and resurrection. That is the indicative (gospel) announcement of the way things are for *all* believers.

So we should be looking for the imperative (command) that follows from it, and as usual, Paul does not disappoint: "Let not sin therefore

reign in your mortal body, to make you obey its passions" (Rom. 6:12).
Then it's back to the indicative: "For sin will have no dominion over
you, since you are not under law but under grace" (Rom. 6:14). He
does not say, "Make sure that sin does not have dominion over you"
or "Here are the principles for how to overcome sin's dominion."
Rather, he simply declares the state of affairs, namely that sin *cannot*
and *will not* rule over those who are in Christ; its tyranny has been
broken decisively.

We still sin, but never in the same way that we did before. Now we
love what we hated and hate what we loved. Romans 7 focuses on this
paradox. However often they find themselves failing in the Christian
life, only believers *struggle* with sin, because sin is both an enduring
reality (with many setbacks) and yet the believer's enemy. Romans 6
and 7 seem almost contradictory. There is the decisive toppling of
sin's dominion, followed by a personal account of repeated failure
in the Christian life. Yet these are not descriptions of two kinds of
Christians (victorious and carnal), or even of two different conditions in which a believer might be at various stages in life. Rather,
everyone who is in Christ is simultaneously defined by this paradoxical
experience. As Paul concludes at the end of chapter 7, the only thing
that can restore our hope in the face of spiritual struggle is the sight
of Christ as he is clothed in his gospel. For our sanctification, it is
not principles for victory, techniques for spiritual ascent, or a new
experience—a "second blessing"—that we need, but the same gospel
through which we were justified.

Nowhere in this lodestar passage for the Christian life does Paul
direct our attention to the imitation of Christ. He has already painted
too dark (realistic) a picture of human depravity to imagine that the
devil, the world, and our sinful hearts could meet their match in our
deeper commitment to follow Christ's example. Christ comes not to
improve our old life but to kill us in order to make us alive in him.
He calls us not simply to imitate Christ but to live out our union
with him. He is not just offering to edit the script we've written for
our lives (or that the culture has written for us) but comes to write
us into his play. Consequently, before he speaks an imperative, he
announces the indicative of the gospel: Christ's saving work has accomplished far more than we imagined. The Spirit's work of uniting
us to Christ makes us not mere imitators but living members of his
body. We are incorporated—baptized—into Christ's death, burial,
and resurrection.

Like many evangelicals, Dallas Willard sees discipleship more in terms of imitating Christ through particular daily spiritual practices. He is careful to add, "We are not speaking here of *perfection*, nor of *earning* God's gift of life. Our concern is only with the manner of *entering into* that life."[4] However, it is not clear, to me at least, how *entering into* that life by our own will and effort differs from *earning* it. In any case, according to Willard, we do not enter into this life in the Spirit except by daily practices that lead to inner transformation.

In my view, this popular perspective is not radical *enough* in its view of disciple making. There is a proper place for imitating Christ's example, but it is not the gospel but the law. It is a command that we imperfectly obey on the basis of the Good News of Christ's obedience, death, and resurrection on our behalf. When it is made a condition of "entering into that life" of grace and the Spirit, imitating Christ becomes a condemning law. It is interesting that Paul calls Timothy to imitate *him*, especially as his "father in Christ Jesus through the gospel" (1 Cor. 4:15). We need good examples to imitate. We are not lone rangers, following our own inner light, but disciples who participate in the life of the church, younger believers learning from older ones. In Christian fellowship, we are formed by wise patterns of godly character and habits that flow from mature depths of life-tested growth in grace. However, this is not the main mission of Jesus Christ. When Paul points to Christ, it is as *Savior and Lord*. Even where we are called to follow Christ's example of loving servanthood, this belongs to the "third use of the law," namely, to guide believers in their grateful response to the gospel. It is a way *of* life, not the way *to* life.

Christ's life is unique. He came not as a mere prototype for others to follow but as the Savior of the world who unites sinners to himself so that they share in *his* victory over sin and death. Because of Christ, we are no longer locked into the vicious circle of striving, mastering, and making everyone else orbit around our sun. Like Christ, we live for others, not merely because we are following him but because we are inextricably united to him by his Spirit.

We find the same message from the lips of our Lord in John 15. His disciples are not only forgiven; joined to him as the life-giving Vine they become living branches, bearing fruit that will remain. We have no life in ourselves, he tells them. By itself, imitating Christ is mere play-acting, like gluing plastic fruit on a dead branch. Only after pressing this point of life through *union* with him does Jesus issue his imperatives to love and serve each other as he has loved and served us.

There is a world of difference between having a role model whose example we fall short of ever reproducing and being broken off of Adam's dead tree in order to be grafted onto the Tree of Life. Doing what Jesus did is different from bearing the fruit of Christ's righteous life. In fact, the most important things that Jesus did cannot be duplicated. Because he fulfilled the law in our place, bore our curse, and was raised in glory to take his throne at the Father's right hand, we can have a relationship with him—and with the Father—that is far more intimate than the relationship of a student to a teacher or a follower to a master.

The Power of God unto Discipleship

Like Richard Foster, Dallas Willard thinks that the real problem is that there has been too much emphasis on grace and justification: "If there is anything we should know by now, it is that *a gospel of justification alone does not regenerate disciples.*"[5] Many passages often treated as "forgiveness passages" are actually about the new birth and transformation, he argues.[6]

We can err in two directions at this point. The first mistake is to subordinate (or assimilate) justification to sanctification. This is usually done out of a concern to rebuff antinomianism (i.e., the view that grace eliminates any need for obedience to God's commands). The second mistake, a reaction against legalism, is to separate justification from sanctification, as if a person could have one without the other.

Yet the glory of the new covenant is that the same gospel that absolves sinners also renews and sanctifies them. Far from creating a morbid subjectivity and individualism, as is often charged, this view frees us from being curved in on ourselves, fretting over our own souls. In a moving letter to Cardinal Sadoleto, Calvin made much the same point when he argued that only by being freed of having to love our neighbor in the service of our own salvation are we able to really love them for their own sake.[7] Sanctification is a life not of acquiring but of receiving from the excess of divine joy that then continues to overflow in excess to our neighbor and from our neighbor to us.

While Rome simply assimilated justification to sanctification, the Reformation position affirmed both as distinct yet inseparable gifts. G. C. Berkouwer replies to those who deny Luther's interest in God's gracious renovation of believers: "To anyone who has had a whiff of Luther's writings this conception is incredible. Even a scanty initiation is enough to be convinced that justification for Luther meant much more than an external event with no importance for the inner man."[8] Like the relation of the doctrine of substitution to other aspects of the atonement, forensic justification not only allows room for other benefits of Christ; it is their source and security. Faith unites us to Christ for justification, sanctification, and glorification. So while we are united to Christ through faith alone, precisely because we are united to Christ, faith can never remain alone. Only because it *receives* every good gift from God, apart from works, can faith be *busy* in good works, looking out to our neighbors in love.

The Reformers saw "Christ for us" (the alien righteousness imputed) and "Christ in us" (the sanctifying righteousness imparted) as not only compatible but necessarily and inextricably related. Grace is both God's *favor* and his *gift*. The gospel is not our conversion experience ("how I got saved"). It is not a report about what happened or happens inside of us. Rather, it is always a message about what God has done decisively and uniquely in his Son for our salvation. And precisely as a saving Word from outside of us, it changes us forever from the inside out.

More than New Habits: The Fruit of the Spirit

In *After You Believe*, N. T. Wright argues that many Christians today are stuck. They trusted in Christ, but now they need to know how to live. Yet they are either paralyzed by a fear of legalism or actually do fall into a merely rule-oriented piety. Wright explains that Christians are called to obedience and that this takes work. It does not just happen. Although he caricatures the views of the Reformers, his point is one that they emphasized. Especially in the Reformed tradition, the sober view of the Christian life as a lifelong struggle—a long walk in the same direction—has been stressed. We do need new habits, and these involve spiritual disciplines that we build intentionally into our busy routines. More than Willard and Foster, Wright emphasizes the importance of the corporate gathering of the saints for preaching and sacrament. Discipleship is "a team sport."[9]

Nevertheless, if it is more than a private affair and imitation of Christ, New Testament discipleship is also more than new habits. Of course, union with Christ bears the fruit of the Spirit, and this in turn motivates new habits, but there is a danger in thinking that new habits themselves are the source of our life. Just as citizens cannot be made good by good laws, believers cannot become good by good habits.

Consistent with Jesus's teaching in John 15, Paul first explained to the Galatians who they were in Christ and then called them to walk in the Spirit, putting to death the fruit of the flesh and bearing the fruit of the Spirit (Gal. 5:16–6:10). The Spirit here is the *Holy Spirit*, not *our* spirit or "inner self." It is the Spirit who testifies to Christ, directing our faith to him alone. United to Christ through faith by the Spirit, we are to live as those who are already defined by this identity.

A new identity yields new attitudes, and new attitudes yield new habits. In Ephesians 4, Paul explains how the gift of pastors and teachers builds up the body of Christ into maturity. Then in chapter 5 Paul adds,

> Therefore be imitators of God, as beloved children. And walk in love, as Christ loved us and gave himself up for us, a fragrant offering and sacrifice to God. But sexual immorality and all impurity or covetousness must not even be named among you, as is proper among saints. . . . Look carefully then how you walk, not as unwise but as wise, making the best use of the time, because the days are evil. (Eph. 5:1–3, 15–16)

The apostle lists some of the fruit of the Spirit in Galatians 5, contrasting these with the fruit of the flesh:

> Now the works of the flesh are evident: sexual immorality, impurity, sensuality, idolatry, sorcery, enmity, strife, jealousy, fits of anger, rivalries, dissensions, divisions, envy, drunkenness, orgies, and the things like these. I warn you, as I warned you before, that those who do such things will not inherit the kingdom of God. But the fruit of the Spirit is love, joy, peace, patience, kindness, goodness, faithfulness, gentleness, self-control; against such things there is no law. And those who belong to Christ Jesus have crucified the flesh with its passions and desires. If we live by the Spirit, let us also walk by the Spirit. (Gal. 5:19–25)

As we mature in the grace and knowledge of Christ, we become more fruitful in our relationships with each other.

However, we live in an age that is full of jealousy and hatred rather than love and peace, immersed in a culture that celebrates the fruit of the flesh. We may *admire* those who are devoted selflessly to the poor and the outcasts, but we would *like to be* the celebrities who attract our gaze on the covers of magazines. In sharp contrast with previous generations, we pay extravagant salaries to celebrities—actors, athletes, models, and business executives—while teachers, laborers, and myriad others who provide essential goods and services live on the edge of poverty. Our own habits reflect our share in this culture of consumerism and celebrity. Would we rather watch the new blockbuster movie or spend the Lord's Day with the people of God? Do we find the mall so attractive that we prefer to be consumers rather than covenant heirs even on the day that God has pledged to spend with us?

Paul warned Timothy that even in the church there will be those who promise health, wealth, and happiness while quoting Bible verses out of context:

> But understand this, that in the last days there will come times of difficulty. For people will be lovers of self, lovers of money, proud, arrogant, abusive, disobedient to their parents, ungrateful, unholy, heartless, unappeasable, slanderous, without self-control, brutal, not loving good, treacherous, reckless, swollen with conceit, lovers of pleasure rather than lovers of God, having the appearance of godliness, but denying its power. Avoid such people. (2 Tim. 3:1–5)

Many of the "fruits of the Spirit" mentioned by Paul might be on any list of positive character traits. For most of its history, Christianity has encouraged the former characteristics over the latter:

Meekness and gentleness	Pride and self-assertion
Faithfulness to the tried and tested	Perpetual innovation and novelty
Slow growth in the same direction	Quick and easy success through efficient methods
Commitment/loyalty/faithfulness	Convenience/fickleness
Responsibility (presence)	Anonymity (absence)
Delayed gratification	Instant gratification
Saving and giving	Spending and consuming
Shepherding/teaching	Entrepreneurship/entertaining
Quiet, patient reflection and wise action	Loud, expressive, and impulsive action
The maturity of old age (growing up)	The fads of youth ("forever young")
Living a godly life	Having a good time
Pleasing God and serving neighbors	Pleasing the crowd and serving oneself

No Christian—much less era of the church—can claim to have mastered godly habits of the heart. Furthermore, the traits in the left column can become a pretense for passivity, false humility, and a dead conservatism. Yet what is different about our culture today—and often our churches, families, and lives—is that at least in actual practice, we have come actually to *celebrate* the latter over the former. If churches themselves are being planted, multiplied, and sustained on the presuppositions of the flesh rather than the Spirit, then it is not surprising when we read of surveys telling us that professing Christians are not really disciples, believing and living no differently from their non-Christian neighbors.

Yesterday I heard an interview with a young girl on National Public Radio. She was asked at a "Read to Grow" rally why she loved reading books even over the summer break. With enthusiasm, the girl talked about the many other worlds she had visited in books. "What would you tell someone who says it's boring and they just can't get into reading?" the interviewer asked. "You've just got to start," replied the girl. "The more you read, the more you want to keep on doing it. Then it becomes a habit and it's what you want to do whenever you can." What if parents and youth pastors took that approach to discipleship more often?

We desperately need to recover good habits: setting apart the Lord's Day, family catechesis and worship, as well as private prayer and meditation. As with any vocation, growing in the grace and knowledge of Christ doesn't just happen. It requires new priorities and concrete decisions every day. Yet it is the fruit rather than the source of entering into that new creation that Christ has won for us already. Both public worship and private spiritual disciplines can become meaningless routines unless they continually expose us to the Triune God who addresses us by his Word and Spirit.

Discipleship Unplugged

Once upon a time, a young American entrepreneur (let's name him Jack) became enamored of the superbly crafted cuckoo clock he picked up one day in a quaint village driving from Geneva to Zurich. A year later, Jack returned with an idea: if he could figure out how the clock he bought was made, he could develop a prototype and put it on the assembly line in China for mass distribution around the world. It could be made more quickly, efficiently, and therefore cheaply once the secrets of its construction were put down on paper. After locating the craftsman who made his clock, Jack opened his laptop, ready to take notes, and began asking details about the clock's construction. Soon, however, the craftsman ran out of answers, so the entrepreneur looked over his shoulder as the craftsman set to work. "How do you make that squiggle?" he asked. "I don't know," the craftsman replied. "I've done it for years. I grew up making these clocks with my father— this is his shop—and it's just in my blood, I guess." Eventually Jack did try to copy the clock, squiggles and all, but it wasn't the same. You just can't make a great piece of culture by formulas that can be routinized and duplicated on an assembly line.

Christian discipleship is a lot like craftsmanship. It can't be produced with formulas, principles, and steps. Disciples don't come off an assembly line. There is no get-spiritual-quick scheme. It takes time, energy, effort, patience, and skill. Certain shared features identify superbly crafted cuckoo clocks, yet each piece is hand crafted, with its own markings. That's part of the charm.

As God's workmanship, each of us is re-created by the Father, in Christ, and is being conformed to Christ's image through the powerful skill of the Spirit. "That's theology," someone may say, "not practical resources and tools for life." All we can say is that it is God himself who tells us, through his Word, that the most practical things we need to know are the amazing truths of what God has done, is doing, and will do for us in his Son. The transformation does not occur through one-size-fits-all formulas but occurs through belonging to a community that immerses us in the drama, doctrine, doxology, and discipleship of "the faith that was once for all delivered to the saints" (Jude 3). It means belonging to the holy commonwealth that passes along habits—many of which cannot be stated explicitly in so many words. The habits of a craftsman are simply different from those of an entrepreneur or industrial manager.

We are increasingly becoming a society that is losing the inherited wisdom and habits of craftsmanship. Not surprisingly, we are becoming a church that is losing its inherited wisdom and habits of discipleship. Some say, "Well, if we can just get the doctrine right, everything else will follow." Others shout back, "No, deeds, not creeds! We just need to get with the program." But neither answer gets the point that growing up into Christ cannot be reduced to intellectualism or activism. There is no doctrinal proposition or spiritual program that will conform us to the image of Christ. The gospel must transform us over a lifetime of quite ordinary and sometimes even plodding habits that we cannot always even articulate.

This is why the disciples walked with Jesus, talked with Jesus, and observed his actions as well as his teaching. In this process, it's often hard to distinguish between doctrinal instruction and practical living. Reading the Gospels, we look over their shoulder and say, "Ah, *that's* what the kingdom is!" That's how God "makes a cuckoo clock."

By contrast, imagine what would happen if parents, teachers, pastors, and others who teach us truths and skills simply left us on our own to teach ourselves? Most likely it would lead to a generation that pounds on the piano without knowing the scale, that builds houses that fall apart, and that creates "community" with few resources other than the limited interests and experiences of a circle of friends.

Repeating the church fathers, John Calvin said that believers need the parental care of the church through their entire pilgrimage. Today one well-known megachurch says that as Christians grow, they need the church less. The church's job is to make people "self-feeders." However, after breakfast with Peter, the resurrected Jesus said to him,

> "Simon, son of John, do you love me more than these?" He said to him, "Yes, Lord; you know that I love you." He said to him, "Feed my lambs." He said to him a second time, "Simon, son of John, do you love me?" He said to him, "Yes, Lord; you know that I love you." He said to him, "Tend my sheep." He said to him the third time, "Simon, the son of John, do you love me?" Peter was grieved because he said to him the third time, "Do you love me?" and he said to him, "Lord, you know everything; you know that I love you." Jesus said to him, "Feed my sheep." . . . And after saying this he said to him, "Follow me." (John 21:15–17, 19)

The Great Commission is a mandate to gather, feed, and protect Christ's sheep until the Great Shepherd himself returns.

Our children as well as new converts to the faith need time to mature, and they need pastors, not programs. They need to belong to a community of disciples—older believers, fellow saints from various walks of life and ethnic backgrounds—who simultaneously show and tell what it means to trust in Christ and love and serve their neighbors. There is no manual for this. Not even the Bible is really a manual of discipleship. Rather, it is the quarry for it, from which faithful shepherds dig each week for our benefit. The Bible is not a how-to program but the unique story that gives rise to the doctrines, the rituals of baptism and the Supper, habits of praise and prayer, fellowship, and witness that it authorizes as our canon.

There is no quick and easy path, a shortcut to success. It takes a lot of work. Although we are not working *for* our salvation, we are working it *out,* as God works in us "both to will and to work for his good pleasure" (Phil. 2:13). Marriage involves a lot of work and only grows with time and patience. No program for "how to raise a family" will actually raise our children and form us to be better parents. To do it well, we often have to change our priorities and daily routines. And we cannot do it alone; we need others. Even more do we need the constant, ordinary, sometimes all-too-familiar habits of family worship, the Lord's Day, fellowship, and personal Bible reading and prayer—especially when the burdens and distractions of our temporal callings threaten to become idols rather than gifts.

Even private spiritual disciples will be of no benefit in shaping our Christian discipleship apart from the ordinary means of grace in the church and the distinct type of piety that arises out of it. Perhaps instead of "the Christian life," we should speak of "the Christian lifetime." Even at the end of our days, we will not be a finished piece of divine craftsmanship. Nevertheless, our strenuous effort is the free and joyful response to the perfect and finished work of Christ. Notice how Paul here links the imperative to the indicative once more:

> Not that I have already obtained this or am already perfect, but *I press on to make it my own, because Christ Jesus has made me his own.* Brothers [and sisters], I do not consider that I have made it my own. But one thing I do: forgetting what lies behind and straining forward to what lies ahead, I press on toward the goal for the prize of the upward call of God in Christ Jesus. Let those of us who are mature think this way, and if in anything you think otherwise, God will reveal that also to you. Only let us hold true to what we have attained. (Phil. 3:12–16, emphasis added)

Only with the gospel in our hearts can we say with Paul's confidence, "The sufferings of this present life are not worth comparing with the glory that will be revealed in us" (Rom. 8:18).

The Strategic Plan

E very mission statement needs a good strategic plan. The one to whom all authority is given not only entrusted his apostles with the message and the mission but also instituted the methods. I have suggested that we are threatened by mission creep. That danger is evident not only in distortions of the message but also in the assumption that we are free to change the strategic plan as we go. Jesus not only gave us the message and the mission statement; he included the strategic plan: *how* we are to fulfill the Great Commission.

6

How to Make Disciples

Go therefore and make disciples of all nations, baptizing them in the name of the
Father and of the Son and of the Holy
Spirit, teaching them to observe all that I
have commanded you.

Matthew 28:19–20

Go into all the world and proclaim the gospel to the whole creation. Whoever believes
and is baptized will be saved, but whoever
does not believe will be condemned.

Mark 16:15–16

And they devoted themselves to the apostles' teaching and the fellowship, to the
breaking of bread and the prayers. . . . And
the Lord added to their number day by day
those who were being saved.

Acts 2:42, 47

There are a lot of strategies today for making disciples. We need to
read the Bible, pray, and engage in personal evangelism. We need

spiritual directors and accountability groups—more living out of the Christian life in community. In addition, we need to be witnesses in word and deed out in the world. Yet all of these concerns are addressed in the Great Commission in terms of the church's public ministry of proclaiming the gospel, baptizing, and teaching. As important as spiritual disciplines and cultural engagement are for Christians, these activities flow from this authorized service that God renders to us in his Son and by his Spirit.

A lot of details are given to us in the New Testament concerning the proper organization and execution of the church's ministry. Throughout the book of Acts, the growth of the church is indicated by the phrase, "and the word of God spread," together with the report of baptisms of adult converts together with their whole households. They gathered regularly for the public ministry of preaching and teaching, fellowship, the Supper, and the prayers. The Lord added those who were being saved daily *to the church* (Acts 2:47). "So the churches were strengthened in the faith, and they increased in numbers daily" (Acts 16:5). There is no distinction in the New Testament between being a disciple and belonging to the church—not just to the invisible church (i.e., of regenerate believers), but to the visible church. Membership in this visible body of Christ is identified by public profession of faith and baptism (in the case of adult converts; reversed in the case of covenant children).

In one sense, this is the easiest section of this book to write, given the simplicity and clarity of our Lord's mandate. Yet it's also the most difficult section, because we seem so far off course from these methods today. Of course, like the message they deliver, these methods have always appeared weak and foolish in the eyes of the world. Yet this judgment seems increasingly prevalent in evangelical circles today. *Preaching?* You mean someone up front telling us what we have to believe and how we should live? *Baptism?* I know Jesus commanded it, but I'm not quite sure why—except to testify to our commitment to follow him. As for the *Lord's Supper*, I can recall some meaningful experiences related to it, and Jesus commanded it, but it's not really central to our worship or to my life as a disciple.

I realize that there are plenty of exceptions, but in my experience these responses are fairly common. So our appraisal of the effectiveness of these means that Christ appointed depends largely on what we believe about them in the first place. If preaching is primarily exhortation on what we need to believe and do, and if the sacraments are chiefly our acts of commitment, then it is understandable that they might wear out their welcome. Yet if they are *means of grace*—that is, *God's* act of raising us from spiritual death by the word of the gospel and ratifying publicly his covenant pledge through baptism and the Supper—then everything changes.

Preaching the gospel, baptizing, and teaching everything—the appointed tools for making disciples—are not just things we do as the entrance to the Christian life. They're not necessary merely for conversion or for planting a church. They are the perpetual means through which disciples—and disciple-makers—are made over the long haul. This is the ministry that Christ has appointed for our home church as well as for our missionaries in a foreign field.

On the basis of the Great Commission—and the many passages that unpack it—the churches of the Reformation affirm that the true church is visible wherever the Word is rightly preached and the sacraments are rightly administered. On the basis especially of passages explored in the next chapter, the Reformed churches added discipline as a third mark.

Today this consensus is no longer obvious. Many of us were raised with evangelistic invitations that distinguished sharply between "getting saved" and "joining a church"; a "personal relationship with Jesus" and "church membership." And this goes back still further, to pietism and revivalism and before that to the radical Protestant movements and still further back to monastic spirituality. The idea is that *real* disciples are formed not in the theater of ordinary Word-and-sacrament ministry and the care of elders and deacons, but in the parachurch enclaves for super-spirituality. Let's look briefly at the methods that Christ included in the Great Commission and then interact with some challenges.

Christ Instituted the Methods for Making Disciples

Paul assures us that we do not have to ascend into heaven or descend into the depths to find Christ, but that he is present in the Word that is preached (Rom. 10:6–8). We are baptized into Christ's death, burial, and resurrection (Rom. 6:1–11). He told the Corinthians that in the Supper we participate in Christ's body and blood (1 Cor. 10:16). And in the context of preaching and church discipline, Jesus promised to be present in the midst of his people through the ministry of the keys—binding and loosing, retaining and forgiving sins (Matt. 16:19; 18:15–20).

Preaching the Word

The entire Bible is the Word of God. However, this Word consists of law and gospel. The law commands, telling us what we must do and threatening death for transgression; the gospel promises, telling us what God has done in Christ for our salvation. Because we are in fact transgressors, the law brings God's judgment, discerning our hidden thoughts and motives as well as our outward actions, so that every mouth is stopped in God's courtroom. The gospel brings the glad tidings that although before God our righteousness is as filthy rags, God clothes us in Christ's perfect righteousness. This is why the apostles emphasize that it is the *gospel* that is "the power of God for salvation" (Rom. 1:16). When I hear preaching, I am a recipient. I do not ascend to heaven, climbing ladders through various spiritual exercises. Rather, I am made a beneficiary of all of God's promises in his Son. Similarly, in baptism, I am not the active party but the recipient of God's covenantal act of ratifying his pledge. God has chosen *means* of grace that fit with the *message* of grace.

Preaching has negative associations in our culture today. Madonna's "Papa, don't preach" captures the prevailing assumption that preaching is basically scolding or at least demanding some form of assent or consent. In other cases, preaching is sometimes reduced to teaching. Teaching holds an important place (as Jesus adds at the end of the Great Commission), but it is not the same as preaching. In preaching, not only is the minister giving us doctrinal and moral instruction (though that is involved), but God is actually killing us and making us alive, writing us out of the "in Adam" story and into his script of the new creation.

Throughout the Scriptures, God's Word through the lips of sinful ambassadors is spoken of as "the power of God for salvation" (Rom. 1:16; cf. Mark 8:38; 1 Cor. 1:18, 24; 2:9) and effective in every mission for which it is sent (Isa. 55:10–11). The Word of God is inherently "living and active" (Heb. 4:12), judging and justifying (vv. 13–14). Peter tells us that we have been "born again . . . through the living and abiding word of God. . . . And this word is the good news that was preached to you" (1 Peter 1:23, 25). The gospel does not merely tell us how to "get saved," as though it were an instruction manual (another command); it is the means through which God actually saves sinners.

Preaching is not a downloading of information from one mind to another. God not only tells us about Christ, but delivers him; not only explains our sinful condition and his saving purposes, but judges and justifies; not only speaks of a new world that we might enter, but brings us into it. God's Word not only tells us to believe—it is the means by which the Spirit gives us faith. In this perspective, preaching cannot be reduced to an intellectual, moral, or experiential exercise, because it is God's work, not ours. And when God speaks, he addresses our whole existence. There is still an important place for doctrinal instruction and moral exhortation, but they are aspects of a deeper and wider work of God. The doctrines explain the unfolding drama that envelopes us in faith and thanksgiving, and the exhortations become the "reasonable service" that we are to offer in view of "the mercies of God" (Rom. 12:1 NKJV).

Therefore, preaching is not an indifferent medium that just happened to be available in the era of Jesus and the apostles but can be replaced with more effective media in our day. There is something intrinsic to the preached Word that makes it essential to the ministry and mission—indeed, the very existence—of the church. It is a word from God, through an authorized messenger, unlocking prison doors. It is not an inner word that wells up from within us in spiritual solitude or from community conversation, but a strange voice from heaven through another sinner like us.

When Luther said that "The church is not a pen-house but a mouth-house," he was pointing out the importance of hearing the Word in the public assembly even over the private reading of the Bible which he had translated into the vernacular.[1] Similarly, the Westminster divines confessed that the Spirit blesses "the reading but especially the preaching of the Word" as a "means of grace" precisely because through it the Spirit is "calling us out of ourselves" to cling to Christ.[2] They were asserting that faithful, meditative, and prayerful reading of Scripture in private or family devotions was essential but nevertheless subordinate to the public ministry of the Word in the common life of the church.

So proclamation is not meant to be merely a form of intellectual enrichment. Another objection that is sometimes heard is that preaching is too static. We need more visual movement and imagery, dance and drama, video clips, and the like. You may have heard some or even all of these criticisms of the centrality of preaching in the church. And minus the video clips, you would have heard a lot of the same arguments in the medieval church where the mass was theater, with stage, lighting, dramatic exits and entrances, and all the props to dazzle the senses. Yet there was a famine of hearing the words of God—especially the gospel of free justification in Christ alone. The invention of new strategies ("mission creep") eventually led to the marginalization, perversion, and finally denial of that message that Jesus told us to proclaim to the world.

The main point to always bear in mind is that God is present where he *promises* to be present. We don't pull him down out of heaven or bring him up from the grave; rather, he comes to us through his Word, especially as it is preached. God is omnipresent, but the question for us is not where he is present in his majesty and glory, but where he is present in his mercy and grace toward us as sinners. Surely God is present in a beautiful sunset, in a violin concerto, in the grandeur of the Grand Canyon, and in the kindness even of my non-Christian neighbors. However, the question is where God is present *in peace*, with the assurance that he accepts me, forgives me, and adopts me as an heir of his estate. This comes only through the gospel—a strange and surprising report that we do not know as a matter of course or learn about through common culture. It is a story that can only be told, Good News that can only be announced.

If preaching is often reduced to informing or exhorting, Christ's charge to "proclaim the gospel" is often reduced to an evangelistic appeal to non-Christians. This is what a lot of people think when they hear us say that the gospel needs to be preached every week. It conjures the image of a formulaic presentation followed by a call to accept Jesus as personal Lord and Savior. However, the gospel is not a call for us to do anything but the Good News about what Christ has done. As I explored in *The Gospel-Driven Life*, this message fills our sails throughout the Christian life, not just at the beginning.

Furthermore, it's easy to say we already know the gospel if it's reduced to a bumper sticker. However, the gospel can be summarized in a single sentence, such as in John 3:16, and also explored in its limitless depth and breadth from Genesis to Revelation.

The Bible stories we learned in Sunday school are not given chiefly as moral examples for us to imitate, but as stories of sinners who, in spite of their unfaithfulness, were beneficiaries of God's gracious promise. Like John the Baptist, they always point away from themselves to "the Lamb of God" (John 1:29). The New Testament itself interprets the story of Abraham in this way. For Jesus and Paul, the patriarch is an example to us as a sinner who was justified through faith in the gospel that he heard (John 8:56; Rom. 4:3; Gal. 3:6). The story of Jonah and the whale is not primarily a lesson about witnessing even when you don't feel like it but a sign pointing to Christ's resurrection from the dead (Matt. 12:39). If we read the prophets so that we can "Dare to be a Daniel," we're missing the point, since the book of Daniel is a lodestar for Jesus's statements about himself as the "Son of Man." David, "the man after God's own heart," is certainly a mixed bag, but his significance is the role that God gives him in the history of redemption, placing David's greater Son on his throne forever.

The Bible is a grand story, from Genesis to Revelation, with Christ as the lead character. The more we hear that story, the more we find ourselves being written into it as characters. We discover ourselves not in the fading scripts of this age or in glossy magazine images but in the story of creation, fall, redemption, and consummation. We are there with Adam and Eve, capitulating to the lie. We are there with Abraham and Sarah, hearing and believing the gospel and being justified. We are walking along with the disciples, not getting it, then getting it, then not getting it again, and then really discovering what his journey was all about. And we are there with the company of heaven, worshiping the Lamb. It is the purpose of preaching and sacrament to put us there, to kill our dead-end character and to write us into God's script.

We have to avoid yet another form of reduction. Although the sermon is the central form of proclaiming the Word, the whole service should be a ministry of the Word. We gather each Lord's Day to hear *God*, not to see inspiring symbols, to express our spiritual instincts, to have exciting experiences, or even merely to hear interesting and informative discourses. Furthermore, we come not only to hear this Word proclaimed in the sermon but to hear God address us throughout the service: in God's greeting, in the law, in the absolution, in the public reading of Scripture, and in the benediction. To each of these divine speaking parts in this script there correspond our lines as well: the invocation, the confession of sin, the "amen" and confession of faith, the offering, and the songs. Therefore, as in our salvation, God's work is always the main event and our involvement is the appropriate response. Even the purpose of singing in church is not to express our individual piety, commitment, and feelings (though it enlists these). Rather, according to Paul, we sing "psalms and hymns and spiritual songs, with thankfulness in your hearts to God"—so that "the Word of Christ [may] dwell in [us] richly, teaching and admonishing one another in all wisdom" (Col. 3:16; cf. Eph. 5:19). Even the sacraments are *visible words*, ratifying before our physical eyes the promise that we have heard with our ears.

The ministry of the Word involves all of these elements and encompasses our whole being in a communion of saints. Although private reading of the Bible is of enormous value in strengthening our faith by deepening our understanding, God has chosen preaching as a social event of hearing that makes strangers into a family. I've surveyed a number of recent books on techniques, methods, and disciplines for Christian growth. In many, the public preaching of the Word (as well as the sacraments) is subordinated to methods that are not prescribed in Scripture. In some, this central means of grace is not even mentioned. However, the methods we come up with usually serve only to drive us deeper into ourselves. By contrast, as the Westminster Larger Catechism teaches, it is "especially the preached Word" that is a "means of grace," since by this method God confronts sinners in their self-enclosed existence, "driving them out of themselves, and drawing them unto Christ."[3] This Word calls us out of our subjectivity and renders us outward-looking and social creatures, but creatures of a particular kind of society that clings to Christ in faith and reaches out to our neighbors in love.

One generation put all the emphasis on the sermon, as if it were not only the primary but the only conveyer of the Word. The liturgical drama of the covenantal conversation between God and his people here and now is surrendered to something more reminiscent of either a lecture hall or a theater. And now their adult children are wondering whether we need the sermon at all. Bit by bit, the Word of God is being heard less in our churches. In fact, "the public reading of Scripture" that Paul regarded as an essential part of his ministry (1 Tim. 4:13) seems to have vanished from many services. It's not surprising that there is so much ignorance of the most basic biblical stories, themes, and teachings. It's not that we don't believe the Bible anymore but that we don't really know it very well. The point of even many niche "study Bibles" seems less to convey the actual content of Scripture than to find (or import) more ostensibly relevant tips for each demographic. Regardless of our professed view of Scripture, do we have liturgies, songs, and sermons substantial enough to convey it to us? Even where there are no clear-cut biblical commands, we have to be wise in the way we think through changes to the liturgy, the songs, the prayers, and other means through which the Word is communicated from generation to generation.

Many people today raised in evangelical churches do not even have a stock of memorized passages. Will the snippets of verses sung repeatedly in choruses today make the Word of Christ dwell in us (and our children) richly with all wisdom? It is indeed a kind of intellectualism for a pastor to assume that his only job is to preach a sermon, while handing off the rest of the service of the Word to a worship committee. The Word is not only taught but caught, and those who grow up in the church often learn more by repeated exposure to the songs and liturgy than by any particular sermon they can recall. It's not just that churches this weak in knowledge of the Scriptures will fail adequately to fulfill the Great Commission; the missionaries themselves may need to be converted.

Conservatives may need to be reminded that the ministry of the Word is more than doctrinal and moral instruction and that it involves more than the sermon. Preaching and sacrament are not merely exercises in remembering timeless truths, or even past events, but the means through which God performs his mighty acts of judgment and deliverance here and now among us. At the same time, we must beware of overreacting, marginalizing the Word in favor of more ostensibly effective media. It's a big day whenever God arrives to speak a new creation into being. Until Christ returns, faith will always come—and come again—through the hearing of the gospel. And I don't think we'll ever get tired of hearing it, especially in heaven when it will make more sense.

Baptizing Them in the Name of the Father, Son, and Holy Spirit

The same assumptions behind a view of preaching as mere instruction in doctrine and morals rather than as a means of God's saving grace are evident when discussing the sacraments. Again, I am not saying that preaching does not involve teaching and exhortation but that these are aspects of a larger communicative event in which the Triune God is not only the central *topic* but the central *actor*. The same is true of baptism and the Lord's Supper. God acts and we respond, not the other way around.

In the covenant of grace, God takes believers and their children into his care, promising them his favor. Abraham believed God and was justified, but he circumcised his infant sons according to God's command. Both sons were heirs of the covenant of grace, even though God's freedom in election was maintained and Isaac received the promise while Ishmael did not. "But it is not as though the word of God has failed. For not all who are descended from Israel belong to Israel, and not all are children of Abraham because they are his off-spring" (Rom. 9:6–7). It is significant that Esau was not outside of the covenant but *rejected* his *birthright*. It is just such examples as these that the writer to the Hebrews evokes in warning participants in the new covenant not to abandon the faith (Heb. 3:12–4:13; 6:4–12; 12:16).

Although the signs have changed and the Spirit is poured out on females as well as males, the New Testament affirms that we belong to the same covenant of grace that believers enjoyed in the Old Testament. Abraham is the father of all who believe in Christ (Gal. 3:7–9), and the children of believers (even of one believing parent) are considered holy (1 Cor. 7:14). The promise of the covenant is for believers and their children.

When the crowd gathered at Pentecost was "cut to the heart" through Peter's proclamation of Christ, they asked, "What shall we do?" (Acts 2:37). And Peter replied, "Repent and be baptized every one of you in the name of Jesus Christ for the forgiveness of your sins, and you will receive the gift of the Holy Spirit. For the promise is for you and for your children and for all who are far off, everyone whom the Lord our God calls to himself" (Acts 2:38–39). In Mark's version of the Great Commission, the command is to "Go into all the world and proclaim the gospel to the whole creation. Whoever believes and is baptized will be saved, but whoever does not believe will be condemned" (Mark 16:15–16).

The public act of being joined visibly to Christ and his church was not walking down an aisle or praying the sinner's prayer, but being baptized. When the Ethiopian official embraced "the good news about Jesus" proclaimed by Philip, he was immediately baptized (Acts 8:34–40). The same was true of Cornelius and the Gentiles accompanying him who believed (Acts 10:34–48). It's the pattern throughout Acts.

Like circumcision, baptism is represented in the New Testament as God's decision and claim on us. Although it obligates us to respond in faith and obedience, baptism is God's sign and seal of his covenant oath. In this act, as in the preached Word, God pledges his commitment to us. In Acts, adult converts are baptized, and there are reports of their bringing their entire family to be baptized (Acts 16:15, 30–33; 1 Cor. 1:16). Of course, many Christians today do not practice the baptism of covenant children, mainly out of the conviction that baptism is chiefly or even exclusively a human act of commitment rather than a divine means of grace. However, Peter's assurance that "the promise is for you and for your children" means that the Great Commission begins with the covenant family and includes "all who are far off, everyone whom the Lord our God calls to himself" (Acts 2:39).

I embraced covenant baptism for exegetical reasons, but it also has enormous practical benefits in the life of the church and its mission. Do we see our children as belonging to the Lord? Do we raise them as Christians, with a view to their professing faith, receiving communion, and becoming active members of Christ's body? Or do we regard them as unbelievers, hoping that they will have an identifiable conversion experience someday? Although there are all sorts of exceptions, do we cling to God's promise to work by his Spirit in the hearts of our children through the ordinary ministry of the church over many years? Or are we looking for a radical conversion experience outside of the Christian home and the church's ministry, maybe at a summer camp or a college retreat?

The way I have put these questions leaves out important nuances. However, in my own experience growing up, the less that my conversion experience had to do with the institutional church and its external ministry, the more genuine it was likely to be considered. (How ironic, since preaching and sacrament are the methods Jesus commanded in the Great Commission!) Sermons and liturgies with public prayers and singing, confession of sin and declaration of pardon were seen as "formal religion." The more informal the context, the more spontaneous and genuine the experience. And as for any notion of clinging to Christ through baptism and the Supper, that would be outright "sacramentalism." In evangelical circles, the personal conversion experience takes precedence over the public means of grace (such as baptism), and the focus of both events is *my* action more than God's.

When baptism is understood chiefly as a promise that I made on a certain date in the past, it loses its sense of relevance for my life in the present, as God's saving promise to which I continually return. Or, if I do continually return to it, is it to God's decision or mine that is decisive for me each day? It makes a lot of difference when you believe that preaching, baptism, and the Lord's Supper are not only Christ's mandate in the Great Commission but also means of grace that God uses to give us faith in Christ and to strengthen that faith to the very end. Every time I witness a baptism today, I participate again in that event. When faced with confusion, temptation, or doubt, I cling not to a decision that I made but to Christ's public certification that he has claimed me and will not let me go. He will not forsake me, and he will not allow me to surrender myself to another lord who would bind and destroy me. This makes a big difference in our life of discipleship.

Baptism has lost its connection to the life of discipleship for many in our day. Many of the testimonies of conversion one hears point to an experience at a summer camp, college ministry event, concert, or evangelistic crusade. A follow-up question might reveal that the person was born into a Christian family, was baptized, and grew up in the church, but these details are often missing from the testimony. There is pressure to ignore these details or even to define the conversion experience over against any prior connection with the church. Sometimes you can gain the impression that Jesus has to take you out of the church, alone in a garden, to *really* experience his grace. However, according to Scripture, the public ministry of the church *is* the garden!

Even if one does grow up in a church in principle, it is increasingly possible to be unchurched in practice. I have met adults who were raised in an evangelical church but were never baptized—even after they professed faith in Christ (which in many cases occurred at a parachurch event). One may go from the nursery to children's church to the youth group to the college campus ministry to small groups to the empty nesters to the golden oldies and never really have been incorporated into the communion of saints. Is it any wonder that those who have never regularly attended the public service of Word and sacrament never join a church in college, although they may be active in a campus ministry? If they do join a church after college, it's often a new experience.

As I was making a similar point at a conference a while back, a youth pastor in a Reformed church challenged me a bit. Youth ministries are so important, he said, because they relate to kids on their own level, "where they are." "That's just it, isn't it?" I asked. "Where are they?" Presumably, their location is "in Christ." They are baptized and are therefore members of the visible body of Christ, his covenant community. *That's* their primary location. Just as they grow up as members of their natural families, with all of the privileges and responsibilities of that home, they grow up in Christ's body. "Let's put it in concrete and practical terms," I suggested. "A teenage boy grows up in the church getting to know an older couple that has encountered the ups and downs of life—a troubled period of marriage, a daughter lost to cancer, and other trials of faith and life." I went on to relate, in this fictional but representative example, that this young man will eventually go off to college or a trade, marry, and discover that he needs something more than warm memories of pizza, retreats, and friends (even a youth pastor) from roughly his own generation. He needs to see how the faith that he has embraced stands up in the howling winds of real life. If he has grown up in the covenant community, he will realize that he needs the covenant community over the long haul. In addition, he needs to be reminded that his primary location is "in Christ," not in his various social demographics determined for him by this fading age. He is not only privileged to belong to Christ; he is obligated to belong to Christ's visible body in a lifelong exchange of gifts.

Genuine discipleship involves the older men and women teaching the younger members, people of different ethnicities and life experiences enriching each other's lives, rich and poor filling up what is lacking in mutual love and service. Covenant children are to be included in the covenant assembly, eagerly anticipating the day when they make their public profession of faith and are admitted to the Lord's Table. If they are raised with the contrast between a personal relationship with Jesus and belonging to the church—and their experience living on the margins of the covenant assembly confirms this—it is little wonder that they fail to join a church or embrace their covenant responsibilities as young adults.

A sign and seal of God's commitment, baptism provokes a response on the part of the recipient (to profess faith publicly in due course) and the parents as well as the whole church (to guide him or her to that end). Although baptism is a one-time event, never to be repeated, it is the gift that keeps on giving. Every day we renew our baptism, dying to ourselves and rising again in newness of life. Is baptism as central today to our public worship and to our identity and daily lives as it was in the book of Acts?

Teaching

When Jesus included in his commission "teaching them everything I have commanded you," he underscored the point I made above that a disciple is first of all a learner—of course, more than that, but not less. This is why the early church gathered regularly for "the apostles' teaching" (Acts 2:42). It is why the ancient church founded catechetical schools and expected converts to go through a rigorous period of detailed instruction in Christian doctrine and practice. It is why the Protestant Reformers wrote up catechisms for the instruction of the people, especially the young, when few adults knew even the Ten Commandments, the Lord's Prayer, or the Apostles' Creed. Judging by the statistics, we are at that point again now in American Christianity.

The Great Commission is God's blueprint for lifelong learners, who have pastors and teachers who care enough to bring them to ever greater maturity in Christ. Evangelism is not just for those outside but for the church as well. We have to reevaluate the common assumption today that we move from being *evangelized* to being *discipled*. These terms are interchangeable. Believers need to be immersed in the gospel every week. They also need to learn God's commands for grateful living in view of his mercies. This can only happen through consistent, loving, patient, and in-depth teaching. Baptism is not just a ritual that we administer at the beginning of the Christian life; it is God's public act of claiming us, to which we are recalled each Lord's Day and throughout the week.

It is not up to us to decide what we think is important and then leave it at that. Dallas Willard is right when he says that discipleship can't be reduced to "fire insurance." It's easy for me to hand off my taxes, my health, and myriad other responsibilities to experts. And we can do the same thing with our faith: "I believe whatever the Bible says." Well, what does it *say*? I'm often asked, "How much do you have to believe to be saved?" But this turns salvation into another version of works righteousness, where we're graded on the most minimal pass/ fail exam. The point to be made is that we are saved by Christ, not by our answers, and that the Christ who saves us expects us to learn *everything* he has to say.

Everything in Scripture is given for our instruction. Paul exhorts even learned Timothy to recall "what you have learned and have firmly believed" through the catechesis of his mother and grandmother, "and how from childhood you have been acquainted with the sacred writings, which are able to make you wise for salvation through faith in Christ Jesus" (2 Tim. 3:14–15). He adds, "All Scripture is breathed out by God and profitable for teaching, for reproof, for correction, and for training in righteousness, that the man of God may be competent, equipped for every good work" (2 Tim. 3:16–17). Next he charges Timothy, "Preach the word" (4:2). Any success in other tasks, programs, and techniques will count for nothing if this one is not fully discharged.

The Lord's Supper

Although it is not mentioned in the Great Commission, the Lord's Supper is included in the command to teach *everything* that Jesus Christ has delivered to his apostles. Jesus instituted the Supper in the upper room on the night before his crucifixion as a sacrament of continual incorporation into his sacrificial death and the blessings of the new covenant (Matt. 26:26–28; Mark 14:22–24; Luke 22:19–20).

In the Supper, Christ ratifies visibly and publicly his last will and testament toward all who receive the sign and seal in faith. Repeating the words of institution, Paul wrote, "For I received from the Lord what I also delivered to you" (1 Cor. 11:23). In fact, so central is this celebration in the ordinary ministry that Paul could refer to it as the event of "coming together as a church" and upbraid the Corinthians for so corrupting the meal by division and scandal that he questioned whether the Supper was actually being celebrated (1 Cor. 11:17–22). "The cup of blessing that we bless," says the apostle, "is it not a participation in the blood of Christ? The bread that we break, is it not a participation in the body of Christ? Because there is one bread, we who are many are one body, for we all partake of the one bread" (1 Cor. 10:16–17).

The emphasis is placed on our participation (*koinonia*) in Christ here and now through eating the bread and drinking the wine. As in preaching and baptism, the Supper provokes our response, but its efficacy does not lie in us and our action—whether our remembering Christ's work in the past or rededicating ourselves to him in the present. While their unbelieving neighbors unite themselves to demons in their pagan rituals, believers are united with Christ and his atoning sacrifice through the Supper (1 Cor. 10:18–22). It may seem as strange to us today as it did to his original hearers when Jesus announces, "Truly, truly, I say to you, unless you eat the flesh of the Son of Man and drink his blood, you have no life in you. Whoever feeds on my flesh and drinks my blood has eternal life, and I will raise him up on the last day" (John 6:53–54). In fact, celebration of the Lord's Supper led to the charge that the early Christians were cannibals. Of course, it is faith that feeds on Christ for everlasting life, but God has given us tangible means for receiving Christ by faith. Along with the apostles' teaching, fellowship, and the prayers, "the breaking of bread" is included as an essential element of worship in the apostolic church (Acts 2:42). Precisely because the Supper is God's gift to us rather than our gift to God, we are filled with thanksgiving (the meaning of *Eucharist*). Precisely because we have truly been given the richest treasure in heaven and on earth, the Spirit forms us through this sacrament into an ever-deepening fellowship with Christ and therefore also with each other.

Like these other elements, the celebration of the Supper is not merely a resource for personal piety but a means through which the Spirit strengthens our faith and builds the whole body up together into Christ as its head. Preaching delivers the promise of the King, and baptism and the Supper are the seals attached to God's covenant pledge, assuring everyone who believes that they are co-heirs of Christ.

Through the preaching of the gospel, baptism, teaching, and the Lord's Supper, the Triune God creates an oasis in the desert. God uses these means not only to teach us about the new creation but to actually create it. The King comes with banners unfurled, proclaiming peace to his enemies and delivering pardons embossed with royal seals. These are not our means of commitment or our strategies for building the church and reaching the world, but God's means of grace. The marks of the church (preaching and sacrament) are grounded explicitly in the Great Commission, as no other strategies—even the ones that come most readily to mind—are not.

Spiritual Gifts, Personal Prayer, and Evangelism: Means of Gratitude

In addition to the public means of grace, there are instructions in Scripture for personal disciplines of prayer, meditation on Scripture, and evangelism. The means of grace—preaching and sacrament—are God's strategies for delivering Christ to us and to the world. The arrow points downward, from God to us. We do not go and get it; God comes and gives it. Yet Scripture mandates a variety of spiritual disciplines for our proper response to this grace. As we see in the covenant that Israel made with God at Sinai, the appropriate response to the terrifying command "Do this and you shall live!" is "All this we will do" (see Exod. 24:7). However, the appropriate response to a free gift is *gratitude*. The Heidelberg Catechism calls prayer "the chief means of gratitude." In addition to corporate prayer in the public service and in family worship, we follow Christ's example of regular times of communion with our Father through the mediation of Christ and the indwelling power of the Spirit. Through the means of grace, the Spirit delivers Christ and gives us the faith to answer back, "Amen!"

Through the means of gratitude, we grow in our response. A baby begins to communicate by crying. Later, parents instruct, "Use your words." Jesus even gave us a model for these appropriate words in the Lord's Prayer. If it is true that one cannot have a personal relationship without knowing certain things about the other person, it is also true that a genuine relationship involves regular conversation. God speaks to us through his Word, and we speak to him in prayer. Even here we are not just left on our own. In the Bible (especially the Psalms) we find not only God's Word—his lines in the script—but our own. Silenced by the fall, we are given our voice back by grace. Learning to pray properly is included in the "all things" that we are to teach to everyone. We don't need more clever strategies for communicating with God: prayer labyrinths, rosary beads, icons, and video clips. We need to meditate on God's Word and pour out our hearts to him in prayer.

For the formal ministry of preaching, sacrament, the prayers, teaching, and discipline, Christ instituted offices. Nevertheless, all believers share in Christ's anointing and are therefore called to address the Father in the name of Christ, without any other mediator, and to witness to Christ with their neighbors.

At various points throughout this book I have suggested that we need to recover important distinctions without letting them turn into oppositions. This is just as true when we consider the relationship between the gifts that Christ gives for the public ministry and the gifts that he gives to all the saints. The New Testament does not allow us either to collapse the distinction between ordained ministry and the wider exchange of gifts in the body of Christ or to create a hierarchical model that separates the servants from the served. Christ does not call all the sheep to be shepherds, but he does call all the sheep to look out for each other. Pastors, elders, and deacons are always servants, never masters, and their service is always toward the flourishing of the whole body. Precisely because the gospel is the announcement of free salvation in Christ, it produces good works. In the same way, a flourishing ministry of ordained officers in the church yields a harvest of gifts.

While Ephesians 4 limits its focus to the gifts of evangelists, pastors, and teachers, Romans 12 and 1 Corinthians 12 list a variety of gifts. Deacons may be called to collect, oversee, and distribute the material gifts and services of the whole body, but all believers are called to hospitality, and some are given a greater measure of this gift than others. Pastors and elders are called to rule as a collective council over the spiritual welfare of the church, but we are all called—even in public worship—to mutual edification and instruction through singing the Word (Col. 3:16). Pastors lead us in public prayer and the confession of our sins, announcing Christ's absolution, but all believers are encouraged to "confess your sins to one another and pray for one another" (James 5:16). Ordination makes some ministers, but baptism makes us all priests. Not everyone holds a particular office in the church, but we all hold the general office of prophet, priest, and king by virtue of our union with Christ.

If we view the offices and order in the church hierarchically, we will conclude that the pastor is the full-time witness to Christ. In a more consumer-oriented culture like ours, this model is literally cashed out in terms of something like this: we pay the pastor to be our substitute disciple. We don't say this, of course, but it is often how we think. The pastor reads the Bible, prays, and evangelizes for us. Maybe we widen the circle a bit and say that the church establishes ministry opportunities for the truly committed disciples to do this for us, relieving us of our responsibilities. So develops the "church within a church," the monks and nuns who live on a higher plane of discipleship and spirituality, while the rest of us are content to be average, ordinary Christians. We're busy with life, after all, and can afford the payoff.

The gifts of pastors, teachers, missionaries, evangelists, elders, and deacons have an essential but limited scope. These officers do not have all of the gifts that a church needs in order to flourish. For a variety of reasons, your pastor may not be the most gifted member at hospitality. And having people over to the house all the time may distract a minister from the ministry of the word of God "to serve tables" (Acts 6:2). However, hospitality is crucial. Happy is the pastor with members who are eagerly engaged in sharing their faith with co-workers—even gathering friends and neighbors for informal discussions of the faith. Richly served, these brothers and sisters have plenty to serve others throughout the week. Elders manage their households well, but other godly parents also manage theirs—and look out for the faith and practice of other young people in the church to whom they made a collective promise in baptism. Thank God for those—especially older saints, widows, widowers, and single members—who are able to contribute more time and talents to prayer and generous service on behalf of the body.

The whole community gathered in the upper room at Pentecost was empowered as witnesses to Christ. The Spirit confirmed his presence among Israel in a single pillar of fire, but at Pentecost "divided tongues as of fire appeared to them and rested on each one of them" (Acts 2:3). The result was not a private prayer language but a supernatural gift of speaking in languages that the speaker had never learned but that were understood by the Jews who had gathered in Jerusalem from many languages and regions for the Feast of Pentecost. The visitors were "amazed and astonished," not because they were speaking ecstatic utterances but "because each one was hearing them speak in his own language. . . . We hear them telling in our own tongues the mighty works of God" (Acts 2:6–7, 11).

Peter preached the Pentecost sermon and many were baptized, but the word of the Lord spread rapidly through the witness of ordinary believers as well. The authorities tried to put out the fire by imprisoning the apostles and killing the deacon Stephen, but God's word continued to spread. In the book of Revelation, the martyrs are triumphant over the world, the flesh, and the devil because of the word of their testimony.

Here again, it is important for us to recognize that personal evangelism is not primarily concerned with testifying to ourselves but with testifying to Christ. There is nothing wrong with relating our Christian experience. In fact, it is often a good way into a conversation with an unbelieving friend or relative. However, it is a mere preamble to the gospel. The apostles and martyrs faced death not because they had a spiritual experience or because their marriages were stronger and they were better people now, but because of their testimony *to Christ*.

If anyone could have testified to the difference that Jesus made in their inner experience and in their relationships with others, it would have been the apostles. Unlike me, they actually did walk and talk with Jesus in a garden! Instead, the record we have is their eyewitness testimony to the most important things that Jesus said and did, and their inspired interpretation. Of course, the gospel changed their hearts and bore fruit in good works, but the testimony was to the events that happened for us all and not just in their own personal experience. Paul related his Damascus road encounter with the risen Christ, but he never suggested that it was normative, much less encouraged others to have their own "Damascus road experience." Rather, the point of his relating this story was to testify to Christ as risen and reigning and to his own calling as an apostolic eyewitness.

I find it easy to talk about myself. I can relate my interpretation of "how I got saved," and who can argue? It's *my* experience. However, believers witness to facts of history with which all people are obliged to reckon. Many believers, much less unbelievers, have never heard an intelligent defense of the Christian claims. So we have to learn the story and the doctrines that arise from it. We have to live in that story, as regular recipients of the ministry of preaching and sacrament. In other words, we have to become disciples.

And the more that we grow in this knowledge and experience of Christ, the more prepared we are "to make a defense to anyone who asks you for a reason for the hope that is in you" and to "do it with gentleness and respect" (1 Peter 3:15). Those who know what they believe and why they believe it do not need to rely on clichés and memorized formulas. They do not need to be coaxed or browbeaten into sharing their faith. It becomes a natural part of everyday relationships and ordinary conversation.

When Christ is being delivered to us weekly in Word and sacrament, the corporate gathering of the saints becomes the field in which a harvest grows. We bring home leftovers from this weekly feast and dine on rich morsels each day. Some pastors print suggested Scripture readings and questions to ponder throughout the week—as takeaway from the last Sunday and in preparation for the next. Sometimes there are also Scripture passages and questions from the catechism recommended for family instruction throughout the week. In all of these ways, the regular banquet of the people of God is the gift that keeps on giving each day.

Home Missions: Making Disciples in Our Families

Our own families are the nearest mission field. Luther called his family "my little parish." In his Pentecost sermon, Peter declared, "The promise is for you and for your children and for all who are far off, everyone whom the Lord our God calls to himself" (Acts 2:39). So the Great Commission is a call not only to foreign missions and church planting but to the succession of covenant blessings from one generation to the next.

Everyone who is baptized is a visible member of the family, and this means that every one of us is not only privileged but responsible to learn the grammar and to live it out among the saints and in the world. No one who is baptized can say that learning and growing in Christian faith and practice is an optional extra. Too busy climbing the professional ladder? We have been bought with a price, not with money but with Christ's blood (1 Peter 1:18–19). Are we too immersed in entertainment, sports, and other cultural pursuits to shepherd Christ's little flock in our home? Baptism distracts us from our distractions. Is the feverish activity of "family life" so all-consuming that we don't have any time for grace? If so, we shouldn't be surprised if one day our children aren't part of the communion of saints.

The Lord's Day

The Lord's Day is not a day of fasting in solitude, but of feasting: eating and drinking in the presence of the Lord—and his people. In this weekly holiday, gathering together with the saints for lively fellowship and communion in Christ, we are made one family together by hearing the same Word and sharing in one Spirit. In this assembly, the kingdom of God is most visibly present in the world in its current form: as an embassy of grace, creating a forgiven and forgiving society.

In giving the Ten Commandments, God based the fourth (Sabbath) command on the imitation of God by his image-bearer: "For in six days the LORD made heaven and earth, the sea, and all that is in them, and rested on the seventh day. Therefore the LORD blessed the Sabbath day and made it holy" (Exod. 20:11). So this command is not based merely on Israel's special relationship to God, but on the original relationship of God and humanity in creation.

To be sure, the new-covenant celebration of the Lord's Day is different from its observance under the old covenant. We are no longer obligated to the ceremonial laws attached to it in the Mosaic covenant. In addition, the seismic impact of Christ's resurrection moved the covenant gathering from Saturday to Sunday: the Lord's Day. This day was set aside entirely for the ministry of Word and sacrament, teaching, the prayers, and fellowship (Acts 2:42; 20:7; 1 Cor. 16:2; Heb. 10:25; Rev. 1:10). This regular assembling of the covenant community is a weekly Easter celebration, the birthday of the new creation. It is not a common day, when we celebrate God's gifts of creation and providence in common grace, but a holy day when we are once again drawn back into the story of Jesus Christ by his Word and Spirit, together with his people.

The Christian Sabbath has been practiced with varying degrees of success in the Reformed tradition. At its best, it has been practiced with joy as well as reverence, anticipation as well as contentment, sumptuous delight in God's gifts as well as a concern to share these gifts with others. It is a day of rest not only for our bodies and minds but also for our souls, as we rest in Christ and cease from relying on our own activity. The emphasis is not what we can't do on the Lord's Day, but what ordinary callings we are freed from to enjoy a foretaste of the everlasting Sabbath. For our temporal welfare as well as for our salvation, we stop working to witness to the fact that God is our provider. We rest in Christ.

Besides attending church services in the morning and the evening for our spiritual nourishment, and resting our bodies, it has been a common Reformed practice to visit shut-ins, hospital patients, retirement homes, and prisons. "Works of mercy," as they are called, belong to the joy and responsibility of the Lord's Day.

This is not the only way that Reformed churches have practiced this discipline. The Lord's Day has often been a burden rather than a delight, buried under a list of written and unwritten traditions and laws that are not commanded in the new-covenant celebration. However, bad celebrations of this day do not justify abandoning it, any more than bad preaching, administrations of the sacraments, prayers, or evangelistic presentations justify abandoning the worship that God has commanded.

The skeptic Voltaire once quipped that if you get rid of the Christian Sabbath, you get rid of Christianity. That is not because of a superstitious attachment but because it is on this day that the Triune God has promised to bless the earth with the in-breaking of his kingdom, creating streams in the desert. Through the means of grace, we enter into God's Sabbath, resting from our works just as God did from his (Heb. 4:9). Each Lord's Day is a foretaste of that everlasting Sabbath glory that awaits us. On this day, in this place, we arrive again as the "salt of the earth" that needs to be resalinized. Give up the Lord's Day, or turn it into something other than the ministry of Word and sacrament, and before long the salt will lose its savor. The promise—which is for us, our children, and all who are far off—will be only faintly heard in the din of the Muzak at the mall (or church!) and the headlines that grab our attention throughout the week. We need to be distracted from the daily news by the news from heaven. And when we are, we actually read the daily news a little differently in the bargain.

Celebration of the Lord's Day may be one of the most challenging practices among Christians today. Yet often the most difficult disciplines are also the ones that draw the sharpest distinctions between citizens of the age to come and citizens of this present age.

Here again we need to work against the growing tendency to collapse the distinction between the holy and the common, the means of grace and the life of service that we render to our neighbors during the week. Common vocations, transactions, tasks, and social activities with our non-Christian neighbors are given to us by God for six days, but on this day we are called out from every nation as Christ's universal priesthood. It is a warm-up for the wedding supper of the Lamb. In a consumer-driven society, we boycott the mall on this day. We refuse to surrender to the culture of entertainment. On this day everyone witnesses to the god they worship. On this day, we witness to the world—and to each other and to ourselves—that *this* is who we really are: "in Christ" rather than "in Adam," claimed by the Spirit and animated by the age to come. Exercising our Christian liberty to eat, drink, play, work, shop, and nurture our hobbies on six days, we jealously guard the Lord's Day because it announces to us and to the world that we were made for more. There is something greater than we can imagine up ahead, and we want to receive every morsel that falls from that table, every scent from that banquet, even now.

It is the Lord's Day, not my day or your day or our group's day. It is not a national holiday but a heavenly holy day. On this day, in the communion of saints, we discover that our deepest identities and affinities are not cultural or socioeconomic. On this day, in this place, there is no time for celebrating our national or ethnic heritage. We are not a society of people with similar interests, hobbies, tastes, and consumer profiles. We do not gather with our circle of friends and neighbors with whom we share similar cultural interests and affinities. We do not arrive with a political agenda. We come because we have heard the promise of "the city that has foundations, whose designer and builder is God" (Heb. 11:10). In this strange place, on this strange day, the older saints teach the younger, the poor enrich the wealthy and the wealthy enrich the poor, outcasts are welcomed, the weary and heavy laden enter into God's Sabbath rest, and autonomous consumers die and are raised with Christ. Take away the Lord's Day and fill it with ordinary callings, entertainments, and pursuits, and you take away that one day on which God has promised to gather, feed, and save his flock, and you stop its witness to the world.

Celebrating Christ's resurrection—and being regularly drawn back into its life-giving energies—this holy day is God's gift for the weekly renewal of his covenant of grace. On this day, in this gathering, the Lord Jesus Christ addresses the world in judgment and forgiveness, baptizes his citizens, feeds and clothes them with spiritual and even material sustenance, and incubates witnesses who penetrate every corner of the world throughout the week. We cannot take seriously the reality of the kingdom of God among us if we do not set this day apart for communion with Christ, just as he has set it apart for us.

Disciples in the Home

I respect the motives of pastors, youth pastors, and parents today who want to keep their children interested in Christ while facing all sorts of distractions and attractions from other directions. Their intentions are not bad. Nevertheless, judging by biblical standards, spirituality among churched young people is in a state of serious crisis. I referred in the introduction to the Barna Research Group report that 60 percent of churched young people become unchurched twentysomethings.[4] The intensive studies by sociologist Christian Smith and his team reflect a vague spirituality that does not differ significantly from that of non-Christians.[5]

Even after a day at school, our children have homework. Merely one day a week, we go to church as a family. There our children are catechized and join us for public worship, and our pastor includes questions for us to go over as a family at home. Throughout the week we read and discuss the Scriptures, pray, and learn the questions and answers of the catechism. Like helping our kids with homework, it is a routine, discipline, and habit. Sometimes it is dull, but it often fills my wife and me with delight as we hear our children ask questions, offer insights, and express their growing faith in Christ. If the school has our children five days a week and still needs parents to help with homework, then discipleship in the faith requires no less attention and focus. We fall short in myriad ways, but my wife and I have come to see in concrete ways the importance of that inextricable link between church and home. Neither of us was raised this way, but we are witnesses now to God's faithfulness to his covenant promise.

It does not take a lot of cultural analysis to realize that if the young people whom Christ has entrusted to the church are dropping out and evidence little serious knowledge of Scripture or the Christian faith, we are failing in the Great Commission at the most basic and local level.

As parents, it is easy for us to treat churches and youth groups as the problem, much as we blame schools for a more general illiteracy. However, even if a church is doing everything it is called to do by Christ, genuine faith and practice will not be real in a young person's life unless it is part of the warp and woof of the home. Children often grow up hearing their parents talk a good game about God and the importance of "spirituality" in their life, while there is little concrete evidence in their daily lives. Even seeing us fail—and return to Christ in confession and assurance of forgiveness—is a crucial learning experience.

Making disciples begins in the home, and parents are the missionaries. This is an important point, because local churches today often expect every member to find a "ministry" in the church. I know fine Christians who, in addition to working two jobs, are spending hours in church-related activities even to the neglect of their own family members, who try not to blame God for keeping their parents or spouse so busy. Then they go to church and everybody scatters to their own group. What would it be like if families came to church together and shared in the same fellowship, and then brought morsels home for family worship throughout the week? Wouldn't they be better served to be salt and light in the home, at school, and at work?

Following the ancient church, reformers like Luther and Calvin drew up catechisms, and they saw it as an essential part of their calling to teach the catechism to the youth themselves. However, the catechism was used primarily in the home, taught by the parents throughout the week. A recent book by J. I. Packer and Gary A. Parrett calls attention to the need for a renewal of catechesis in the church today, observing that such regular instruction requires a concerted effort between the church and the home.[6] At the grammar stage, eagerness to memorize is ideal for learning the catechism's questions and answers along with the supporting biblical passages. Then, as children become teenagers, they need the freedom—indeed, the encouragement—to question their inherited faith in an environment where their explorations can be guided and their questions can be answered. Furthermore, they need to see the relevance of the Christian faith in the lives of their parents.

It's possible to have "head knowledge" without "heart knowledge," but it's impossible to have the latter without the former. We have to know at least some things in order to be moved to praise, maturity, and obedience. Contrary to the deep anti-intellectualism of many

Christians, no one has ever abandoned the Christian faith because they thought too much or knew too much. Sanctification is as much about the head as it is about the heart and actions. In fact, it is as our minds are renewed by the Word that we are able to offer our bodies as a living sacrifice.

As we meditate on Scripture, we step into its drama and are instructed in its doctrines. In prayer, we respond with praise, questions, cries, thanksgiving, anxieties, and hope. We find ourselves living in this new world in a personal relationship with our Lord. And then we look out to the world and our callings in it as servants to our neighbor who needs us. We are to "grow in the grace and knowledge of our Lord and Savior Jesus Christ" (2 Peter 3:18).

Dripping with the corrosive acids of our own sins as well as the cultural assumptions that ooze from our own pores even as Christians, we lose our saltiness and become indistinguishable from the world. Only by being constantly transformed by the renewing of our minds can we be "resalinized" by the Spirit through the Word (see Rom. 12:1–2).

7

Disciples and Discipline

"Teaching Them to Observe All That I Have Commanded"

As a child, I exasperated my piano teacher because I stubbornly insisted on playing by ear instead of benefiting from her expertise. I didn't need to learn the notes; I could teach myself to play. And the result today, of course, is that I'm limited to a narrow repertoire of show tunes.

Even in a good church, there are few Mozarts, but pastors and elders are called because they are more mature in teaching and playing God's music. Submitting ourselves to the discipline of officers in the church is often viewed as threatening to one's personal relationship with Jesus. However, becoming a disciple of Christ means living in the story, learning the doctrine, joining our brothers and sisters in praise and grateful obedience. If we only play by ear, we'll never grow up in Christ. Our repertoire will be limited to whatever we have taught or experienced on our own.

The key to acquiring skill in any field, hobby, sport, or relationship is *discipline*—submitting ourselves to the rules and to the expertise of teachers. This may seem rote, especially at the beginning, and we now have an entire culture that is losing its patience with this stage. In addition, our culture prizes individual autonomy. We're a nation of adults who brush off submission to instruction with the childish response, "I know, I know." Everyone is competent already. We just need tools and resources. And this cultural habit is carried over into do-it-yourself discipleship.

In contrast with that assumption, this chapter explores the offices that Christ established for building his body. The Great Commission speaks first of the *ministry* of Word and sacrament, because this is not only the ministry *of* the church but the ministry that creates, sustains, and expands the church. The means of grace are God's ministry to us, not our tools for self-help. The church not only *fulfills* the Great Commission; it is the *offspring* of the Great Commission—and not only in its founding but each and every time it is gathered. The church exists because of the ministry, not the other way around.

And yet Christ created a visible church with particular structures and offices. The Spirit disrupts and disorganizes our lives, human society, and cultural assumptions, only to reorganize us into his people. Although the church is not commissioned to administer the affairs of secular states, it is indeed a political institution. It is Christ's embassy in the world. Whether we take the visible form of the church seriously or not, our churches cannot help but exhibit a particular political order. At one end is a *hierarchical* government, where the authority comes from an earthly head. At the other end is a *democratic* government, where authority lies primarily in the individual (collectively, "the people"), who may or may not recognize external authorities. Between these extremes lies a *covenantal* government in which Christ as the sole head of the church disperses his delegated authority through a network of mutual accountability, locally and more broadly.

We do not make God our Savior any more than we make him our Creator. Because Christ *is* Savior and Lord, and is present in saving activity wherever he has promised to be, there is a visible church that administers his everlasting peace in his name. The church does not arise either from the leadership of an earthly head or from the will of the people but from the saving work of God in Jesus Christ. The first principle of any sound doctrine of the church is that Christ alone is its living head.

Often in the ancient Near East, rulers were described metaphorically as shepherds over their kingdom, and the Bible appropriates this imagery for its Shepherd-King:

> Know that the LORD, he is God!
> It is he who made us, and we are his;
> we are his people, and the sheep of his pasture.

> Enter his gates with thanksgiving,
>   and his courts with praise!
> Give thanks to him; bless his name!
> For the LORD is good;
>   his steadfast love endures forever,
>   and his faithfulness to all generations. (Ps. 100:3–5)

Yet, like sheep, we have all gone astray, each to his own way (Isa. 53:6; Jer. 50:6), but God promised our forebears that he would gather his sheep under a Good Shepherd (Ezek. 34:11; Micah 2:12).

The church is a people (sheep), but it is also a place (a fold) where the Good Shepherd feeds, protects, and disciplines his flock. Sheep by nature go astray, looking for their own patch of grass—and they get lost. We do not need fitness coaches who help us to become self-feeders; we need shepherds who lead us and keep us in the rich pastures of God's Word.

The New Testament not only gives us the message, mission, and methods of the Great Commission but even gives us instruction on the government of the church. Of course, we do not find every detail in Scripture, but there are basic principles: (1) Christ alone is the head of the church; (2) Christ has authorized certain offices for the maintenance of the public ministry and spiritual care of the saints (pastors and elders) as well as for their temporal needs (deacons); (3) there is an organic relationship between local churches that expresses itself in organizational unity.

Christ's Ordained Offices in the Church

As I argued in the previous chapter, we cannot outsource our discipleship to ordained ministers. Baptism qualifies all believers as prophets, priests, and kings. We have all been given gifts for the benefit of the whole body, as Paul lays out in 1 Corinthians 12 and Romans 12.

At the same time, all of these gifts come from the Spirit through the ministry of the Word. Paul explains this in Ephesians 4. First, he says, "There is one body and one Spirit—just as you were called to the one hope that belongs to your call—one Lord, one faith, one baptism, one God and Father of all, who is over all and through all and in all. But grace was given to each one of us according to the measure of Christ's gift" (vv. 4–7). God is "over all and through all and in all" believers (v. 6). Every believer shares equally in the gift of grace. Yet we have differing gifts in that one body. Paul continues: "Therefore it [Ps. 68:18] says, 'When he ascended on high he led a host of captives, and he gave gifts to men.' . . . (He who descended is the one who also ascended far above all the heavens, that he might fill all things.) And he gave the apostles, the prophets, the evangelists, the shepherds and teachers" (vv. 8, 10–11). In this context, the gifts that Christ gave (and gives) in his ascension are church officers. I have already argued that the offices of prophets and apostles have come to an end, as the foundation-laying era of the church ended. Now we have evangelists, pastors, and teachers.

What is the purpose for these gifts? In many of our modern translations, the next verses read, "to equip the saints for the work of ministry, for building up the body of Christ, until we all attain to the unity of the faith and of the knowledge of the Son of God" (vv. 12–13). The Greek verb translated "to equip" (*katartismon*) can also be rendered "to complete or perfect," as in fact it was in older English translations. If so, then it is through the work of pastors and teachers that the Spirit completes or perfects the body. This makes the most sense with Paul's analogy of a building. It is the saints in general who are being built up into a structure with Christ as its head. They are equipped not *for* this ministry but *by* this ministry for other godly callings in the church and in the world.

Another point: *eis* can be translated either as "into/unto" (purpose) or as "by or with" (instrument). The translation makes all the difference. Are pastors and teachers given "to equip the saints for the work of ministry" or "to complete the saints by/with the work of ministry"? It could go either way, except for the fact that this clause is the first in a series of others: "*for* building up the body of Christ, *until* we all attain to the unity of the faith and of the knowledge of the Son of God, to mature [adulthood], to the measure of the stature of the fullness of Christ, *so that* we may no longer be children, tossed to and fro by the waves and carried about by every wind of doctrine" (vv. 12–14, emphasis added).

In other words, Paul is saying that Christ has given the church the gift of pastors and teachers for the following purpose: to complete the saints with the ministry of the Word so that they will be united in the faith and in the mature knowledge of Christ instead of being children who are carried about by every wind of doctrine. The result is that the whole body is served, so that "speaking the truth in love," we are joined to each other in a common faith with Christ as our head and every part of the body in working order. In this way, the whole church is prepared to live a new life in the world, no longer walking "as the Gentiles do, in the futility of their minds" (v. 17). The whole body is the beneficiary of the ministry of pastors and teachers, not only so that everyone may be built up together into Christ through sound doctrine, but also so that they may love and serve each other.

In the Great Commission itself, the strategic plan already determines the church as a visible and embodied institution in history, a covenant community running across all times and places. Because the kingdom is in every moment the work of the Triune God, descending from heaven, it cannot be reduced to a historical institution. Nevertheless, Christ's kingdom doesn't hover over the world, calling souls to ascend upward, out of their bodies, history, and the world. Rather, like in the incarnation itself, this kingdom comes into the world, fully embodied. Preaching is audible. Baptizing and communion are physical, embodied, public, and tangible events. Confessing Christ takes place in the public service and spills out into the streets as believers testify to the gospel and live in view of God's mercies. The Word is heard, not only in the preaching but in the public singing, the prayers, and other responses of the saints. This same Word is practiced in a community in which strangers become brothers and sisters, co-heirs of Christ and each other's material as well as spiritual support. Wandering sheep are brought back. And it is even visible in its political organization as a society of forgiven and renewed sinners under the saving lordship of its ascended King.

The Good Shepherd exercises his care through under-shepherds. Far from being a secular corruption, the offices of pastor, elder, and deacon are identified explicitly in Scripture, with specific qualifications (1 Tim. 3–4; 2 Tim. 2:14–4:8; Titus 1:5–3:11) and instructions for proper order among the rest of the members, including public worship (1 Cor. 10–12; 1 Tim. 5).

The Gifts He Gave: Offices in the Church

Although all believers are priests, not all are pastors. As a friend of mine put it, the Scriptures do not teach that every sheep is a shepherd. Nevertheless, the church is not an oligarchy ruled by clerics any more than it is a democracy ruled by the people. Rather, it is a kingdom of servant leadership, with authority spread out between pastors who teach and elders who rule. Though ordained, elders are not ministers but representatives called out by Christ through the acclamation of his people. They do not represent the people, but Christ to his people.

As busy as Paul was in apostolic ministry, he did not consider a church plant properly constituted until it had elders. "This is why I left you in Crete," he reminds Titus, "so that you might put what remained into order, and appoint elders in every town as I directed you" (Titus 1:5). The term "elders" (*presbyteroi*) is often an overarching term for the spiritual leaders of the church, including pastors (sometimes called *episcopoi*, meaning "overseers") as well as the elders who rule but do not preach or administer the sacraments. "Let the elders who rule well be considered worthy of double honor," Paul tells Timothy, "especially those who labor in preaching and teaching. . . . Do not be hasty in the laying on of hands" (1 Tim. 5:17, 22). In fact, James adds, "Not many of you should become teachers, my brothers, for you know that we who teach will be judged with greater strictness" (James 3:1). Ministers are not called to be CEOs, marketing directors, or life coaches. Rather, Paul exhorts Timothy to "devote yourself to the public reading of Scripture, to exhortation, to teaching. Do not neglect the gift you have, which was given you by prophecy when the council of elders [*presbuteriou*] laid their hands on you" (1 Tim. 4:13).

Disciples do not float in and out of church like shoppers (a contract). Their baptism is not only the sign and seal of their participation in the covenant blessings; it inducts them into a new language, a new family, and a new way of living (a covenant). They do not create the covenant; the covenant creates them.

Just as there are families for forming people and social and political structures for forming citizens, *discipleship* requires *discipline*. Although the English word has a negative connotation in our culture, discipline simply means "instruction," and a disciple is someone who is instructed. Disciples are lifelong learners. They do not decide for themselves what they will believe and how they will live, but they submit to the yoke of Christ through his ordained officers.

The last two chapters of Hebrews remind us to be committed to regular church attendance and to submit to the discipline of those whom God has placed over us. Like a good Father, the Lord disciplines those whom he loves (Heb. 12:3–17). He does so not out of disappointment, irritation, or impatience, but out of a gracious determination to prepare us for the glories of the age to come. "Therefore let us be grateful for receiving a kingdom that cannot be shaken, and thus let us offer to God acceptable worship, with reverence and awe, for our

God is a consuming fire" (Heb. 12:28–29). God has given us shepherds to lead us safely to our heavenly city:

> Remember your leaders, those who spoke to you the word of God. Consider the outcome of their way of life, and imitate their faith. . . . For here we have no lasting city, but we seek the city that is to come. . . . Obey your leaders and submit to them, for they are keeping watch over your souls, as those who will have to give an account. Let them do this with joy and not with groaning, for that would be of no advantage to you. (Heb. 13:7, 14, 17)

Again, note that this discipline is not a burden under which we chafe. Rather, it is *to our advantage* that we submit to those who watch over us. Formed by this ministry of Word and sacrament, the saints exhibit—and are called to exhibit more and more—fellowship in body and soul with each other and also hospitality to strangers (Heb. 13:1–3).

So important is this work of pastors and elders that the office of deacon was established so that the apostles could fulfill their ministry of the Word and prayer without being distracted by the necessary work of caring for the temporal needs of the flock (Acts 6:1–4).

Church Discipline

We have seen that becoming a Christian is a lifelong process. And the church is the mother of the faithful. The Great Commission is never completed, even for lifelong believers, during their pilgrimage. Private spiritual disciplines are important, but they cannot be a substitute for the discipline of the church.

There is a lot of talk today about spiritual directors and life coaches. People sense the need for mentorship in areas of life where pastors, elders, and wise family members used to fill the bill. What happened? In part, institutional bonds have broken down. Social dynamics have made us more anonymous, separated demographically as well as geographically from our extended families. Pastors are often too busy being CEOs to mentor their members, and it has become too easy simply to hand covenant children over to youth ministries and others to various counselors, support groups, or other parachurch outreaches.

The "divide and conquer" principle in our culture of marketing separates even family members from each other. Aging grandparents have their "home," parents are occupied with adult responsibilities, tasks, and groups, while older children may be as divided from their younger siblings by targeted "needs" as they are from their parents. This segmenting logic, which turns marketing opportunities into perceived needs, has engulfed our churches like an oil spill. Younger believers can become sealed off from the wider fellowship by appealing to the alleged uniqueness of their generation's needs, tastes, and interests. The niche marketing that inundates families during the week, separating the generations psychologically, emotionally, and intellectually, spills over into the church.

Regardless of what we say, in practice we often work against God's pledge to be our God and the God of our children. Now we have a couple of generations of professing evangelicals who do not know the basic grammar of the Christian faith. Is it any wonder that the lives and values of professing Christians do not differ significantly from those of the surrounding culture?

Jesus calls us to abide in him by abiding in his *words* (John 15:7). His words create the new world that we indwell in the power of the Spirit. And it is *his* world that is enduring, while what we call "the real world" is fading away. As with learning to play musical notes or to pedal a bike, eventually we not only look *at* this or that doctrine but look *through* them and see the world—and live in it—differently. They are no longer simply "objects" external to us but become the "feelers" through which we interpret reality.

So in the Christian life, the key is to focus directly on the doctrine, not as an end but in order to gain the expertise to focus directly on one's activity in the world (i.e., discipleship). This is why God gave us pastors, teachers, and elders. They teach us to play the music— and then to live in and through it until we're no longer staring at our hands but looking up to God in faith and out to our neighbors in love. Because this is a never-ending lesson, we never outgrow the need for teachers.

Although there is a lot of interest in private spiritual disciplines, *church* discipline is increasingly neglected and sometimes abused, particularly where orderly structures and offices are not present. In fact, neglect often leads to abuse, as strong personalities—whether a domineering leader or self-appointed vigilantes—run roughshod over the appropriate and authorized "due process" of discipline.

Jesus promised the church that he would be present "where two or three are gathered in my name" (Matt. 18:20). This verse is often used to support the idea that Jesus is present in informal as well as formal church settings. However, in context, Jesus is addressing the question of church discipline. If a brother or sister sins, the matter is dealt with privately, with "two or three witnesses." Jesus adds,

> If he refuses to listen to them, tell it to the church. And if he refuses to listen even to the church, let him be to you as a Gentile and a tax collector. Truly, I say to you, whatever you bind on earth shall be bound in heaven, and whatever you loose on earth shall be loosed in heaven. Again I say to you, if two of you agree on earth about anything they ask, it will be done for them by my Father in heaven. For where two or three are gathered in my name, there am I among them. (Matt. 18:17–20)

The context is not an informal gathering of believers. It is not even a regular gathering of the church. Rather, it is a disciplinary action, to be overseen by the apostles and elders and then by the ordinary ministers and elders after the apostolic era.

All believers are called to do their part in teaching, encouraging, reproving, and correcting each other. However, Christ established offices in the church, giving his own authority to pastors for the ministry of Word and sacrament and to the elders for spiritual oversight. Together, ministers and elders exercise the office of the keys (binding and loosing) by proclaiming the forgiveness of sins and by barring those who are unrepentant in doctrine or in life from the Lord's Table.

Therefore, we are all under church discipline to one degree or another, as pupils of Christ who are receiving, learning, and growing in our faith and obedience. Even the church's censures are meant to lead us to repentance, not to punish or to drive away. This is an important point, because in recent years it has become increasingly common to hear pastors boast that their ministries are finally successful after they were able to drive away certain people. This can be a form of passive-aggressive, informal excommunication that a pastor exercises in his person rather than in his office (together with the elders), and it is far from the proper discipline that leads a shepherd to leave the ninety-nine to bring back the one sheep that has strayed.

The alternative to an intentional, formal, and active order in the church is not freedom, love, and tolerance but the "Wild, Wild West," with the townsfolk either cowering in fear under a thug or taking justice into their own hands. I have seen numerous cases in which wider bodies of church courts (a presbytery or synod) have saved a local church from a despotic minister or elders and spared local churches from the brush fire of gossip and vigilante lynchings that occur when there's no law and order in town. When we discipline in decency and in order, following due process, we guard the accused and the wider church from false charges and gossip. Private sins are dealt with privately, and public sins are dealt with publicly. In fact, I've witnessed cases in which the accusers were disciplined more seriously than the offender because they took matters into their own hands, seeking vengeance rather than reconciliation.

The Corinthian church had become a "Wild, Wild West" church, like many today. The church had come to mirror the worldliness of its litigious, proud, selfish, greedy, immoral, and power-grabbing society. It was an immature church, more like a fraternity house than the family of God. However, unlike a lot of us (and perhaps some Corinthian believers), Paul does not blame this condition on the world. He does not offer a single jeremiad against the Corinthian culture or encourage a march on city hall. Nor does he even say that the Corinthian saints need to avoid any contact with unbelievers. He says,

> I wrote to you in my letter not to associate with sexually immoral people—not at all meaning the sexually immoral of this world, or the greedy and swindlers, or idolaters, since then you would need to go out of the world. But now I am writing to you not to associate with anyone who bears the name of brother if he is guilty of sexual immorality or greed, or is an idolater, reviler, drunkard, or swindler—not even to eat with such a one. For what have I to do with judging outsiders? Is it not those inside the church whom you are to judge? God judges those outside. "Purge the evil person from among you." (1 Cor. 5:9–13)

For some reason, we have become accustomed to judging the world, while discipline is lacking in the church.

In the churches with which I am familiar in my own ministry, excommunication is the last resort, after repeatedly failed attempts to reconcile erring members to Christ's tutelage. Even in that tragic case, the goal is still to encourage repentance and faith in Christ, with the door left open wide for prodigal sons and daughters.

Like many pastors, I can attest to the gracious effects of the Spirit through ministers and elders who labor prayerfully, patiently, and consistently in this difficult yet rewarding aspect of their calling. I'll never forget the sister who left her husband for another man and then, after repeated attempts at correction in private, was publicly barred from the Lord's Table. A couple of years later, she returned repentant.

She related that the Lord brought her back through the Word that she had learned and couldn't get out of her head and heart, the tragic loss of not living out her baptism and sharing with the saints in the Supper, and the prayers that she heard were being offered by the whole church for her return.

It is as easy to just leave a church as it is for pastors and elders to just let someone go. Laziness can always be spun as tolerance. Love requires a greater burden from everyone involved.

Disciples and Denominations

A representative, covenantal, and connectional government was present in the post-apostolic church. There were already divisions in the apostolic church over doctrine, as well as over sectarian attachment to persons. Nevertheless, the church was led by pastors and elders (presbyters) together in local and broader assemblies. Early after the apostolic era, moderators of presbytery became identified as bishops, and this developed into a distinct office. Interestingly, Orthodox theologian John Zizioulas and Pope Benedict both acknowledge presbyterian polity as the earliest form of church government.[1] However, churches in both the East and the West began to imitate the hierarchical political system of the empire.

In the face of various internal challenges, a broad ecumenical consensus was achieved through general synods and councils. Nevertheless, the hierarchical tendency led to the Western papacy, contributing to the Great Schism between Eastern and Western churches in 1064. The idea of starting a new church was far from the minds of the Protestant Reformers. That is why they were *reformers*, not new prophets or apostles.

Nevertheless, under the Protestant umbrella today there is a bewildering array of denominations. It may be easier for us to see how the ancient church was warped by its imperial culture, and that the churches of the Reformation were still held together more by an alliance with the state, but our democratic and egalitarian culture today has also shaped—and misshaped—our understanding of the church. Today, even groups that began as free-wheeling movements of the Spirit have become institutionalized. The processes of modernity that lead to entrepreneurial start-ups and bureaucratic agencies are as evident in denominations as they are in businesses and governments.

In the modern era, after the tragedy of religious wars, Protestants at least have settled for the existence of separate denominations with different confessions. At their best, they have preserved catholicity by recognizing other denominations as true churches, or at least as communions that retain something of the marks of the church. At their worst, they have identified their own tradition—even their own denomination—as the only true church.

In this confusion, however, many Christians have pursued a "non-denominational" or "post-denominational" approach. Some groups do not even have church membership. Nevertheless, each of these new movements eventually becomes a denomination in practice, if not in theory. Often, they become even more hierarchical and personality-driven than the denominations they left.

Is there any way forward, or should we just learn to accept the divided condition of the visible church? After defending the connectional principle, I will explore some ways in which we might be able to apply it even in a fragmented world of denominations.

The Church and Churches: Organic Connectionalism

Some of the Pauline epistles are addressed to specific churches in which there were various local congregations. Yet the letters are addressed to "the church in Rome," "the church in Corinth," and so forth. Furthermore, the New Testament refers to the church in an even broader sense, including the whole visible church. Just as the local church reflects the principle of "many in one and one in many," so too local churches are many but together form one church in all times and places. Every local church is a microcosm of the "one holy, catholic, and apostolic church." In fact, the authority of broader assemblies or synods consists in the fact that they are delegated and representative meetings of the local churches. Nevertheless, their decisions are binding on the local churches they represent.

In Acts we learn that the question of including Gentiles in the church without requiring that they adopt Jewish practices aroused considerable controversy. This a great place to see in concrete terms how the drama gives rise to the doctrine, doxology, and discipleship. The radical Good News is that Christ has borne the curse of the law for Jews and Gentiles alike and that they now receive justification and new life through faith in him. The dividing wall between God and humanity and between Jew and Gentile has been torn down in Christ.

This headline is unpacked in a variety of doctrines. What can we do in the face of this but celebrate the lavish grace of God? However, it means that a lot is going to have to change on the ground. There will be a lot of discomfort and strangeness as Jewish Christians find themselves being baptized, eating of the same bread and drinking from the same cup, and sharing their spiritual and temporal goods with "the great unwashed" (Gentiles). What happens when someone brings pork chops to the potluck? The drama transforms what discipleship looks like in real life.

Things heated up when Paul and Barnabus returned to Antioch (in Syria) and reported on the advance of the gospel among the Gentiles: "And when they arrived and gathered the church together, they declared all that God had done with them and how he had opened a door of faith to the Gentiles. And they remained no little time with the disciples" (Acts 14:27–28). However, in Acts 15, a group came down to Antioch from Judea, insisting, "Unless you are circumcised according to the custom of Moses, you cannot be saved" (v. 1). After some debate, "Paul and Barnabus and some of the others were appointed to go up to Jerusalem to the apostles and the elders about this question" (v. 2). It is interesting that although Paul was an apostle, the Antioch church *appointed* him, along with Barnabus and others, to represent it in Jerusalem. It was a *delegated* embassy, even for Paul.

The result of this overture from the Antioch church (probably consisting of various congregations) was the calling of a special synod or council. The phrase "the apostles and the elders" occurs repeatedly throughout this event, because the church was to be governed not by the apostles alone (much less by Peter alone) but by the common assent of delegated assemblies. "The apostles and the elders were gathered together to consider this matter" (v. 6). It was to be a representative government, not a monarchy, oligarchy, or democracy.

After initial debate, Peter gave a moving speech about how God had revealed that the Gentiles were equal members of Christ: they "hear the word of the gospel and believe," the same Holy Spirit is given to them, "and he made no distinction between us and them, having cleansed their hearts by faith. Now, therefore, why are you putting God to the test by placing a yoke on the neck of the disciples that neither our fathers nor we have been able to bear? But we believe that we will be saved through the grace of the Lord Jesus, just as they will" (vv. 7, 9–11). Then Paul and Barnabus related their stories of conversions among the Gentiles. "After they finished speaking,

James replied, 'Brothers, listen to me. Simeon has related how God first visited the Gentiles, to take from them a people for his name'" (vv. 13–14). After teaching that the prophets' word was now being fulfilled, he urged the assembly to refrain from placing this burden of Jewish identity on the Gentiles (vv. 12–21).

Now came the time for a decision:

> Then it seemed good to the apostles and the elders, with the whole church, to choose men from among them and send them to Antioch with Paul and Barnabus . . . with the following letter: "The brothers, both the apostles and the elders, to the brothers who are of the Gentiles, in Antioch and Syria and Cilicia, greetings. Since we have heard that some persons have gone out from us and troubled you with words, unsettling your minds, although we gave them no instructions, it has seemed good to us, having come to one accord, to choose men and send them to you with our beloved Barnabus and Paul. . . . We have therefore sent Judas and Silas, who themselves will tell you the same things by word of mouth. For it has seemed good to the Holy Spirit and to us to lay on you no greater burden than these requirements: that you abstain from what has been sacrificed to idols, and from blood, and from what has been strangled, and from sexual immorality. If you keep yourselves from these, you will do well. Farewell." (vv. 22–29)

We see that "the whole church" is represented by delegated officials, "apostles and elders," from the various local churches.

No longer are Gentile believers to be unsettled by self-appointed judges, because the whole church has spoken with one voice in this written decision. In fact, it is called a *dogma* (decision) in Greek. The Antioch church rejoiced in hearing the verdict of the assembly through the delegates. In the next chapter, we learn that Paul met Timothy and made him his associate. The son of a Jewish believer and a Greek father, Timothy was not circumcised, yet he accepted circumcision for the sake of the weaker conscience of Jewish Christians. "As they went on their way through the cities, they delivered to them for observance the decisions that had been reached by the apostles and elders who were in Jerusalem. So the churches were strengthened in the faith, and they increased in numbers daily" (Acts 16:4–5).

Given the fact that there had been considerable tension between James and Paul over this question, with Peter alternating between them, the unity arrived at during this council is remarkable. It is the principle of mutual accountability and admonition at work. The goal of church unity is consensus in doctrine and life, not the power of an apostle or even all of the apostles themselves. Even with the living apostles, the decision was reached in communion. The official practice of the church was not determined by a single apostle, nor even by the college of apostles, but by delegated representatives (apostles and elders). Furthermore, the decision was not delivered from a single church to the rest of the body, nor left to the judgment of each local church. Rather, it was reached by these representatives from all the churches in assembly together.

If this was true in the apostolic church, it is surely to be the case in the post-apostolic era. Paul said, "For no one can lay a foundation other than that which is laid, which is Jesus Christ" (1 Cor. 3:11). The apostles laid that foundation by their extraordinary calling and ministry, while the ordinary ministers who follow them will build on that foundation (1 Cor. 3:9–17).

The foundation is not still being laid. The ministers and elders like Timothy are called not to add to the deposit but to "guard the good deposit entrusted to you" (2 Tim. 1:14). "You then, my child, be strengthened by the grace that is in Christ Jesus, and what you have heard from me in the presence of many witnesses entrust to faithful men who will be able to teach others also" (2 Tim. 2:1–2). In the face of heresy and schism, the ordinary ministers and elders are to "contend for the faith that was once for all delivered to the saints" (Jude 3).

There are no apostles today. There are no successors of the apostles today. It was an extraordinary office for an extraordinary era, as the Holy Spirit delivered a normative canon for the church's faith and practice. The apostles were called directly by Jesus Christ and therefore had unique authority. Now, however, church officers are called by Christ through the voice of the church, with a ministerial authority under the Word. Paul may be strengthened in his work by recalling his immediate calling by Jesus on the road to Damascus—"an apostle— not from men nor through man, but through Jesus Christ and God the Father, who raised him from the dead" (Gal. 1:1)—but he encourages Timothy to recall his ordination day, "when the council of elders laid their hands on you" (1 Tim. 4:14). The ordinary ministry of Word and sacrament is *founded on* Christ and the apostles, but it is not a *continuation* of that extraordinary ministry.

The same Spirit who inspired the words of the prophets and apostles now illumines the hearts and minds of the pastors and teachers, as well as elders and deacons, to lead the church in its Great Commission. The

church is not constituted hierarchically (from above), nor democrati-
cally (from below), but covenantally (in a web of interdependence).

So the New Testament teaches a connectional model of church
government in which ministers and elders share leadership—even
during the ministry of the apostles. And it is connectional in the wider
fellowship of particular churches. At the congregational level, there
is a distinction between officers and the rest of the body, yet always
in service to the whole church. The officers are servants, not masters.
Christ alone is the head of the church, but he exercises his office as
Chief Shepherd through under-shepherds. Just as the congregation is
"many in one" and "one in many," the congregations are united in one
body in every city through their delegated officers (pastors and elders),
and these churches are united in one broader church spread across all
times and places, meeting in wider assemblies. These assemblies have
real authority from Christ and under Christ to determine the proper
interpretations of God's Word for faith and practice.

Connectionalism and Denominations

There were sects even in the apostolic church, people claiming to
be "of Apollos," "of Paul," "of Cephas [Peter]," and so forth. However, visible and institutional as well as organic unity was preserved
through the ministerial authority of pastors and elders in assembly.
So how can we preserve the New Testament's connectional principle
in a denominational and post-denominational world? For example, it
would be pretentious for me to imagine as a Reformed minister that
the general assemblies and synods of our denominations are equivalent
to the Council of Jerusalem in Acts 15 or even to the post-apostolic
ecumenical councils that our churches accept.

*First, a connectional principle cannot be maintained as perfectly in
this situation as it was in the apostolic era, but this must not lead to
apathy concerning it.* Trusting in the sovereign power of the Triune
God, we can hope that this situation will change, but the church's sanctification, like that of individual believers, is only partial in this age.
Nevertheless, we strain toward the prize. We cannot ignore Christ's
commands simply because we cannot keep them perfectly. Can denominations be proximate ways of realizing in concrete ways that
genuine catholicity of a representative and connectional relationship
between local churches, even though they are not exhaustive expressions of it? I believe that they can, insofar as they provide umbrellas

under which various congregations can share in the organic connections of mutual instruction and admonition that Christ wills for his
church. The tragic division of denominations today does not justify
further division into independent congregations.

*Second, I wonder if we can see our way toward greater agree-
ment on terms for different levels of union and communion between
denominations.* The Protestant Reformers were not separatists but
reformers. They were burning the midnight oil in conferences in the
hopes of reaching agreement on the divisive issues when the Roman
Catholic Church issued its fatal anathemas against justification by
grace alone, through faith alone, on the basis of Christ's merits alone.
Excommunicated and subject to the imperial ban, the churches of
the Reformation nevertheless believed that they were part of the continuing catholic church that was being reformed according to God's
Word. To separate from a true, visible church they regarded as an
act of schism.

However, today it is not only individual believers who shop from
church to church, but churches also seem to conclude that disunity is
tolerable merely on the basis of different histories, ethnic backgrounds,
and consumer profiles. We have seen that the New Testament speaks
of our unity in "one Lord, one faith, one baptism" (Eph. 4:5), a
common confession and a common hope, contending for "the faith
that was once for all delivered to the saints" (Jude 3). There can be
no unity where there is fundamental disagreement on these points.
Nevertheless, do such differences account for the 33,820 Protestant
denominations today? According to the *World Christian Encyclopedia*,
this number has grown from 8,196 in 1970, and an estimated 270–300
new denominations are born each year.[2] What does Christ's objective
status as King mean subjectively for the life and government of our
churches in this context?

Is there not a cause for encouraging churches and denominations to
pursue (1) organic, visible, connectional unity wherever there is a common confession of faith; (2) cooperation wherever possible (especially
in missions and mercy ministries); and (3) forums for mutual instruction and admonition on matters of church-dividing disagreements?

At the first level are particular churches as well as denominations
that share a common confession, even if they have different confessional documents. Umbrella bodies already exist, ostensibly to
facilitate greater cooperation between conservative denominations.
Can churches overcome the distinctive character of their historical

circumstances, ethnic hegemony, and indifferent traditions in service to Christ's explicit mandate for unity? It would seem that confessional Reformed churches were more ecumenical in the sixteenth and seventeenth centuries than they are today. For example, Calvin and other Reformed leaders were willing to compromise even on church government for the sake of a united witness. Reformed churches from a variety of nations in Europe came together at the Synod of Dort (1618–1619), joined by representatives from the Church of Scotland and the Church of England. Yet today, even denominations that confess the same faith and practice (including church government) remain divided.

At the second level, even where there is not yet agreement on a common confession on all points, could there be official interdenominational committees for studying areas of agreement as well as disagreement and creating a shared map for church planting and foreign missions? Of course, these mission endeavors would be entirely funded and directed by each denomination. Yet the concern would be to "preach the gospel, not where Christ has already been named, lest I build on someone else's foundation, but as it is written, 'Those who have never been told of him will see, and those who have never heard will understand'" (Rom. 15:20–21). The Great Commission, not market share, would be the objective. Within this belt of church relationships, participating bodies would recognize each other as legitimate churches, albeit with different confessions that reflected still-important disagreements. In addition, coordinated efforts in mercy ministries could also be established. Even if some member churches did not allow shared exchanges in their own official ministry, they could cooperate by coordinating their own ministries in recognition of the valid ministry of others.

Then finally, could there be a third concentric circle of engagement in which denominations participated in conversation and in mutual instruction and correction, even where mutual recognition as true churches, much less organic unity, seems unlikely to us at the present time?

The Westminster Confession reminds us that the church, like individual believers, remains simultaneously justified and sinful:

> This catholic church hath been sometimes more, sometimes less visible. And particular churches, which are members thereof, are more or less pure, according as the doctrine of the gospel is taught and embraced,

ordinances administered, and public worship performed more or less purely in them. The purest churches under heaven are subject both to mixture and error; and some have so degenerated as to become no churches of Christ, but synagogues of Satan. Nevertheless, there shall be always a church on earth, to worship God according to his will.[3]

The descriptions "sometimes more, sometimes less visible" and "more or less pure" underscore the importance of discernment.

Of course, there are challenges to pursuing these various levels of interdenominational engagement. In confessional (Reformed and Lutheran) Protestant churches, genuine differences have grown into caricatures. Similar to the hardening of arteries that followed the schism between East and West in the eleventh century, interconfessional divisions between the churches of the Reformation rely as much on mistrust and misunderstanding as they do on serious and remaining differences. Even among confessional denominations *within the same tradition*, the commitment to visible church unity seems less important than in any previous period. Denominations become brands, like Pepsi and Coke, vying for their market share. Or they become custodians of a dead tradition, clinging to the *heroes* of the past more than the *faith* that animated them in their generation. Ecumenical apathy is an act of collective disobedience to Christ's commands, as wrong as any other act of making peace with our personal sins over against the call to sanctification. Denominations remain valid, but denominationalism is a form of collective narcissism.

Often this lack of ecumenical vision in confessional circles is influenced by the downplaying of the visible church in broader evangelicalism. While encouraging grassroots ecumenism among Christians in different traditions, evangelicalism is a movement, not a church. It is identified visibly not by a single leader like the pope (despite George Marsden's famous definition of an evangelical as "anyone who likes Billy Graham"). Furthermore, many of today's evangelicals exhausted themselves in disappointment and fatigue in mainline denominations that seemed committed to self-destruction. As the visible church-as-institution has succumbed to bureaucracies that compromise genuine faith and practice, it is no wonder that it has lost its credibility. Therefore, all of this talk about connectional unity and ecumenical conversations sounds like a waste of time to many. Besides, who would represent "the evangelical church" in consultations with various denominations? Once more, evangelicals pour themselves into parachurch agencies for grassroots cooperation, but what if this enormous vitality were invested in the greater unity of the visible church?

It's not that I think that the goal of evangelical reunion is impossible as much as I think it vacuous. Jesus Christ did not found a political action committee, a spiritual formation center, a website, or a circle of friends. He promised that he would be with his *church* to the very end, wherever the Word is preached and the sacraments are administered. I think I know what it would look like if there were a merger of Baptists and Pentecostals or of Lutherans and Anglicans, but it's hard to imagine what it would mean for evangelicalism to be united in anything like concrete terms. Ecumenism needs churches, not parachurch networks and famous leaders.

Denominations matter because churches matter. By themselves, denominations are merely organizational umbrellas for the connectional unity between churches to flourish and for churches to help each other fulfill the Great Commission. To the extent that they facilitate this mission and strategic plan of our Lord, they are useful. To the extent that they become bureaucratic enclaves of pride and introspection, they are obstacles. Denominations may come and go, but the parts of Christ's body that they feed and encourage—that is, the actual churches—form the indispensable organism that is created by and fulfills the Great Commission.

Church and Parachurch

If evangelicalism is largely a network of *parachurch* agencies and Christ entrusted the Great Commission to his *church*, is there no place for the former? I have quoted Dallas Willard's insightful comment that "Discipleship on the theological right has come to mean preparation for soul winning, under the direction of parachurch efforts that had discipleship farmed out to them because the local church really wasn't doing it."[4]

This is a stinging indictment of the church. In one sense, it is on target. In every age, the church is tempted toward either energetic mission creep (distraction) or lazy self-satisfaction (survivalism). For many different reasons, the church can take its eye off of the ball and fail miserably. Yet the answer is not to siphon away the energies of sound and mission-minded believers from the church and pump them into parachurch ministries. Rather, the answer is to *reform the churches*.

At the same time, I'm convinced that there is still an important place for parachurch efforts. The prefix *para* means "alongside." When groups of Christians come alongside the church to form publishing houses, schools, social agencies, and other voluntary organizations, they can be enormously helpful resource-generating engines. The Rafiki Foundation (www.rafiki-foundation.org) has created numerous orphan villages across Africa. Partnering with local churches, Rafiki provides infrastructure (including housing), job training, and medical treatment (especially targeting HIV/AIDS). Churches are neither commissioned nor equipped to tackle these challenges, but Christians have come together to meet essential physical needs. These are the sorts of endeavors, coming alongside the church, that express Christ's love in word and deed.

The same can be said of colleges, seminaries, and organizations that promote the work of the church without replacing it. Although I am a minister at my local church and serve on denominational committees, most of my time is spent as a full-time professor at an independent seminary that prepares graduates for various denominations. I also lead an organization with a broadcast called *The White Horse Inn* as well as a magazine, *Modern Reformation*. I write books like this one for parachurch publishers and speak at parachurch conferences. In all of these activities, I am responsible to my church. Nevertheless, none of these organizations claims to be doing the work of the church. There is an important place for preparing ministers to participate in the Great Commission and helping people more generally to understand it. Yet assisting is different from actually executing this commission.

By providing support systems, parachurch agencies can help churches to stay focused on execution, but they transgress their limits when they assume the role that Christ entrusted to his church. They are not authorized to make disciples. They have no commission to proclaim the Word, to administer baptism or the Lord's Supper, to determine faith and practice, or to exercise spiritual discipline. Whatever they do must be in service to this ministry of the church rather than as a substitute parent.

Christians are called to do many things that the church is not called to do. The place where believers are *made* salt and light is wherever the Word is preached and the sacraments are administered, but the primary place where believers *are* salt and light is the world. Some believers are called to offices in the church, but most are called to offices in the world. We take up that subject in the next chapter.

8

The Great Commission and the Great Commandment

Evangelism and Social Justice

A while back, I asked the general secretary of the World Council of Churches if his organization still holds to its old slogan, "Doctrine divides; service unites." Chuckling, he said, "Good grief, no." He went on to relate that the group has learned over the decades that *service* divides. Some think capitalism is the way forward, while others insist on socialism. The pie cuts a thousand ways. "But then we've found that when we go back to talking about the Nicene Creed or some such thing, there is at least a sense of people coming back into the room and sitting down with each other to talk again." It's worth mentioning that the WCC emerged out of an evangelical missionary conference in 1910 and reminds us that it is usually in the name of mission that we become distracted from the message and mission of Christ.

In a recent issue of *Christianity Today*, Fuller Seminary president Richard Mouw relates the story of his article submission to the flagship evangelical magazine, then under the leadership of Carl Henry.[1] Henry himself had challenged evangelicals to engage with social concerns in his book *The Uneasy Conscience of Modern Fundamentalism* (published in 1947). However, he told the young graduate student that he needed to tweak some of the arguments in his article.

Though grateful that Henry was considering the article, Mouw recalls, "I was also troubled by the change he was proposing. This was a period in my life when I had often felt alienated from evangelicalism because of what I saw as its failure to properly address issues raised by the civil rights struggle and the war in Southeast Asia. As a corrective, I wanted the church, *as church*, to acknowledge its obligation to speak to such matters."[2]

Henry wouldn't budge. Where Mouw insisted it was the *church's* duty to address these issues directly, Henry wanted him to say it was the *Christian's* duty. The church has a responsibility to proclaim God's Word, even with specific application, wherever it speaks. It has the authority from God to announce a final judgment of oppression, wanton violence, and injustice and to call all people (including Christians) to repentance and faith in Christ in the light of this ultimate day in court. However, "The institutional church," said Henry, "has no mandate, jurisdiction, or competence to endorse political legislation or military tactics or economic specifics in the name of Christ."[3]

Henry quoted Princeton University ethicist Paul Ramsey: "Identification of Christian social ethics with specific partisan proposals that clearly are not the only ones that may be characterized as Christian and as morally acceptable comes close to the original New Testament meaning of *heresy*."[4] At the same time, Henry argued that evangelicals are not only authorized but commanded to proclaim God's clear "No!" to excessive violence, racial injustice, and other serious moral crises. God's Word shapes the moral conscience of its hearers, but where it does not offer specific policy prescriptions, the church has no authority to speak.

Upon reflection, Mouw concludes, "Henry was right, and I was wrong." Drawing on his Reformed heritage, especially the legacy of Abraham Kuyper, Mouw points out that there is an important place for *Christians* thinking and working together to apply biblical teaching to such issues. However, the *church* must not exceed its mandate.

Today the mantra "deeds, not creeds," is likely to be heard as frequently from the quarters of evangelical Protestantism as it has been now for a century in mainline Protestantism. In part, this is an understandable reaction to an apparent lack of concern for *bodies*, and not only for human bodies but for the creation itself. If salvation is all about the soul's escape from the body and this earth will be destroyed (both ideas explicitly rejected in Scripture), what's the point of getting all worked up over social injustice? Bad creeds feed bad deeds: sins of omission as well as commission.

It is always incumbent on churches to be "teaching [disciples] to observe all that I have commanded you" (Matt. 28:20)—not just our favorite parts, but "the whole counsel of God" (Acts 20:27). As we become more aware of climate change and its attendant threats to our whole planet, it is theologically erroneous and spiritually irresponsible for churches to remain silent on God's command for stewardship. Anchored in the past work of God (creation) and his ever-vigilant providence, the church's hope is oriented toward the restoration of the whole creation (Rom. 8:20–25). Slavery and segregation in the US and apartheid in South Africa were justified morally and theologically by gross distortions of God's Word. It was when churches did what only they were authorized to do (that is, declare such exegesis to be heretical) that there was a widespread change in Christians doing what they were authorized to do as citizens: to work alongside non-Christians in dismantling the laws and social patterns that such preaching had helped to legitimize.

The church executes its commission—"teaching them to observe all that I have commanded you"—when it proclaims God's judgment on specific evils and teaches believers how to think and live differently as his disciples. However, when the church turns to policy prescription, it enters the realm of the properly coercive exercise of legal power. The spiritual sword of the Word and Spirit becomes confused with the temporal sword of state. Pontificating on matters beyond its expertise and authority, the church actually loses that considerable spiritual authority that it has to address the world in Christ's name as his official embassy. At one extreme is the view that Christians should not be interested in, much less participate in, the social and political process for the common good. At the other extreme is the view that this is the mission of the church. Historically, these positions are identified with Anabaptist and Roman Catholic traditions, respectively. At least in theory, the churches of the Reformation held that Christians are citizens of two kingdoms simultaneously—each kingdom being distinct yet intersecting in the life of every believer.

In my late teens, I was becoming enchanted not only with the doctrines of grace but with the wider vision of Reformed theology. I was amazed at the historical impact of Reformed Christianity on the rise of literacy, education, science, the arts, literature, and other fields. I devoured the late 1970s writings of Francis Schaeffer, who was just as concerned about racism (*True Spirituality*) and environmental stewardship (*Pollution and the Death of Man*) as he was about abortion and euthanasia. Salvation became a lot larger than "going to heaven after you die." I felt challenged and liberated by it all.

Years later, I took a course at the International Institute of Human Rights in Strasbourg, France, and spent late nights with people from various countries who recounted atrocities committed with the direct or indirect support of the United States. As I read liberation theologians, I resonated with their affirmation of creation and the redemption of bodies, not just souls. Yet the more I read, the more dissatisfied I became. While they saw that sin is not only private and personal behavior but public and systemic injustice, they seemed ironically to reduce sin to actions much as fundamentalists. What both seemed to miss is the fact that sin is first of all a *condition* and that it goes so deep that we cannot liberate ourselves from it—either individually or corporately. The interpretation of Scripture, drawing a one-to-one correspondence between Israel's liberation from Egypt and political revolution, seemed just as selective and self-serving. Their eschatology seemed overrealized: the kingdom of glory here now, being brought to completion by our efforts. They would make the kingdoms of this world the kingdom of Christ. But isn't that the sort of faulty exegesis that led to "Christendom" in the first place? Furthermore, trying to turn the kingdoms of this age into the kingdom of Christ often ends in self-righteous violence and disillusionment. Instead, we should participate, alongside non-Christians, in acheiving more modest—and less eschatologically ultimate—improvements in our common societies.

It is more difficult to distinguish our dual citizenship when we think that our own culture (or political party) is right—perhaps even "Christian" (or at least "Judeo-Christian"). For several decades, evangelicals seemed to be the Republican party at prayer. But now the movement risks merely changing its political affiliation, tying the gospel to a different political agenda. Christians have an obligation to active love and service to their neighbors, but this is different from the Great Commission that Christ has entrusted to the church's official ministry.

Through preaching and sacrament, God calls us out of the dance of death and seats us at the wedding feast with Abraham, Isaac, and Jacob. Turned in on ourselves, we are spin doctors. In our self-preoccupation, we either wallow in despair or exult in self-righteousness. Yet this Word calls us out of ourselves, out of our introspective navel-gazing, out of our despair and self-righteousness, and out of the circle of friends like us, to look up to God in faith and out to our neighbors in love. United to Christ by his Spirit, we are united to brothers and sisters we did not choose for ourselves. As Christ is the gift of the Father and the Spirit to us, he makes us gifts to each other. Through preaching, baptism, the Supper, and the spiritual care of elders, we are driven outside of ourselves: in faith toward Christ and in love toward our neighbor.

Yet the evidence that Christ's kingdom is present among us is not only restricted to the spiritual care that he provides as our prophet, priest, and king; it extends to the welfare that he exercises for our temporal needs as well. The heart of my challenge in this chapter is to recognize the distinction between the Great Commission and the Great Commandment without separating them. This argument works in concentric circles, from the work of the *church* in its mission of mercy to the work of *Christians* in their various vocations.

Mercy Ministries

Christ, through his apostles, instituted the office of deacon. This makes the care of temporal needs part of the Great Commission itself. Mercy ministries belong to the "everything" that Christ called his apostles to teach.

The Sermon on the Mount introduces a radically new ethic for the kingdom of God. The old covenant is fading away under Jesus's ministry; the new has come. It is not a revival of the Sinai covenant. Instead of driving out the enemies of God, this conquest will take the paradoxical form of suffering and loving prayer for and service toward persecutors. It establishes a new regime—not one that Christians impose on the regimes of this world but one that they begin to exhibit in the church as a colony of heaven.

In his parable of the great banquet, Jesus said, "When you give a dinner or a banquet, do not invite your friends or your brothers or your relatives or rich neighbors, lest they also invite you in return and you be repaid. But when you give a feast, invite the poor, the crippled, the lame, the blind, and you will be blessed, because they cannot repay you" (Luke 14:12–14). In other words, if you invite your friends and relatives to this holy feast, that's no different from any common meal. Common meals are fine. You can get together with your friends and relatives. We all know how to play the game of inviting over the boss or wealthy neighbors who can return the favor in one way or another. But at this holy banquet of the kingdom, you are to go *looking for* the poor and the weak as your guest—"and you will be blessed, *because they cannot repay you.*" Church is a weird place.

Isn't this exactly the way it works with all of us who come to the feast, eating and drinking with God together? It is interesting that Paul says that "at the right time Christ died for the ungodly" (Rom. 5:6). What's "the right time"? It is "while we were still weak," "while we were still sinners," "while we were enemies" (Rom. 5:6, 8, 10). God gave his Son at just the right moment: when we were in no position to repay him. This unspeakable goodness is now meant to propel us to look beyond the ordinary rules of social behavior and to pursue actively the poor, the weak, and the outcast. Often we join a church precisely because it is made up of people who are like us—or people we would like to be like. Yet the kingdom has different priorities. It is not simply that we have people with needs in our churches and should look out for them, but that we should be reaching out to those who are *not* a part of our circle of friends, who are *not* people with whom we feel comfortable, who do *not* share our cultural tastes or socioeconomic position, and who are in *no* position to scratch our back if we scratch theirs.

In this communion of saints, we are not in a debt economy but in a gift economy. We are not owners but heirs. A Christian owner of a bank is obligated to demand that loans be paid, but believers do not call in personal loans on each other. A Christian police officer may have to use force to apprehend a criminal, but a believer must endure suffering in the face of persecution for his or her faith. The Triune God is the giver of all good gifts, and when he brings us into the fellowship of that exchange of gifts between the Father, Son, and Spirit, we find ourselves filled and overflowing. In this economy, as Calvin pointed out, wealthier believers need the poorer saints just as much as the reverse. Consistent with the logic of grace, we all get what we need precisely in the process of giving ourselves away. Because God has time for us, we have time for each other. Because we have been richly blessed with every provision, we bless each other.

This is not just a good idea but a concrete reality in the world whose details Christ has included in his constitution for the new covenant. Everything that Christ commanded for the life of his church is included in the New Testament. He cares not only for the invisible church but also for its visibility. The church is not just a spiritual creation; it is a real, historical, tangible institution. It is created and sustained through the spoken Word, water, bread, and wine. And it is not just souls that are saved but bodies as well. If we will be raised together in glory on the last day bodily, then we are obligated to care for each other as whole persons here and now.

Instituting the Office of Deacon

The office of deacon is as essential to the proper discipline of the church as the office of minister or elder. Jesus Christ is not only our *prophet*, proclaiming his Word through preachers, and our *king*, ruling us through elders; he is also our *priest* who not only intercedes for us but also cares for our physical needs through deacons. Jesus calls the church not only to save souls, but to care for bodies.[5]

The institution of the diaconate is reported in Acts 6:

> Now in these days when the disciples were increasing in number, a complaint by the Hellenists arose against the Hebrews because their widows were being neglected in the daily distribution. And the twelve summoned the full number of the disciples and said, "It is not right that we should give up preaching the word of God to serve tables. Therefore, brothers, pick out from among you seven men of good repute, full of the Spirit and of wisdom, whom we will appoint to this duty. But we will devote ourselves to prayer and to the ministry of the word." (vv. 1–4)

Stephen and several others were chosen. "These they set before the apostles, and they prayed and laid their hands on them" (v. 6). In ordinations like this, we hear the echo of Jesus's words to the apostles as he gave them the keys of the kingdom: "Again I say to you, if two of you agree on earth about anything they ask, it will be done for them by my Father in heaven" (Matt. 18:19). They operated with Christ's power of attorney, as his ambassadors.

As it turned out, the temporal needs of the believers were better served by deacons, and the apostles were able to continue their embassy undistracted. "And the word of God continued to increase, and the number of disciples multiplied greatly in Jerusalem, and a great many of the priests became obedient to the faith" (Acts 6:7). The ministry of word and sacrament is distinct from the ministry of mercy to temporal needs. If they were the same, then Peter and the other apostles would not have seen "waiting on tables" as a distraction from their ministry. Yet they saw this care for temporal needs as so integral to the life of the church that a separate office was established for it.

The qualifications for deacons are clearly explained in 1 Timothy 3. In addition to being of upstanding character, "They must hold the mystery of the faith with a clear conscience. And let them also be tested first; then let them serve as deacons if they prove themselves blameless" (vv. 9–10). Paul even greets the Philippian church, "To all the saints in Christ Jesus who are at Philippi, with the overseers and deacons" (Phil. 1:1).

The Collection for the Saints: An Apostle's Obsession

Paul was obsessed with the gospel—and with getting it to the Gentiles, which is why he was so ambitious to make it all the way to Rome before he died. However, there is something else with which he seemed almost obsessed, something that I'd missed for many years while reading his epistles. It was a collection from all of the mostly Gentile churches to take back to the struggling believers in Jerusalem. We can easily miss this repeated reference along with all of the incidental greetings and instructions to particular people at the end of his epistles, but it was heavy on Paul's heart. And as we will see, it was inextricably linked to (though not identical with) his ministry of the gospel.

I will start with Paul's mention of this collection in 1 Corinthians. Throughout this letter, Paul has exhorted the Corinthians to grow up. However, the group to which he is writing is not a biker club, a veterans' association, or even a family. It is not a natural community at all but an outpost of Christ's heavenly kingdom in this present evil age. It is united not by family ties, by cultural affinities, or even by personal choice but by God's electing, redeeming, justifying, and sanctifying grace.

Divided into factions over leadership personalities and such matters as spiritual gifts and eating meat that had been used in pagan ceremonies, this was a community in disarray. Similar to the complaint of the writer to the Hebrews, Paul says that by now they should be teachers, but instead they are themselves acting like unspiritual "infants in Christ" (3:1). Besides engaging in sectarianism and ungodly contention, they had even used the Lord's Supper and spiritual gifts as an occasion for their one-upmanship instead of for the building up of the body in Christ. Instead of a choir, the church had become a stage for virtuoso performances: an ecclesiastical version of *American Idol*. Instead of being a beachhead for the Spirit's

creation of a colony of the heavenly city, the Lord's Table had become
a parody of Holy Communion. Yet in all of this, the recipients of
these stern rebukes remain the subjects identified in the beginning
as "the church of God that is in Corinth, . . . those sanctified in
Christ Jesus" (1:2).

After proclaiming the gospel indicative once again ("Christ and
him crucified"), Paul issues his imperatives to be what they are in
Christ. Basically, 1 Corinthians is a call to the reform of the church
in terms of its visible marks: faithful preaching of the gospel (chaps.
1–2); proper administration of the sacraments, especially the Supper
(chaps. 10–11); and discipline in the worship and life of the church
so that it functions as a body (chaps. 5–7; 12–14).

It is within this context that Paul speaks of a project that was near
and dear to his heart: a collection for the saints in Jerusalem:

> Now concerning the collection for the saints: as I directed the churches
> of Galatia, so you also are to do. On the first day of every week, each of
> you is to put something aside and store it up, as he may prosper, so that
> there will be no collecting when I come. And when I arrive, I will send
> those whom you accredit by letter to carry your gift to Jerusalem. If it
> seems advisable that I should go also, they will accompany me. (16:1–4)

At first this may seem like a passing remark in the signing-off section
of Paul's epistles. But it is actually more than that.

First, the collection was occasioned by a desperate need. Political
agitation by various groups of Jewish zealots had led to another
Roman crackdown, and this included what amounted to a block-
ade of basic necessities to Jerusalem. Many died of starvation. It
was during this time (the mid-40s) that James wrote his epistle,
addressing the social conflict in the Jerusalem church between the
rich and the poor and calling believers to be doers and not merely
hearers of the word.

Second, the collection was especially formal. It wasn't just another
collection taken "on the first day of the week," as Christians have been
taking collections in the public service ever since. Paul assumes some
general familiarity with this project: "Now concerning the collection
for the saints" (v. 1), which he has only mentioned here for the first
time in this letter.

Third, the collection was catholic (universal). It was not merely
the initiative of one local congregation: "as I directed the churches

of Galatia, so you also are to do" (v. 1). It is an apostolic injunction
to be received and obeyed by all of the churches.

Fourth, although all churches are to participate, each collection was
local, to be taken up each Lord's Day in every church. No last-minute
fund drive when Paul comes! The believers in Corinth are called to
make this collection part of their weekly worship service. Thus, it isn't
a top-down enterprise, but it is a movement of charity from all local
assemblies to another local assembly. This expresses genuine catholicity. Although the injunction is apostolic, the administration is to be
determined by each church's officers (most likely the deacons). "And
when I arrive, I will send those whom you accredit by letter to carry
your gift to Jerusalem" (v. 3). Paul respects the integrity of this local
church and its officers. As an apostle, *he* will send the officers (most
likely deacons) with the gift to Jerusalem, but he will send "those
whom you accredit by letter." He even adds, "*If it seems advisable
that I should go also, they will accompany me*" (v. 4, emphasis added).
Paul really wanted to be there for the giving of the grand collection,
but he cedes that personal right to the officers of that church.

Paul refers to this collection also in Romans 15:

> I myself am satisfied about you, my brothers and sisters, that you
> yourselves are full of goodness, filled with all knowledge and able to
> instruct one another. But on some points I have written to you very
> boldly by way of reminder, because of the grace given me by God to be
> a minister of Christ Jesus to the Gentiles in the priestly service of the
> gospel of God, so that the offering of the Gentiles may be acceptable,
> sanctified by the Holy Spirit. In Christ Jesus, then, I have reason to be
> proud of my work for God. For I will not speak of anything except
> what Christ has accomplished through me to bring the Gentiles to
> obedience—by word and deed, by the power of signs and wonders,
> by the power of the Spirit of God—so that from Jerusalem and all
> the way around to Illyricum I have fulfilled the ministry of the gospel
> of Christ; and thus I make it my ambition to preach the gospel, not
> where Christ has already been named, lest I build on someone else's
> foundation. (vv. 14–20)

But wait a minute! This is not talking about taking an offering for the
saints in need. Paul is talking here about his calling to "the priestly
service of the gospel of God," making the *Gentiles* an acceptable
offering to God.

True, but let's read on:

This is the reason why I have so often been hindered from coming to you. . . . At present, however, I am going to Jerusalem bringing aid to the saints. For Macedonia and Achaia have been pleased to make some contribution for the poor among the saints at Jerusalem. They were pleased to do it, and indeed they owe it to them. For if the Gentiles have come to share in their spiritual blessings, they ought also to be of service to them in material blessings. When therefore I have completed this and have delivered to them what has been collected, I will leave for Spain by way of you. I know that when I come to you I will come in the fullness of the blessings of Christ. (vv. 22, 25–29)

Paul concludes by asking for prayer "that I may be delivered from the unbelievers in Judea, and that my service for Jerusalem may be acceptable to the saints, so that by God's will I may come to you with joy and be refreshed in your company. May the God of peace be with you all. Amen" (vv. 31–33).

Why is this collection so central to Paul's apostolic mission? In Romans, it is a concrete expression of the goal of Paul's entire ministry. His priestly ministry of offering up the Gentiles as a sacrifice—not of atonement, but of thanksgiving—to God the Father, in the Son, and through the Spirit is expressed in tangible, material, and temporal terms through this offering for Jewish believers. Jerusalem is where it all happened; "salvation is from the Jews." The Great Commission goes out from Jerusalem to Judea and Samaria to the uttermost ends of the earth. So it is only proper that the spiritual gift that goes out to the Gentiles comes back to the Jewish saints in material blessing.

Central to Paul's gospel is that in Christ the wall of partition between Jew and Gentile has been removed. And now the collection expresses that truth. The drama leads to doctrine, doxology, and discipleship. "Put your money where your mouth is," as they say. Paul seems to imply in Romans 15:14–15 that the Roman Christians, though "filled with all knowledge and able to instruct one another," needed a strong admonition to care for the saints.

And this was probably as much of a test of discipleship for the Jewish believers as it was for the Gentiles. Accepting charity was an embarrassment in the ancient world even more than today, but Jews had been especially careful to avoid the charity of their Roman occupiers. There would have been members of the Jerusalem church who were demanding that Gentile converts adopt Jewish circumcision and dietary laws. Then in walks Paul, the former persecutor of that very Jerusalem church, now an apostle to the Gentiles, flanked by representatives (probably deacons) from far-flung Gentile churches, carrying a treasure to lay at the feet of suffering brothers and sisters. Nothing drives home the gospel and challenges spiritual arrogance more than being destitute—even physically—and depending on the kindness of "foreigners." Yet in this very act, the Jewish believers were bound more deeply to their Gentile co-heirs than they were to their Jewish neighbors. They were no longer strangers and aliens.

So how did the Corinthians do when Paul finally came around for this collection? We find out in his second letter to the church (2 Cor. 8:1–9:15). Paul provokes the Corinthians to jealousy by recounting the generosity of the Macedonian churches in spite of their poverty: "We want you to know, brothers, about the grace of God that has been given among the churches of Macedonia, for in a severe test of affliction, their abundance of joy and their extreme poverty have overflowed in a wealth of generosity on their part" (8:1–2). They even were "begging us earnestly for the favor of taking part in the relief of the saints. . . . Accordingly, we urged Titus that as he had started, so he should complete among you this act of grace" (8:4, 6).

So Paul clearly saw this collection as connected to the gospel itself. It is not the gospel but the reasonable response to it. They must stop thinking of this collection as a tax—see it not as "an exaction" but "as a willing gift" (9:5). The Corinthians had excelled in knowledge; now it was time for them to excel in generosity (8:7–8). "For you know the grace of our Lord Jesus Christ, that though he was rich, yet for your sake he became poor, so that you by his poverty might become rich" (8:9). He reminds them that they started this project of collecting funds in Corinth a year ago, and he urges them now to finally complete it. Just as we build up each other through the diversity of our spiritual gifts, so also through the diversity of our material means. The poor need the rich, and the rich also need the abundance of gifts that the poorer members bring to the body (8:12–15).

The first Christians were not an early communist society. Each person gave *freely*, distributing goods and services to any who had need. Yet they gave freely precisely because the laws and values governing society are not ultimate and the church's practice was based on its view that the earth is the Lord's, we are the Lord's, and therefore we share all things together in common (Acts 2:44–45). No one was expected to sell his or her home and give the money to the common fund, though some did. In fact, believers often met in private homes. There is not even a word about making this practice public policy for the Roman

Empire. Nevertheless, generosity is to characterize the communion of saints. As all that the Father has belongs to the Son and the Spirit (and vice versa), all that each believer has belongs to the whole body.

We often seem more eager to say that the early Christians weren't communists than we are to say what these texts clearly affirm: namely, that in a real sense, giving to the needs of the poor among us is not charity but justice—not the justice that is appropriate for the kingdoms of this age, but the justice that can only be a foretaste of the age to come. The saints shared Christ in common through baptism, the apostles' teaching, the breaking of bread, and the prayers, so why not everything else? These are the people with whom we are on pilgrimage together throughout our lives to the Holy City. They are our true brothers and sisters, mothers and fathers. Although the focus was on the care of the saints, there was an expression of common living and fellowship in Christ that spilled over into every area of their lives together.

According to the New Testament, making and serving disciples involves ministering to the material needs of believers. This extends not only to members of the local congregation but also to the wider communion of churches. Just as the pastors and elders are representatives from local to broader assemblies, so too are deacons in their collecting, overseeing, and dispensing the goods and services of Christ's body to those members in need.

I wonder if we take this seriously enough today. It's estimated that 200 million Christians are under the threat of arrest, imprisonment, mutilation, and death right now. (Not to downplay early church persecution, but the highest scholarly estimates place the total martyrdoms under the Roman emperors at one hundred thousand, while a couple million Christians have been martyred in recent years alone.) Are our resources being pooled sufficiently, like Paul's collection, to serve as a witness to the power of the gospel? Are we really caring for the household of God? Are families of martyrs in Nigeria being assisted by gifts from churches in New England? What if every local church in North America formed a concrete relationship with a particular local church somewhere in a depressed area—either in our own country or in another part of the world? Or with a struggling church in a place where victims of persecution stand in dire need of material supplies? What if local churches "adopted" churches destroyed in a natural disaster, helping them to rebuild their meeting place and their lives?

Often today, deacons are treated as "elders in waiting." We're not always sure what they do. Sure, they clean up after coffee time, take offerings, and set up chairs, but the office seems to have lost something of its dignity.

I have had the pleasure of serving in churches where some of the deacons were successful in business. They dispense funds generously where needed, but they also give generously of their time and talents in counseling members who have lost their job or who need a plan for getting out of debt. Although most would make fine elders, I am delighted when they find their niche in the diaconate and don't want to leave it. They know that caring for the temporal welfare of Christ's flock is just as important as the spiritual care of pastors and elders. Just as there is no hierarchy of the soul over the body, there is no hierarchy of pastors and elders over the deacons. The priests are equal to the prophets and kings. They just do different things.

Historians observe that Geneva became a model for other cities during the Reformation, with former monks and nuns serving in a reactivated diaconate. Much to the chagrin of many Geneva elites, the city swelled with refugees fleeing religious persecution. The diaconate oversaw and administered a vast network of services. Caring for fellow saints is the work of the church; it is our burden of common fellowship in Christ, not a burden that we place merely on our fellow citizens.

Mercy Ministries and Social Justice

The more difficult question we face today is whether mercy ministries are limited to the saints or are to be coupled with evangelism as an essential outreach to unbelievers. Paul says, "So then, as we have opportunity, let us do good to everyone, and especially to those who are of the household of faith" (Gal. 6:10). Hebrews 13 exhorts, "Let brotherly love continue. Do not neglect to show hospitality to strangers, for thereby some have entertained angels unawares. . . . Do not neglect to do good and to share what you have, for such sacrifices are pleasing to God" (vv. 1–2, 16). Entertaining angels unawares is probably a reference to Abram's unwitting hospitality to strangers who were actually angels sent to save him and his family from the destruction of Sodom. In any case, the reference to strangers here, like the prisoners mentioned in verse 3, is most likely to believers who were showing up on doorsteps of fellow saints seeking a hiding place from the authorities.

Jesus had already prepared his disciples for this scenario. One place is Matthew 24–25, where he speaks of what will happen in between his ascension and return in glory. There will be persecution. Believers in Christ will be cast out of the synagogues, their own relatives will hand them over to the authorities, and there will be wars and rumors of wars, until the gospel is preached to every nation. And then Jesus speaks of the last judgment when he separates the sheep from the goats:

> Then the King will say to those on his right, "Come, you who are blessed by my Father, inherit the kingdom prepared for you from the foundation of the world. For I was hungry and you gave me food, I was thirsty and you gave me drink, I was a stranger and you welcomed me, I was naked and you clothed me, I was sick and you visited me, I was in prison and you came to me." (Matt. 25:34–36)

What is especially striking is that the righteous answer, "'Lord, when did we see you hungry and feed you, or thirsty and give you drink?' . . . And the King will answer them, 'Truly, I say to you, as you did it to one of the least of *these my brothers*, you did it to me'" (vv. 37, 40, emphasis added). Meanwhile, the reverse happens in the case of the goats: Jesus indicts them for turning their back on the saints—and therefore on him—while they protest the charge and defend their righteousness (vv. 41–45).

The bond between the Head and his body is so inextricable that when the ascended Jesus appeared to Saul on the Damascus road, he asked, "'Saul, Saul, why are you persecuting *me*?' And he said, 'Who are you, Lord?' And he said, 'I am Jesus, *whom you are persecuting*'" (Acts 9:4–5, emphasis added). Paul would never forget—and only grow in his understanding of—the significance of this bond of union between Christ and his church.

In my view, therefore, none of the principal passages usually adduced actually supports the emphasis on social action (i.e., service ministries to the civil community) as an element of the Great Commission.

The Great Commandment and the Great Commission

Just at this point, some readers will understandably object: "Are you saying that the church has no commission to extend Christ's love to non-Christians through charitable work?" First, I don't believe that there is any command forbidding the church to give to the needs of non-Christians. Yet if regular, sacrificial giving is required of all believers (as I believe it is), then churches have to be careful about where they disburse these gifts beyond Christ's explicit institution.

Churches are binding the consciences of believers by Christ's authority whenever they preach, so they had better be certain that they are preaching God's Word and not their own doctrines and commands. The same is true of giving. Millions of evangelical Christians in mainline Protestant denominations who gave generously and regularly in obedience to Christ's command and love for their neighbors have had to watch their regular offerings go in part to support political revolutions all over the world. The same thing can happen in more conservative churches, as support is sent for causes with which particular members may in good conscience disagree.

In many denominations, quotas are expected to be sent from each local church for the support of church-related colleges, hospitals, relief organizations, and myriad other programs. Doubtless, we need these kinds of social institutions, but the church has no commission from Christ to own and to operate them. The church has all of the authority in heaven and on earth to proclaim God's law and gospel—and to require its members to support the work that Christ has authorized. However, it is a misuse of church power to force consciences, against their will, to give to concerns that cannot be drawn as a good and necessary conclusion from Scripture.

I am not suggesting that the church should only extend diaconal services to its professing members or that a church cannot support relief efforts in the aftermath of a natural disaster. Obviously, deacons have to use their own discretion on the ground. What I am suggesting is that there are myriad causes that are good, bad, and indifferent for which the church has no special competence or commission. Why do we think that if something is worthwhile for a Christian (or group of Christians) to invest in, it has to be done by the church as an official activity? Christians supporting a worldwide relief organization will probably be much more effective than a church that is trying to become one. Christians with a background in law, business, economics, health, and science will be in a much better position than a pastor or group of church leaders to integrate their faith with social questions of the day.

Abraham Kuyper was, as they say, a man of many parts. Besides being a pastor and theologian, he founded a major newspaper and a university, and in 1901 he became prime minister of the Netherlands. Nevertheless, he advocated the independence of the various spheres. Not only is the state not over the church, the church is not over the state, or the arts, or science, or other cultural fields. Furthermore, he distinguished between the church as an *organization* entrusted with the means of grace and the church as an *organism* consisting of believers who were salt and light in these various spheres. It is these spheres and this distinction between the church as place and the church as people that become confused in contemporary talk about the church transforming society.

The *Great Commandment* is different from the *Great Commission*, but Christians are responsible to both. A young lawyer asked Jesus, "Teacher, which is the great commandment in the Law?" (Matt. 22:36). Jesus replied, "You shall love the Lord your God with all your heart and with all your soul and with all your mind. This is the great and first commandment. And a second is like it: You shall love your neighbor as yourself. On these two commandments depend all the Law and the Prophets" (Matt. 22:37–40). Jesus was simply repeating Moses (Lev. 19:18; Deut. 6:5). The second commandment is like the first because love of God is inextricable from love of neighbor.

We have seen a tendency to confuse these mandates, as if the Great Commandment were the Great Commission and good works were the gospel. There is nothing in the Great Commission about transforming culture. However, the Great Commandment calls every person— believer and unbeliever alike—to works of love and service in our daily lives. If some confuse these mandates, others separate them, as if our high calling in Christ had no connection with responsible stewardship and citizenship in the world.

Christians and non-Christians alike are obligated to the same moral law that requires personal and social justice—even love—between every person. Nevertheless, like the Beatitudes that precede it, the Sermon on the Mount is the new-covenant law of love that is given specifically to the fellowship of saints, not a blueprint for the wider society. Paul's commands in 1 Corinthians are consistent with this sermon of our Lord: Christians are not to sue each other in secular courts, but are to settle disputes in church courts. Yet there is no evidence that Christians were not involved in secular courts, either as litigants or as officers. The New Testament forbids any use of force in the Great Commission, yet Roman soldiers—even high officers— repent and believe in Christ without any mention of their having to surrender their secular vocation (Luke 7:9; Acts 10:1–48).

Confusing These Mandates

If we *confuse* these mandates, then the Great Commission becomes the Great Society: another try at "Christendom." The church is no longer able to reach out to the world effectively with the gospel because it is not itself properly evangelized. Instead of being the resalinization plant for the people of God who are then scattered into the world throughout the week, where they can actually serve non-Christians, the church itself loses its distinctive ministry and the salt loses its savor. At the same time, loving our neighbor easily becomes a pretense for evangelism instead of being the rightful claim of an image-bearer of God (believer or unbeliever) on my time, energy, and support. It's easy in this line of thinking either to replace evangelism with social work or to use the latter merely as a carrot for conversion. Again, this not only turns the gospel ("evangel") into our works; it assumes that loving and serving our neighbor has to be justified on the basis of the Great Commission.

Because everyone is created in God's image and knows God's moral law (even if it is suppressed in unrighteousness), a believer can work with non-Christians for the common good of society. Special revelation not only gives us the gospel; it gives us the proper spectacles through which to view the law. Nevertheless, we can appeal to the law of God that rings in the consciences of our neighbors whether or not they recognize it as such. Although unbelievers "by their unrighteousness suppress the truth" (Rom. 1:18), they cannot suppress everything at the same time. Furthermore, Christians are often wrong. Regeneration does not make us more intelligent or skilled in cultural affairs; in fact, non-Christians have often corrected Christians in helpful and responsible ways. We can reach a working consensus with non-Christians on a variety of moral, social, and political issues that face us.[6] Non-Christians as well as believers have contributed to the rise of religious liberties in the modern age, scientific advances, just laws, and world relief. As a divinely commissioned institution, the church does not pursue its mandate through marches, secular courts, and legislative assemblies. However, Christians alongside non-Christians pursue their mandate (loving neighbors) through these and all sorts of other cultural activities.

However, when we confuse the Great Commission with the Great Commandment, three tragedies inevitably follow. First, we confuse the gospel with the law. Second, we now give the impression that we are trying to legislate and enforce the gospel rather than defend the civil rights and good of our neighbors. Third, instead of appealing to the general revelation that extends to believer and unbeliever alike, we end up dividing not only the culture but the church along political and ideological lines.

On paper, black and white Protestants in the United States share similar beliefs. However, African-American and suburban white churches have each become "home base" for a particular political and social agenda more than outposts of Christ's kingdom in the world. Generally speaking, white suburban churches and black urban churches have become less known for their forthright proclamation of Christ than for being predictable organs for the Republican and Democratic parties. The influence that all of these millions of Christians might have, shaken out into their communities as they rub shoulders with non-Christians, is undermined by their determination to be a "voting bloc." Every politician knows that he or she always has a spot in the pulpit come election time.

Fulfilling Both Mandates

What I am arguing for here is radically different from the social gospel of the left and the right today. For Charles Finney and the Second Great Awakening generally, the church was conceived as a society of moral transformers. With no distinction between the church as organization and as organism, Finney replaced the church's official ministry with a series of specific commands that are not found anywhere in Scripture and were to be made public policy through legislation and enforcement. The Great Commission was to provoke people through "excitements sufficient to induce repentance" and then to bring moral and social righteousness to the nation. At the end of the nineteenth century, evangelist D. L. Moody adopted a more pessimistic view of social change, concluding that Christians should try to save as many souls as possible on a sinking ship.

We are trapped between these two extremes today: a social gospel (on the left and the right) that confuses the Great Commission with the Great Commandment and a dualism that sees no connection between the church's calling and the Christian's calling in the world.

As Christ's official embassy, the church is authorized to announce to the whole world the claims of God's moral law and the gospel of grace. However, it has no authority to determine policies that are negotiated and enforced through the properly coercive arm of civil government. Yet Christians (like non-Christian) citizens are called to be engaged in this political process. Where Scripture does not bind their conscience, the church cannot do so. In their common vocations, citizenship, and service, Christians are free to exercise their own wisdom. Christians are not free to withhold their love from their neighbors, separating themselves into pious enclaves that avoid the claims of citizenship. However, this neighbor-love is not the gospel; it is the law that obliges Christian and non-Christian alike.

This view contradicts the conclusions of social gospel voices on both sides of the aisle. It requires that people defend their views in the arena of public opinion. It requires that we argue for certain policies not because they are Christian but because they are for the common good that Christians and non-Christians must adjudicate as citizens, legislators, judges, and elected officials.

The rhetoric on the evangelical left and right in politics today strikes me as simplistic both in interpreting Scripture and in applying it to public policy. Just as the religious right lifts Old Testament passages out of their redemptive-historical context for patriotic celebrations, moral crusades, and military campaigns, the religious left does the same with the prophets and Jesus. Both approaches seem to assume that these passages offer timeless truths that apply to all people and nations everywhere at all times. Sensitivity to the complexity of the different covenants and administrations must not get in the way of a really useful proof text!

Of course, in these passages God teaches us about his intrinsic character and care for victims of violence and injustice. Nevertheless, the political policies were explicitly included by God in the *book of the covenant*. Which covenant? The covenant that Israel swore at Mount Sinai. When God took Israel as his special nation, salvation and social policy went hand in hand. Once we recognize that the Sermon on the Mount is a new-covenant ethic for God's people, in common nations ruled ultimately by God's providence rather than in a theocracy ruled immediately by God's written decrees, our Bible quoting becomes more complicated. As I've said, there just is not that much in the New Testament about how to order society. That does not mean that it isn't important, but that it is a matter of common grace, left to the variety of histories, cultures, and governments that exist in this present age.

Besides exhibiting simplistic exegesis, evangelical politics often strikes me as simplistic in its policy solutions. And when God is on your side, there's no place for negotiation and compromise. Yet forming common policies through negotiation and compromise is where the institutions of democratic republicanism shine. Ideology gets chastened by the actual state of affairs. Arguments for a wide spectrum of policies are set forth in the public arena. At the end of the day, complexities are given more due and compromises emerge. There was little room for that in Israel, with a divine law that prescribed the personal and public life of God's people to exacting detail. However, we now live east of Eden and Jerusalem.

I have Christian friends on both sides of the political aisle who have been called to public office out of the same sense of neighbor-love, with the same theological convictions, who nevertheless disagree with each other on the best way of honoring the Great Commandment. Christians holding the same faith and practice also hold positions on environmental policy, taxes, and health care which cover the whole political spectrum. This is not because the Bible is unclear or because one group believes the Bible and the other doesn't. It is because the Bible is not a policy manual or political platform. So Christians, like non-Christians, are responsible to investigate the data and the arguments for particular issues and vote their conscience. Like the gospel of the Great Commission, the moral law at the heart of the Great Commandment is the same in every time and place. Yet the law of love must be interpreted and applied in concrete and often difficult

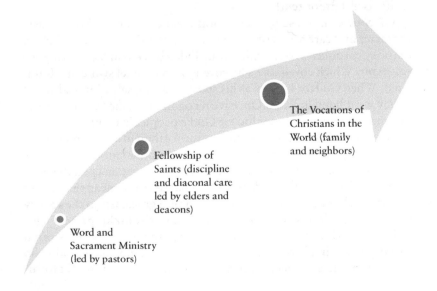

The Vocations of Christians in the World (family and neighbors)

Fellowship of Saints (discipline and diaconal care led by elders and deacons)

Word and Sacrament Ministry (led by pastors)

contexts where compromises have to be made. And it is actual neighbors we encounter, not "the neighbor" in the abstract, to whom the Great Commandment directs our concern.

The Great Commission establishes a narrow mandate for the church in its official ministry, yet this very specific ministry shapes us for our myriad callings in the world.

Wilberforce: A Case Study

One of the ironies of history is the way in which different Christian movements have influenced the wider culture. The early Christians suffered persecution—even martyrdom—for their witness to Christ. One one hand, they didn't withdraw into monasteries but fulfilled their callings in the world alongside non-Christians. On the other hand, they didn't have a social agenda for transforming the Roman Empire. And yet, transformed by the gospel, they became salt and light in their communities, and this brought common grace blessings to the wider culture.

For at least a century and a half, American Protestants have evidenced a marked preference for "deeds over creeds," and yet, since Finney's announcement that the church is a society of moral reformers, the church seems less genuinely evangelized and Western culture is dominated by secularist impulses. In fact, this irony (among others) has been explored with great insight by sociologist James Davison Hunter in his book *To Change the World: The Irony, Tragedy, and Possibility of Christianity in the Late Modern World.*[7]

In this light, I have found William Wilberforce (1759-1833) an exceptional figure in his age. A Church of England layperson, Wilberforce was came to a public profession of his faith through reading the Puritans. Wilberforce was convinced by his friend and pastor, John Newton (author of the hymn "Amazing Grace"), to enter politics. One of the chief ambitions that the two men shared was the abolition of the slave trade. However, Newton knew that his calling was to preach, teach, and shepherd Christ's flock. Yet, gripped by this gospel and steeped in its truths, Wilberforce could use his considerable gifts in politics for the common good. Humanly speaking, one could say "No Newton, no Wilberforce." This may serve as a historical example of the point I'm making: *The ministry of the church as an institution or embassy instituted by Christ*—identified by preaching, baptizing, communing, and teaching everything Christ delivered—is *where disciples are made*. Worldly vocations are where disciples are *sent*.

In his remarkable book *A Practical View of Christianity* (1797), Wilberforce contrasts authentic Christianity with the nominal Christianity then prevalent in England. One of the most striking emphases in the book is the author's conviction that the "grand defect" of our time is "neglect of the peculiar doctrines of Christianity."[8] We are used to hearing in American evangelicalism today that we have the correct doctrine but are not living it out—and yet I found in Wilberforce's description of the vague Christianity of his day a remarkable parallel to our own malaise of "Christless Christianity."

Wilberforce argued that the collapse of vital Christian practice had its source in widespread ignorance among professing Christians concerning what they believed and why they believed it. He says that he wrote out of a concern that "the bulk of those who belong to the class of orthodox Christians" nevertheless seem to possess "scarcely any distinct knowledge of the real nature and principles of the religion which they profess."[9] The problem was not creeds without deeds, but a vague moralism that denied the power of the gospel:

> If we listen to their conversation, virtue is praised, and vice is censured; piety is perhaps applauded, and profaneness condemned. So far all is well. But let anyone, who would not be deceived by these "barren generalities" examine a little more closely, and he will find that not to Christianity in particular, but at best to Religion in general, perhaps to mere Morality, their homage is intended to be paid. With Christianity, as distinct from these, they are little acquainted; their views of it have been so cursory and superficial, that far from discerning its characteristics and essence, they have little more than perceived those exterior circumstances which distinguish it from other forms of religion.[10]

No longer taught the basics of the Christian faith, the children easily succumb to skepticism or simply ignore their superficially Christian background when they arrive at college. They are "shaken by frivolous objections . . . which, had they been grounded in reason and argument, would have passed them 'as the idle wind,' and scarcely have seemed worthy of notice."[11] They have become easy prey. You don't even need rank atheism to undermine this kind of shallow spirituality.

This "poverty of superficial religion," this "voluntary ignorance," necessarily weakens not only the faith of believers but causes them to go along with the flow of the culture.[12] God's supernatural revelation

gives us new truths that we could never have known otherwise, not
just "maxims of worldly policy or a scheme of mere morals."[13] The
heart of this Word is the gospel, the promise of the Savior. All of the
Old Testament saints looked forward eagerly to his coming, but many
churches today seem to proceed as if nothing had ever happened.[14]

Wilberforce then prosecutes his case, in his second chapter, by
examining "inadequate conceptions of the corruption of human nature." "Had we duly felt the burden of our sins, that they are a load
which our own strength is wholly unable to support, and that the
weight of them must finally sink us into perdition, our hearts would
have danced at the sound of the gracious invitation, 'Come unto me,
all ye that labor and are heavy laden, and I will give you rest.'" Yet in
spite of the evangelical creed and liturgy of the Church of England,
most professing Christians are confident in their own righteousness.[15]
Rather than lodging their acceptance with God in Christ's sacrifice,
"they really rest their eternal hopes on a vague, general persuasion of
the unqualified mercy of the Supreme Being" or, "still more errone-
ously, they rely in the main on their own negative or positive merits."[16]
They may close their prayers with Christ's name, but they "disclaim
a Savior, or avowedly relinquish their title to a share in the benefits
of his death." They imagine that God is "more lenient" now than he
may have been in the past.[17] It is beneath them to acknowledge that
they are "guilty and helpless sinners." "They have never summoned
themselves to this entire and unqualified reununciation of their own
merits, and their own strength; and therefore they remain strangers to
the natural lostness of the human heart. . . . They consider not that
Christianity is a scheme 'for justifying *the ungodly*' [Rom 4:5], by
Christ's dying for them '*when yet sinners*'" and instead they make the
fruits of holiness "the cause rather than the effects" of justification and
reconciliation.[18] Only this ignorance of the gospel itself can explain
the lack of affection for Jesus Christ and the Word of God among
nominal Christians. Only the gospel of grace in all of its fullness
gives meaning to the otherwise vague phrase, "believing in Jesus."[19]

The *doctrines* of vague liberal moralism are barren and therefore
cannot bear even the fruit of righteousness that they seek to incul-
cate.[20] All of Christianity's calls to practical obedience and love arise
from its doctrinal core, leading to a radically different discipleship in
the world.[21] The gospel is not subsumed under religion and morality,
but gives rise to a particular kind of practice, with grace as the basis
and God's glory as the goal.[22]

Ill-equipped by this distinctive message and hope, nominal Christianity becomes dependent on "the desire for human estimation and applause."[23] Once again, Wilberforce grounds his call to humility and faithfulness in a recovery of Christian doctrine. Sin is not merely a mistake. "Sin is considered in Scripture as rebellion against the Sovereignty of God, and every different act of it equally violates his law, and, if persevered in, disclaims his supremacy. To the inconsiderate and the gay this doctrine may seem harsh, while, vainly fluttering in the sunshine of worldly prosperity, they lull themselves into a fond security."[24]

Some content themselves with their progress in moral reformation, while others are led to despair after successive attempts at renewing strict obedience, and many of these finally end up in infidelity. Nothing less is needed than for Christians to "lay afresh the whole foundation of their Religion," to rediscover the truths that they profess in the creed.[25] In particular, they need to recover the grace of God in the gospel.[26] "These gigantic truths retained in view would put to shame the littleness of their dwarfish morality."[27] "Looking unto Jesus" is the only way of living grateful lives of love and service to our neighbors.[28] "These peculiar doctrines constitute the center to which [the real Christian] gravitates! The very sun of his system! The soul of the world! The origin of all that is excellent and lovely! The source of light, and life, and motion, and genial warmth and plastic energy!"[29]

It is certainly true that Christianity has raised the morals of cultures where it has prevailed. Yet people of various religions—or no religion—can conform themselves outwardly to social practice. In view of the distinctive doctrines of the gospel, these are "superficial appearances."[30] In sharp contrast with believers under the cross of persecution, true Christianity in Britain has been weakened by civil religion and general prosperity.[31] "Their effect is sure; and the time is fast approaching when Christianity will be almost as openly disavowed in the language as in fact it is already supposed to have disappeared from the conduct of men; when infidelity will be held to be the necessary appendage of a man of fashion, and *to believe* will be deemed the indication of a feeble mind and a contracted understanding."[32]

On the contrary, grounded in its core doctrines, Christianity makes its appeal to the mind as well as to the heart and the actions. "Improving in almost every other branch of knowledge, we have become less and less acquainted with Christianity," exchanging its doctrines for "a mere system of ethics."[33]

Let us remind ourselves that the author of this argument was zealously committed to the betterment of humanity and the title of this work is *A Practical View of Christianity*! The kind of liberal moralism that was identified in his day as the "Socinian" heresy cannot even produce the transforming effects that it has substituted for the power of the gospel. The faith that Wilberforce commends is simply "Christianity in its best days," as in "the religion of the most eminent Reformers" and so clearly inculcated in the liturgy and confession of the Church of England.[34] "Let the Socinian and the moral teacher of Christianity come forth, and tell us what effects they have produced on the lower orders. They themselves will hardly deny the inefficacy of their instructions." Yet wherever the gospel of free grace is proclaimed, whole neighborhoods and communities of the poor are being transformed.[35] "But fruitless will be all attempts to sustain, much more to revive, the fainting cause of morals, unless you can in some degree restore the prevalence of Evangelical Christianity."[36]

At the same time, Wilberforce realized that even these modest claims for the wider social effects of the gospel might turn it into merely a means to the end of civil morality, "as though the concern of Eternity were melted down into a mere matter of temporal advantage or political expediency."[37] The gospel has powerful effects because it is true and life-giving, not because of its practical usefulness.

In short, Wilberforce knew that a generation of professing Christians that ignores its treasures or takes them for granted will surrender them without a struggle. He also knew that if families and churches avoided the depths of doctrine for the shallow end of the pool, all distinctively and authentically Christian resources for resistance against the powers and principalities would be lost. The problem is not that we have creeds without deeds but that our practice no longer seems to be informed by our faith. "Let our churches no longer witness that unseemly discordance which has too much prevailed between the prayers and the sermon which follows."[38] At the same time, he warns against orthodox Christians who assent fully to the doctrines, but in a general kind of way. They are nominal Christians of a different but no less serious sort.[39] A doctrinal Christianity severed from life is no more likely to produce fruit than an activistic moralism severed from Christian doctrine.

Wilberforce is one example of the way forward here, especially as a recent Pew study reports that atheists and agnostics score higher on knowing basic details of the Bible and Christian teaching than do evangelicals. (Mormons and Jews were a close second.)[40] From him we learn at least two vital lessons. First, we learn that the church as an institution (like the family) is commissioned with a task that differs from that of the believer in his or her calling in the world. If the church does not fulfill its unique commission, no other institution will pick up the slack. Second, we are encouraged to return to the "first things": the core doctrines of Christianity that transform our thinking and lead us to doxology, which feeds our way of life in the world. In the great truths of the faith we find not only things to which we assent, but food for our souls, music to our ears, and a true motivation for active service to our neighbors in the world.

Forgiving Sins and Doing Good

As Christ's embassy of grace, the church is commissioned with the most important vocation in the cosmos right now: the forgiveness and renewal of sinners. The church's ministry—preaching the gospel, baptizing, communing, and caring for the growing flock—is already determined by its ascended King. To say that this is the most important work to be done in the world right now is not to say that it is the only important work to be done. The church cannot say or do everything that needs to be said and done by Christians working alongside non-Christians in society.

What about Jesus's miraculous signs? Aren't they indicative of the all-encompassing renewal of creation? Jesus not only forgives and renews but heals and raises the dead. Yes, all of this is true. The kingdom is just this all-encompassing, but not everyone was healed. Not only were the resurrections few in number, but the beneficiary ended up dying again on another day. They were not raised in glory, as Jesus was and we will be one day. What we have in these miraculous signs is a testimony to Christ and his kingdom's inauguration, not a pattern for our work of consummating it. The age to come is breaking in on this present evil age, but it's still this present evil age. Jesus healed the paralytic and said, "Take heart, my son; your sins are forgiven," provoking charges of blasphemy from the religious leaders (Matt. 9:2). Knowing their thoughts, Jesus said, "'Why do you think evil in your hearts? For which is easier, to say, "Your sins are forgiven," or to say, "Rise and walk?" But *that you may know that the Son of Man has authority on earth to forgive sins'*—he then said to the paralytic—'Rise, pick up your bed and go home'" (Matt.

9:4–6, emphasis added). Jesus's works were signs that all authority was given to him to judge and to forgive, not object lessons for our fulfillment of the Great Commission.

Churches that bind the consciences of their members on issues not explicitly addressed in Scripture are violating the catholicity of the church and the freedom of the Christian. In short, they are adding something to the gospel as an essential condition of community. I want to talk politics when I come to church. It's just that I want to talk about—and hear about—the politics of heaven that is even now breaking in on this present evil age. It's amazing how reluctant churches are these days to allow Christ to speak clearly and authoritatively on "divisive" issues of doctrine and practice, while they often seem quite willing to divide the church over cultural and political matters.

A recent *Newsweek* article by Lisa Miller reported that evangelicals who publicly supported Barack Obama's presidential campaign are growing impatient with the apparent failure of an as yet unfulfilled consummation of history. "When Barack Obama was running for president, an outfit called Matthew 25 helped him get elected. Through ads and outreach, this group convinced legions of moderate evangelicals that Obama represented them. . . . In Matthew 25, Jesus promises his disciples that they will be rewarded in the next world for feeding the hungry and caring for the sick."[41] Miller reports, "'We need a leader,' [Jim] Wallis told me, 'to call not for incremental change but transformational politics. The president could do that.'" Just change the agenda and it sounds like the Moral Majority all over again. Political messianism binds the left and the right. However much conservatives bemoan "big government," everybody seems to want the President of the United States to usher in the millennium. Richard Cizik, former NAE lobbyist, cofounded the New Evangelical Partnership for the Common Good, "which aims to redefine the Christian agenda." There's also the progressive think tank Third Way. Former Republican senator and Obama critic John Danforth says this is the time to find common ground between evangelical progressives and conservatives. Danforth adds, "I think Matthew 25 is a very good place to start."[42]

I beg to differ. The moral law, inscribed on the conscience of every human being, is the place to start. I have argued above that Matthew 25 is not about alleviating world hunger and poverty any more than the angels' Christmas announcement of peace on earth is a general story about Jesus winning the Nobel Peace Prize. Jesus provoked division in Israel and still divides families, although he strictly forbids the use of force in this mission. However, any serious alleviation of temporal want and violence *requires* the use of legitimate force through legislation and enforcement. As citizens of earthly kingdoms, especially in democracies, Christians are necessarily involved in this political process. We want just laws, and we want national and international powers to back them up, for the good of our neighbors. However, is this the way that Jesus's kingdom is growing, from a mustard seed to a great tree with its branches covering the globe? It is in part the confusion of Christ's present reign in grace with his future reign in glory that provokes the disillusionment of some Obama supporters, just as conservatives lost faith in George W. Bush.

But we should all be praying—especially as Christians—that politics be incremental rather than transformational, measured rather than messianic. Often with altruistic intentions, "transformational" leaders with political power have become despots and dictators. Since their motives are right (justice, freedom from oppression, alleviation of poverty), their vision and strategy must be enacted at all costs. They must burn the old order to the ground and start over. Only if we think we can build God's kingdom this way are we likely to swing like a pendulum from "Hosanna!" to "Crucify him!" as we do in modern Western politics. I, for one, am glad that I live in a nation where the political process curbs the messianic pretensions of those who advocate "redemptive" leadership. Christians on the left and on the right have a delusional obsession with politics that verges on idolatry. It not only distracts the churches from their Great Commission but also assumes that cultures are shaped more by what happens in general elections every four years than by families, neighborhoods, schools, and the wider spheres such as the arts and sciences, entertainment, and technology.

The church must always address the whole Word of God, and its drama, doctrine, and doxology shape our discipleship not only in the church but in the world. C. S. Lewis put it eloquently: "I believe in Christianity as I believe that the sun has risen—not only because I see it, but because by it, I see everything else."[43] As they apply the Ten Commandments, the Reformation catechisms teach that this includes positive responsibilities to look after our neighbors—not only by refraining from causing them harm but by acts of justice and charity. God tells us that we are created in a covenant not only with him and with each other but with all creatures, under the mandate to care for creation rather than to exploit and plunder it. And in the gospel he tells us what he has done, is doing, and will do to make all things new. Through his Word, the Spirit is creating a new society within the secular kingdoms of this age as a sign of the new creation. God's moral vision for his world has not changed. The commandment to love God and neighbor itself does not change. It remains the standard of divine righteousness for every era and for every person. What has changed is the transition from "this present age" (under sin and death) to "the age to come" (bringing righteousness and life), and that makes all the difference.

This transition is recognized in 1 John 2, where the apostle calls the saints to love each other: "Beloved, I am writing you no new commandment, but an old commandment that you had from the beginning. The old commandment is the word that you have heard. *At the same time, it is a new commandment* that I am writing to you, which is true in him and in you, *because the darkness is passing away and the true light is already shining*" (vv. 7–8, emphasis added). Hearing this commandment "in Adam," under the reign of sin and condemnation, leaves us without any hope. It only tells us what we *haven't* done. However, hearing this commandment "in Christ," under the reign of justification and eternal life, we are summoned to a new way of existence.

In our culture especially, we often pit law against love, but in the Bible law is simply the stipulation of love's duties. The command to love is just as damning—more damning, in fact—than the command simply to refrain from acts of violence. Jesus demonstrated in the parable of the Good Samaritan and elsewhere that the genuine fulfillment of the law (that is, love) is far more demanding than outward conformity to a system of rules.

The point in 1 John 2, then, is that the promised era of the new covenant, when the Spirit would give us new hearts to love God and neighbor—*on the basis of the forgiveness of sins* (Jer. 31:31–34)—has dawned. With Christ's resurrection as the firstfruits, the age to come has broken into this present evil age, and even those who are only outwardly members of the covenant community participate in these previews of coming attractions through the Word and sacraments (Heb. 6:4–8).

For believers, the command to love deepens in its summons and intensity. That is why the Sermon on the Mount is even more demanding than the giving of the law at Mount Sinai. Loving our *enemies*? The Psalms include prayers that call down God's curses on his enemies, but Jesus says that we are now to pray for the good of those who persecute us for our faith. Sharing our worldly goods with the poor, especially with our fellow saints? Showing hospitality to strangers, with no expectation of anything in return? Freely sharing our material resources with our brothers and sisters as God's gifts rather than our own treasure? Yes, this is the pattern not only for super-saints and monks but for every believer. And it is no longer a burden, because the threat of judgment for failures in executing this calling adequately is no longer hanging over us. We love and serve our neighbors now as those who have been justified and are being renewed day by day, conformed to the image of our Savior. So the Great Commandment is an old commandment, but in another sense it is new. It comes to us now as those who share in Christ's resurrection life.

Although the command to love remains, for believers who find their justification in Christ's righteousness, it no longer comes with a threat. It is not the precepts of the law that are cancelled, according to Colossians 2, but "the record of debt that stood against us with its legal demands" (v. 14).

The church proclaims God's claim on the world in creation. It announces the dawn of the new creation that gives us a new way even of seeing the Great Commandment. And it witnesses not only to the intermission of grace in the gospel but to the coming judgment of Babylon, the city of oppression. "And the merchants of the earth weep and mourn for her, since no one buys their cargo anymore"—cargo of precious jewels, linens, wood, spices, oil, chariots, "and slaves, that is, human souls" (Rev. 18:11–13). And in the body of Christ, we are called already to a radical form of existence as a foretaste of the city of God. In the church there is to be no distinction between slave and free (Matt. 20:27; Gal. 3:28; Col. 3:11) or rich and poor (1 Cor. 11:17–34).

Yet in their civil affairs the only exhortations are for masters and servants to treat each other with mutual respect (Eph. 6:9; Col. 3:22; 4:1; 1 Peter 2:18). This was not a slavery based on kidnapping, and even Rome in its decadence treated slaves as persons. In contrast with modern slavery, it was part of an economic system in which a debtor could buy or work one's way out of slavery—or be redeemed by another. Surely a full-orbed view of neighbor-love would eventually overthrow even this version of slavery, but the New Testament did not provide the mandate or the blueprint for dismantling it. Christians, working alongside non-Christians, eventually did abandon this social institution. The Scriptures do not teach capitalism or socialism, nor do they give us any instructions about building social infrastructure or managing international debt relief.

Saving Grace and Common Grace

So the New Testament fundamentally alters our way of being in the world, without giving us specific instructions on a host of matters that we address every day in common with our unbelieving neighbors. In addition to the triumphant indicatives of the gospel, God's Word gives us clear imperatives as to how this new creation changes our relationships on the ground. However, in spite of the many details for the church's message, mission, ministry, offices, and patterns of Christian discipleship, when it comes to our vocations in the world, we are simply told to respect and pray for those in authority over us and to love and serve our neighbors. In view of Christ's return, Paul urges the Thessalonians "to aspire to live quietly, and to mind your own affairs, and to work with your hands, as we instructed you, so that you may live properly before outsiders and be dependent on no one" (1 Thess. 4:11–12).

Loving and serving our neighbors in our common callings is not "kingdom work." It is the service that all human beings are obligated to offer to their neighbors. When it comes to service projects, community programs, and other forms of assistance, we are free to work alongside non-Christians to provide for our neighbors' needs. Christians are also free to form associations together for common projects and concerns: hospitals, relief agencies, pregnancy centers, homeless shelters, political think tanks, and societies for Christian lawyers, doctors, and so forth. Yet whether they work alongside mainly Christians or non-Christians, their labors are common rather than holy.

Work does not need to be holy in order to be important and God honoring, any more than marriage needs to be a sacrament in order to be a divinely ordained institution. Not only the church but "the earth is the LORD's, and everything in it" (Ps. 24:1 NIV). God engages in common labor every day by giving us and our unbelieving neighbors what we need for daily sustenance. Our common work—this laboring "east of Eden"—is crucial, but it is *east of Eden*: the work of God in common grace, not in saving grace. When we fix a roof or mop a floor or argue a case before the Supreme Court, we are not ushering in the kingdom of God but are fulfilling our divine calling in the world as fellow citizens. As we do these things to the glory of

God, in the light of our high calling in Christ and participation in his new regime, even sweeping the floor is filled with nobility. However menial and insignificant a task may seem, *God* is loving and serving our neighbors *through our hard work.*

We do not need more political, moral, and cultural crusades. Instead, what we need are "salty" Christians whose robust faith and discipleship shape the way they think, live, and exercise their gifts, training, and wisdom in their callings. We do not need more churches called to active duty in the culture wars. What we need are more churches that are resalinization instead of desalinization plants, churches that are dedicated to making disciples who are not only forgiven and renewed in Christ but also well taught and actually active in the world—in their families, neighborhoods, schools, workplaces, and volunteer organizations, loving their neighbors through their vocational excellence as well as through their witness to Christ.

Indicatives and Imperatives

Biblical *imperatives* are always the reasonable response to biblical *indicatives.* In other words, God's commands are grounded in God's works. As covenant heirs, believers are given two mandates: the Great Commission and the Great Commandment. *The Great Commandment is rooted in God's act of creation.* Loving God and our neighbors is the reasonable response to the work of the Triune God in creating, caring for, and ruling over his world. "The earth is the LORD's and the fullness thereof" (Ps. 24:1). *The Great Commission is rooted in God's act of redemption.* Bringing the Good News of Christ's victory to the ends of the earth is the appropriate response to his saving work. As a beneficiary of the Great Commission, the believer will see even the Great Commandment in a new light, be liberated to embrace it from the heart, and live toward its full realization in the everlasting Sabbath.

All authority in heaven and on earth belongs to Christ, but in two senses: as the mediator of creation and as the mediator of redemption. The Great Commandment and the Great Commission have their authorization in these distinct works. The following chart helps to explain this point:

"All authority in heaven and on earth has been given to me. Therefore, . . ."

The Great Commission	The Great Commandment
Proclaim the gospel to everyone	Love God and neighbor
Baptize	Do justice and love mercy
Serve Communion	Live righteously, defend righteousness
Teach and obey	Live wisely
Care for the saints in body and soul	Live compassionately
Witness to neighbors	Serve neighbors through callings

The Great Commission reflects the holy (saving grace) and is where disciples are made. The Great Commandment reflects common grace and is where our discipleship goes.

The Kingdom We Are Receiving: Following the Flow of Gifts

James reminds us, "Every good gift and every perfect gift is from above, coming down from the Father of lights with whom there is no variation or shadow due to change. Of his own will he brought us forth by the word of truth, that we should be a kind of firstfruits of his creatures" (James 1:17–18). Similarly, Paul told the Athenian philosophers that God does not need anything but supplies all good things for our sustenance (Acts 17:24–25). God is the giver, not the receiver, of all gifts: "'Or who has given a gift to him that he might be repaid?' For from him and through him and to him are all things. To him be glory forever" (Rom. 11:35–36).

Gifts come down to us and then flow through us to our neighbors. This is one of Martin Luther's most helpful practical emphases for our spirituality in the world. God gives us salvation, along with our daily bread, and then calls us to be means through whom he serves our neighbors in our callings and in our witness. We do not present our good works to God, as though he might repay us, but to our neighbors as those who are free to love without threats and rewards. We have to understand the direction in which God's gifts flow:

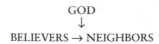

Biblical history doesn't exactly lead us to conclude that *we* are the ones building the kingdom of God. More characteristically, the church in both testaments is ambiguous in its identification with the kingdom of God, much less to be credited with redeeming the world. In fact, the writer to the Hebrews reminds us that even the old-covenant theocracy was a frail, temporary, and now obsolete kingdom. Everything that *can* be shaken *will* be shaken, he says, until all that stands in the midst of the rubble is the house that God built. "Therefore, since we are receiving a kingdom that cannot be shaken," he instructs, "let us . . . worship God with reverence and awe" (Heb. 12:28 NIV). It is a redemptive kingdom, not a civil one, and the Triune God is the architect and builder (Heb. 11:10). Our response is gratitude and witness, not self-congratulation and ambitious social planning. We are not creating a kingdom of priests to our God. Rather, Christ is acclaimed in heaven: "[F]or you were slain, and by your blood you ransomed people for God from every tribe and language and people and nation, and *you have made them* a kingdom and priests to our God, and they shall reign on the earth" (Rev. 5:9–10, emphasis added).

It is actually a great relief to learn that we are not called to redeem the world or to transform it. We are freed up to proclaim the gospel when we know that we are *receiving* a kingdom that cannot be shaken. And we are actually liberated to love and serve our neighbors when we know that *God* will transform the kingdoms of this age when Christ returns to the earth. Unburdened by the impossible demands of redeeming and transforming the world, we are liberated to fulfill the Great Commission and the Great Commandment in concrete, specific, and usually unnoticed acts toward concrete and specific neighbors each day.

It's hard enough to really believe that we are recipients of rather than contributors to our own redemption. The further challenge is to believe that we are receiving rather than building an unshakable kingdom. We may be saved by grace, but now the focus has to be on our transforming work. It's very difficult for us to really believe that all good gifts come from God to us and through us to our neighbors. We want to reverse that direction. Like Peter, we are often too pious to let God serve us; we will serve him (John 13:3–20). But all good gifts come from God to us and through us to our neighbors, not from us to God and neighbor.

Brian McLaren raises an important point: "Can't seeking my personal salvation as the ultimate end become the ultimate consumerism or narcissism?"[44] Indeed, it can. In a consumer-oriented society, *everything* is for sale, and there is a kind of narcissism in making our own salvation the ultimate end of our existence. However, there are two ways of dealing with this. The first is to say, with McLaren, that the gospel is a call to love God and our neighbors—and this is salvation. The second is to say, with the Scriptures, that we were created for God's glory, that we are incapable of fulfilling this ultimate end (not because we are "so often ignorantly wrong and stupid" but because we intentionally suppress the truth in unrighteousness), and that the gospel consists exclusively in the announcement of what God has done to redeem his creation in Christ.

This second answer was Calvin's counsel to Cardinal Sadoleto. The reformer said that when our salvation is placed in our hands, we are always fretting over our souls. Every pious emotion or activity is calculated in terms of whether it will improve our relationship with God. However, he argued, when we give over our salvation to Christ alone, relying on his merits, we are able for the first time to love and serve others without a selfish preoccupation with rewards and punishments. Since we have already been given every spiritual blessing in heavenly places, we can give our neighbors what they need without concern for what we will get out of it.[45] Yet this is not possible if Christ did not fulfill the law in our place and bear God's wrath for our transgressions. "Until people are persuaded that God is the fountain of all of our good, and that he has left no part of our salvation to them," Calvin insists, "they will never devote themselves wholly, truly, and sincerely to him."[46] Grace inspires gratitude. "There is . . . an exact parallel in this respect between piety and faith," notes B. A. Gerrish. Only because of the forgiveness of sins that comes from Christ can the uneasy conscience ever be assured that God is indeed good and the source of all good.[47]

From God alone, therefore, all good and perfect gifts come to the world and are then distributed by us for the feast. The church is the *place* where sinners are gathered to receive, yet it is also the *people* who are scattered to fulfill their common callings. In the latter, the church has no dominion. It cannot command the covenant community to embrace particular political ideologies, policies, parties, or politicians. It can only witness to the kingdom of grace, not inaugurate the kingdom of glory. Hence, Calvin as well as Luther refers to "two kingdoms" that must be kept distinct in the present age, although the believer participates in both.[48]

Gustav Wingren nicely summarizes Luther's concern with the neighbor as the recipient of the believer's good works. Instead of living in monasteries, committing their lives in service to themselves and their own salvation, or living in castles, commanding the world to mirror the kingdom of Christ, Luther argues, believers should love and serve their neighbors through their vocations in the world, where their neighbors need them.[49] "God does not need our good works, but our neighbor does."[50] When we offer our works to God, we simultaneously "attempt to depose Christ from his throne" and neglect our neighbor, since these works "have clearly been done, not for the sake of [our] neighbor, but to parade before God."[51] Wingren notes that "In his [Luther's] *Treatise on Christian Liberty*, the main thought is that a Christian lives in Christ through faith and in his neighbor through love."[52]

> In faith, which accepts the gift, man finds that it is not only "heaven that is pure with its stars, where Christ reigns in his work," but the earth too is clean "with its trees and its grass, where we are at home with all that is ours." There is nothing more delightful and lovable on earth than one's neighbor. Love does not think about doing works, it finds joy in people; and when something good is done for others, that does not appear to love as works but simply as gifts which flow naturally from love.[53]

The regime of grace is therefore not in conflict with that of creation, but fulfills it. The commandment to love, Luther insists, is natural law.[54] Yet that law written on the conscience in creation is engraved in living letters by the Spirit on the hearts of those who are swept into the new creation.

9

Mission Creep

Inventing Our Own Strategic Plan

Now that I've laid out a positive case for what I take to be the heart of our Lord's commission to his church, this chapter engages more critically with contemporary challenges. My concern is that we have moved away from the message, mission, and strategic plan that we have been given for this time between Christ's two advents.

The message of the kingdom determines its mission, and both determine the strategy. If we think of the kingdom of God as primarily a transformation of the inner self, we will look for strategies that facilitate personal growth. If the kingdom is chiefly concerned with transforming society, then we will focus on strategies that promote greater justice, peace, morality, and ecological stewardship in the world.

I have argued that the kingdom of God centers on the delivery of Christ, clothed in his gospel, to the ends of the earth through the ministry of Word and sacrament. The kingdom does not emerge within us, nor does it evolve through our moral and cultural programs. It descends from heaven, breaking into this present age in the power of the Spirit, beginning the renovation of creation that will only be consummated at Christ's return. In this phase, the kingdom of God is the forgiveness of sins, the new birth, and living in this new-creation reality together with all the saints as we grow up into Christ, who is the head of the body. The kingdom's *effects* will be evident in the good works of the saints as well as their witness. Nevertheless, the kingdom is *identified with* the delivery of Christ in the gospel.

The strategy Jesus commands is consistent with this view of the kingdom. Since it is a kingdom that we are *receiving*, it makes sense that God has instituted these means in his Great Commission. We are made recipients of Christ and all of his benefits by hearing an external Word. It does not well up within us, nor is it an action plan we have devised for building a kingdom. It is God's word to us, not our words to or about God. It is the indictment and the Good News brought to us by an ambassador. God seals his promise in baptism and regularly in the Lord's Supper—once again, *God's* gracious activity is front and center. Our covenant Lord graciously gives us pastors, elders, and deacons to care for our spiritual and material needs. We are not self-feeders but are richly fed and cared for by Christ through his officers. This disciple formation instituted by Christ generates a new society of forgiven and renewed sinners, a strange communion that ignores the divisions and demographics of this present age and frees these disciples to be salt and light in the world through their relationships and callings.

This kingdom comes to us from outside of ourselves, but it brings inner transformation and harbingers of the age to come that transform our relationships in the world. So far from ignoring these crucial aspects of the new creation, I am arguing that true transformation of anyone or anything in this present evil age can only come about through the forgiveness of sins that is regularly announced and ratified in the ministry of the gospel. Recipients of this ministry will be transformed inwardly and in their relationships with others as they live and work in the world.

When we add our own strategies, much less substitute them for Christ's appointed means, mission creep is inevitable. Christ's ordained means of grace are inseparable from the mission, and the mission is inseparable from the message. Among other things, that is the point that Paul makes in Romans 10. The message of "the righteousness that is through faith" is opposed to "the righteousness that is by works," he says, and each message has its own methods. If the gospel is confused with our striving, then we will create methods for ascending into the heavens to bring Christ down or into the depths to bring him again from the dead. Instead, Paul teaches, we need to receive Christ where he has descended to us and still meets us today.

There are a lot of complaints today about the church being lazy, about true discipleship being rare. I'm not so sure. Of course, there is a lot of hypocrisy and nominal commitment, as has always been the case. Bad theology leads to bad practices, and even with sound teaching we are often unfaithful to our calling. Others may know better, but in my experience there are many Christians who are doing what they think they're supposed to do and many churches that are as busy as beehives. We have "Martha" all over us today: industrious, entrepreneurial, actively engaged in all sorts of church-related enterprises. We have myriad outreach programs, social programs, missions programs, and so forth.

From where I sit, the problem is not so much that the church is *lazy* but that it is *distracted*. The greatest danger that the church faces in any age is not that it might not be busy enough but that it might not be *Christian* enough, either in its outreach to unbelievers or its weekly ministry to the saints. Even where the message and the mission have not yet been altered in explicit terms, we can bury the church's ministry in a heap of programs and strategies of our own making.

We are all inveterate idolaters by nature since the fall. Adam and Eve turned from the Light of the World to their own inner light. They wanted to determine for themselves truth and error, good and evil instead of hearing and submitting to the external Word of their covenant Lord. Instead of bringing the sacrifice for guilt that God had appointed for directing faith to Christ, Cain brought his own offering, and both he and his worship were rejected by God.

Aaron bowed to the pressure of the Israelites to fashion a golden calf. No longer filled with fear by hearing God speak, "the people sat down to eat and drink and rose up to play" (Exod. 32:6). In what has to be the classic expression of pastoral self-defense, Aaron appealed to Moses, "Let not the anger of my lord burn hot. You know the people, that they are set on evil" (Exod. 32:22). Evidently, Moses hadn't read the polls. It's a tough job keeping the people happy. Years later, upon adding a ceremony to God's worship, Aaron's sons Nadab and Abihu died on the spot.

The writer to the Hebrews reminds us that we hear God's voice today not in the thundering of Mount Sinai but from the heavenly Zion and Christ our mediator. Yet he says that this is all the more reason for us to listen to God's Word. "Therefore let us be grateful for receiving a kingdom that cannot be shaken, and thus let us offer to God acceptable worship, with reverence and awe, for our God is a consuming fire" (Heb. 12:28–29).

As Protestants, we can be pretty smug. We know idolatry when we see it, especially in strange rituals and ceremonies, icons and statues, altars and prayers to Mary and the saints. We might have witnessed a service in which various rites were added that are nowhere found in Scripture and wondered at so much "man-made religion." Less obvious to us are the myriad examples of our own accumulated additions to God's strategic plan.

In spite of the clarity of the Great Commission's mandated strategies (preaching, sacrament, teaching), Protestantism has become just as creative in usurping Christ's sovereign authority to determine such things. Where is the "altar call" found in Scripture, for example? Isn't it more than ironic that many churches that would never call the communion table an altar nevertheless have an altar for a new sacrament? How did the sinner's prayer become a more important certification of belonging to Christ than baptism? And how did the daily quiet time become more central for communion with Christ than the Supper? Given the explicit strategies of the Great Commission—and its practical outworking in Acts and the Epistles—where did we ever get the idea that it had so little to do with the church?

"New Measures": Getting Creative with the Great Commission

Even in the Great Awakening there were evangelists who encouraged believers to look for the extraordinary work of the Spirit in spectacular revivals rather than relying on the Spirit's ordinary work through the means of grace.

In the nineteenth century, however, Charles Finney explicitly subordinated the ordinary means of grace to the periodical revival meeting with its "new measures." Denying original sin, the substitutionary atonement, and justification through faith alone, he argued in no uncertain terms that we are saved by our own works.[1] Finney inveighed against critics who insisted that the new birth was the work of God and that revival was not in our hands. A revival could be planned, staged, and managed. God was as hands-off in determining the methods as he was in conversion itself. The Great Commission just said, "Go," says Finney. "*It did not prescribe any forms*. It did not admit any. . . .

And [the disciples'] object was to make known the gospel in the *most effectual way* . . . so as to obtain attention and secure obedience of the greatest number possible. No person can find any *form* of doing this laid down in the Bible."[2]

To invoke Romans 10 again, Finney's message was "the righteousness that is by law," and the methods followed consistently. The church was defined as "a society of moral reformers" rather than as a society of forgiven and renewed sinners regularly evangelized by the Word and directed to love and serve their neighbors in their callings.

Like Finney, revival leaders did not think they needed any special education for their calling. In fact, that might dampen their enthusiasm and distract them from the practical training they could receive from itinerant evangelists. After all, it is deeds rather than creeds that propels the church's mission in the world. Garry Wills observes,

> The camp meeting set the pattern fôr credentialing Evangelical ministers. They were validated by the crowd's response. Organizational credentialing, doctrinal purity, personal education were useless here—in fact, some educated ministers had to make a pretense of ignorance. The minister was ordained from below, by the converts he made. This was an even more democratic procedure than electoral politics, where a candidate stood for office and spent some time campaigning. This was a spontaneous and instant proclamation that the Spirit accomplished. The do-it-yourself religion called for a make-it-yourself ministry.[3]

Wills repeats Richard Hofstadter's conclusion that "the star system was not born in Hollywood but on the sawdust trail of the revivalists."[4]

Eschewing "churchianity" in favor of "following Jesus," the Jesus Movement spawned various networks of nondenominational denominations. Each new movement has been announced as a fresh move of the Spirit, a revival, new wine that could not be contained in the old wineskins of traditional churches. The church is not an organization, but an organism, an invisible kingdom of zealous believers over against the visible church with its humdrum ministry.

Yet this succession of self-proclaimed prophets announcing independence from the establishment have succeeded merely in setting up remarkably closed and protected circles of leadership around each charismatic founder. What was an egalitarian movement in southern California in the 1970s has now become a fairly hierarchical denomination led by its patriarch. Indeed each of these movements eventually became institutionalized as a separate denomination, settling into its own patterns of organization.

Sources of Our Dilemma

Across a broad spectrum of churches today, one may discern a series of dichotomies that distort the Great Commission and distract us from the strategies that Christ gave us. Let me suggest a few.

Contract vs. Covenant

This dichotomy is not a false choice. It is a real fork in the road. Many Christians think of salvation as a transaction. God offers a great deal. He will make sure that we go to heaven when we die, and perhaps also experience transformed lives and communities in the meantime, if we will follow a few simple demands. God makes salvation possible, but we have to cooperate and do our part. Even the new birth is described as an event that we can bring about by following the right instructions, as in the title of a bestseller years ago, *How to Be Born Again*. Our part of the bargain may be minimal (like saying a prayer or going forward at an evangelistic meeting). Or it might be more demanding, requiring dedication to regular spiritual disciplines, moral earnestness, and perhaps a second conversion experience that brings us into the higher life of the Spirit. Some may even go so far as Charles Finney, making perfect obedience to God's law the basis for salvation, but that kind of strictness is rare these days.

For the most part, the contract is offered as a relatively easy and rewarding exchange. In any case, the individual is in the driver's seat. As the bumper sticker says, "God is my copilot." Since salvation is grounded in my choice, after weighing the pros and cons, belonging to the church is a choice. I am autonomous, free to come or go as I please. And if I'm not completely satisfied, I can return the unused portion for a full refund.

In sharp contrast is the covenant of grace. In this paradigm, the Triune God is front and center. I am not the sovereign chooser. The plan revolves around God and his purposes, not around me and mine. The Father has chosen me in his Son and has united me to Christ by his Spirit. Although his people are unfaithful, he remains faithful because of his promise (2 Tim. 2:13). In this covenant, God pledges to forgive his people's sins and to give them a new heart (Jer. 31:31–34).

He will not only justify sinners but will renew them and conform
them to the image of his Son. So this is not just "fire insurance." It
is not a contract, even with minimal requirements; it is a covenant,
with maximal blessings. Yet that means that our lives will be filled
with conflict, pain, and constant turmoil as God weans us from this
present evil age that has defined our hopes and fears—our very lives.
The indwelling presence of the Spirit will throw our tidy house into
disrepair as he opens us up to the renewing energies of the age to
come. Furthermore, this sovereign grace creates a community, not
just a collection of saved individuals. Like the vertical relationship
with God, the horizontal relationship to my brothers and sisters has
its source in his grace. This is not the group of friends I would have
chosen for myself, but God chose them for himself—and for me. We
are all co-heirs with Christ in the family of God.

In a contractual paradigm, means of grace become means of works:
resources for personal or social transformation. As a result, the church
is conceived primarily as a resource provider. Far from being the
"mother of the faithful" from which we never depart, a study by the
Willow Creek Community Church concludes that the church's job
is to turn believers into "self-feeders." Like a personal trainer at the
gym, the church provides a workout plan, but as individuals follow
it, they need the church less and less.[5] Taken to its extreme, contractual thinking easily leads to the view expressed by George Barna, an
evangelical pioneer of church marketing: "Think of your church not
as a religious meeting place, but as a service agency—an entity that
exists to satisfy people's needs."[6]

The evangelical emphasis on the "invisible church" (emphasis on
invisible) reaches wild proportions in the internet age. Barna now
celebrates the growing abandonment of local churches for internet
communities and resources.[7] In fact, he has introduced a new demographic: the "Revolutionaries," the "millions of believers" who are
advertised as those who "have moved beyond the established church
and chosen to be the church instead."[8] The Revolutionaries have found
that in order to pursue an authentic faith they had to abandon the
church.[9] Intimate worship, says Barna, does "not require a 'worship
service,'" just a personal commitment to the Bible, prayer, and discipleship.[10] Where Luke reports that the church gathered regularly for
the apostles' teaching, the fellowship, the breaking of the bread, and
the prayers (Acts 2:42–47), Barna suggests that preaching is simply
"faith-based conversation" and the means of grace are no more than

whatever it takes for "intentional spiritual growth," "love," "resource investment," and "spiritual friendships."[11]

Whereas a covenantal approach begins with God's Word and forms a communion of saints, in Barna's paradigm everything begins with the individual's personal decision, strengthened by more personal disciplines, and ends with the abandonment of the visible church. God's ordained means of grace are replaced with whatever is calculated to facilitate our own means of commitment. "Scripture teaches us that devoting your life to loving God with all your heart, mind, strength, and soul is what honors Him. Being part of a local church may facilitate that. Or it might not."[12]

In an earlier book, Barna summarized the ominous data from his religion surveys as follows: "To increasing millions of Americans, God—if we even believe in a supernatural deity—exists for the pleasure of humankind. He resides in the heavenly realm solely for our utility and benefit. Although we are too clever to voice it, we live by the notion that true power is accessed not by looking upward but by turning inward."[13] Barna laments this prevailing condition, especially highlighting the tragedy that apparently it characterizes evangelicals as much as others. And yet, instead of a cure, his prescriptions seem to offer more of the disease that he has diagnosed. This disconnect—not just between faith and practice but between our *formal* faith on paper and the *operating* faith that we actually bring to questions of practice—lies at the heart of our inability to recognize our own capitulations to the human-centered and contractual assumptions of a market-driven culture.

As the embodied communion of the saints is replaced by the internet explorer, the phrase "invisible church" takes on a new and ominous meaning. Yet it is part of a long history in which the public gathering of the covenant community for the means of grace was made subordinate to conventicles or "holy clubs." In the name of reaching the unchurched, evangelicalism increasingly tends to unchurch the churched.

Like Finney, George Barna asserts that the Bible offers "almost no restrictions on structures and methods" for the church.[14] Indeed, he believes that the visible church itself is of human rather than divine origin. Nature abhors a vacuum, and where Barna imagines that the Bible prescribes no particular structures or methods, the invisible hand of the market fills the void. Barna recognizes that the shift from the institutional church to "alternative faith communities" is largely due to market forces to which he frankly insists we must conform.[15] The foretaste of heavenly catholicity surrenders to the powers of this present age in Barna's vision.

"So if you are a Revolutionary," Barna concludes, "it is because you have sensed and responded to God's calling to be such an imitator of Christ. It is not a church's responsibility to make you into this mold. . . . The choice to become a Revolutionary—and it is a choice—is a covenant you make with God alone."[16] Though he employs the word "covenant," his assumptions are more suggestive of a contract: a consumer's decision to accept certain terms in exchange for certain goods and services. In the covenant of grace, the spotlight is on God's electing, redeeming, and regenerating activity, which results in a communion of saints. In a contractual model, the customer is king, the sovereign chooser, who may or may not belong to the covenant community.

More recently, Barna and Frank Viola coauthored *Pagan Christianity: Exploring the Roots of Our Church Practices*. As the title and subtitle suggest, this book is a sweeping dismissal of the official ministry, both the elements of public worship and particular offices. In fact, the authors suggest, "We believe the pastoral office has stolen your right to function as a full member of Christ's body." [17] By contrast, the authors emphasize spontaneous and informal events that eschew any fixed order of worship or official leadership. Of course, the Reformation brought changes, but Luther and Calvin basically continued to follow a Roman Catholic paradigm, with its formal offices and liturgies, and an ordinary supper transformed into "a strange pagan-like rite."[18] Given the intent to recall contemporary Christians to "New Testament Christianity," the lack of any serious engagement with New Testament passages clearly instituting the church's offices and public ministry is disappointing.

In *Reimagining Church: Pursuing the Dream of Organic Christianity*, Viola asserts that even in its public worship the early church lacked "human officiation"[19] and everything was "electric" and "free and spontaneous."[20] In this way, "the Lord Jesus Christ presides invisibly" through every-member ministry.[21] In fact, the Lord's Supper was originally nothing more than a "potluck dinner" that included bread and wine (or grape juice), where people offered (spontaneously, of course) a "toast" to Jesus throughout the meal.[22] However, again the question may be raised: if "the New Testament doesn't supply us with a detailed blueprint for church practice,"[23] why do writers like

Barna and Viola think that we have fallen away from the "original blueprint" for these nearly two thousand years? And why do they offer their own urgent blueprint as the original pattern?

As much as the emergent or missional movement emphasizes its novelty, there are many continuities with evangelical pietism. The shift from proclamation of the gospel to conversation about the community's world-transforming activity is evident in the worship gathering. Tony Jones describes Jacob's Well, a pioneering emergent community in Kansas City: "To the classic Presbyterian sanctuary with dark-stained pews and a choir loft, JW has added the requisite video screens and replaced the pulpit with a band. All of the speaking takes place at the floor level—*only the musicians are on stage*" (emphasis added).[24] (One might wonder how exactly this differs from the model pioneered by the megachurches.) As the predominantly white audience gathers, there is a table off to one side with a quote from the contemporary Anabaptist theologian John Howard Yoder, suggesting, Jones says, that "the visible church is not to be the bearer of Christ's message, but to be the message."[25]

Reacting against the individualism in consumer-driven approaches, the emergent movement stresses the importance of community. The question is whether, by continuing to follow other assumptions that shape the revivalistic heritage, this value can become anything more than a group of friends who are bound by similar stories and cultural demographics.

Most of the early pietists remained in the established churches but formed *ecclesiolae in ecclesiam* (churches within the church), where the serious work of discipleship was reserved for the most committed members. They still joined their mediocre brothers and sisters for public worship, but the real action happened in these small groups more than through the corporate ministry of Word and sacrament. The Wesleys founded "holy clubs" within Anglican churches that eventually became a separate denomination: Methodism. Indeed, evangelicalism itself is not a church, but a network of renewal movements—sometimes within churches and sometimes outside of, and even over against, any visible church.

In spite of its sharp criticisms of evangelicalism, the emergent movement is not really a serious departure from this heritage. As if similar sentiments had never been expressed by Thomas Müntzer, George Fox, John Robinson, Charles Finney, and a host of more recent luminaries, Tony Jones announces, "In the twenty-first century, it's

not God who's dead. It's the church. Or at least conventional forms
of church. . . . Indeed, churches still abound. So do pay phones. . . .
Of course, the death of the pay phone doesn't mean that we don't
make phone calls anymore. In fact, we make far more calls than ever
before, but we make them differently."[26] As Finney would say, we need
"new measures."

Similarly, Jones's own church, Solomon's Porch in Minneapolis (led
by Doug Padgitt), transforms the traditional service into a conversation. "The point is to jettison the magisterial sermon that has ruled
over much of Protestantism for five hundred years," Jones explains.
"Here the sermon is deconstructed, turned on its head. The Bible is
referred to as a 'member of the community' with whom we are in
conversation, and the communal interpretation of a text bubbles up
from the life of the community."[27] Bread and grape juice and wine are
offered in "a loud, party atmosphere, and an optional quiet meditation room," but "this aspect of the worship is not guided by a cler-
gyperson." Sometimes communion is introduced with a poem or "a
testimony about 'what the Lord's Supper means to me,' and another
week with the traditional 'Words of Institution' from the Book of
Common Prayer." After this, "We sit down again for announcements,
and the kids then begin to fight over the leftover communion bread,
since it's usually cinnamon raisin or chocolate chip or cheddar jalapeño
sourdough." It's messy. "But true worship of God is a messy endeavor.
I make no bones about that. It's not meant to be done 'decently and
in order,' but messily and with only a semblance of order, and with
a great deal of joy."[28]

Minus the cheddar jalapeño sourdough, this setting might seem
familiar in a pietist community or Wesley's "Holy Club" at Oxford,
or to someone with a Quaker or Plymouth Brethren background. Far
from representing a radically new approach for a postmodern era,
these descriptions remind me of the house church movement I was
raised in during the 1970s and 1980s.

In all of these movements, the public ministry of Word and sacrament is either subordinated to or even replaced by informal gatherings
without any ordained leadership. The Friends (Quakers) reject baptism
and the Lord's Supper, and even the weekly gathering has at least historically been characterized by a circle of fellowship with each person
sharing a reflection believed to be given by the Spirit through an inner
light. Collapsing the Great Commission into the Great Commandment, the Salvation Army dispensed with the commanded institutions

of baptism and the Lord's Supper, although it has requirements that are not found in Scripture (such as abstinence from alcohol). In the light of this summary, Dietrich Bonhoeffer was probably not far off the mark when he described American Christianity as "Protestantism without the Reformation."

Inner vs. Outer

Condescending to us, God works inwardly in us by his Spirit through external and creaturely means. Our souls are not divine, with a direct and immediate relationship with God. We are embodied creatures and God relates to us as such. It is not by spirits rising up to heaven but by God becoming flesh that we have been redeemed. And it is by the Spirit working through ordinary human language, water, bread, and wine that Christ is delivered to us today.

Of course, external means are not enough. Preaching and sacraments are means of grace, not the source or cause of grace. In other words, these external means themselves do not do anything. Rather, *God* works through them, as he chooses. After being baptized, receiving communion, and hearing years of sermons, one might nevertheless disown his or her birthright (Heb. 6:4–12). Yet God has *promised* to work through these creaturely means, and they remain what they are—means of grace—even if the reality (Christ and his benefits) is not embraced. God's Word stands regardless, but hardens instead of softens the heart. Baptism and the Supper retain their efficacy, even if they confirm the unbelieving and unrepentant in judgment rather than life.

The radical inner-outer (or external-internal) contrast was most fully exploited by the ancient Gnostics, who tried to blend Christianity with Greek philosophy. Although the church decisively confronted this heresy, Greek (especially Platonic) assumptions remained influential, especially in monastic movements. Wherever Platonism is most evident, there is a tendency to treat creaturely signs merely as aids to contemplation. They may aid our spiritual experience and intellectual ascent, or—with the addition of the contractual element I've discussed—provide an opportunity for us to exercise our will. However, they are not regarded as means of grace.

The inner-outer dualism led to various spiritualist movements in the Middle Ages. Some of these groups disowned any "external church" with its preaching, sacraments, and discipline. Others remained in the church but downplayed the corporate means of grace in favor of private spiritual disciplines.

A Franciscan monk named Joachim of Fiore (1135–1202) wrote a commentary on the book of Revelation that would have enormous impact beyond the Middle Ages. In that work, he divided history into three ages: the Age of the Father (law, and the order of marriage), the Age of the Son (grace, and the order of the clergy), and the Age of the Spirit. In the third age of "the eternal gospel," the whole earth would become a monastery, with every person knowing God directly and intuitively in their hearts without the aid of Scripture, preaching, sacraments, or the church. Many enthusiastic leaders of the Radical Reformation set dates for the dawn of this Age of the Spirit.

The tendency of the Anabaptists at least historically was to drive a wedge between the creaturely sign and its heavenly reality, the external and the internal, the formal and the informal, the visible (institutional) church and the invisible society of true disciples.[29] All of this was roughly equivalent to the Platonic dualism between soul and body. The Reformers called it "enthusiasm," meaning "God-within-ism," since the tendency at least was to subordinate the external Word to the inner light. Everything external to the inner self is viewed as a burden, a threat, the prison house of the soul. It is not the outer Word that beats the air but the inner word or light to which we should give our attention. This presupposition is evident in the downplaying or outright rejection of preaching and sacrament by radical Protestants, in favor of spiritual conversations and private disciplines. The inner light trumped the external ministry.

When we come to the Enlightenment, we can see that it was a very religious movement. Joachim of Fiore's third age became "secularized" as the Age of Enlightenment. Drawing on the expectations of "the enthusiasts of the thirteenth century" concerning a coming Age of the Spirit that would transcend all need for creaturely mediation (including Bible and church), G. E. Lessing (1729–81) boasted that this day had arrived. Employing an antithesis between letter and spirit in an interpretation that had been often employed by the ancient Gnostics, the mystics, and some radical Anabaptists, Lessing urged, "In short, the letter is not the spirit, and the Bible is not religion. Consequently, objections to the letter and to the Bible are not also objections to the spirit and to religion."[30] In fact, in Lessing's *The Education of the Human Race*, "the speculations about 'the eternal gospel' are connected with the anticipations in Joachim and the spiritual Franciscans."[31]

Like Thomas Müntzer, he correlated the contrast between "letter" and "Spirit" with the Bible and true spirituality.[32] For Immanuel Kant, this contrast was drawn in terms of the "pure religion" of inner morality ("the moral law within") and the "ecclesiastical faiths" with their particular creeds and rites.

In Romanticism, the turn inward was complete. In the early nineteenth century, Friedrich Schleiermacher (1768–1834) advised the "cultured despisers" of Christianity in his day to "turn away from all that is usually called religion" and fix their gaze on the "God-inspired" feelings and actions of noble souls.[33] The creeds and official administrations of the external ministry represent the "letter" rather than the "spirit." Whether conceived in terms of inner reason (Descartes), "the moral law within" (Kant), or "pious feeling" (Schleiermacher), modernity turned a deaf ear to any external authority.

American transcendentalism (Emerson, Thoreau, James, and others) was the version of Romanticism that attracted a wide following among Boston intellectuals. Emerson had written, "The height, the deity of man is to be self-sustained, to need no gift, no foreign force"—no external God, with an external Word and sacraments or formal ministry.[34] Finney's revivalistic legacy represents, in the words of Garry Wills, "an alternative Romanticism," a popular version of self-reliance and inner experience, "taking up where Transcendentalism left off."[35]

In the light of this history, we can understand why surveys consistently reveal that Americans consider themselves "spiritual, but not religious." Suspicious of institutional churches, creeds, preaching, and sacraments, they nevertheless believe that they have a vital relationship with God. Wade Clark Roof's findings are hardly surprising when he reports, "The distinction between 'spirit' and 'institution' is of major importance" to spiritual seekers today.[36] "Spirit is the inner, experiential aspect of religion; institution is the outer, established form of religion."[37] He adds, "Direct experience is always more trustworthy, if for no other reason than because of its 'inwardness' and 'withinness'—two qualities that have come to be much appreciated in a highly expressive, narcissistic culture."[38] In fact, Roof comes close to suggesting that evangelicalism works so well in this kind of culture because it helped to create it.

In his latest book, *A New Kind of Christianity*, Brian McLaren follows liberal theologian Harvey Cox in announcing the arrival of "the Age of the Spirit." In this era of emerging peace and justice, the church vanishes into "faith communities." Buddhists, Muslims, Jews, Christians, and even atheists will come increasingly to cooperate in creating the kingdom of God. The externals that divide religions must give way to universal human flourishing. As humankind matures, it advances from the primitive views of God (especially in the Old Testament) to the peaceable kingdom that Jesus launched. This is *most*-modern, not postmodern. McLaren's interpretation of the Bible as reflecting an evolving spiritual consciousness from primitive to more mature ideas about God is as old as Lessing's *Education of the Human Race*. In fact, McLaren alludes to this title.[39]

Yet even in less extreme proposals, the impulse of radical Protestantism is prevalent in evangelicalism today. In *Celebration of Discipline*, Richard Foster's survey of spiritual disciplines that he judges essential does not even include baptism and the Lord's Supper. In fact, the emphasis is on spontaneity and freedom, over against forms. "Until God touches and frees our spirit we cannot enter this realm. . . . Our spirit must be ignited by the divine fire. As a result, we need not be overly concerned with the question of a correct form for worship. . . . When Spirit touches spirit the issue of forms is wholly secondary."[40] The subtitle of this important work is *The Path to Spiritual Growth*, and he treats as essential many methods of personal piety that are not commanded in Scripture. Yet there is no mention of the means of grace that Christ explicitly mandated for making disciples.

Willard continues that emphasis in *The Great Omission: Reclaiming Jesus' Essential Teachings on Discipleship*, arguing that most Christians today are satisfied with a gospel of forgiveness that omits the inner transformation of souls. He offers what appears to be his own translation of the Great Commission: "I have been given say over all things in heaven and in the earth. As you go, therefore, make disciples of all kinds of people, submerge them in the Trinitarian Presence, and show them *how to do* everything I have commanded. And now look: I am with you every minute *until the job is done*" (emphasis added).[41] In this misleading paraphrase, the means of God's saving grace (Word and sacrament) are replaced with methods for our activity. Although the "keys of the kingdom" that Jesus gave to the apostles are associated with the church's official ministry of preaching, sacrament, and discipline (Matt. 16:18–19; 18:15–20), Willard identifies "solitude, silence, and fasting" as the "keys of the kingdom."[42] The "keys" become tools or techniques for unlocking our inner world: "We are using the keys to access the Kingdom."[43] "I almost never meet someone in spiritual coldness, perplexity, distress, and failure," he says, "who is regular in the use of those spiritual exercises that will be obvious to anyone familiar with the contents of the New Testament."[44]

Willard argues that the heart of the gospel is inner renewal: "The gospel is new life through faith in Jesus Christ."[45] We are transformed in our character by "carefully planned and grace-sustained disciplines."[46] These disciplines of obedience are not only the means but the source of our inner transformation.[47] "Jesus is actually looking for people he can trust with his power."[48]

When asked in an interview to identify "the discipline that you think we need to be exploring more at this point," Foster answered, "Solitude."

> It is the most foundational of the disciplines of abstinence, the *via negativa*. The evangelical passion for engagement with the world is good. But as Thomas à Kempis says, the only person who's safe to travel is the person who's free to stay at home. And Pascal said that we would solve the world's problems if we just learned to sit in our room alone. Solitude is essential for right engagement.[49]

Foster shares Willard's conviction that an emphasis on God's grace has paralyzed the pursuit of inner transformation. Where Scripture teaches that Christ's objective work outside of us in public history is the gospel—"the power of God for salvation," Foster writes,

> The most important, most real, most lasting work, is accomplished in the depths of our heart. This work is solitary and interior. It cannot be seen by anyone, not even ourselves. It is a work known only to God. It is the work of heart purity, of soul conversion, of inward transformation, of life formation. . . . Much intense formation work is necessary before we can stand the fires of heaven. Much training is necessary before we are the kind of persons who can safely and easily reign with God.[50]

Willard helpfully points out the significance of the largely abandoned Sabbath practices of earlier generations.[51] However, even this crucial discipline loses the corporate character that it has in the New Testament and becomes another opportunity for private solitude. "Silence completes solitude, for without it you cannot be alone."[52] To quote Willard again: "It is a tragic error to think that Jesus was telling us, as he left, to start churches, as that is understood today."[53] I am not entirely sure what is intended by "as that is understood today," but it seems evident from the New Testament that the apostles understood the Great Commission precisely as starting churches.

In this view, the public, corporate, and audible ministry of the keys becomes assimilated to a spirit-body dualism that has always been prominent in the monastic traditions. "The flesh stands, basically, for the natural. . . . What then is *spirit*? Spirit is *unbodily personal reality and power*."[54] God is seeking true worshipers. "I believe that that means people who in the core of their being, beyond all appearance in the physical world by means of their body, want to stand clear and right before God. And they are people who wholly devote their innermost being—the heart, will, or human spirit—to doing so."[55] This Platonic tendency is also evident in Foster's work.[56] But is this the New Testament definition of Spirit and flesh?

Following Plato, many Christians in the contemplative tradition have understood spirit (*pneuma*) and flesh (*sarx*) in terms of the "higher world" of eternal reality and the "lower world" of mere appearances. The spirit (or mind) is regarded as the higher, true self, the immortal spark of divinity, while the body and its senses belong to the realm of ever-changing shadows: mere appearances.

However, in the New Testament the contrast between Spirit and flesh refers to the Holy Spirit's regenerating power versus the impotence of human nature in its fallen condition. Where Platonism thinks of spirit versus flesh in terms of *two worlds* (spiritual versus material), the New Testament speaks of the Spirit and the flesh in terms of *two ages* (this age versus the age to come). With Christ, the final resurrection of the dead has already begun. Our head has been raised and glorified, beyond the reach of sin, condemnation, and death. Furthermore, the Spirit has been poured out on all of the saints, indwelling them as the deposit on their own resurrection in glory. Far from driving us deeper within, biblical eschatology directs us outside of ourselves to the descent of the kingdom in history. It is not our gradual ascent up the ladder of spiritual contemplation but the descent, ascent, and return of Christ in the flesh that drives Christian faith, hope, and love.

Instead of taking flights of solitude, ascending upward from spirit to Spirit, we need to live in this world as those who have already "tasted the heavenly gift, and have shared in the Holy Spirit, and have tasted the goodness of the word of God and the powers of the age to come"

(Heb. 6:4–5). The whole earth is not yet renewed in its consummated glory, but we live in that hope even now, on the basis of Christ's resurrection. Even our private disciplines of prayer and meditation on Scripture serve this goal of making us extroverted creatures: looking up to Christ in faith and out to our neighbor in love.

The contrast between external means and inner transformation is also emphasized by Stanley Grenz, a theological pioneer of the emergent movement. In fact, he draws inspiration from evangelicalism's pietist heritage. "Although some evangelicals belong to ecclesiological traditions that understand the church as in some sense a dispenser of grace," he observes, "generally we see our congregations foremost as a fellowship of believers."[57] We share our journeys (our "testimony") of personal transformation.[58] Therefore, Grenz celebrates the "fundamental shift . . . from a creed-based to a spirituality-based identity" that is more like medieval mysticism than Protestant orthodoxy.[59] "Consequently, spirituality is inward and quietistic,"[60] concerned with combating "the lower nature and the world,"[61] in "a personal commitment that becomes the ultimate focus of the believer's affections."[62]

Nowhere in this account does Grenz locate the origin of faith in an external gospel; rather, faith arises from an inner experience. "Because spirituality is *generated from within the individual,* inner motivation is crucial"—more important, in fact, than "grand theological statements" (emphasis added).[63]

> The spiritual life is above all the imitation of Christ. . . . In general we eschew religious ritual. Not slavish adherence to rites, but doing what Jesus would do is our concept of true discipleship. Consequently, most evangelicals neither accept the sacramentalism of many mainline churches nor join the Quakers in completely eliminating the sacraments. We practice baptism and the Lord's Supper, but understand the significance of these rites in a guarded manner.[64]

In any case, he says, these rites are practiced as goads to personal experience and out of obedience to divine command.[65]

Grenz realizes that this view "exchanges the priority of the church for the priority of the believer."[66] However, this is merely to state explicitly the working theology that evangelicals assume, Grenz notes:

> "Get on with the task; get your life in order by practicing the aids to growth and see if you do not mature spiritually," we exhort. In fact, if a believer comes to the point where he or she senses that stagnation

has set in, evangelical counsel is to redouble one's efforts in the task of exercising the disciplines. "Check up on yourself," the evangelical spiritual counselor admonishes.[67]

The emphasis on the individual believer is evident, he says, in the expectation to "find a ministry" within the local fellowship.[68]

All of this is at odds with an emphasis on doctrine and especially, Grenz adds, an emphasis on "a material and a formal principle"— referring to the Reformation slogans *sola fide* (justification by Christ alone through faith alone) and *sola scriptura* (by Scripture alone).[69] In spite of the fact that the Scriptures declare that "faith comes by hearing, and hearing by the word of God" (Rom. 10:17 NKJV), Grenz says, "Faith is by nature immediate."[70]

Consistent with his emphasis on the priority of inner experience, Grenz urges "a revisioned understanding of the *nature* of the Bible's authority."[71] Our own religious experience today needs to be included in the process of inspiration.[72] Accordingly, Grenz believes that this will "chart the way beyond the evangelical tendency to equate in a simple fashion the revelation of God with the Bible—that is, to make a one-to-one correspondence between the words of the Bible and the very Word of God."[73] So instead of God's Word coming to us from outside of ourselves, giving us faith and bringing inner transformation in its wake, even Scripture becomes the pious expression of the experience of the individual or community.

Yet this is simply to return to the moribund enthusiasm of Friedrich Schleiermacher. It is not a postmodern innovation but a revival of Romanticism—and, before that, the doctrine of the inner light held by radical Protestants.

Writing at the beginning of the twentieth century, G. K. Chesterton recalled a recent editorial in the newspaper. Chesterton summarized its main argument that "Christianity when stripped of its armour of dogma (as who should speak of a man stripped of his armour of bones), turned out to be nothing but the Quaker doctrine of the Inner Light." "Now, if I were to say that Christianity came into the world specially to destroy the doctrine of the Inner Light, that would be an exaggeration," Chesterton responded. "But it would be very much nearer the truth."[74] The Romans of the first century (especially the Stoics) were advocates of the Inner Light. However, Chesterton concludes that "of all horrible religions the most horrible is the worship of the god within."[75] "Christianity came into the world firstly in order to assert with violence that a man had not only to look inwards, but to look outwards, to behold with astonishment and enthusiasm a divine company and a divine captain. The only fun of being a Christian was that a man was not left alone with the Inner Light, but definitely recognized an outer light, fair as the sun, clear as the moon, terrible as an army with banners."[76]

Mystics and rationalists imagine that the inner self is the most nearly divine part of us, but the New Testament identifies the inner self in its fallen condition as "the old self" and "the flesh," belonging to the old creation that is passing away. It is almost as if this dying "old Adam" in us is revived and rejuvenated every time we turn inward to gaze upon it to comfort it or perhaps even to worship it.

It is the work of the Spirit to destroy this idol by the preaching of the law and to call us out of ourselves into the bright light of day with Christ as the sun. When this happens, we become ecstatic creatures instead of introspective ones. We look up to our God in faith and out to our neighbor in love. This is what makes Christianity an intrinsically *missionary* faith while also affirming the active participation of Christians in the world through their secular callings.

Living the Gospel vs. Proclaiming the Gospel

I mentioned above that calls to discipleship often divide into two emphases—*personal change through spiritual disciplines* and *social change through cultural engagement*—and that these reflect older rivalries between the *contemplative* and the *active* life.

The emphasis in the spiritual disciplines movement is on the contemplative life. For example, bestselling author Richard Foster observes that there is a lot of interest these days in "social-service projects." "Everyone thinks of changing the world, but where, oh where, are those who think of changing themselves?"[77] Yet for the Franciscan heritage, discipleship is above all the imitation of Christ—particularly his concern for the poor and oppressed in the world. A similar emphasis is struck in evangelicals today in the emerging church movement.

There is no hard and fast division here. In fact, emergent leaders look to medieval and Anabaptist spiritualities, acknowledging the influence of Dallas Willard and Richard Foster. Both movements emphasize deeds over creeds and are somewhat suspicious of formal church structures as inhibiting free-spirited transformation. Both emphasize the imitation of Christ more than the uniqueness of his person and work, without denying the latter. Nevertheless, there is a subtle difference in emphasis, with a younger generation of emergent Christians seeking a more outward-looking, culturally engaged pattern of discipleship through transformation.

One tie that binds these various approaches is the call to "live the gospel." It is often reflected in the proposed shift from thinking of Christianity as a *missionary* faith to a *missional* faith, or in terms of *saving souls* versus *redeeming the world*. The call to missional Christianity by writers like the missionary bishop Lesslie Newbigin meant that our mandate is not only to send missionaries to other parts of the world but to be Christ's witnesses where we are. Newbigin reminded us that the church isn't called merely to *engage* in missions but that it *is* a mission. Newbigin was terrific at holding together what is often separated today: namely, the priesthood of all believers and the importance of the visible church with its public ministry of the means of grace.[78] As we can see even in the titles of his major works, the heart of the Great Commission remained for Newbigin the proclamation of Christ: *Truth to Tell: The Gospel as Public Truth*; *The Open Secret: An Introduction to the Theology of Mission*; and *The Gospel in a Pluralistic Society*.

There are still many who use the term "missional" in this helpful way. However, increasingly "missional" not only *supplements* the "missionary" model; it often *supplants* it. As a consequence, the priesthood of all believers (the church as the people who are disciples) is often emphasized in contrast with the formal ministry (the church as the place where disciples are made). Darrell Guder's *The Missional Church* helped to turn a concept into a movement.[79]

In spite of important differences, the emergent and spiritual disciplines movements share a view of discipleship that stresses a number of important contrasts.

The emergent movement is reacting against extremes—some real, others caricatures—and like most reactions, it has become its own extreme, offering a bevy of false alternatives. Nevertheless, we must first hear what these brothers and sisters are saying and ask why they have found evangelical churches so inhospitable to embodying the forgiveness and grace that they proclaim to the world. What are so many younger Christians reacting against that makes them long for genuine community of engaging, forgiving, and loving friendship? What are the realities that provoke their indictment of hypocrisy, dogmatism, and inwardly focused lives and churches? I believe that at least part of the answer lies in the fact that many traditional and megachurch environments are bored by or distracted from the gospel and its delivery through the ministry of Word and sacrament.

I have heard the emergent critique, and I have been challenged by it personally. Nevertheless, I am left with the nagging suspicion that half-truths have been mistaken for whole truths and the things that are in the foreground of the biblical drama are pushed into the background. I will focus on two major contrasts that seem to dominate the emergent agenda, although they reflect an older and broader tendency in evangelicalism.

The spiritual disciplines movement may focus more on personal transformation and the emergent movement more on social transformation, but from both one often hears common evangelical refrains: deeds, not creeds; life, not doctrine; internal reality, not external forms. Brian McLaren explains, "Anabaptists see the Christian faith primarily as a way of life," focusing on Jesus's Sermon on the Mount rather than on Paul and doctrines concerning personal salvation.[80]

Furthermore, there seems to be a distrust of preaching and teaching as a means of transformation. Words are habitually twisted, distorted, and abused in our culture—even by authority figures. Cynicism is bound to set in when there seems to be a lack of connection between talking the talk and walking the walk. In this context, it's not surprising that words become seen as merely external, formal, and perfunctory, instead of living and active.

In contrast to the megachurch world in which many were reared, emergent Christians are interested in theology. They don't want the Christian faith to be pared down to "40 Days of Purpose" or "Four Spiritual Laws," Tony Jones explains. "Warren's book, a forty-day experience of purposeful living, boasts about a thousand Bible verses, the vast majority of them coming with little explanation and no context," Jones complains.[81] He also criticizes Robert Schuller for transforming "the gospel of Jesus Christ into the 'power of positive thinking (with Jesus).'"[82]

These populist versions of American Christianity wandered a bit from the apostle Paul, who proclaimed that the cross on which Jesus hung was a "scandal." Both Schuller and Warren are progenitors of the "seeker-sensitive" church movement, which dominated American evangelicalism in the 1980s and 1990s. Preaching about concepts like sin was avoided, opting instead for sermon series on "how to be a better Christian family."

Emergents know that the answers aren't that easy, and they are looking for greater depth, for more serious—theological—answers to the big questions.[83] Yet like the megachurch movement, emergent conversations evidence little interest in or awareness of the resources of the Reformation.

Like Dallas Willard, many emergent leaders today see genuine discipleship more in terms of transformation over against the forgiveness of sins, and extending Christ's redeeming work by following his example rather than emphasizing Christ's vicarious atonement and justification through faith alone. As Jones describes,

> In an emergent church, you're likely to hear a phrase like "Our calling as a church is to partner with God in the work that God is already doing in the world—to cooperate in the building of God's Kingdom." Many theological assumptions lie behind this statement, not least of which is a robust faith in God's presence and ongoing activity in the world. Further, the idea that human beings can "cooperate" with God is particularly galling to conservative Calvinists, who generally deny the human ability to participate with God's work. This posture, however, is too passive for most emergents, who see the Bible as a call for us to contribute to God's purposes.[84]

What are we to make of this contrast between the gospel lived and proclaimed?

The gospel is referred to in Scripture exclusively as something that is *proclaimed*. In fact, that is the mandate of the Great Commission: "preach the gospel." The call to deeds over creeds contradicts both the historical claims of the earliest Christians and the doctrinal interpretation of those claims in the New Testament.

First, the historical claims. To be sure, there are verses that speak of living *in view of* the gospel, in a manner *worthy of* the gospel, and bearing the *fruit of* the gospel. However, there is no passage that says that we are to *live the gospel*. Those who believe that the gospel is a call to transforming the kingdoms of this age are inventing a message that runs counter to the central claims that provoked Jesus's crucifixion and the persecution of the earliest believers.

The building ire of the religious leaders toward Jesus coalesced around his making himself equal with God (John 5:18) and forgiving sins in his own person, directly, over against the Temple and its sacrificial system (Mark 2:7). In fact, at his trial he is charged by the Jewish council with announcing the destruction of the temple, and

asked by the high priest, "'Are you the Christ, the Son of the Blessed?'
And Jesus said, 'I am, and you will see the Son of Man seated at the
right hand of Power, and coming with the clouds of heaven'" (Mark
14:61–62). With that, "the high priest tore his garments and said,
'What further witnesses do we need? You have heard his blasphemy.
What is your decision?' And they all condemned him as deserving
death" (Mark 14:63–64).

Jesus was never charged on the grounds of trying to cultivate the
inner life through spiritual disciplines. Nor was he brought to trial for
trying to bring world peace. In fact, he said, "Do not think that I have
come to bring peace to the earth. I have not come to bring peace, but a
sword. For I have come to set a man against his father, and a daughter
against her mother, and a daughter-in-law against her mother-in-law.
And a person's enemies will be those of his own household. Whoever
loves father or mother more than me is not worthy of me" (Matt.
10:34–37). Jesus's opponents never included a revolutionary blueprint
for improving world conditions among the indictments against him. In
fact, his mission was an utter failure for those who saw him as a leader
of political revolution. He told his followers up front that they would be
harassed and that some of them would die for their testimony to him.

The response of imperial Rome also focused on the historical and
theological claims of the early Christians. They were not persecuted
for following the example of Jesus. In fact, Gentiles expressed admira-
tion for the close bond of the believers and their care for each other's
material as well as spiritual needs. So what was everybody so worked
up about when it came to the Christians?

In a letter written to Emperor Trajan about AD 112, Pliny the
Younger, Caesar's supervisor of Bithynia (now central-northern Tur-
key) explains that informers would come to him with the names of
their own relatives and friends who were Christians. One charge was
that they "chant antiphonally a hymn to Christ as to a god."[85] What
stood out to Pliny, however, was the intractability of these "criminals":
all they had to do in order to be sent home freely was to curse Jesus
and offer incense to the emperor. Yet this they would not do, even up
to the moment of their execution.[86]

The indictment of both Jewish and Roman authorities centered on
the confession of Jesus as the Christ, God incarnate, King of Kings
and the Savior of the world. Throughout the New Testament, believers are said to suffer specifically "for my sake" and "for my name's
sake" (Matt. 10:18, 22). The temple authorities warn the Jerusalem

Christians to stop speaking about Jesus (Acts 4:17–18; 5:40), Stephen
is stoned on the charge of blasphemies about Jesus (Acts 6:8–8:1),
and Paul refers to his many persecutions as suffering for the name of
Christ (2 Cor. 11:22–29 and others).[87] In fact, before his conversion
Paul is described by Luke as persecuting those who invoke Jesus's
name (Acts 9:14, 21). Paul himself relates that during those years
his goal was "to do many things in opposing the name of Jesus of
Nazareth" and that he tried to make Jewish Christians "blaspheme"
Jesus's name (Acts 26:9, 11). This charge of blasphemy indicates not
only the central charge of their opposition, but the central conviction
of the earliest Christians: Jesus Christ as God and the only Savior.

Gathering evidence from external testimony (including Pliny's),
New Testament scholar Larry Hurtado summarizes the core of early
Christian faith and practice. They would gather regularly for the
following practices:

1. hymns about Jesus sung as part of early Christian worship;
2. prayer to God "through" Jesus and "in Jesus' name," and even
   direct prayer to Jesus himself, including particularly the invocation of Jesus in the corporate worship setting;
3. "calling upon the name of Jesus," particularly in Christian
   baptism and in healing and exorcism;
4. the Christian common meal enacted as a sacred meal where
   the risen Jesus presides as "Lord" of the gathered community;
5. the practice of ritually "confessing" Jesus in the context of
   Christian worship; and
6. Christian prophecy as oracles of the risen Jesus, and the Holy
   Spirit of prophecy understood as also the Spirit of Jesus.[88]

Pliny was concerned about the rapidly spreading faith in Christ,
as we see in his complaint to Caesar that the pagan temples were "almost deserted," and as a result, the enormous economic trade in the
various cults and sacrifices was disappearing.[89] The Romans accused
the early Christians of atheism and of undermining the civil religion
of the empire by refusing to participate in the cult of the emperor.
The Roman senator and historian Tacitus relates that "an immense
multitude" was arrested, upon acknowledging they were Christians,
on the charge of "hatred of the human race."[90] Yet these martyrs
even used their trial as an occasion to articulate, explain, and defend
the gospel (besides the many examples in Acts, see 1 Peter 3:15–16).

In the external as well as internal sources, then, there is no evidence that Christians were persecuted merely because they were following the example of Jesus. Philippians 2:6–11 calls believers to have the same mind of Christ in humbling themselves, but the analogy clearly breaks down. Hurtado observes, "We have no reason to think that the intended readers were expected to aspire to an equivalent exaltation for themselves, with the entire cosmos acclaiming them as divine 'Lord.'"[91] These early Christians performed many worthy deeds, but they were martyred for their creed, which was fleshed out in their public worship.

Second, this slogan, "living the gospel," confuses the law with the gospel. This is about the greatest mistake believers can make in interpreting Scripture. "Now we know that the law is good, if one uses it lawfully" (1 Tim. 1:8). The law is good not only because it exposes our sin, despite all of our efforts at spin and self-justification, and sends us to Christ for justification, but also because it guides us. It tells us as believers what pleases God. Indeed, God's moral law is nothing other than the stipulation of what it means to love God and neighbor. But we don't *live the gospel*. We *believe the gospel* and we *follow the commands*. The gospel is the announcement that a life has already been lived perfectly for us, surrendered for us, and taken back up as the firstfruit of the new creation. Believing this Good News, we then offer ourselves not as sacrifices of atonement but as living sacrifices of thanksgiving, spreading the aroma of Christ (Rom. 12:1; 2 Cor. 2:15).

Nothing that you, or I, or all of us together do can add one task to Christ's completed mission. His mission is connected to our mission as the basis for its effects, but they are qualitatively different. He is the Savior and we are the saved; he redeemed and we are redeemed; he is building his church and we are receiving a kingdom that cannot be shaken. All of this is a gift. And it's a gift that is meant to be opened, explored, wondered at, and used. It is also a gift that is to be given: always dispensed without ever being diminished.

Third, Christ mandated proclamation of the gospel. It is not for us to decide whether preaching the gospel is adequate to our current situation. To be sure, our hypocrisy repels and our love attracts, but the Spirit's work is inseparable from the word—specifically, the word of the gospel concerning Christ. This is why the central mandate of the Great Commission is to "proclaim the gospel to the whole creation" (Mark 16:15). "So faith comes from hearing, and hearing through the word of Christ" (Rom. 10:17). Faith is *expressed* through our love and good works, but it does not *come* from them. Peter says that we are "born again . . . through the living and abiding word of God. . . . And this word is the good news that was preached to you" (1 Peter 1:23, 25).

The apostle Paul saw the renewing of our minds by the Word as the source of being transformed rather than conformed to the pattern of this age (Rom. 12:1–2). If masses of Christians are not living in accordance with their profession, the answer is not to switch from creeds to deeds but to immerse ourselves in the creed that gives rise to the right sort of practical living. If ever there was a church of consumers imitating the narcissistic patterns of its culture, it was the Corinthian church. Yet Paul doesn't just assume that they understand the gospel. He reminds them that while he was with them he preached nothing but Christ and him crucified (1 Cor. 2:2). "Aha!" some of Paul's adversaries might have replied, "That's why their church is so messed up! If you had been more balanced in your teaching, emphasizing the need for inner transformation and the imitation of Christ, you wouldn't be writing this disciplinary letter." However, Paul not only doesn't think he made a mistake; he goes right back to the gospel again, reminding them of who they are in Christ. Only after doing this does he upbraid them for living inconsistently with this gospel that they profess. Paul's assumption is that if a church is failing to live out its creed, then maybe it does not really understand it yet.

The Spirit creates faith through the gospel, and this faith yields the fruit of righteousness in our daily living. We need the law to define the righteousness *of* God and the gospel to announce to us the righteousness *from* God that is a gift in his Son. There is a lot for us to do, as prescribed in the Bible's commands, but the gospel tells us what has been done for us. That is why it is Good News. This gospel is meant to be proclaimed, recited, unpacked, administered in baptism and Eucharist, sung, prayed, and discussed in the fellowship of saints. Even singing in the church is another way of making "the word of Christ dwell in you richly, teaching and admonishing one another in all wisdom, singing psalms and hymns and spiritual songs, with thankfulness in your hearts to God" (Col. 3:16).

This gospel ministry drives us out of ourselves to Christ and to our brothers and sisters, and then out into the world. It reshapes our sense of who we are and where we are going. God created and sustains the world through his Word. God redeems through his living and active speech. There's no way of salvation apart from good words. We need the gospel as much today as we did when we first believed. The gospel "re-words" us, from the aimless plot of existence "in Adam" to the amazing drama of being "in Christ." So the gospel is something we *hear*; the law is something we *do* because of it.

Part of the problem is that this rich and inexhaustible gospel from Genesis to Revelation has been reduced to slogans on T-shirts and coffee mugs. Like coins that lose their embossing with constant handling, familiarity breeds contempt. What we need are not fewer words but better, deeper, richer, and more profound words. We need to be constantly steeped in God's Word and communicate the Word to each other and to the rest of the world. And we need to ask how our lives, our relationships, and our churches are being shaped by this gospel word that we have heard, sung, prayed, and shared with others.

Of course, emergent groups still use words, but it's more in the style of conversation. Tony Jones adds, "Further, emergents are enamored of story, particularly of telling their own stories and listening to others' stories."[92] How is this different from the string of "before" and "after" testimonials and "what this verse means to me" Bible studies that have characterized traditional evangelicalism for a long time? And how is talking about ourselves going to drive us out of the kind of inward focus that creates a circle of friends like us, opening us up to a communion of saints who are united only by having heard and embraced the same Savior?

We need to hear *the* story, with Christ as the lead character. We need to have our character killed off again in this scene, raised with a new identity in Christ. It's a lot easier to talk about ourselves and our journeys than it is to talk about God's journey from creation to exodus, conquest, and consummation through biblical exposition. Yet talking about ourselves doesn't really lead to community, at least not to the kind of community that finds its story in the biblical plot. We come together with our own stories about being a white guy from Iowa who wrestles with his sexuality, a black woman from Atlanta who lost her house in the market crash, a lonely Puerto Rican immigrant, a teenager struggling with his faith, an elderly woman who just lost her husband to cancer, a normal couple facing normal challenges of marriage and raising a family, or a CEO or a janitor who was just laid off. All of these stories contribute to the diversity that enriches and is enriched by the whole body. Yet when we gather to hear the "Christ story," we become a family. It's "one Lord, one faith, one baptism" (Eph. 4:5). In other words, it's the Great Commission: the gift that keeps on giving, not just on the foreign mission field but also here at home every week.

Stop the recital of this grand narrative and the only sound we'll hear is the cacophony of chatter of a culture that loves to talk to itself about itself. We're overwhelmed every day by a rushing torrent of propaganda from advertising, politics, entertainment, and pop psychology. We are being baptized and catechized every day into the wisdom and ephemera of this passing age, which makes faithful Christian ministry all the more essential. We are not just pooling our ignorance or sharing our experiences. We are being given new truths and experiences that we never anticipated.

Speaking more generally of the evangelical movement (especially in the United States), the antidoctrinal tenor of our churches is consistent with the anti-intellectual tenor of our times. We have become worldly at the places where we thought we were most pious. It is not a mark of faithfulness, but of worldliness, to identify Christian discipleship merely with emotional experience or a moral and social activism that eschews doctrine. "Deeds, not creeds" equals "law, not gospel." Ultimately, it means that we are left talking about ourselves rather than Christ. Even doxology becomes vague self-expression unless it is a response to God's Word. "Let's just praise the Lord." *Why?* "Let's just follow Jesus and do what he would do." Again the question presses upon us: *Why?* We live "in view of God's mercies." That means that we cannot even be transformed except by the Word of God that renews our minds, exposing us again and again to the disrupting news of God's redeeming work.

Our lives may attract people to or repel them from the word of the gospel. However, Dan Kimball is simply wrong when he (like Jones above) invokes St. Francis's advice about a wordless preaching of the gospel and says, "Our lives will preach better than anything we can say."[93] Everything in the New Testament points to instruction in the faith that yields true discipleship, genuine maturity, and generous fruit-bearing. My life does *not* preach better than the prophetic and apostolic witness to Jesus Christ, but I can still be saved—even from my hypocrisy—by hearing that gospel again every week.

Mere imperatives to more faithful living will only drive one to either despair or self-righteousness (or a little of both). We are transformed not by hearing more about ourselves and each other but by hearing more about God and his mighty acts of salvation throughout history. Our Buddhist cousins, Muslim neighbors, and burned-out churchgoers need to encounter disciples of Christ who point away from themselves, witnessing to Christ as the Savior of *sinners*—even Christians like ourselves who still fall short of the glory of God. They need to be introduced to the Good News that is greater than all of our sin, including the sins of Christians. They do not need to see more Christians holding up their lives as the gospel, only to watch them fall; they need more Christians holding up Christ as the gospel as they confess their sins and receive his priestly absolution. They need to encounter Mary Magdalenes who have sat at our Lord's feet to feast on his person and work and then rise to love and serve their neighbors.

And ironically, when we are seeking Christ rather than a generic social and moral impact on the society, one that we could have apart from him, something strange happens. A communion emerges around the Lamb, drawing people together "from every tribe and language and people and nation" into "a kingdom of priests to our God" (Rev. 5:9). From a justifying and sanctifying communion with Christ that they share together, there emerges a foretaste of genuine peace, love, and justice that can orient our ordinary lives and animate our activity in our worldly callings. Start with the regular proclamation of the gospel and you get everything else thrown into the bargain: faith, justification, sanctification, and glorification. Start with anything else, and it's business as usual with pious window dressing. With Paul, we should all be able to say, "For I am not ashamed of the gospel, for it is the power of God for salvation to everyone who believes" (Rom. 1:16).

The older emphasis in evangelical revivalism was on "soul saving." The world is going to be destroyed, but our commission is to get as many people as we can to say the sinner's prayer so that they can go to heaven when they die. It was revolutionary for me when I encountered writers who related the wider biblical horizon of a new creation that encompassed all of creaturely reality. Of course, the resurrection of the body had always been an article of faith that I embraced, but it wasn't part of a cosmic restoration of the world. I remember J. I. Packer saying at a conference that whereas fundamentalism is "world-denying," Reformed theology is "world-affirming." That makes all the difference in the world, quite literally.

At this point we find an area of shared interest between Reformed and emergent emphases. Tony Jones observes, "The evidence is in: millions of individuals 'inviting Jesus Christ into their hearts as their personal Lord and Savior' at megachurches and Billy Graham crusades has done little to stem the moral dissolution of America. And ironically, it's the very individualism engendered by evangelicalism that has resulted in this predicament."[94] According to Jones, "too many evangelical churches have emphasized the vertical, just-me-and-Jesus relationship to the exclusion of the horizontal relationships with other human beings and with all of creation. In fact, a major study in the 1990s showed that the individualism inherent in American evangelicalism is directly responsible for evangelicals' inability to diagnose and solve systemic social issues like racism and abortion."[95] Maybe the analysis is a little simplistic, but I think there is a lot of truth in Jones's indictment. Yet Jones's cure seems to me at least to be worse than the disease.

There is a direct correlation between collapsing the gospel into law, Christ's person and work into ours, preaching the gospel into "living the gospel," this age into the age to come, and the sacred ministry of the church into the secular service of believers in the world. McLaren commends the missional model for eliminating "old dichotomies like 'evangelism' and 'social action.'"[96] The church as institution (with the Great Commission) is collapsed into the church as believers (with the commission to witness to others and serve them through their callings). Dichotomies aside, there is a crucial distinction to be made between evangelism (proclaiming the gospel, baptizing, and teaching) and social action (loving and serving our neighbors, especially in our families and secular callings). *Christians* have many callings in the world, but *the church* has one calling to the world.

It is one thing to say that we are partners with God in bringing the Good News to the world and loving our neighbors in our callings and quite another to say that we are partners with God in redeeming and reconciling the world. According to Anglican bishop N. T. Wright, "The church is called to do the work of Christ, to be the means of his action in and for the world. . . . God intends to put the world to rights; he has dramatically launched this project through Jesus. Those who belong to Jesus are called, here and now, in the power of the Spirit, to be agents of that putting-to-rights purpose."[97]

Though still central and essential, Jesus seems to be more like the one who gets the ball rolling than the unique person whose saving work in his first and second advents is unrepeatable and inimitable. Jesus dramatically launches the project. So the kingdom of glory is already present, unfolding by degrees. "God is rescuing us from the shipwreck of the world, not so that we can sit back and put our feet up in his company, but so that we can be part of his plan to remake the world."[98] Isn't this precisely the kind of thinking that led to the fusion of Christ and culture in Christendom?

Similarly, McLaren redefines the Great Commission as completing Christ's reconciling activity: "To say that Jesus is Savior is to say that in Jesus, God is intervening as Savior in all of these ways, judging (naming evil as evil), forgiving (breaking the vicious cycle of cause and effect, making reconciliation possible), and teaching (showing how to set chain reactions of good in motion)."[99] He mentions Jesus's suffering, but only as bearing the wrath of human beings. Jesus forgives from the cross, but does he bear God's judgment of sinners on the cross? If so, there is no mention of it. "Then, because we are so often ignorantly wrong and stupid, Jesus comes with saving teaching, profound yet amazingly compact: *Love God with your whole heart, soul, mind, and strength*, Jesus says, *and love your neighbor as yourself*, and that is enough." This is what it means to say that "Jesus is saving the world."[100] Although Jesus called this the summary of the *law* (Matt. 22:37–40, citing Deut. 6:5), for McLaren it becomes the summary of the *gospel*.

These writers remind us of the danger in disconnecting the vertical relationship with God from the horizontal relationship to our neighbors. In fact, after summarizing the first table of the law as love of God, Jesus adds, "*And a second is like it*: You shall love your neighbor as yourself" (Matt. 22:39, emphasis added). However, these writers risk making the same mistake, only this time by focusing on the horizontal relationships apart from the vertical. When this happens, sin is easily reduced to bad things we do to each other that leads to a brokenness in interpersonal relationships. It is no longer seen as a transgression of God's covenant that brings God's judgment and therefore a curse into every other relationship. "Indeed, many emergent Christians will concur that we live in a sinful world, a world of wars and famines and pogroms," Jones says. "But they will be inclined to attribute this sin not to the distance between human beings and God but to the broken relationships that clutter our lives and our world." This means that on Good Friday, Christ's crucifixion became "the impetus for healed and healing relationships in a world that desperately needs them. And the concentration on correct doctrine is also the reflection of an earlier time."[101]

Jones confuses the vertical relationship of human beings (indeed, creation) to God with individualism. These are different issues. The

Bible focuses on the vertical breach of God's law as the source of weal or woe in horizontal relationships. The curse of original sin and guilt is God's judgment based on his unalterable holiness and righteousness. The word "curse" belongs to the world of ancient Near Eastern diplomacy, with its threats for violating a treaty. God's curse upon humanity (and creation because of humankind) was the sanction that God warned about when he commissioned Adam as his covenant servant.

It is striking that even though he had seduced Bathsheba and then had her husband sent to his death in battle, David's confession begins with the cry, "Against you, you only, have I sinned and done what is evil in your sight, so that you may be justified in your words and blameless in your judgment. Behold, I was brought forth in iniquity, and in sin did my mother conceive me" (Ps. 51:4–5). Can we identify today with that sharply vertical sense of sin—even horrible atrocities committed against our neighbor—as first and foremost an offense against *God*?

The impression that we often get today is that sin offends God only indirectly—because it hurts other people or ourselves, not because it is first and foremost an act of treason against our good and faithful Creator. Ironically, fundamentalism and the emergent movement sound alike at this point. The former may single out sex, drugs, and rock and roll while the latter targets militarism, greed, and environmental recklessness. However, both reduce *sin* primarily to *sins* (bad behaviors) apart from seeing the latter as the fruit of a moral condition that has swallowed our entire race and provoked the wrath of God: "None is righteous, no, not one; no one understands; no one seeks for God. All have turned aside; together they have become worthless; no one does good, not even one" (Rom. 3:10–12, citing Pss. 14:1–3; 53:1–3).

Once we lose the vertical dimension of sin—that makes it truly sinful—there is no longer any place for understanding the cross as that marvelous paradox of love and wrath, mercy and justice. No longer a vicarious and propitiatory sacrifice (as if there were anything like God's wrath to worry about), Christ's work simply becomes a paradigmatic act of healing and restoring relationships between human beings and the environment. By following his example, we can do our part in the redemption of the world.

If we acknowledge the priority of the vertical relationship, the impact of sin and Christ's saving work on the horizontal plane make sense. When we obscure the former (much less deny it), even the moral seriousness of our sins against each other loses its weight.

Like a massive meteor strike, the impact of Adam's transgression not only leaves a crater but sends its fatal smoke and ash into the atmosphere, enveloping the globe. The problem is vertical, with horizontal effects. So too is the solution. With Isaac Watts's famous hymn, "Joy to the World," we sing of a redemption that extends to every nook and cranny of creation: "far as the curse is found." The gospel announces that "death is swallowed up in victory" (1 Cor. 15:54) because the *legal* basis for the curse has been dealt with. Death is not just something that invades our lives and makes us victims. Rather, as God warned in the terms of the original covenant, death came into the world through Adam as the judicial penalty for transgression (Rom. 5:12–21). Not *feelings of* condemnation and guilt, but *God's judgment*, is the source of our woes: "For the wages of sin is death, but the free gift of God is eternal life in Christ Jesus our Lord" (Rom. 6:23). "The sting of death is sin, and the power of sin is in the law" (1 Cor. 15:56). Christ's death and resurrection have secured not only the salvation of our souls but the redemption of our bodies—indeed, the restoration of the whole created order (Rom. 8:19–21). Yet this second act awaits Christ's return. "But if we hope for what we do not see, we wait for it with patience" (Rom. 8:25).

If Christ's work of redemption does not address the *judicial crisis* of sinners before a holy God and the *condition* of bondage that pumps out all of our specific sins, then the world still lies under the shroud of death, violence, oppression, and injustice forever. What's the point of trying to do *anything* about the immediate problems in our world, in our neighborhood and family, in ourselves if, at the end of the day, we still lie ultimately under the dominion of death and hell?

To be sure, there is more to the cross than propitiation, forgiveness, and justification. At the cross Jesus also became the victor over the powers and principalities of this present evil age. Yet even in the primary passage for this view, Christ's conquest over the powers is based on the fact that in his cross work Christ bore our sins, "having forgiven us all our trespasses," not by overlooking them, but "by cancelling the record of debt that stood against us with its legal demands. This he set aside, nailing it to the cross. He disarmed the rulers and authorities and put them to open shame, by triumphing over them in him" (Col. 2:13–15).

In addition to phrases such as "living the gospel" and calls to continue Christ's incarnation and saving work, we often hear appeals to participate in Christ's reconciling work. Often this is drawn from

Paul's reference to "the ministry of reconciliation" in 2 Corinthians 5:18–6:2. In this passage we are told, first, that this reconciliation—all of it—is "from God." Second, it is all "in Christ." Third, he has entrusted his ambassadors with "the ministry of reconciliation," which he defines in strictly vertical terms—that is, peace with God through the cross of Christ, where our debts were cancelled.

Of course, this reconciliation with God generates myriad effects on the horizontal plane in our lives and interpersonal relationships. However, Paul clearly defines the gospel of reconciliation as the message concerning Christ's vicarious atonement. Someone might be willing to die for a good person, says Paul,

> but God shows his love for us in that while were still sinners, Christ died for us. Since, therefore, we have now been justified by his blood, much more shall we be saved by him from the wrath of God. For if while we were enemies we were reconciled to God by the death of his Son, much more, now that we are reconciled, shall we be saved by his life. (Rom. 5:8–10)

This reconciling work is not done by us, but for us. It is not something to complete but something to rejoice in and to announce to others: "More than that, we also rejoice in God through our Lord Jesus Christ, through whom we *have now received* reconciliation" (Rom. 5:11, emphasis added).

This reconciling work fulfilled by Christ is distinct from the ministry of reconciliation entrusted to Paul. The apostle does not say that he participates in the work of reconciliation. The work of reconciliation is not an ongoing movement or process unfolding in history. In fact, he says that "in Christ *God was* reconciling the world to himself, not counting their trespasses against them, and *entrusting to us* the *message* of reconciliation" (2 Cor. 5:19). What continues—and what Christ's ambassadors are called to participate in as co-workers with God—is the ministry of heralding this Good News to the ends of the earth. Through this ministry, strangers and enemies experience and embrace the reconciliation that Christ achieved more than two millennia ago. Consistent with the Great Commission, Paul clearly identifies the ministry of reconciliation with the ministry of the keys: that is, with delivering Christ with his gospel, through Word and sacrament. The ministry of the church is the visible form of Christ's reign in the world right now. This is how we become citizens of the age to come and introduce others to it, while we also participate in the common life of our non-Christian neighbors.

Jones adds, "Nor is there any such thing as a 'sacred-secular divide.' Regardless of the City of God versus City of Man of Augustine (354–430) or the 'two kingdoms' of Luther (1483–1546) or the myriad other articulations of a Platonic divide between the things of God and the things of this world, emergents see the whole culture and creation as one big mess in which God is moving."[102] Is there really no distinction at all between the church and the world, or between being gathered with Christ's flock for the Word, baptism, communion, fellowship, and the prayers, and Christians going to a concert with their friends from work?

Once again, it is not Plato's two worlds but the New Testament's two ages that led the Reformers to distinguish between the kingdom of grace and its consummation in glory as well as saving grace and common grace. The Reformers called believers out of the monasteries and into the world, to marriage and families and to their neighbors in secular callings. Platonic dualism doesn't lead to the world-embracing sense of vocation with which historians credit the Reformation. This movement not only led to the reevangelization of "Christendom" and launched modern missions; it also had an enormous impact on education, the arts, science, family life, social relief, and a host of other concerns. Believers were liberated to glorify and enjoy God in their secular callings. The Reformers criticized the Anabaptists for a dualistic worldview that advocated a retreat from common culture. In fact, contemporary Anabaptist historians acknowledge their tradition's debt to Platonism's matter-spirit dualism.[103]

Luther distinguished between the kingdom of power (secular government) and the kingdom of grace (the church's ministry), but he called them "the kingdom of the left hand" and "right hand," respectively. Whose hands? They are *God's* hands, which the Father exercises in the Son and by his Spirit. The whole earth is the Lord's (Ps. 24:1). Yet in this time between Christ's two advents we do not yet see the assimilation of the kingdoms of this age to the kingdom of Christ. So the question is not whether Christ's redeeming work extends to bodies as well as souls, but the timing. What are we to do in the meantime? We are to fulfill the Great Commission and our daily callings both as disciples and as co-workers and fellow citizens of temporal kingdoms. "But the one who *endures to the end* will be saved. And this gospel of the kingdom will be proclaimed throughout the whole world as a testimony to all nations, and *then* the end will come" (Matt. 24:13–14, emphasis added).

In our churches and in our relationships with non-Christians, we are called to reflect the servant leadership of Jesus Christ, who "came not to be served but to serve, and to give his life as a ransom for many" (Matt. 20:28). But what does real sacrificial living, genuine servanthood, look like if we no longer believe that Jesus himself died as a vicarious sacrifice, bearing God's just wrath, in the place of sinners who deserved it? To be sure, we need to reconnect the vertical with the horizontal, our holy calling in Christ with our common callings in the world. But if Christ's death was not a vicarious sacrifice for his enemies, bearing their wrath in forgiving grace, how can we be called to reflect Christlike servanthood in our own interpersonal reconciliation with and between enemies, forgiving their faults even while they rage against us?

Dispense with the radical character of God's activity in Christ's cross and you lose any basis for radical, cruciform discipleship. Because Christ's vicarious sacrifice is unique, ending all such sacrifices for sin, our sacrificial living is not a matter of bearing the wrath of God. Whatever we bear from others, whatever injustices we suffer from enemies, whatever disloyalties we endure from friends are well short of having to face God's righteous anger.

Furthermore, this liberates a wife from having to accept the violence of an abusive husband, a minority group from having to bear the guilt for social turmoil projected onto it by the majority, or a victim of economic injustice from having to sit out his or her sentence passively. There are no more sacrifices for the sins of others, no scapegoats to bear the guilt of their oppressors.

There is an obvious connection between the false antitheses that are encouraged by the emergent movement. If the gospel is something that we live instead of something that we proclaim, then the gospel itself must be something other than the announcement that God has become flesh to save us from death and hell and to reconcile us to God. And if the gospel is a call to partner with God in his mission to transform the world by imitating Christ's example, then the church must be an informal group of Jesus-followers rather than a formal embassy entrusted with the means of grace. If the focus is on us and what we do, then preaching is replaced by motivational conversation, shifting from God's story to ours; baptism and the Supper become our acts of commitment rather than God's gift of his Son; and we just need to live more consistently before our non-Christian neighbors rather than proclaim the gospel as a life-and-death issue.

Seen in this light, the emergent movement is less radical than advertised. It merely takes modern evangelicalism to the next stage. In fact, Jones describes his movement from Campus Crusade to a more emergent approach through encountering "lifestyle evangelism" (or "friendship evangelism") in college. "The basic premise is that *how one lives* makes a more compelling case for Christian faith than what one says. Or as Saint Francis of Assisi purportedly said, 'Preach the gospel always, and if necessary, use words.'"[104]

However, if we affirm both the church as *organism* (scattered as salt and light into the world) and the church as *organization* (commissioned to deliver God's means of grace), there is a proper place for commending the gospel through the way we live before our neighbors. We do not have to go to work each day with the primary goal of converting our co-workers. By doing our work "as unto the Lord," winning the respect of others, and developing natural friendships, our lives should provoke co-workers to ask questions about what makes us tick. As we work beside non-Christians as volunteers and love neighbors in our community, our light will no longer be hidden in *church-related* social projects. We will be contributing to the common good in the common culture whose burdens and delights we share with unbelievers. And because we have been well instructed in the faith by our churches, we will be ready to give to everyone an answer for the hope that we have. So we don't have to preach the gospel all of the time, but we dare not substitute our own lives for this proclamation.

The promising emphasis on serious discipleship today is a bracing challenge to the consumer-oriented passivity that reduces salvation to "fire insurance" and "going to heaven when you die." However, it is often threatened by a strong tendency to reduce following Christ to moral and social activism—apart from (and sometimes even against) a concern for sound doctrine. It is especially risky when the gospel is no longer the word concerning Christ and his work but our own redeeming and reconciling activity. As Paul reminds us in Romans 10, we do not save either ourselves or our world by ascending into the heavens or by descending into the depths to bring Christ up from the dead. Rather, the resurrected Christ comes to us in his Word. It's time to look outside of ourselves and away from ourselves, to the Triune God who descends to us. Only then can we truly look out to our neighbors and our world not really as "ours" at all, but as God's, and live in that world as truly transformed citizens of Christ's kingdom.

The Marks of the Church vs. the Mission of the Saints

Closely related to the call to "live the gospel" is the priority given to *being the church* over *going to church*. It is a contrast between the marks (Word, sacrament, discipline) and the mission (personal and social transformation). The church is not a place where certain things happen, we are told, but a people who do certain things.

As George Marsden has shown, the Second Great Awakening is in many respects the common source of both Protestant liberalism and fundamentalism.[105] Even when announced as new and "emerging," this dichotomy belongs to a long history in radical Protestantism, from Thomas Müntzer to representatives as varied as the nineteenth-century evangelist Charles Finney and liberal contemporary theologian Harvey Cox.

In *The Secular City* (1965), Cox wrote, "The insistence of the Reformers that the church was 'where the word is rightly preached and the sacraments rightly administered' will simply not do today." Rather, he says, "the church appears" wherever "a new inclusive human community emerges" through social action.[106] This is consistent with Finney's description of the church as "a society of moral reformers." Dallas Willard comments, "It is a tragic error to think that Jesus was telling us, as he left, to start churches, as that is understood today. . . . He wants us to establish 'beachheads' or bases of operation for the Kingdom of God wherever we are. . . . The outward effect of this life in Christ is perpetual moral revolution, until the purpose of humanity on earth is completed."[107] So this is the real question for true disciples: "Will they break out of the churches to be his Church?"[108] Similarly, Dan Kimball says, "We can't *go* to church because *we are* the church."[109] From this Kimball draws the familiar contrast between evangelism (mission) and the marks of the church (means of grace). Appealing to Darrell Guder's *The Missional Church*, Kimball thinks that things went wrong at the Reformation:

> The Reformers, in their effort to raise the authority of the Bible and ensure sound doctrine, defined the marks of a true church: a place where the gospel is rightly preached, the sacraments are rightly administered, and church discipline is exercised. However, over time these marks narrowed the definition of the church itself as a "place where" instead of a

"people who are" reality. The word church became defined as "a place where certain things happen," such as preaching and communion.[110]

However, I see at least three problems with this increasingly widespread thesis. *First, it is another example of confusing the law and the gospel.* Unless the church is first of all a place where God judges and justifies the guilty, renewing them constantly by his Word and Spirit, it cannot be a people who constitute anything more than another special interest group. Believers are called to do a great many things, but this is the third use of the law (to guide believers), not the gospel. As the effect of the gospel, our good works bring glory to God and service to our neighbors. However, to suggest that they (or we) *are* the gospel itself is a fatal confusion.

Second, this view introduces a dilemma between the church's essence and its mission that is not found in the New Testament. There is not first of all a church assembling by its own decision and then certain things that the church does. Rather, the church itself comes into being, is sustained, and grows through the same Word that it proclaims to the world. Wherever this gospel concerning Christ is proclaimed to sinners and ratified in the sacraments, a fragile piece of this passing evil age becomes a theater for God's performance and the site of a mysterious intrusion of the powers of the age to come. In that precarious crevice between these two ages, a church is born, grows, and becomes an embassy of Christ's heavenly reign on earth. Christ himself instituted a visible new-covenant assembly, delivering not only its message but its public rites and offices.

From the Great Commission and the book of Acts, we hear of a kingdom that descends from heaven and expands to every nation precisely through the marks of preaching, sacrament, and discipline. There are many things besides these marks that identify a *healthy* church, such as the gifts of hospitality, generosity, administration, and service. We are indeed called *to be* the church, but we can only become the church through the public ministry that Christ has promised to bless. All of these gifts are given and strengthened through the Word and the sacraments. Hence, a church that lacks friendliness is unhealthy, but a church that lacks the Word is *not a church.*

We do not need a proliferation of marks (almost all of which shift the focus from God's action to our inner experience and activity) but need to fulfill the Great Commission each week, delivering Christ to the sheep already gathered ("you and your children") and to "all who are far off" (Acts 2:39 NIV). A church that is not missional is not faithfully proclaiming the Word, baptizing, and teaching all that Christ delivered, just as a church that is not faithful in executing these marks is not missional as defined by the Great Commission.

Third, this view confuses the church-as-gathered with the church-as-scattered. Or, to put it differently, it tends to assimilate the visible church to the invisible church. We do not have to choose between the church as place and as people. Therefore, we must *go* to church if we are to *be* the church.

Just as we cannot choose between the external means of grace and the internal work of the Spirit, we cannot choose between the church as a historical institution authorized by Christ as his embassy and the church as a people who are gathered in fellowship and scattered as salt and light in their callings.

The suggestion that we cannot go to church because we are the church invites the obvious question as to why we should participate regularly in church services at all. As George Barna has reminded us, resources for personal spirituality and social action may be found on any number of internet sites. However, if we are not self-feeders needing resources for our own workout plan but sheep who need a shepherd, then we need to go to church in order to be the church. God works from the outside in and through the marks of the church he pursues his mission.

Besides denying implicitly the clear Scriptural testimony to our being united in sound doctrine and membership in one visible body, as well as any difference between the general office of believers and the special offices of pastors, elders, and deacons, Jones says, "But true worship of God is a messy endeavor. I make no bones about that. It's not meant to be done 'decently and in order,' but messily and with only a semblance of order, and with a great deal of joy."[111] In 1 Corinthians 14, Paul upbraids the Corinthians for their spiritual immaturity, illustrated in chaotic ("messy") worship. "Let all things be done for building up," he says (v. 26), not for personal self-expression. "For God is not a God of confusion but of peace" (v. 33). And if the phrase that Jones has in quotes sounds familiar, it is because it comes from verse 40: "But all things should be done decently and in order."

Finally, the trajectory that leads to private spiritual disciplines and transformative conversations over the corporate means of grace and that threatens to turn the visible church into an internet café is something like a new Gnosticism. Although emergent folks especially affirm the importance of Jesus and of being incarnated, concrete, bodily communities, the visible church seems to evaporate into thin air. For all of the emphasis on community, Jones echoes Barna's fascination with the disembodied fellowship of saints: "I consider über-blogger Bob Carlton of San Francisco one of my closest friends, although we've never been in the same room."[112]

Is this just a further adaptation of the church to its marketplace, a more consumer-driven vision than even the megachurches realized? Ironically, given the solid criticisms of evangelical consumerism, emergent writers like Tony Jones share the fascination with the internet analogy: "There is no Internet headquarters. You can't drive to an office building, park in the parking lot, and walk in the front door of Internet, Inc. When it comes to the Internet, there's no *there* there." It exists, but as a "scale-free network," with lots of hubs.[113]

Coining the term "Wikichurch," Jones says that the emergent movement is a lot like the online encyclopedia Wikipedia. "The term wiki has come to refer to an Internet technology that allows any user to modify the content in a database, with few or no restrictions. . . . Wiki is a Hawaiian word meaning 'quick,' and wikis are developed to be quickly and easily accessible. . . . One can look at the qualities of Wikipedia and analogize them to many other scale-free networks, including the emergent church."[114]

Can discipleship, as defined by Scripture, be a disembodied relationship via email? And can the church that Christ creates be generated by the values of "quick" (wiki), "developed to be quickly and easily accessible," modifying content "with few or no restrictions"? Is this really postmodern or most-modern? Is it a radical call to living in community or a welcoming embrace of a false catholicity of a wired world? Is this something that can pass a treasure down from generation to generation and around the world in different cultures? And can there really be anything like a New Testament church if the fellowship of the saints around the Word and water and bread and wine is exchanged for just another circle of friends, including "best" friends with whom you have never actually been in the same room?

There is a danger in assuming that the spiritual warfare between the gospel and unbelief is a matter merely of private ideas and behaviors—just affirming a few fundamentals and abstaining from sexual immorality. We often assume that cultural patterns are neutral. The message does not change, but the methods are always changing, determined by the most effective technologies at hand.

Specialists in media ecology have observed that we not only use technology; technology uses us. Or to be more precise, the tools we use actually shape us and our lives as societies. For all of its amazing usefulness—even for communicating the gospel—the internet is also altering our way of being human. MIT professor Sherry Turkle observes that people are increasingly living in alternative realities: synthetic communities that circumvent the kind of "real life" societies that embodied interaction generates. "As more people spend more time in these spaces, some go so far as to challenge the idea of giving any priority to the RL [Real Life] at all. After all, . . . why grant such superior status to the self that has the body when the selves that don't have bodies are able to have different kinds of experiences?"[115]

The marks of the church are examples of a "real life" society that requires bodily presence. It's not just that isolated souls assemble in one place; the Word that we hear together with our ears, in the power of the Spirit, actually creates, grows, and expands the church every week. We are baptized with real water and eat and drink a real meal, which as a Reformed Christian I confess as nothing less than "the true and natural body and blood of Christ."[116] In these events, Christ himself is present and delivers himself to his people in the power of his Spirit. He is the life-giving Head, and we are his members. A "real life" participation in Christ's body and blood also generates a "real life" communion of saints. The church is the body of Christ, not the spirit of Christ.

By putting us in touch with people we might not have met otherwise, the internet may *facilitate* community, but it cannot *constitute* community. The communion of saints is constituted by speech, water, bread, and wine, and it exists bodily as an actual fellowship of persons. Far from anonymous Web surfers and emailers, we are placed in a relationship of mutual submission. We offer our bodies, not just our souls, as a living sacrifice of praise. Far from being passive voyeurs or spectators, we are active participants in each other's lives.

If we spiritualize all of this away, there is no reason why we should object to the substitution of invisible digital community for the visible household of faith. The Great Commission forms churches, not websites. In this way, God is colonizing his fallen world with the life-giving energies of the age to come. So it is not enough to yield intellectual assent to "the resurrection of the body and the life everlasting" while denying this hope in our actual lives—particularly in the way in which we live out the Great Commission.

Precisely because we need to be disciples instead of consumers and communities united in Christ by the Spirit rather than freelance individuals, we need a view of the Great Commission and its effects that is fuller, deeper, richer, and more faithful to the New Testament. The church is pretty messy, all right, just as each of us is as well. And it will be messy until Christ returns. Part of that messiness is because God is disordering our lives by his judgment and grace. However, the God who disorders also reorders; the God who tears down also builds up; the God who makes a mess also cleans it up. Our continuing messiness is a sin to be confessed, not a virtue to be celebrated.

Church vs. Kingdom

There is a ditch on each side of this question. On one side is the tendency simply to *identify* the church with the kingdom of God. There is no ambiguity, no precariousness to the church's existence in this present age. The visible church, including its external offices and ministry, is the kingdom of Christ unfolding in history. On the other side is the danger of *separating* the kingdom from the church, sometimes even setting them over against each other. There is the kingdom over here and the church over there. Don't let the church get in the way of the kingdom of Christ!

The liberal Catholic Alfred Loisy famously quipped that Jesus announced a kingdom and instead it was the church that came. Enthusiastic devotees of a kingdom fully consummated here and now easily become disenchanted critics when things do not seem to pan out. That was why Jesus was rejected by many of the throngs who hoped he would bring political liberation. Of course, Jesus will bring glorious liberation to captives in the most concrete, political, physical, and earthly terms when he returns. On that day his kingdom will not be limited to believers and the church but will encompass the whole earth, and everyone will know when it arrives.

Although divided over capitalism and socialism, prosperity evangelists and advocates of the social gospel share what is called an "over-realized eschatology." That is, both confuse Christ's kingdom of grace in its present phase with his kingdom of glory and power at his return. They expect Christ's heavenly reign on earth over the political kingdoms of this age to begin now, bringing prosperity, cessation of violence, and justice for all. The *church* may be obsessed with preaching, administering sacraments, and caring for the flock, but the *kingdom* is where the action is—really making a difference in the world. In this view, building the Great Society is more interesting than fulfilling the Great Commission. As a result, a chasm grows between what is derisively called "maintenance ministry" (the means of grace) and "missional outreach."

Playing the kingdom off against the church can also happen in more pietistic circles, assuming that the kingdom of God is a purely inner and personal reality that is related only ambiguously to the visible church with its external Word, sacraments, and government. The Campus Crusade mission statement reads: "Launching spiritual movements by winning, building, and sending Christ-centered multiplying disciples." Campus Crusade has done a lot of good. Nevertheless, in the university contexts with which I am familiar, there is often a tendency for such groups to become an alternate church. There is preaching and even sometimes baptism and communion, and there is certainly discipline—in some cases, pretty heavy-handed "oversight." However much visible church membership might be encouraged, a student might reasonably wonder why he or she should even join a church. And given the near absence of the church and its official ministry in the most representative writings of the spiritual disciplines movement, most of one's spiritual growth seems to happen elsewhere.

There is a long history of parachurch agencies assuming the role that Christ gave to his church. Monastic movements often arose in the Middle Ages as a way of calling the truly committed disciples away from the world—and even from a worldly church—as communities of vital spirituality.

Whereas traditional churches distinguish between clergy and laity, Tony Jones announces in a bit of a Marxian flourish that "emergent churches are doing away with these class distinctions."[117] "You might think of this as an inherent trust in human nature, the opposite of the Augustinian doctrine of Original Sin (which says that we're all inherently tainted with a sinful nature). In some ways, that's correct. . . . If anything, the pastor in this scenario is a broker of a conversation—*that's* how she teaches."[118] Jones relates, "Emergents downplay—or outright reject—the difference between clergy and laity."[119]

However, Jones adds that Wikipedia—the analogy he drew above for emergent churches—isn't a complete free-for-all. There are developers, stewards, bureaucrats, administrators, and overseers. "And founder Jimmy Wales has unparalleled access to the users and content on Wikipedia. Only he can ban a user for life." Similarly, Jones argues, emergent churches have leaders, but they are facilitators rather than "predetermining what the church will do, what congregants will believe, or anything else."[120] So if it is not a common confession and body of elders to whom everyone is accountable, including the ecclesiastical equivalent of Jimmy Wales, what becomes the criterion for such an apparently abusive exercise of power such as "banning a user for life"? Is this the point at which free-wheeling movements require a despot at the top to manage the chaos?

It is certainly true that (1) the church is not just a visible organization but a Spirit-created and Spirit-filled organism; (2) it is not only a place where certain things happen (like preaching and sacrament) but a people who are called as salt and light into the world; (3) God's Word gives us not only a gospel to believe but commands to obey; (4) believers not only receive God's gift in the public assembly but share these heavenly and material gifts with each other and with their neighbors; and (5) God serves the world not only with his saving gifts through the holy ministry but with temporal gifts through the common vocations of believers (and unbelievers). Yet the trend today is simply to collapse the former in each of these pairs into the latter. The visible church is collapsed into the invisible church, and therefore the official means of grace become reduced to the informal gathering of believers.

Once again we see that the message, mission, and strategy all hang together. If your paradigm is mainly the imitation of Christ, then preaching focuses on holding up models and exhortations, baptism shows that we really mean business, and the Supper gives us periodical opportunities to remember Christ's model and rededicate ourselves to it.

The distinction between the invisible and visible church is helpful here. These are not two different churches, much less associated with Plato's two realms. Rather, once again, it is the two-age eschatology that provokes a distinction between the church as it is known to God in his electing grace and as it is known to us visibly in the world right now. In his counsel to Timothy in the midst of frustrations over divisions and false teaching, Paul assures the young pastor, "But God's firm foundation stands, bearing this seal: 'The Lord knows those who are his'" (2 Tim. 2:19).

Just as in the Word and sacraments there is a union of the creaturely sign with its eschatological reality, the visible church is neither identical with the fully consummated kingdom (i.e., the invisible church) nor separate from it. In every local church there are those who publicly profess Christ but are not actually converted. Nevertheless, the apostles address their letters to the visible church: "To the church of God that is in Corinth," and so forth. The visible church does not consist of all those who are elect and truly regenerated but consists of all professing Christians together with their children.

So the church's identity is determined by God's sanctifying action—he makes the whole field holy as the land that he plants, waters, and tends. Even though there are weeds among the wheat, they will be separated by the Lord himself at the harvest (Matt. 13:24–30). In that day, there will be no distinction between the visible and invisible church. The sheep will be recognized and welcomed into the everlasting kingdom prepared for them since the foundation of the world.

Obviously, in this conception, the church is defined as not only the people who are truly born again, but the place where Christ is at work by his Word and Spirit bringing about the new birth. This is as true for a two-hundred-year-old church in Illinois as it is for a mission station in Cambodia. Where the Word is proclaimed and the sacraments are properly administered, there is a church, even if many of the members are faking it, although it is through that faithful ministry that the Spirit brings genuine conversion. The church is a visible institution in history, not just an invisible association of saved individuals.

As the body of Christ to be revealed on the last day, the church is indeed the kingdom of God: restored humanity together with a renewed creation, with the enthroned Lamb as its center. As it is now—visibly apparent to us today—the church is a colony of this heavenly kingdom. It is a mixed body, with wheat and tares, and even the wheat often looks like tares. That is why Jesus warns his ambassadors not to pull up the wheat until he comes for the harvest (Matt. 13:24–30). In fact, it is to that astounding hope that we turn our attention in the final chapter.

10

Until He Comes

The Great Assurance

And behold, I am with you always,
to the end of the age.
Matthew 28:20

This book opened with, "Before You Go," exploring the triumphant announcement that justifies the Great Commission. It
concludes with, "Until He Comes," Christ's assurance that the Great
Commission will not fail.

The gospel is not the "Oh, of course" that we can take for granted
as the message we take to the world. Rather, it is the first and last word
that Jesus gives us in the Great Commission itself. Actually, it is the
Great Commission that is the "of course"—the reasonable service
that we render simply because of the fact of Christ's victory in the
past, his presence today, and his promise for the future.

Jesus is not waiting for us to fulfill the Great Commission before
he returns in glory; rather, he is fulfilling the Great Commission by
his Word and Spirit and will return on the day that the Father has set.
This relieves us of an impossible burden, liberating us to participate in
the missionary movement in which the Triune God has been engaged
from the beginning of the world.

294

The Paradoxical Promise

Jesus pledged to be present with his church even to the end of the age right at the moment that he ascended to heaven. At the very moment that the disciples finally understood the point of Jesus's journey to the cross and, through the cross, to the resurrection, *he left*! As the firstfruits of the harvest, Jesus ascended bodily to the right hand of the Father. What a time to leave, though, just when things were really getting started. What is a kingdom without a king?

Yet he had already prepared them for his departure (John 14–16). He would not leave his people as orphans, but would send the promised Spirit to lead them into all truth, illuminating their hearts and minds to understand and to embrace everything that he had taught and empowering them to bring this witness to the ends of the earth. Jesus said, "I tell you the truth: it is to your advantage that I go away, for if I do not go away, the Helper will not come to you. But if I go, I will send him to you. And when he comes, he will convict the world concerning sin and righteousness and judgment" (John 16:7–8). Because Christ did ascend and sent the Spirit, we today know Jesus Christ better even than the disciples before this event. The Spirit unites us to Christ, seating us with him in heavenly places, and through the ministry of the gospel raises up from the valley of dry bones a mighty army of kingdom heirs.

Our Lord's commission began with a triumphant indicative and now concludes with a solid promise. Lodged in the precarious crevice of his Word, where the powers of this present age are being assaulted by the powers of the age to come, the church appears weak and foolish in the eyes of the world. It does not look like the one holy, catholic, and apostolic church that its Lord nevertheless says it is.

Jesus's promise to be with his church to the end of the age is nothing like the pagan sentimentalism that speaks of loved ones as "still with us" through their spirits or memories. The Spirit whom Jesus promised is a person: the third person of the Trinity. Although Jesus is absent from us in the flesh, the Spirit unites us to the whole Christ in heaven by his mysterious grace.

As I argued in my opening chapters, nothing can compensate for Jesus's absence in the flesh. Not even the Holy Spirit is a substitute for our Living Head; in fact, the Spirit's indwelling presence provokes within our hearts the cry for Jesus's return when our exile will be ended and we will join him in the everlasting Sabbath. If not the Spirit, then no mere human being will suffice to make up for the bodily absence of our Lord. There is no "vicar of Christ" who replaces Jesus in the flesh. Even the apostles did not replace Jesus but were his ambassadors in this world, and there are no living successors to St. Peter or any of the other apostles today. Not even the people of God as a community on earth can fill in for Jesus.

Rather, the church endures and even conquers from age to age and nation to nation in dependence on the Spirit who unites us to our ascended Lord and gives us every blessing in heavenly places. It is the Spirit who even now has seated us with Christ, enthroned over death and hell. It is the Spirit who inspired the words of the prophets and apostles as the Word of God, a Word through which Christ continues to address his little flock. It is the Spirit who binds us to Christ in baptism and the Lord's Supper, so that we can be bathed by our Lord and fed with his own body and blood.

How can Jesus announce his departure in the flesh, even telling his disciples that he will return bodily only at the end of the age, and yet at the same time promise, "And behold, I am with you always, to the end of the age" (Matt. 28:20)? The only possible answer is the one that he gave his disciples in the upper room and repeated at his ascension: the outpouring and indwelling of the Holy Spirit, working through the Word.

It is not through confidence in its programs, strategies, achievements, or publicity but through dependence on the Spirit and confidence in his Word that the church fulfills this Great Commission. So a renewed commitment to this mandate requires not only a deeper understanding of the gospel indicative that justifies it and a fuller appreciation for the means of grace that he has ordained for it; it also requires a more profound understanding of and dependence upon the person and work of the Spirit in this time between the ascension and return of Christ in the flesh.

Jesus for President!

Protestants reject the claim that any pastor or leader can be the head of the whole church. Christ did not leave his people orphans, to be looked after by someone in his place. Rather, the Good Shepherd continues to guard and increase his flock through under-shepherds who serve but never replace his direct sovereignty over it. Jesus presides over his church, and not by our election.

However, there are Protestant ways of making a similar mistake. It is easy for us to look for substitutes and surrogates. We may look for a charismatic leader who exudes spiritual energy and power. We may become attached to an ancient tradition or to a new movement rather than to Christ. There are myriad ways to shift the focus from Christ and the kingdom that he is building to ourselves and our own kingdom building.

After Moses remained on the mountain with God for over a month, the people below grew restless. "When the people saw that Moses delayed to come down from the mountain, the people gathered themselves together to Aaron and said to him, 'Up, make us gods who shall go before us. As for this Moses, the man who brought us up out of the land of Egypt, we do not know what has become of him'" (Exod. 32:1). The result was the golden calf. Instead of representing Moses in his physical absence, Aaron took over the reins. Instead of gathering the people to hear the word of the Lord, Aaron allowed the people to gather themselves together to him. They bullied him: "Up, make us gods who shall go before us." They were ready to move on, with or without "this Moses . . . who brought us up out of the land of Egypt." Of course, Moses did come down pretty quickly, as God informed him that the people were breaking the laws that God was giving him on the mountain.

How much more tragic it is when one greater than Moses has brought us up out of death and hell and ascended to intercede with the Father on our behalf—and is forgotten and replaced with substitute messiahs. Like Israel, we are impatient. In Christ's physical absence, we demand new mediators, media, and experiences to give us some visible, physical, tangible presence of God. Unlike the terrifying experience of hearing God's voice, Israel had a silly idol that they could control because they had just made it. We too grow weary of waiting for Christ to return bodily, dissatisfied with hearing his voice and relying on his indwelling Spirit. We are tired of waiting for the return of our mediator to lead us into the Promised Land. We will take Canaan and build the kingdom ourselves. It's time to move on.

Christ's Program, Not Ours

We do not ascend to God; God descended to us and continues to descend by sending us his Word of Christ through preachers. Christ is as near to us today as the Word that we hear proclaimed. This is Paul's point in Romans 10, as we have seen. We have to keep our focus on the historical pattern of Christ's descent in the flesh, death and resurrection in the flesh, ascension in the flesh, and return at the end of the age in the flesh. Descending into our history, he has forever transformed it, opening up a fissure in that history of death by his resurrection. By his Spirit, Christ keeps that fissure opened for the proclamation of the gospel, so that our lives even now become united to the new history of everlasting joy that he has already entered as our pioneer. It is neither the ascent of the soul nor the gradual ascent of humanity toward a better world but the in-breaking of the kingdom of Christ to which the church bears witness. Christ has redefined history for us and for the whole earth.

In *Christless Christianity* I explored the state of contemporary Christianity in America. Drawing on various surveys and analyses, I tried to articulate some of the contours of and reasons for the dominance of what sociologist Christian Smith labels "moralistic, therapeutic deism." We come to the Great Commission with *our* questions, many of which are shaped by the culture in which we live. As Paul reminded Timothy, the last days are marked by narcissism, greed, disloyalty, and selfishness. It follows that we gradually transform the Commission's *message* into something about us rather than something about God and his saving purposes, work, and destiny for us in Jesus Christ. Consistent with this new message, we transform the Commission's *mission* into a kingdom that we are building rather than receiving, and we exchange its *methods* of delivering Christ through preaching and sacrament for our own clever programs, techniques, and principles for effecting real transformation of ourselves and the world.

However, the result has been not only an increasing failure to reach the lost but a growing tendency to lose the reached. We place our hope in laws, principles, programs: things that we do to ascend to pull God down to us, instead of in the gospel that is brought to us by a herald as completely counterintuitive Good News.

In an interview with Billy Graham's *Decision* magazine, C. S. Lewis was once asked, "Do you feel, then, that modern culture is being de-Christianized?" Lewis responded,

> I cannot speak to the political aspects of the question, but I have some definite views about the de-Christianizing of the church. I believe that

there are many accommodating preachers, and too many practitioners in the church who are not believers. Jesus Christ did not say, "Go into all the world and tell the world that it is quite right." The Gospel is something completely different. In fact, it is directly opposed to the world.[1]

Like Athanasius, our motto should be, "Against the world, for the world." It is in the world's best interest that we stand up to it, refusing to conform our message, mission, or methods to the pattern of this passing age.

We believe, live, and act on the basis of the covenant that was made between the persons of the Trinity before all time for our redemption, the saving work of Christ that is already completed. And we believe, live, and act on the basis of Christ's promise to be with us by his Word and Spirit until the very end, when he returns bodily in glory. This promise with which Jesus assures the shaky apostles at the end of his Great Commission is similar to the one that he issued in Matthew 16, when he gave them the keys of the kingdom: "I will build my church, and the gates of hell shall not prevail against it" (v. 18).

Again and again we meet this emphasis of our Lord on the kingdom that he is building and we are receiving. Jesus told his disciples not to be anxious about the future. "Fear not, little flock, for it is your Father's good pleasure to give you the kingdom" (Luke 12:32). In John's vision in Revelation 5, the heavenly choir sings its hymn to the Lamb on the throne who not only "ransomed people for God from every tribe and language and people and nation," but who "*made them* a kingdom and priests to our God" (vv. 9–10, emphasis added). It is not what we make of Christ, or of the world, but what Christ makes of us that makes his kingdom evident in the world. We may build all sorts of things. We may build movements, personalities, programs, and publicity-generating organizations. However, only Jesus can build his church. It is his church, not ours; his ministry, not ours. He builds it through means, to be sure, but it is the means that he has instituted and promised to bless with his saving presence.

This church may not look pretty. It may be full of internal contradictions, weakness, strife, and error. It may be persecuted for the truth and sometimes, tragically, even persecute those who testify to the truth. Nevertheless, our Lord's promise is not only that hell will not be able to prevail *over* the church but that the gates of hell will not prevail *against* it. In other words, the church is on the offense, not the defense, in this present evil age. Regardless of the church's outward appearance, even its suffering, Christ's promise trumps all earthly powers. Wherever this church is preaching Christ, baptizing, administering the Supper, confessing its sins, receiving Christ's absolution, confessing its faith in the gospel, caring for the sheep, and unleashing its salty saints in ever-widening circles of mission, witness, and service in their ordinary vocations, Satan's kingdom is falling piece by piece. We are storming the Bastille, that wretched prison which holds Christ's blood-bought treasure of captives. We are bringing the Good News that the long night is over and the Light has come into the world.

We have seen how Paul, in Ephesians 4, describes the triumphal entry of Christ through the gates of Paradise, claiming his victory, with captives in his train. From his throne he distributes the spoils of his victory to the saints through the ministry of his gospel. Similarly, in 2 Corinthians 2:14–17 we read,

> But thanks be to God, who in Christ always leads us in triumphal procession, and through us spreads the fragrance of the knowledge of him everywhere. For we are the aroma of Christ to God among those who are being saved and among those who are perishing, to one a fragrance from death to death, to the other a fragrance from life to life. Who is sufficient for these things? For we are not, like so many, peddlers of God's word, but as men of sincerity, as commissioned by God, in the sight of God we speak in Christ.

A Pilgrim People

If you want to know *who* you are in history, it helps to know *where* you are in history. Throughout the New Testament, Jesus locates his disciples in that precarious intersection between this present evil age and the age to come. That's why the apostles address us as "strangers and exiles" (Heb. 11:13), like the Jews in Babylon rather than in the old-covenant theocracy.

Like Cain, the modern person was (and is) a master. The master's kingdom is of this world—something that he or she is building, a tower reaching to the heavens. A constant stream of masters has washed over our civilization, sweeping millions of victims into its deadly current. Partly in reaction, the postmodern person is a vagrant, or perhaps a tourist, with no utopian aspirations. The tourist just wants to take in the sights, sauntering from booth to booth at Vanity Fair.

If you have the money and power, it's easy to be a master. It's also easy to be a tourist, dispensing with all the fuss about arriving safely at any particular destination. A totally free itinerary, without following any set of prescribed directions, the tourist's schedule is set by whim and passing intrigue. It's fun to be a tourist, for a while at least, but as a way of life, it's pure consumerism, ignoring the responsibilities of local ties.

The really difficult thing to be in this age of sin and death is a *pilgrim*. By definition, a pilgrim lives in the tension of the "already" and the "not yet." Pilgrims are impelled by the promise of a city that they have heard about but have never seen. Focusing on a solid destination, they cannot meander. They cannot interrupt their pilgrimage to wander down whatever interesting highway catches their eye. They are on their way somewhere, and the days are growing shorter. However, they only have a promise, confirmed by a bath, and a table set in the wilderness along the way for their refreshment as a foretaste of the banquet awaiting them upon their arrival.

It's hard for us to be pilgrims. It's always been difficult, of course. Everything in Satan's arsenal is directed against our confidence in Christ. As strange as it may seem in the light of our riches in Christ, our own hearts are still impressed with this passing evil age. Even in the church, distractions abound: easier, simpler, and faster ways to have our best life now. Pilgrimage—the long, often difficult and tedious, and self-denying path to Zion—is about the most un-American idea one can imagine.

To be called like Abram out of his moon-worshiping family in Ur, or like Peter to drop his nets and follow Jesus even to Calvary, is the most difficult vocation to embrace. In fact, it is impossible. As Abram, Peter, and all believers ever since have come to realize, becoming a Christian pilgrim is a gift of grace. Everything about this journey to Zion seems odd, surprising, and counterintuitive. Abram knew that God's promise contradicted the facts of his own experience. Assuming that glory rather than the cross awaited them, Peter did not understand the point of his master's journey from Galilee to Jerusalem until after he denied Jesus three times and was nevertheless restored by his victorious Savior after his resurrection. Judging by the winding and often daunting path of Bunyan's Pilgrim, the Christian pilgrimage is not easy. Often, Pilgrim meets his greatest obstacles not in the form of obvious giants who block his path to the Celestial City, but in the subtler form of distractions and distortions of the faith that promise to make the trek easier.

Going beyond Bunyan's image of a lonely pilgrim, we have in Scripture the confidence of a "cloud of witnesses" (Heb. 12:1) who cheer us on from the heavenly stands. Though further along, not even they have arrived finally at their destination, as they wait with us for their resurrection and glorification. On that day, we will all have arrived and the body of Christ will be as glorious as its Head. One day we will not need faith to believe with the hymn writer, "Solid joys and lasting treasures, none but Zion's children know."[2]

We may sing, "We're Marching to Zion," but most of the time we feel like we're limping. Sometimes we may even wonder if "Zion" is like the lost city of Atlantis: a collage of human dreams projected onto a mythological map.

However, we know that Zion is a real destination because Jesus Christ has already arrived there. It was he who promised that he would fulfill all righteousness and lead his people safely through the raging waters of death to the other side in resurrection splendor. His resurrection is not a myth; it's a historical fact, with evidence that is available for public scrutiny. Therefore, since our Head has already arrived in regal splendor, announcing his conquest, with liberated hosts in his train, we are assured that we as his body will arrive in due course.

In the meantime, the pilgrimage is a struggle. Don't let anyone tell you differently. It's false advertizing to invite people to Christ as a panacea for trouble, disappointment, and temptation. As a believer, you are a co-heir with Christ to God's entire estate. The devil knows that you are equipped with all of the necessary weapons for bringing down his kingdom as you spread the gospel through your witness.

It is true that Satan is described as "the god of this world" (2 Cor. 4:4). Yet far from serving as a proof text for our collective exorcism of territorial demons and generational curses, Paul goes on to give us the sense in which he intends the phrase, "god of this world." First of all, it has to do not with spiritual technology but with the gospel: "And even if our gospel is veiled, it is veiled only to those who are perishing. In their case the god of this world has blinded the minds of the unbelievers, to keep them from seeing the light of the gospel of the glory of Christ, who is the image of God. For what we proclaim is not ourselves, but Jesus Christ as Lord" (2 Cor. 4:3–5). In other words, Satan has deluded the world into denying the God who has made them, and then when the redeemer is proclaimed, the world rejects him now as it did when he appeared (cf. John 14–16).

In other words, we are dealing here in the realm of faith and unbelief, not magic.

Because of our own indwelling sin and the weakness of our faith, the spiritual warfare described in Scripture is far more challenging than the science fiction alternatives. Yet it is also more assuring. The most exciting and liberating thing that a believer can hear in the middle of spiritual and physical distress is not that there is a secret battle plan for defeating the powers of darkness if we will only come together and follow its fail-proof steps, but the announcement that Jesus Christ has already accomplished this for us in his first advent. After Jesus sends out the seventy-two disciples into the harvest, they return elated: "Lord, even the demons are subject to us in your name!" And Jesus replies, "I saw Satan fall like lightning from heaven," giving them authority over Satan and his minions who blind the world. "Nevertheless," Jesus adds, "do not rejoice in this, that the spirits are subject to you, but rejoice that your names are written in heaven" (Luke 10:17–20).

A clear theme is emerging here: the binding of Satan and the powers of darkness occurs with the arrival of the kingdom, and it centers on the spiritual blindness of which the physical restoration of sight is but a sign. The healings and exorcisms performed by Jesus and his apostles are signposts announcing that the kingdom of the gospel has finally arrived: "But if it is by the Spirit of God that I cast out demons," Jesus declares, "then the kingdom of God has come upon you. Or how can someone enter a strong man's house and plunder his goods, unless he first binds the strong man?" (Matt. 12:28–29).

Furthermore, this kind of spiritual warfare that the New Testament describes is not that of a lonely pilgrim making his way to the Celestial City; it is of a great throng making their way from slavery in Egypt to the Promised Land. The call to spiritual warfare is not an appeal to a general program for our defeat of Satan but the confession of Jesus as "the Christ, the Son of the Living God" that evokes Jesus's further announcement in Matthew 16:18–19: "And I tell you, you are Peter, and on this rock I will build my church, and the gates of hell shall not prevail against it. I will give you the keys of the kingdom of heaven, and whatever you bind on earth shall be bound in heaven, and whatever you loose on earth shall be loosed in heaven." The authority to bind and loose is exercised wherever and whenever the gospel is proclaimed, wherever the devil's fortress is looted and his prisoners are baptized, transferred from the kingdom of sin and death to the kingdom of life everlasting. The cosmic battle, according to the Gospels, turns on faith in Christ and admission to his kingdom. Spiritual warfare is all about the gospel. It is when Peter's confession is heard on the lips of men, women, and children from Jerusalem to the ends of the earth that we see the sun setting on Satan's empire.

The most obvious proof text for spiritual warfare is Ephesians 6. There are allusions to Isaiah 59 in this passage. In that Old Testament courtroom scene, Yahweh arraigns his people and pronounces them guilty based on clear evidence. They admit their guilt, but Yahweh is astonished that there is no mediator, no one to intercede. So he clothes himself with judgment and salvation, donning a breastplate of righteousness and bearing a sword in his hand.

In Ephesians 6, then, Paul draws on this cosmic trial and relates it to our own individual Christian experience. Satan comes to us, as he came to Adam, Israel, and Jesus, and promises us the kingdoms of the world if we will serve him. Those who have renounced Satan and his lies are targeted for persecution, temptation, and suffering. All we have—and it is enough—are the weapons that God has provided. And notice that the military dress and weapons Paul lists are identical to those mentioned by Isaiah—with one crucial difference. In Isaiah 59, they are worn by Yahweh himself, the Redeemer who comes to Zion. In Ephesians 6, they are worn by us. This is what Paul means earlier in the letter when he tells us to "put off your old self" or "put on the Lord Jesus Christ" (Eph. 4:22; Rom. 13:14; cf. Rom. 6:6; Col. 3:9–15).

None of these defenses mentioned are our own. We do not read here about our marvelous Christian experience, our love for the saints, our progress in obedience, our passion for God. These are some of the effects that we experience when we "put on Christ" in this spiritual battle, but the armor itself must be nothing less than Christ himself, with his Word, his righteousness, and his gospel. Don't go onto the battlefield in your street clothes—or in your own protective gear. Don't dare to enter this conflict in your own righteousness, zeal, or strength. Donning someone else's armor, we are standing in someone else's strength. The testimony that prevails in this battle is not about us and what we have done or how we have improved ourselves or the world, but a witness to God and what he has done in Christ. Pointing away from ourselves to Christ is the only sure defense when Satan accuses us in God's courtroom.

There is *the belt of truth*. How can we answer the devil's accusations and twisting of Scripture if we do not ourselves know God's Word? Bad theology is deadly. Sound doctrine is not, as many seem to assume today at least implicitly, a distraction from the real life of Christian discipleship, but preparation for it.

Then there is *the breastplate of righteousness* that we wear—that "alien righteousness," as the Reformers called it, Christ's own righteousness imputed to us although we are wicked in ourselves. This righteousness alone stands in God's judgment and therefore in the face of Satan's accusations. After all, Satan is often right when he accuses us, and he terrifies our conscience with the fear that we have fallen out of favor with God. If somehow he can undermine our faith in Christ and the sufficiency of his righteousness, what could constitute a more sterling victory? But he cannot succeed in this if we are wearing Christ's righteousness and not relying on our naked chest to preserve us from his blows.

Next, *the gospel of peace* is our shoes that make us ready to run the race set before us. Like the belt of truth and breastplate of righteousness, the gospel is not about us but about someone else: Christ's "It is finished!" Further, Satan cannot penetrate *the shield of faith*. If we were to do battle with our experience, our intellect or our works, we would fall quickly, but faith too points away from ourselves to Christ who intercedes for us.

Finally, Paul mentions *the sword of the Spirit*, which is not a fanciful lightsaber to be wielded by spiritual heroes but is nothing else than "the word of God" (Eph. 6:17). Nothing in us or done by us is victorious in spiritual battle. We can only extinguish the flaming arrows of doubt, fear, and anxiety by directing the world, the flesh, and the devil to our Captain at the Father's right hand, who has crushed Satan's head and rendered his accusations and efforts futile. All of these pieces Paul mentions are really one person: Jesus Christ. He is our peace. He is our breastplate. Faith in him shields us from every enemy. His Word is our only sword.

With all of this in mind, Paul concludes by encouraging his readers to continually pray "for all the saints," not just for themselves, and particularly for Paul, and not just for him personally because of his importance, nor indeed that he would be kept from all suffering, but in order "that words may be given to me in opening my mouth boldly to proclaim the mystery of the gospel, for which I am an ambassador in chains, that I may declare it boldly, as I ought to speak"

(Eph. 6:18–20). This does not mean that we should not pray for a whole host of other things, *including* tangible physical needs, but it does mean that even the role of prayer in spiritual warfare centered for Paul on the progress of this gospel of Christ to the ends of the earth. This, after all, is how Satan's kingdom is crushed and the kingdom of grace is erected on top of its ashes.

Yet for now, the snapshot in Revelation 12 reminds us that Satan "knows that his time is short" (v. 12), and so in an act of desperation, he turns his final violence toward the prisoners whom Christ has freed. We will not grow without a fight, without sharing in his sufferings. Unlike justification, our sanctification is a lifelong struggle—so much for "let go and let God." We are only *beneficiaries* of Christ's victory in the war of the heavens, but we must "work out [our] salvation with fear and trembling" in the meantime, "for it is God who works in [us], both to will and to work for his good pleasure" (Phil. 2:12–13). Small victories are prized; battles lost are soon forgotten, extracting lessons for the next. None of our enemies—the world, the flesh, or the devil—will simply move aside and put up a white flag. And yet, in our fighting we cannot hide our unrestrained anticipation, prefigured in the arrival of Israel in the Promised Land, of the time when at last the land will be truly at rest from war. Until then, we fight as those who belong to the Warrior-God who has already conquered with his own right arm.

Born from above in the precarious crevice between the ascension and return of its risen Head, the church is its own distinct culture. In one sense, it is a counterculture. After all, we belong to the new creation, where already we have tasted the powers of the age to come. We have already received God's verdict of the last judgment: "There is therefore now no condemnation for those who are in Christ Jesus" (Rom. 8:1). We have already been transferred from the reign of sin and death to the reign of righteousness and life; once "not a people," we are "the people of God" (1 Peter 2:9–10 NKJV).

Yet the church too is simultaneously justified and sinful; definitively claimed by the Triune God in grace, but still far from arriving at its destination in the City of God. In this present age, the church becomes visible not to the extent that it is a counterculture, but to the extent that it points away from itself to Christ—who *has* arrived as our forerunner in heaven. With this gospel and by his Holy Spirit, Christ is building "a kingdom that cannot be shaken" (Heb. 12:28). In receiving and witnessing to this gospel, the transformation that issues in a truly different way of thinking, feeling, and acting becomes partially realized in our time and place.

At the same time, we are also citizens of secular culture. Here we are guided by biblical truth, to be sure, but also by godly prudence, reflected in a variety of cultural styles, preferences, and social-political views. The church is not meant to be a subculture, creating its own alternative novels, movies, hangouts, political action committees, and clubs. Rather, as it focuses particularly on its unique calling to fulfill the Great Commission, it shapes the way that we live as Christians in our worldly callings with unbelievers and believers alike. Like Jeremiah's letter to the exiles in Babylon, Peter reminds us,

> Therefore, preparing your minds for action, and being sober-minded, set your hope fully on the grace that will be brought to you at the revelation of Jesus Christ. As obedient children, do not be conformed to the passions of your former ignorance, but as he who called you is holy, you also be holy in all your conduct, since it is written, "You shall be holy, for I am holy." And if you call on him as Father who judges impartially according to each one's deeds, conduct yourselves with fear throughout the time of your exile, knowing that you were ransomed from the futile ways inherited from your forefathers, not with perishable things such as silver or gold, but with the precious blood of Christ, like that of a lamb without blemish or spot. He was foreknown before the foundation of the world but was made manifest in the last times for your sake who through him are believers in God, who raised him from the dead and gave him glory, so that your faith and hope are in God. (1 Peter 1:13–21)

Homecoming

Preparing his disciples for his departure and the sending of the Spirit, Jesus included in that upper room speech the following promise:

> Let not your hearts be troubled. Believe in God; believe also in me. In my Father's house are many rooms. If it were not so, would I have told you that I go to prepare a place for you? And if I go and prepare a place for you, I will come again and will take you to myself, that where I am you may be also. . . . Peace I leave with you; my peace I give to you. Not as the world gives do I give you. Let not your hearts be troubled, neither let them be afraid. You heard me say to you, "I am going away, and I will come to you." If you loved me, you would

have rejoiced, because I am going to the Father, for the Father is greater than I. And now I have told you before it takes place, so that when it does take place, you may believe. (John 14:1–3, 27–29)

Jesus did not escape the world into which he was now calling his disciples to suffer and witness. Nor is he merely waiting in heaven to return someday.

Every day that passes on earth is a productive delay of the last judgment. In the meantime, Jesus is gathering a people for himself on earth, forgiving and renewing them by his Word and Spirit, interceding for his co-heirs, and preparing his heavenly sanctuary for our arrival.

This whole creation will be wholly saved, and yet wholly new. If our goal is to be liberated from creation rather than the liberation of creation, we will understandably display little concern for the world that God has made. If, however, we are looking forward to "the time for restoring all the things which God spoke by the mouth of his holy prophets long ago" (Acts 3:21) and the participation of the whole creation in our redemption (Rom. 8:18–21), then our actions here and now pertain to the same world that will one day be finally and fully renewed.

Raising our eyes in faith toward God, we reach out to our fellow saints and to our neighbors with our hearts and hands in love. As God serves us with his heavenly gifts through the ministry of the church in his own Great Commission, he also serves our neighbors with common blessings through our worldly callings. Let us live out our discipleship as those who know that all authority in heaven and on earth belongs to our Redeemer, that he is with us until the end of the age, and that he will at last return bodily to judge the living and the dead and to make everything new. "Christ has died, Christ is risen, Christ will come again!"

Notes

Introduction

1. Jim Hoagland, "Prepared for Non-Combat," *Washington Post* (April 15, 1993).

2. Read Mercer Schuchardt, "Hugh Hefner's Hollow Victory," *Christianity Today*, December 2003, 23.

3. LaTonya Taylor, "The Church of O," *Christianity Today*, March 22, 2002, 12.

4. Ralph Waldo Emerson, "Harvard Divinity School Address," in *American Philosophic Addresses, 1700–1900*, ed. Joseph I. Blau (New York: Columbia University Press, 1946), 588–604.

5. The Barna Group, "Most Twentysomethings Put Christianity on the Shelf Following Spiritually Active Teen Years" September 11, 2006, http://www.barna.org/barna-update/article/16-teensnext-gen/147-most-twentysomethings-put-christianity-on-the-shelf-following-spiritually-active-teen-years?q=twentysomethings+put+christianity+shelf.

6. Terry Eastland, "Sunday Morning, Staying at Home," *The Wall Street Journal*, September 2, 2008; Julia Duin, *Quitting Church* (Grand Rapids: Baker, 2008).

7. Ed Stetzer, "Chicken Little Was Wrong," *Christianity Today*, January 2010, 37.

Chapter 1 Before You Go

1. Christopher J. H. Wright, *The Mission of God: Unlocking the Bible's Grand Narrative* (Downers Grove, IL: InterVarsity Academic, 2006).

2. Ibid., 21–38.

Chapter 2 Exodus and Conquest

1. Wright, *Mission of God*, 10.

2. Jon Levenson, *Resurrection and the Restoration of Israel: The Ultimate Victory of the God of Life* (New Haven: Yale University Press, 2008); see also Kevin J. Madigan and Jon Levenson, *Resurrection: The Power of God for Christians and Jews* (New Haven: Yale University Press, 2008).

3. Kim Riddlebarger, *A Case for Amillennialism* (Grand Rapids: Baker, 2003), 56.

4. Brian McLaren writes, "*Parousia*, in this way, would signal the full arrival, presence, and manifestation of a new age in human history. It would mean the presence or appearance on earth of a new generation of humanity, *Christ again present, embodied in a community of people who truly possess and express his Spirit, continuing his work.* This would be the age of the Spirit and grace rather than law and lawkeeping. . . . If this alternative understanding has merit, the *parousia*—the arrival or

presence—of the new era or covenant began
after an in-between time during which the
old era or covenant coexisted with the new."
He adds, "When the cataclysmic 'last days'
of the old era ran their course, the new age,
new covenant, new testament, or new era
was brought to full term, and its *parousia*
has come. Our call, in this view of things,
is not to wait passively for something that
is not present (*apousia*), but rather to participate passionately in something that is
present (*parousia*)—*fully present, but not
complete in its development*, and so calling
for our wholehearted participation." Brian
McLaren, *A New Kind of Christianity: Ten
Questions That Are Transforming the Faith*
(New York: HarperOne, 2010), 198–99, emphasis added.
    5. Raymond B. Dillard, "Intrabiblical
Exegesis and the Effusion of the Spirit in
Joel," in *Creator, Redeemer, Consummator: A Festschrift for Meredith G. Kline*,
ed. Howard Griffith and John R. Muether
(Greenville, SC: Reformed Academic Press,
2000), 90.
    6. Lewis Sperry Chafer, *Major Bible
Doctrines*, revised by John Walvoord (Grand
Rapids: Zondervan, 1974), 136.
    7. Ibid.
    8. Brian McLaren, *A Generous Ortho-
doxy* (Grand Rapids: Zondervan, 2004),
206.
    9. McLaren, *A New Kind of Chris-
tianity*, 138.
    10. John Calvin, *Harmony of the Evan-
gelists*, trans. William Pringle (Grand Rapids: Baker, 1996), 179.
    11. Ibid., 201.

Chapter 3 An Urgent Imperative

    1. Quoted by Douglas Farrow, *Ascen-
sion and Ecclesia* (Grand Rapids: Eerdmans,
2009), 115, from *Orat.* 1.6–2.5.
    2. Augustine, *The City of God*, trans.
Henry Bettenson (New York: Penguin Clas-
sics, 2003). See the excellent study by Robert
Markus, *Saeculum: History and Society in
the Theology of St. Augustine* (Cambridge:
Cambridge University Press, 1989), as well
as his more recent (and slightly revised)
reflections in *Christianity and the Secular*

(South Bend: University of Notre Dame
Press, 2006).
    3. Robert Payne, *The Dream and the
Tomb: A History of the Crusades* (New
York: Stein & Day, 1985), 34.
    4. Michael Novak, quoted in David Van
Biema, "The Passion of the Pope," *Time*,
November 19, 2006, 6.
    5. The Pew Forum on Religion and Pub-
lic Life, "U.S. Religious Landscape Survey,"
Nov. 16, 2009, http://religions.pewforum
.org/reports/. See "Portraits: Beliefs & Practices: Evangelical Churches."
    6. Joseph Cummings provides a very
helpful survey of these positions in "Muslim Followers of Jesus?" *Christianity Today*,
December 2009, 32–35.
    7. Pew Forum, "U.S. Religious Land-
scape Survey."
    8. John Hick, "The Pluralist View"
in *Four Views on Salvation in a Pluralist
World*, ed. Dennis L. Ockholm and Timothy R. Phillips (Grand Rapids: Zondervan,
1996), 27–59.
    9. Brian McLaren, *A Generous Ortho-
doxy*, 109–10..
    10. Ibid.
    11. Ibid., 112, 114.
    12. The best recent critique of inclusiv-
ism I have encountered is a collection of es-
says edited by Christopher W. Morgan and
Robert A. Peterson, *Faith Comes by Hearing: A Response to Inclusivism* (Downers
Grove, IL: InterVarsity, 2008). In addition,
the following resources are recommended:
R. Douglas Geivett and W. Gary Phillips,
"A Particularist View: An Evidentialist Ap-
proach," in *Four Views on Salvation in a
Pluralistic World*, ed. Dennis L. Okholm
and Timothy R. Phillips (Grand Rapids:
Zondervan, 1995); D. A. Carson, *The Gag-
ging of God: Christianity Confronts Plu-
ralism* (Grand Rapids: Zondervan, 1996);
Ajith Fernando, *The Supremacy of Christ*
(Wheaton, IL: Crossway, 1995); Paul R.
House and Gregory A. Thornbury, eds.,
*Who Will Be Saved?: Defending the Bibli-
cal Understanding of God, Salvation, and
Evangelism* (Wheaton, IL: Crossway, 2000);
Douglas Moo, "Romans 2: Saved Apart
from the Gospel?" in *Through No Fault of
Their Own?: The Fate of Those Who Have
Never Heard*, eds. William V. Crockett and

James G. Sigountos (Grand Rapids: Baker, 1991), 137–45; Daniel Strange, *The Possibility of Salvation Among the Unevangelized: An Analysis of Inclusivism in Recent Evangelical Theology* (Carlisle, UK: Paternoster Press, 2002).

13. Larry W. Hurtado, *How on Earth Did Jesus Become a God? Historical Questions about Earliest Devotion to Jesus* (Grand Rapids: Eerdmans, 2005), 59.

14. Canons of Dort, Chapter 1, Art. 17, in the *Psalter Hymnal: Doctrinal Standards and Liturgy of the Christian Reformed Church* (Grand Rapids: Board of Publications of the CRC, 1976), 95.

15. Karl Barth, *Church Dogmatics* vol. 2 pt. 2, 13; vol. 4 pt. 2, 271; vol. 4 pt. 3a, 3. See also Karl Barth, *The Word of God and the Word of Man*, trans. Douglas Horton (New York: Harper & Brothers, 1956, 1957), 120. However, Barth shied away from affirming universal salvation (vol. 2 pt. 2, 417).

16. On Moltmann's view, see especially Jürgen Moltmann, "The Logic of Hell" in *God Will Be All in All: The Eschatology of Jürgen Moltmann*, ed. Richard Bauckham (Edinburgh: T & T Clark, 1999), 43–48.

17. Terrance L. Tiessen, *Who Can Be Saved: Reassessing Salvation in Christ and World Religions* (Downers Grove, IL: InterVarsity, 2004).

18. Clark Pinnock, "Overcoming Misgivings about Evangelical Inclusivism," *Southern Baptist Journal of Theology* 2, no. 2 (Summer 1998); 33–34. He adds, "I agree that inclusivism is not a central topic of discussion in the Bible and that the evidence for it is less than one would like. But the vision of God's love there is so strong that the existing evidence seems sufficient to me" (35).

19. Ibid., 34: "Scripture speaks in different ways about how people are saved subjectively. For example, it says that God loves seekers and rewards them, even if they are not Jews or Christians (Heb. 11:6). It says that Christ will save some people who have no idea who Jesus is but who showed by their deeds that they love God's kingdom (Matt. 25:37)." It should be noted that neither of these passages even implies that the subjects are outside of the covenant community. On the contrary, for example, in Matthew 25

Jesus speaks of a final separation of sheep and goats, with the former told, "'Come, you who are blessed by my Father, inherit the kingdom *prepared for you from the foundation of the world*'" (v. 34, emphasis added). The good deeds that Jesus then goes on to describe are consequences and evidences of their being in Christ, not the means, and the context is the immanent threat of persecution, when believers will be cast into prison for their faith in Christ. Pinnock appeals to "Declaration on the Relationship of the Church to Non-Christian Religions," par. 2 in *The Documents of Vatican II*, ed. Walter M. Abbott, trans. ed. Joseph Gallagher (New York: Herder & Herder, 1966), 662.

20. Ibid., 35–36: "I find support in Paul's statement that people may search for God and find him from anywhere in the world (Acts 17:27). I appreciate him saying that the gentiles have God's law written on their hearts (Rom. 2:16) and may be given eternal life when, by patiently doing good, they seek for glory and honor and immortality (Rom. 2:7). As a Catholic might put it, there are people with a desire for baptism who have not been able to be baptised."

21. McLaren, *A Generous Orthodoxy*, 254–55.

22. Ibid., 260, 264.

23. Tony Jones, *The New Christians: Dispatches from the Emergent Frontier* (San Francisco: Jossey-Bass, 2008), 76.

24. Ibid., 96.

25. Ibid., 99.

26. James L. Kugel, *Traditions of the Bible: A Guide to the Bible As It Was at the Start of the Common Era* (Cambridge: Harvard University Press, 1988), 276–78.

27. These examples often put forward by inclusivists, as well as other principal arguments from this camp, are treated respectfully and carefully in Christopher W. Morgan and Robert A Peterson, eds., *Faith Comes By Hearing: A Response to Inclusivism* (Downers Grove, IL: InterVarsity Academic, 2008).

28. McLaren, *A New Kind of Christianity*, 216.

29. McLaren, *A Generous Orthodoxy*, 101.

30. Brian McLaren, *Finding Our Way Again: The Return of the Ancient Practices* (Nashville: Thomas Nelson, 2008), 202.

31. Ibid.

32. H. Richard Niebuhr, *The Kingdom of God in America* (New York: Harper & Row, 1959), 193.

33. George Hunsinger, *Disruptive Grace: Studies in the Theology of Karl Barth* (Grand Rapids: Eerdmans, 2000), 76.

34. Ibid., 80.

35. Ibid.

36. G. K. Chesterton, *Orthodoxy: The Romance of Faith* (New York: Doubleday, 1959), 32.

37. Ibid., 31.

38. Dinesh D'Souza, *What's So Great About Christianity?* (Washington, DC: Regnery Publishing, 2007), 3.

39. Ibid.

Chapter 4 One Gospel and Many Cultures

1. Christopher J. H. Wright, *The Mission of God: Unlocking the Bible's Grand Narrative* (Downers Grove, IL: InterVarsity Academic, 2006), 38.

2. Philip Jenkins, *The Next Christendom: The Coming of Global Christianity* (Oxford: Oxford University Press, 2002).

3. Wright, *The Mission of God*, 43.

4. John Franke, *The Character of Theology* (Grand Rapids: Baker, 2005), 142.

5. Wright, *The Mission of God*, 42.

6. Ibid., 42n14.

7. Ibid., 44.

8. Ibid., 45.

9. Andrew Carey, "African Christians: 'Just a Step from Witchcraft'?" *Church of England Newspaper*, July 10, 1998.

10. Wright, *The Mission of God*, 47.

11. Jones, *The New Christians*, 25.

12. Ibid., 56.

13. John de Gruchy, *Liberating Reformed Theology: A South African Contribution to an Ecumenical Debate* (Grand Rapids: Eerdmans, 1991), 23–24. See also Allen Boesak, *Black and Reformed: Apartheid, Liberation and the Calvinist Tradition*, ed. Leonard Sweetman (Maryknoll, NY: Orbis, 1984), 87.

14. Donald McGavran, *Understanding Church Growth*, ed. and rev. C. Peter Wagner (Grand Rapids: Eerdmans, 1970), 163, 174–75. C. Peter Wagner defended McGavran's approach in *Our Kind of People: The Ethical Dimensions of Church Growth in America* (Atlanta: John Knox, 1979).

Chapter 5 The Goal

1. James C. Wilhoit, *Spiritual Formation as if the Church Mattered* (Grand Rapids: Baker Academic, 2008).

2. Dallas Willard, *The Great Omission: Reclaiming Jesus' Essential Teachings on Discipleship* (New York: HarperOne, 2006), 11.

3. Ibid., 53.

4. Ibid., 10.

5. Ibid., 62, emphasis in original.

6. Ibid., 47.

7. John Calvin, *A Reformation Debate: Sadoleto's Letter to the Genevans and Calvin's Reply*, ed. John C. Olin (Grand Rapids: Baker, 1966), 56.

8. G. C. Berkouwer, *Studies in Dogmatics: Faith and Sanctification* (Grand Rapids: Eerdmans, 1952), 29.

9. N. T. Wright, *After You Believe* (New York: HarperOne, 2010).

Chapter 6 How to Make Disciples

1. Martin Luther, *Church Postil* of 1522, quoted in Stephen H. Webb, *The Divine Voice: Christian Proclamation and a Theology of Sound* (Grand Rapids: Brazos, 2004), 143.

2. Westminster Shorter Catechism in *The Book of Confessions* (PCUSA: General Assembly, 1991), Question 89.

3. Westminster Larger Catechism in *The Book of Confessions* (PCUSA: General Assembly, 1991), Answer 155.

4. The Barna Group, "Most Twentysomethings Put Christianity on the Shelf Following Spiritually Active Teen Years" September 11, 2006, http://www.barna.org/barna-update/article/16-teensnext-gen/147-most-twentysomethings-put-christianity-on-the-shelf-following-spiritually-active-teen-years?q=twentysomethings+put+christianity+shelf.

5. Christian Smith and Melinda Linquist, *Soul Searching: The Spirituality of America's Teens* (New York: Oxford University Press, 2007).

6. J. I. Packer and Gary A. Parrett, *Grounded in the Gospel: Building Believers the Old-Fashioned Way* (Grand Rapids: Baker, 2010).

Chapter 7 Disciples and Discipline

1. John Zizioulas, *Being as Communion* (Crestwood, NJ: St. Vladimir's Seminary Press, 1997), 195: "On the one hand [the bishop] was understood as a 'co-presbyter,' i.e. as one—presumably the first one—of the college of the presbyterium." "This is clearly indicated by the use of the term *presbyters* for the bishop by Irenaeus (Haer. IV 26:2). This should be taken as a survival of an old usage in the West, as it can be inferred from *I Clement* 44, 1 Peter 5:1, etc." (195n85). In *Called to Communion*, trans. Adrian Walker (San Francisco: Ignatius Press, 1996), Pope Benedict (then Cardinal Ratzinger) acknowledges that *presbyter* and *episcopoi* are used interchangeably in the NT (pp. 122–23).

2. David Barrett, George Kurian, and Todd Johnson, *World Christian Encyclopedia*, 2nd ed. (Oxford: Oxford University Press, 2001), 3.

3. Westminster Confession of Faith, 25.IV–V in *The Trinity Hymnal*, rev. ed. (Atlanta: Great Commission Publications, 1990), 863.

4. Willard, *The Great Omission*, 53.

Chapter 8 The Great Commission and the Great Commandment

1. Richard Mouw, "Carl Henry Was Right," *Christianity Today*, January 2010, 30–33.

2. Ibid., 30.

3. Ibid., 32.

4. Ibid., 33.

5. For a helpful treatment of this three-fold office and its connection to the church, see Derke Bergsma, "Prophets, Priests, and Kings: Offices in the Church," in *The Compromised Church*, ed. John Armstrong (Westchester, IL: Crossway, 1998), 117–32.

6. See David VanDrunen's outstanding survey, *Natural Law and Two Kingdoms in the Reformed Tradition* (Grand Rapids: Eerdmans, 2010).

7. James Davison Hunter, *To Change the World: The Irony, Tragedy, and Possibility of Christianity in the Late Modern World* (New York: Oxford University Press, 2010).

8. William Wilberforce, *A Practical View of Christianity*, ed. Kevin Charles Belmonte (Peabody, MA: Hendrickson, 1996), 176.

9. Ibid., xxxv.

10. Ibid., 1.

11. Ibid., 2.

12. Ibid., 4–5.

13. Ibid., 6.

14. Ibid., 7.

15. Ibid., 38–39.

16. Ibid., 67.

17. Ibid., 68.

18. Ibid., 69–70.

19. Ibid., 71–72.

20. Ibid., 85.

21. Ibid., 87–88.

22. Ibid., 96–97.

23. Ibid., 116–137.

24. Ibid., 160–161.

25. Ibid., 177–178.

26. Ibid., 179.

27. Ibid., 180.

28. Ibid., 181–89.

29. Ibid., 189.

30. Ibid., 209.

31. Ibid., 210.

32. Ibid., 213.

33. Ibid., 214.

34. Ibid., 215.

35. Ibid., 229.

36. Ibid., 234.

37. Ibid., 235.

38. Ibid.

39. Ibid., 262.

40. The Pew Forum on Religion and Public Life, "U.S. Religious knowledge Survey," September 28, 2010.

41. Lisa Miller, "Heaven Help Him: Religious Centrists Bail on Obama," *Newsweek*, February 8, 2010, 18.

42. Ibid.

43. C. S. Lewis, "Is Theology Poetry?" in *C. S. Lewis: Essay Collection* (London: Collins, 2000), 21.

44. McLaren, *A Generous Orthodoxy*, 97.

45. John Calvin, *A Reformation Debate: Sadoleto's Letter to the Genevans and Calvin's Reply*, ed. John C. Olin (Grand Rapids: Baker, 1966), 56.

46. John Calvin, *Institutes*, ed. J. T. McNeill, trans. F. L. Battles (Philadelphia: Westminster Press, 1962), 1.2.2.

47. Ibid., 3.3.19.

48. Ibid., 4.20.1–3.

49. Gustav Wingren, *Luther on Vocation*, tr. Carl C. Rasmussen (Evansville, IN: Ballast Press, 1994), 2.

50. Ibid., 10.

51. Ibid., 13, 31.

52. Ibid., 42.

53. Ibid., 43.

54. Ibid., 44.

Chapter 9 Mission Creep

1. Charles G. Finney, *Systematic Theology* (Minneapolis: Bethany, 1976), 31, 46, 57, 179–80, 206–9, 236, 320–22.

2. Quoted in Michael Pasquarello III, *Christian Preaching: A Trinitarian Theology of Proclamation* (Grand Rapids: Baker Academic, 2007), 24, emphasis added.

3. Garry Wills, *Head and Heart: American Christianities* (New York: Penguin Press, 2007), 294.

4. Ibid., 302.

5. Greg L. Hawkins and Cally Parkinson, *Reveal: Where Are You?* (Northbrook, IL: Willow, 2007), 4, 39, 42–44, 49, 53, 65.

6. George Barna, *Marketing the Church* (Colorado Springs: NavPress, 1988), 37.

7. George Barna, *Revolution: Finding Vibrant Faith Beyond the Walls of the Sanctuary* (Carol Stream, IL: Tyndale House Publishers, 2005).

8. Ibid., back cover copy.

9. Ibid., 17.

10. Ibid., 22.

11. Ibid., 24–25.

12. Ibid., 37.

13. George Barna, *The Second Coming of the Church* (Nashville: Word, 1998), 7.

14. Barna, *Revolution*, 175.

15. Ibid., 62–63. Following "the 'niching' of America" on the part of global marketing in the effort to "command greater loyalty (and profits)," we now have "churches designed for different generations, those offering divergent styles of worship music, congregations that emphasize ministries of interest to specialized populations, and so forth. The church landscape now offers these boutique churches alongside the something-for-everybody megachurches. In the religious marketplace, the churches that have suffered most are those who stuck with the one-size-fits-all approach, typically proving that one-size-fits-nobody."

16. Ibid., 70.

17. Frank Viola and George Barna, *Pagan Christianity: Exploring the Roots of Our Church Practices* (Ventura, CA: BarnaBooks, 2008), 136.

18. Ibid., 197.

19. Frank Viola, *Reimagining Church: Pursuing the Dream of Organic Christianity* (Colorado Springs: David C. Cook, 2008), 55, 65–66.

20. Ibid., 31, 40, 54, 56, 63, 137, 220.

21. Ibid., 234.

22. Ibid., 80–81.

23. Ibid., 244.

24. Jones, *The New Christians*, 177.

25. Ibid., 177–78.

26. Ibid., 4.

27. Ibid., 216.

28. Ibid., 217–18.

29. Recent scholarship has confirmed the existence of three major types of groups that have often been lumped together under the name "Anabaptist": the rationalists, the inspirationists, and the Anabaptists. See William Estep, *The Anabaptist Story: An Introduction to Sixteenth-Century Anabaptism* (Grand Rapids: Eerdmans, 1996), 10–28.

30. G. E. Lessing, *Lessing's Theological Writings*, ed. Henry Chadwick (Palo Alto, CA: Stanford University Press, 1957), 18.

31. Ibid., 53.

32. Ibid.

33. Friedrich Schleiermacher, *On Religion: Speeches to Its Cultured Despisers*, trans. Richard Crouter (Cambridge: Cambridge University Press, 1996), 15.

34. Quoted in Wills, *Head and Heart*, 273.

35. Ibid., 302.

36. Wade Clark Roof, *A Generation of Seekers: The Spiritual Journeys of the Baby*

Boom Generation (San Francisco: Harper-Collins, 1993), 23.

37. Ibid., 30.

38. Ibid., 67.

39. McLaren, *A New Kind of Christianity*, 103–4.

40. Richard Foster, *Celebration of Discipline: The Path to Spiritual Growth* (New York: HarperOne, 1988), 159.

41. Willard, *The Great Omission*, xiii.

42. Ibid., 34–35.

43. Ibid., 37.

44. Ibid., 30.

45. Ibid., 64.

46. Ibid., 65.

47. Ibid., 65–66.

48. Ibid., 16.

49. Interview by Mark Galli with Richard Foster, "A Life Formed in the Spirit," *Christianity Today*, September 2008, 32.

50. Richard Foster, "Spiritual Formation Agenda: Three Priorities for the Next 30 Years," *Christianity Today*, February 4, 2009, 40.

51. Willard, *The Great Omission*, 35.

52. Ibid., 36.

53. Ibid., xiii.

54. Ibid., 46–47.

55. Ibid., 46.

56. For example, external forms are contrasted with the inner spirit that is ignited directly by "Spirit" in *Celebration of Discipline*, 159.

57. Stanley Grenz, *Revisioning Evangelical Theology: A Fresh Agenda for the 21st Century* (Downers Grove, IL: InterVarsity, 1993), 32.

58. Ibid., 33.

59. Ibid., 38, 41.

60. Ibid., 41–42.

61. Ibid., 44.

62. Ibid., 45.

63. Ibid., 46.

64. Ibid., 48.

65. Ibid.

66. Ibid., 51.

67. Ibid., 52.

68. Ibid., 55.

69. Ibid., 62.

70. Ibid., 80.

71. Ibid., 88.

72. Ibid., 122.

73. Ibid., 130. At stake in this loss of *sola scriptura* (by Scripture alone) are the corollaries: *solo Christo* (by Christ alone), *sola gratia* (by grace alone), *sola fide* (through faith alone), and *soli Deo gloria* (to God alone be glory). These stakes are not too high for Brian McLaren, for example, who scolds Reformed Christians for "their love-affair for the Latin word '*sola*.'" Brian McLaren, *A Generous Orthodoxy*, 23.

74. Chesterton, *Orthodoxy*, 75.

75. Ibid., 75–76.

76. Ibid., 76.

77. Richard Foster, "Thirty-Year Vision," *Christianity Today*, January 2009, 41.

78. See especially Newbigin's excellent book *The Household of God* (Carlisle, UK: Paternoster, 2002).

79. McLaren, *A Generous Orthodoxy*, 105: "The term missional arose in the 1990s, thanks to the Gospel and Our Culture Network. It was popularized by the Network's important book called *The Missional Church* (Darrell L. Guder, et al., Grand Rapids: Eerdmans, 1998)."

80. Ibid., 206.

81. Jones, *The New Christians*, 108.

82. Ibid.

83. Ibid., 109.

84. Ibid., 72.

85. Pliny (the Younger), *Epistles*, in *A New Eusebius: Documents Illustrative of the History of the Church to A.D. 337*, ed. J. Stevenson (London: SPCK, 1974), 13–15, quoted in Hurtado, *How on Earth Did Jesus Become a God*, 13.

86. Hurtado, *How on Earth Did Jesus Become a God?*, 15.

87. Ibid., 69–72.

88. Ibid., 28.

89. Ibid., 81.

90. Ibid., 79.

91. Ibid., 79.

92. Jones, *The New Christians*, 142.

93. Dan Kimball, *The Emerging Church: Vintage Christianity for New Generations* (Grand Rapids: Zondervan, 2003), 185, 194.

94. Jones, *The New Christians*, 13.

95. Ibid., 17.

96. McLaren, *A Generous Orthodoxy*, 108.

97. N. T. Wright, *Simply Christian* (San Francisco: HarperCollins, 2006), 201, 204.

98. N. T. Wright, *Justification: God's Plan and Paul's Vision* (Downers Grove, IL: InterVarsity, 2009), 24.

99. McLaren, *A Generous Orthodoxy* (Grand Rapids: Zondervan, 2004), 96.

100. Ibid., 97.

101. Jones, *The New Christians*, 79.

102. Ibid., 75.

103. Thomas N. Finger, *A Contemporary Anabaptist Systematic Theology* (Downers Grove, IL: InterVarsity, 2004), 216–219, 291, 305, 321, 468.

104. Jones, *The New Christians*, 101–2.

105. George M. Marsden, *The Evangelical Mind and the New School Presbyterian Experience: A Case Study of Thought and Theology in Nineteenth Century America* (New Haven: Yale University Press, 1970).

106. Harvey Cox, *The Secular City* (London: SCM Press, 1965), 145. More recently, see his *The Future of Faith* (New York: HarperOne, 2009).

107. Willard, *The Great Omission*, xiii-xiv.

108. Ibid., xv.

109. Kimball, *The Emerging Church*, 91.

110. Ibid., 93.

111. Jones, *The New Christians*, 218.

112. Ibid., 189.

113. Ibid., 180.

114. Ibid., 182.

115. Sherry Turkle, *Life On the Screen* (New York: Simon and Schuster, 1995), 14.

116. The Belgic Confession, Article 35.

117. Jones, *The New Christians*, 183.

118. Ibid., 183–84.

119. Ibid., 204.

120. Ibid., 186.

Chapter 10 Until He Comes

1. The interview with Sherwood Wirt in *Decision* magazine is included in C. S. Lewis, *God in the Dock* (Grand Rapids: Eerdmans, 1970), 265.

2. John Newton, "Glorious Things of Thee Are Spoken," 1779.

Michael S. Horton (PhD, University of Coventry and Wycliffe Hall, Oxford) is J. Gresham Machen Professor of Systematic Theology and Apologetics at Westminster Seminary California and associate pastor of Christ United Reformed Church in Santee, California. He co-hosts *The White Horse Inn* radio broadcast and is editor-in-chief of *Modern Reformation* magazine. He is the author or editor of more than twenty books, including *Christless Christianity* and *The Gospel-Driven Life*. He also serves on the advisory council of the Laussane Committee on World Evangelization.

Information on White Horse Inn

White Horse Inn (www.whitehorseinn.org) is a multimedia catalyst for reformation. Our mission is to help Christians "know what they believe and why they believe it" through conversational theology. The conversations take place in talk show, magazine, event, book, blog, and social media formats. Our vision is to see a modern reformation in our churches through a rediscovery of God, the gospel, and the classic Christian confessions proclaimed during the sixteenth-century Reformation.

More than just a talk show and a magazine, White Horse Inn is a conversation for reformation. C. S. Lewis famously remarked that "mere Christianity" is like a hallway. In this hallway, real conversations between Christians of different convictions can begin and develop over time as we emerge from these various rooms to speak of Christ and his gospel to one another. For twenty years, White Horse Inn has hosted this conversation both on the radio (*White Horse Inn*) and in print (*Modern Reformation*) in the spirit of that great hallway of "mere Christianity," bringing the rich resources of the Reformation to bear on American evangelicalism.

At the center of our work are six core beliefs:

1. **The five "solas" of the Reformation are more than slogans to be recovered; they are the messages that will renew the church's mission in our age.**

2. **Gospel-centered preaching that rightly distinguishes between law and gospel rescues the church from "Christless Christianity" while enabling Christians to grow in grace.**

3. **Word and Sacrament ministry realigns the church's mission and identity from program-driven pragmatism to the means of grace that Christ has ordained for the creation, sustenance, and expansion of his kingdom.**

4. **A properly missional mindset will identify the church as distinct from but engaged with the world, encouraging individual Christians to pursue their God-honoring vocations.**

5. In order to know what they believe and why they believe it, Christians need to be well catechized and grounded in the central doctrines of the faith.

6. Withstanding the onslaught of heresy and persecution requires a confessing church grounded in the witness of the ages and animated by deeds of loving service and witness.

Our vision is to see nothing less than a "modern reformation" take hold in the hearts and lives of Christians here in America and around the world. It is our prayer that God would once again pour out his Spirit, granting the church a modern reformation. For Christ's sake. Amen.

White Horse Inn is home to the *White Horse Inn* radio broadcast and *Modern Reformation* magazine.

MODERN REFORMATION

White Horse Inn · 1725 Bear Valley Parkway · Escondido, CA 92027
1-800-890-7556